D1636485

Free Trade

Free Trade

Neither Free Nor About Trade

Christopher D. Merrett

Montréal/New York
London

Black Rose Books No. Y231
Hardcover ISBN: 1-55164-045-7 (bound)
Paperback ISBN: 1-55164-044-9 (pbk.)

Canadian Cataloguing in Publication Data

Merrett, Christopher Douglas

Free trade : neither free nor about trade

Includes bibliographical references and index.
ISBN 1-55164-045-7 (bound).—
ISBN 1-55164-044-9 (pbk.)

1. Free trade—Canada. 2. Free trade—United States.
3. Canada—Economic conditions—1991- . 5. Free trade.
I. Title.

HF1776.M47 1995 382'.971073 C95-900733-4

Mailing Address

BLACK ROSE BOOKS
C.P. 1258
Succ. Place du Parc
Montréal, Québec
H2W 2R3 Canada

BLACK ROSE BOOKS
340 Nagel Drive
Cheektowaga, New York
14225 USA

A publication of the Institute of Policy Alternatives of Montréal (IPAM)

Printed in Canada

Contents

Acknowledgements

This project could not have been completed without help from many supportive individuals and institutions. First, I would like to gratefully acknowledge the assistance of the Government of Canada which provided financial support through its Canadian Studies Fellowship Program. I would also like to thank the Canadian Centre for Policy Alternatives and the Business Council on National Issues for their cooperation, publications, and valuable insights into the free trade debate in Canada. I would also like to acknowledge three anonymous reviewers and the editors of Black Rose Books whose insights have helped me to improve upon earlier versions of this text. Closer to home, I would like to thank Norman Walzer, John Gruidl, and Jeff Crump from the Illinois Institute for Rural Affairs located at Western Illinois University. I would also like to acknowledge the generosity and support provided by David Reynolds, Rex Honey, Rebecca Roberts, Claire Pavlik, and Shelton Stromquist at the University of Iowa, Fred Shelley at Southwest Texas State University, Abdi Samatar at the University of Minnesota and Richard Peet at Clark University. I also owe a debt of gratitude to the following close friends who read portions of the text, listened to my ideas and buoyed my spirits when it seemed as though the writing would never end: Mike Allard, John Luxton, Mike Smith, Seth Feaster, Doug Jones, John Kupfer, Mary Skopec, Bill Schwarz, Dave Riley, Jay Emerson and Gail Hollander. Of course, I alone am responsible for any remaining inconsistencies. My brother and his wife, Ron and Wendy Merrett, and their children, John and Rebekah, have been a lifelong source of joy and so I would like to say thank you to them. Of course I owe a considerable debt to my parents, Stan and Edna Merrett, who have offered me their unqualified love and support in whatever endeavor I have pursued throughout my life. Finally, I would like to express my love and gratitude to my wife, Mary Kiritsy, who has been a never-ending source of love and encouragement. I am fortunate to have such a supportive network of colleagues, friends and family.

Figures

List of Abbreviations

ACA	Advisory Council on Adjustment
ACTRA	Association for Canadian Cinema, Television and Radio Artists
AFL-CIO	American Federation of Labor — Congress of Industrial Organizations
APMAC	Automotive Parts Manufacturers Association of Canada
BCNI	Business Council on National Issues
CA	Cooperation Apparatus
CAC	Canadian-American Committee
CAP	Canada Assistance Plan
CATJO	Canadian Alliance for Trade and Job Opportunities
CAW	Canadian Auto Workers
CBC	Canadian Broadcasting Corporation
CCA	Capital Cost Allowance Program
CCPA	Canadian Centre for Policy Alternatives
CCF	Canadian Commonwealth Federation
CDC	Canadian Development Corporation
CIA	Canadian Importers Association
CLC	Canadian Labour Congress
CMA	Canadian Manufacturers' Association
CPI	Consumer Price Index
CPR	Canadian Pacific Railroad
CRTC	Canadian Radio-Television and Telecommunications Commission
ECC	Economic Council of Canada
EPF	Established Programs Financing
FIRA	Foreign Investment Review Agency
FTA	Canada-United States Free Trade Agreement
GATT	General Agreement on Tariffs and Trade
GDP	Gross Domestic Product
GPMC	Grocery Products Manufacturers of Canada
IMF	International Monetary Fund
IRDI	Industrial Relations and Disputes Investigations
IRPP	Institute for Research on Public Policy
ITC	International Trade Commission
MBS	Management-by-stress

MLA	Meech Lake Accord
MNC	Multinational Corporations
MPAA	Motion Picture Association of America
NAFTA	North American Free Trade Agreement
NCC	National Citizens' Coalition
NDP	New Democratic Party
NEP	National Energy Policy
NFB	National Film Board
Norad	North American Aerospace Defense Command
NPR	National Public Radio
OECD	Organization for Economic Cooperation and Development
OSAP	Ontario Student Assistance Program
PATCO	Professional Air Traffic Controllers Organization
PC	Progressive Conservatives
UAW	United Auto Workers
USTR	United States Trade Representative

Reciprocity, Reciprocity, Reciprocity
Recipe for paucity.

John Boyle, *This Magazine*

No nation was ever ruined by trade.

Benjamin Franklin, *Essays, Thoughts on Commercial Subjects*

Chapter 1

Free Trade and Social Change

Voltaire once said about the Holy Roman Empire that it was neither holy, Roman, nor an empire. In similar fashion, it can be argued that the Canada-United States Free Trade Agreement (FTA) is neither free, about trade, nor an agreement supported by a majority of Canadians. Many commentators believe that the Canada-United States FTA, implemented on January 1, 1989, has had its greatest impact not on trade, but on the sweeping social and political changes that were initiated or accelerated within Canadian society.[1] This book aims to identify these changes, assess their significance and explain how and why free trade affected them by adopting a political economy perspective known as Regulation theory.

The economic crisis of the 1970s and 1980s represents the most important factor driving the proliferation of free trade policies that exist between the United States and Canada (and now Mexico), Australia and New Zealand and between countries of the European Community.[2] Alliances between multinational corporations (MNCs), financial institutions and national governments have formed to promote free trade agreements as part of a larger agenda. Their goal has been to restore corporate profits by restructuring industrial societies. Proponents of free trade have supported social reforms under the banner of "increasing competitiveness."[3] Canada's most powerful business lobby, the Business Council on National Issues (BCNI), stressed that its prime objective in supporting the FTA is the "urgent and continuing need to secure an improved position for Canada within the rapidly changing and increasingly competitive global economy."[4] The ideology of free trade therefore fits into the broader strategy of enhancing the position of capital with respect to labour and the State.

Increased capital mobility has forced workers and governments around the world into internecine competition to attract investment. Corporations use the threat of relocation to force concessions out of workers, to restrict workers' rights and to force cuts in Welfare-State spending — all designed to increase corporate flexibility and economic growth. Free trade agreements facilitate social restructuring by drawing countries into closer contact while supranational market forces erode the policy-making powers of the Nation-State. National standards for wages, taxes, investment and social spending are harmonized to a continental standard. All this is argued to have occurred in response to the economic crisis of the 1970s and 1980s.[5]

It is important, however, to place economic crisis and free trade into a broader context. The capitalist world economy has endured periodic cycles or waves of economic growth and crisis during its development.[6] Current social change in industrial societies can be linked to a crisis of capital accumulation within the most recent long wave of economic development. Economic growth in each long wave depends upon a model of development characterized by a unique configuration of labour, capital and the State. Eventually, fundamental contradictions within capitalism undermine each model of development. A new wave of economic growth will not occur until a new model evolves to regulate these contradictions. Free trade agreements and related policies such as monetarism, deregulation, and the geographic relocation of production represent attempts to mediate the contradictions of capitalism by restructuring or bypassing restrictions imposed by the Nation-State. Hegemonic coalitions of corporate and State interests aim to create a continental model of development capable of supporting a new wave of prolonged economic growth.[7]

Free trade agreements therefore herald a diminishing role for the Nation-State in a rapidly restructuring world economy. An examination of the Canada-United States FTA will show how the development of continental trading blocs reduce the salience and sovereignty of the Nation-State. The FTA has initiated or accelerated substantial change in Canada through closer political-economic articulation with the United States. Transformations can be identified by paying specific attention to the impact of free trade on the Canadian economy, society, and the State. Significant overlap between these categories exists because they each provide different perspectives for examining the same process — the periodic development and crisis of capitalism.

The details of this argument will be made clear according to the following outline. The remainder of chapter one explains the theoretical framework used for analyzing free trade. Chapter one also describes the economic growth and crisis in the United States and Canada after 1945. This background information helps explain why a hegemonic alliance of Canadian and American corporate and State interests would use the FTA to create a continental model of development in the 1980s. It needs to be stressed that the FTA is not the only source of social change in Canada. The FTA needs to be distinguished from other catalysts of social change such as recessions and deindustrialization. Therefore, chapter two provides the historical context in which debates over free trade took place in order to elucidate the underlying agenda of free trade proponents. Given the content of free trade discourse, it can be shown that hegemonic Canadian and American interests wanted to enhance corporate flexibility and profitability by restructuring North American society using continental market forces.

Chapters three, four and five will examine the specific impacts of free trade on Canada. Chapter three examines the development of Canada's economy in greater detail, moving on to reveal how free trade and continued American protectionism have affected the performance of the Canadian economy in the 1980s and 1990s. Chapter four outlines the development of Canadian labour relations. Free trade is then examined for its impact on Canadian labour given the threat of labour market restructuring and job relocation. Chapter five looks at the role of the State in industrial societies during the postwar period, followed by an examination of the impact of the FTA on the Canadian Welfare State and national sovereignty. Chapter six offers some final thoughts including the future of Canada under the influence of a broader hemispheric free trade agreement that could extend to much of Latin America.

A Framework For Studying Free Trade

According to Regulation theory, economic and social crises caused by overproduction or underconsumption should be the norm in capitalist society. However, capitalism has experienced long periods when what society produces is co-ordinated with what society consumes to generate predictable economic growth. During these times contradictory social and class relations that define capitalism reproduce themselves in a coherent manner to ensure economic stability. The economic policies that co-ordinate consumption with production constitute a "regime of accumulation." The maintenance of a regime of accumulation depends upon a particular set of political and social policies which can be described as a "mode of regulation." A mode of regulation tempers individual behaviour and expectations through social compromises between labour, capital and the State. Institutions such as unions, organized religion, the State, international relations and supranational organizations also contribute to social stability. Together, a regime of accumulation and a mode of regulation form a model of development.[8]

Regulation theorists borrowed the term "Fordism" from Antonio Gramsci to describe the model of development underpinning industrial democracies from the 1940s to the 1970s. Gramsci was an Italian political economist who first used the term to describe American industrial development prior to World War II.[9] Henry Ford had just introduced the radical idea that mass production of automobiles or any other product could be sustained only if accompanied by mass consumption. In order to have mass consumption the minimum wage had to be raised to allow workers to buy more than just the bare necessities. Ford's idea was never put into practice because wage increases alone were not enough to stimulate demand prior to the Second World War. After 1945 the expansion of the Welfare State and military spending helped to realize Ford's idea that sustainable mass production could only exist with comparable levels of mass consumption.

Fordism is much more complex than a simple co-ordination of consumption with production. Ford's ideas must be seen in the context of organizational and technological innovations that had been introduced to the manufacturing world during the late nineteenth and early twentieth centuries. The corporate form of organization, inspired by the railroad companies, revolutionized the way businesses arranged their production process.[10] Labour productivity was increasing because industrialists were applying the ideas espoused by F. W. Taylor in *The Principles of Scientific Management* (1911). Taylor showed how productivity could be increased by breaking a job down into its component parts and then assigning a worker to complete just one particular stage of the manufacturing process. This detailed division of labour accelerated the deskilling process which lowered the training time required for each labourer and increased management's control over the labour process. Further productivity gains could be achieved by separating out the management, conception, control and execution processes into a social hierarchy. Ford combined Taylorism and the corporate business format in his new automobile factories. He realized that this revolution of the production process could only be achieved if mass production was matched with mass consumption. In order to create this match Ford saw the need to build a new "rationalized," modernist and populist democratic society.[11]

Gramsci was fascinated by Ford's attempt to "create a new type of man for a new type of work."[12] It was apparent to him that questions about the new forms of work were inseparable from questions of sexuality, views of the family, forms of moral coercion and consumerism. This assertion was borne out when Ford sent social workers into the homes of his "privileged" workers to make sure that the new mass-production labourer had views on family life, morality and rational consumption appropriate to corporate needs.[13] Ford so firmly believed in the ability of corporate power to reorder society that he increased wages despite the onset of the Great Depression. He believed that higher wages would boost demand for consumer goods and revive the depressed economy. However, the Depression was too severe. Ford was forced to lay off workers and lower wages or face bankruptcy. It would fall to President Roosevelt, The New Deal, and the Second World War to revive capitalism by accomplishing through State intervention what Ford had hoped to achieve through wage increases alone.[14]

Despite the efforts of Ford to increase consumption norms in society during the Depression, the required increase in consumer demand did not really occur until after the Second World War. Two fundamental problems blocked the widespread implementation of Fordist practices prior to 1939. The first challenge was to convince an antagonistic working class to submit to a production system that forced workers to spend long hours in regimented tasks over which they had little control. Ford experienced high rates of worker turnover in his automobile factories because people quickly tired of the repetitive nature of the work.[15]

The second obstacle confronting Fordism lay in the inadequate impact of State intervention in the economy. By the early twentieth century, capitalism had shown repeatedly that it was prone to depressions and recessions. The crisis of the 1930s was particularly vicious because factories using mass production techniques were producing far more commodities than could be absorbed by consumers. Individual capitalists were unable to stimulate effective demand to revive the economy and it fell to the State to save capitalism. The challenge was to discern what the new State role should entail and how Nation-States could interact in a predictable manner with each other. Planners and politicians generally agreed that the Depression was due to a lack of effective demand. An ominous solution was sought by fascists in Japan, Italy and Germany. They believed that democratic governments were impotent to solve the crisis because they did not discipline workers and rationalize production in an appropriate manner. Excess capacity was absorbed in fascist countries through much needed expenditures on infrastructures to facilitate production and consumption. Demand was also bolstered through increased military expenditures. Many politicians and intellectuals thought that the policies implemented by Japan, Germany and Italy provided a viable way out of the depression if they could be stripped of their appeals to mythology, racism and militarism. Schumpeter supported the New Deal because he saw it as a benign form of the policies adopted by the Axis countries.[16]

John Maynard Keynes also believed that the State could moderate the cyclical nature of economic growth through fiscal and monetary policy without resorting to the repression, militarism and nationalism inherent in fascist governments. Keynesian philosophy underpinned the New Deal in the United States. There is some evidence to suggest that it improved economic conditions. However, it was the massive expenditures of the Second World War which ultimately lifted the American economy out of the doldrums. It is worth noting that the Keynesian policies of the New Deal were significant for improving the quality of life for a large segment of the American population and therefore heading off dissent. Furthermore, the New Deal legitimized the idea of strong government involvement in the economy — an essential element to the period of rapid economic expansion that followed the Second World War.[17]

Ford's goal to match rates of consumption with rates of production was finally achieved after the Second World War as industrial economies experienced unprecedented economic growth. Keynesian economics and the rise of the Welfare State combined to stimulate consumer demand. Yet even after 1945, the development of the Fordist regime of accumulation was not a straightforward process. The foundation of Fordism was based on the rise of a series of industries that had developed after the First World War, but which had achieved new levels of productivity only during the Second World War. Huge production complexes blossomed in the North American Midwest, the British West Midlands, the German Ruhr-Rhineland and the Japanese Tokyo-Yokohama industrial district, which produced cars, ships, steel, electrical consumer goods, and petrochemicals. The "privileged workers" within these industries represented one component of a rapidly increasing effective demand. A second component in the expansion of Global Fordism was the role of State-sponsored development policies. The most important programme was the reconstruction of war-torn European economies through the Marshall Plan.[18] American surplus productive capacity would not have to remain idle with consumer demand created by a functioning European economy. The State also spurred the suburbanization process in the United States through low-interest home loans, zoning bylaws and highway building, triggering a huge expansion in the demand for consumer durables.[19]

Epochal postwar growth depended on a series of compromises between major actors in the capitalist economy. Fordist production processes were not widely implemented until the State defused resurgent working class militancy. Fascist governments in Italy and Germany undermined the European labour unions in the 1930s. In the United States, the Wagner Act (National Labor Relations Act) of 1935 had given workers the right of collective bargaining if they relinquished powers in the realm of production. After the war, American unions attempted to regain control over the workplace. McCarthyism and ultimately the Taft- Hartley Act (Labor-Management Relations Act) of 1947 subdued the most radical aspects of labour activism.[20]

Labour was not totally defeated, however. As corporations and their associated work forces increased in size, the threat of renewed activism also increased. Corporations grudgingly accepted increased union memberships in order to co-opt union leaders. Union leaders promised to control their membership and promote increased productivity in exchange for higher wages. Postwar labour-management compromises stimulated effective demand in just the way that Henry Ford had hoped. Capital, with the help of its ideological supporters in the State, finally solved the class problems that had impeded the implementation of Fordism. The capitalist class had achieved what Gramsci referred to as "hegemony" over the production process.[21]

The State assumed a variety of new roles to minimize the turbulence of capitalist development. Stable growth was promoted by the State by using fiscal and monetary policy to counter any downturns in the economy. Risky large-scale infrastructural projects such as the interstate highway system and hydro-electric power dams were all constructed to assist the American economy. Unlike governments in the early 1930s, industrialized countries under Fordism promoted full employment and were committed to increasing the social wage by subsidizing or providing free health care, education, housing and social security. Postwar Fordism therefore required compromise and co-operation between large capital, the State and labour in order to create a new society willing to match ever-expanding production with increased rates of consumption.

The development of Fordism also required a politically stable and closely integrated international economy. The United States guaranteed a stable international environment for accumulation through an elaborate system of alliances and agreements backed up by its massive military force. Policy-makers wanted to avoid another descent into the autarky that characterized international relations during the 1930s. They proposed a new world system where capital could circulate freely in a world divided up into independent countries each possessing the ability to create a national economic policy.[22] The Bretton Woods Agreement, which created the International Monetary Fund (IMF) and the World Bank (International Bank for Reconstruction and Development), represents one pillar supporting the new international economic framework. Signatories to the Bretton Woods Agreement agreed to impose monetary constraints on their external economic relations and to tie their currencies to the American dollar which became the "global" reserve currency. The United States acted as the reserve banker to the world by backing up its dollar in gold. A second pillar was the General Agreement on Tariffs and Trade (GATT). The export orientation of the expanding American economy would benefit from freer access to foreign markets. In order to reduce barriers, the United States sponsored GATT, which was designed to lower tariffs and provide a more liberal environment for international trade and investment.

It must be pointed out that Fordism diffused in an uneven manner from the United States to the rest of the world. Even within the United States large sectors of the population did not benefit from collective bargaining or access to the job market. The benefits fell mainly to the predominantly white, male, unionized labour force. The worst effects of deskilling and authoritarianism in the workplace were felt by women and minorities. To this must be added the resentment felt by people of the developing world who expected the modernization process to improve their quality of life. Instead, articulation with the global economy facilitated the destruction of local cultures and brought capitalist domination in the form of "peripheral Fordism" and "bloody Taylorism" in return for very few material gains.[23] However, the mode of regulation in the United States and the global economy was able to ameliorate these tensions and ensure over twenty-five years of steady economic growth in the industrialized world.

Many reasons have been given for the collapse of the Fordist model of development starting in the late 1960s. In general terms, the crisis developed because the Fordist mode of regulation was unable to contain the contradictions of capitalism. Why this occurred remains open to debate. One reason given is that the United States had lost its hegemonic position within the global economy. American business interests retained their hegemonic position as long as Japan and Europe remained weak. As the war-ravaged economies were rebuilt, Americans faced increasingly stiff competition both at home and abroad. Markets in Japan and Europe became increasingly saturated with domestic products. Increased competition forced a decline in the rate of profit of American-based companies. Declining rates of profit were also linked to rigidities in long-term, large-scale investments of fixed capital locked into mass-production systems. Fordist manufacturers, using mass-production techniques, assumed that consumer markets would experience steady upward growth and consumer preferences would remain unchanged.

When foreign goods reached American shores, people began to purchase them in large quantities. The American manufacturers were unprepared to cater to the changing tastes of the American consumer.

Rigidities in Fordist labour forces also led to declining rates of profit. Labour became increasingly militant as their wages and benefits failed to keep up with inflation. Frustrations felt by labour became manifest in the rash of strikes from 1968 to 1972. The State introduced new social programmes in an attempt to maintain its legitimacy. Money to pay for the new programmes came from increased corporate taxes which further decreased profitability. The only flexible American response to the crisis was through State monetary policy. The government had the ability to print money at whatever rate was necessary to keep the economy stable. The circulation of more money only aggravated a volatile situation by triggering another wave of inflation. The inflation- driven crisis of capital accumulation became manifest in the breakdown of the Bretton Woods monetary system.

American dollars were used as foreign exchange reserves and as hard currency in international trade. In the 1960s Americans increased their imports of European goods. The result was a build up of Eurodollars (American dollars held in European countries). The supply of dollars was increased further by U.S. deficit- spending needed to pay for the Vietnam War and Lyndon Johnson's Great Society programmes.[24] Financial instability increased when it was realized that the United States had printed much more money than it could convert into gold. Fixed foreign market exchange rates began to destabilize in 1971 when speculation in U.S. currency increased. As U.S. gold reserves depleted, President Nixon suspended the convertibility of American dollars into gold. By 1973, it was agreed to allow all currencies to float freely on the international market. A global market based on flexible exchange rates is inherently unstable because the investor and trader are not sure what the long-term relationship will be between currencies. Fluctuations in currency exchange rates can cut into the profits of people trading in the global market. Instability in foreign exchange rates represents one reason why some countries eventually entered into free trade agreements and monetary unions. In 1978, members of the European Economic Community created the European Monetary System to stabilize trade and investment by instituting fixed, although adjustable exchange rates amongst member States, while maintaining a floating rate with the outside world.

In the early 1970s, the deteriorating U.S. economy experienced a small reprieve because the oil-producing OPEC countries accepted payment only in American dollars. But a large portion of these petro-dollars ended up as risky loans to underdeveloped and newly industrializing countries which further destabilized the global monetary system. The supply of American dollars circulating in the world economy continued to increase as the United States exported its dollars to cover mounting trade imbalances. Speculation in American dollars increased. Economic instability created by American actions prompted member countries of the Organization for Economic Co-operation and Development (OECD) to unanimously agree that inflation was the most serious problem facing world capitalism. The failure of Keynesian policies to slow inflation convinced the American government to turn to the monetarist policies of economists at the University of Chicago.

Monetarism has been the policy of choice for classical liberals and neoconservatives who abhor the notion of governmental interference in the economy.[25] According to monetarist theory, inflation can be controlled by simply using interest rate policy to adjust the money supply in relation to economic growth. In 1973, Milton Friedman, a leading economist at the University of Chicago, showed that monetarism could work by helping General Pinochet to control inflation in Chile. The fact that unemployment rose from 7 to 30 percent did not seem to be an issue. Monetarism was further legitimized as a policy by the *McCracken Report* commissioned in 1977 by the OECD. The official title of this report was paradoxically called *Towards Full Employment and Price Stability*. Despite the reassuring tone of its title, the report questioned all Keynesian policies adopted in the postwar period. It went on to recommend that countries plagued with inflation adopt a tight money policy (high interest rates), fiscal restraint (low taxes), cuts in social spending (attack on the Welfare State) and the deliberate increase of unemployment. The *McCracken Report* assured OECD countries that inflation could be reduced and profitability restored through the implementation of the "democratic disciplinary state."[26]

In 1979, it appeared as though the international monetary system was on the verge of total collapse. The price of gold was soaring and the value of the U.S. dollar was falling. World economists and bankers warned Paul Volker, then chairman of the U.S. Federal Reserve Board, and William Miller, U.S. secretary of the treasury, that the disastrous run on the dollar would worsen if drastic steps were not taken. In October 1979, the Carter administration formally adopted a monetarist policy, abandoning the State-centered policies of Keynesian economics for the market-centered strategy of monetarism. The Federal Reserve declared a policy of tight money by increasing U.S. interest rates. Unwittingly, Carter sounded the death knell of Fordism by adopting monetarist policies. Ronald Reagan accelerated the demise of Fordism by implementing an even more draconian version of monetarism.

The United States was not the only OECD country to reject Keynesian cures for economic maladies. Monetarism was adopted by almost every OECD country in the 1970s and 1980s. Neoconservative governments believed that a solution to the economic crisis would be found through the "invisible hand of the market-place."[27] Thatcherism in Britain abandoned the consensus-building role of the Welfare State. West German Social Democrats adopted monetarist policies as early as 1973 and the right-wing government of France followed suit in 1976. Even the social democratic countries of Scandinavia adopted tight money policies. By late 1980, it was obvious that the world was slipping into the deepest recession since the Great Depression of the 1930s. Figure 1 and Figure 2 show that most OECD countries experienced drops in the annual percentage increase of their real gross domestic product (GDP) over a twenty-five year period from 1966 to 1991.

Some of the OECD countries rebounded from the recession of the early 1980s. However, any apparent rebound must be interpreted with care because as the last line in Figure 1 shows, recovery for all OECD countries combined has been slight. Even though some countries did improve their rates of economic growth in the late 1980s, growth never regained the momentum of the 1960s and 1970s. Also, countries that did improve in the 1980s based that improvement on regressive tax policies and on extreme debt build- up, versus a firm foundation for long-term growth.

Recovery cannot be discerned simply by measuring the GDP or any other single economic indicator. Unemployment statistics reveal that all European Community countries experienced higher unemployment rates in 1991 than in 1979, prior to the recession. Even though the real GDP of many countries experienced renewed growth, many people permanently lost their jobs. In those countries where unemployment dropped, the labour force has been restructured. Corporations increasingly use flexible production techniques requiring only part-time or temporary labour. The end result for labour is the loss of many benefits including job security and trade union recognition achieved during the Fordist era.[28]

Following the crisis of Fordism, the tax structure in the nineteen most industrialized countries became increasingly regressive. From 1975 to 1985, sales tax, income tax and social security tax have increased as a percent of total tax revenue. Corporate and property tax rates have remained stable. Increasingly

Figure 1
Annual Percentage Increase in the Real GDP of OECD Countries

Country	1966-78	1974-79	1980-85	1986-91
Canada	5.3	4.2	2.4	3.0
France	5.5	3.1	1.1	2.9
Italy	5.4	2.6	1.4	3.2
Japan	9.4	3.6	4.0	4.4
United Kingdom	3.1	1.5	1.2	2.5
United States	3.4	2.5	2.5	3.1
West Germany	4.1	2.4	1.3	3.3
OECD Average Growth	4.5	2.7	2.3	3.3

Source: "OECD Economic Outlook," *OECD Observer* 161 (February 1991): 33.

regressive tax rates represent just one element in a litany of policies adopted by neoconservatives attempting to erect a post-Fordist model of development.[29] In addition to monetarism and regressive tax structures, neoconservative policies also include reduction of social services offered by the State. George Bush's "thousand points of light" called for increased private contributions to shore up the gap left by cuts in the American Welfare State. Neoconservatives advocate the deregulation of business, finance and banking, transportation, communications, environmental controls, health and safety standards and any other impediment to investment.

The ideology of free trade also dominates the corporate agenda, particularly in the United States where exporters have long been frustrated by their inability to penetrate Japanese and some European markets. New Right governments are vehemently anti-union. This was graphically displayed in President Reagan's firing of striking American air traffic controllers and Prime Minister Thatcher's treatment of the British coal miners' unions. Capital became increasingly aggressive and "disciplinary" in its attempt to implement a new model of development.[30] It is in this context that one must view the crisis of capital

Figure 2
Annual Percentage Increase in Real GDP of OECD Countries

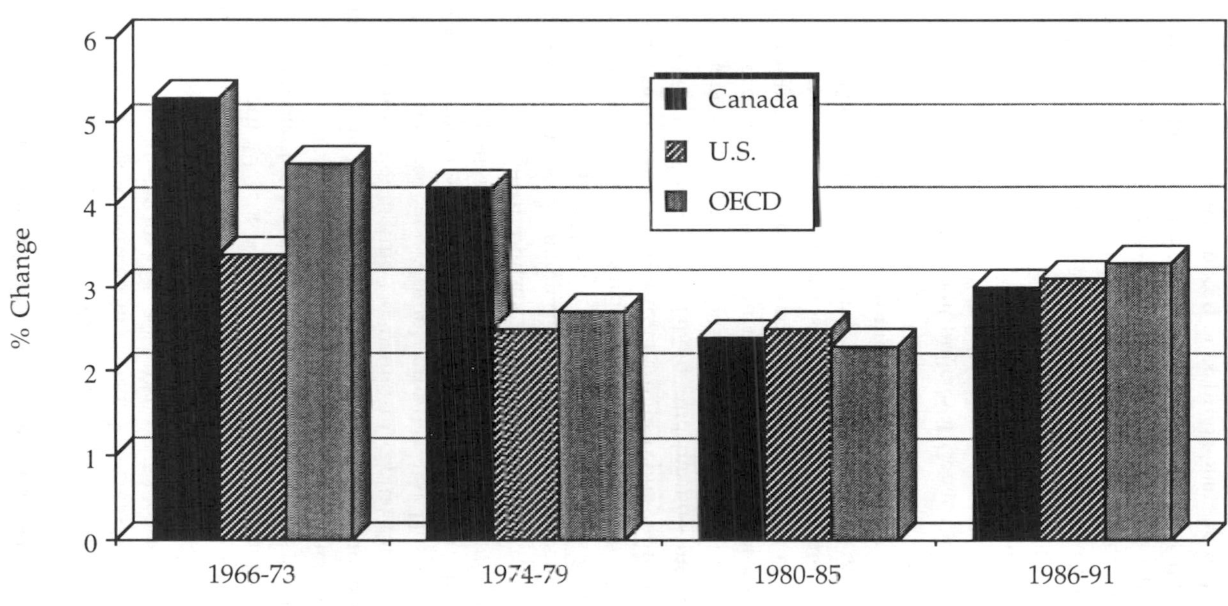

Source: "OECD Economic Outlook," OECD Observer 161 (February 1991): 33.

accumulation in Canada and the free trade agreement between Canada and the U.S.

The inflation plaguing the rest of the world afflicted Canada as well. The impact of the crisis is revealed in Canada's decreasing rate of economic growth during the 1970s and early 1980s (see Figure 1). Canada's Fordist labour-management compromise became increasingly strained as wages lagged behind the rate of inflation. Strike activity increased dramatically in the early 1970s as workers attempted to keep inflation from eroding their purchasing power. In 1974, consumer prices increased by 10.9 percent. The governor of the Bank of Canada announced the gradual implementation of monetarist policies.[31] In theory, a monetarist policy fights inflation by slowing the circulation of capital through higher interest rates and reduced money supply growth rates. This strategy had little effect as evidenced by the 9.1 percent inflation rate in 1980.

In the face of inflation and decreasing rates of profitability, the Canadian government appointed Donald Macdonald in 1982 to chair the Royal Commission on the Economic Union and Development Prospects for Canada to find a remedy for the ailing economy. This commission, which came to be called the Macdonald Commission, held hearings across Canada listening to testimony from groups representing Native Canadians, churches, farmers, women, labour, and business interests. The Macdonald Commission agreed with business interests when it concluded that Canada needed to rely more on market forces to solve economic problems. Government interventions to counter the effects of recessions were deemed unrealistic and unnecessary. The Welfare State needed to be streamlined. The capstone to the report was that a bilateral free trade agreement should be negotiated with the United States. In the words of the Macdonald Commission chairman, Canadians needed to take a "leap of faith" and adopt radically different policies if Canada was to embark on the road to economic recovery.[32]

One of the reasons for recommending the FTA was that it would provide Canadian industries secure access to a larger market. Canadian industries could become more efficient by expanding their production facilities to take advantage of economies of scale. The more likely reason for recommending the FTA was that it would enable the Canadian government and business elites to restructure the Canadian economy along the lines of the Reagan/Thatcher agenda in order to restore corporate profitability. According to this view, Fordist social relations and institutions operating at the level of the Nation-State — national unions, national restrictions on investment, State monopolies, regional development programmes, cultural development programmes, the expansive Canadian Welfare State, subsidies and tariffs — impose restrictions on the circulation and profitability of multinational capital. These impediments, anchored at the level of the Nation-State, have blocked attempts made by multinational capital to restore lagging profitability — a product of the crisis of Fordism. By bringing Canada and the United States into closer contact, continental market forces would enable the Canadian government and an international business elite to restructure the Canadian economy along neoconservative lines.

What is the logic behind this neoconservative agenda? The United States is a more market-oriented society than Canada. Social programmes have been dismantled under Reagan and Bush. The Left and trade unions are much weaker in the United States than their counterparts in Canada. Knowing this, the Canadian government did not want to lose legitimacy by directly confronting labour while simultaneously dismantling social welfare programmes. The implementation of free trade offers a more subtle, yet strategic approach. As articulation between the two economies increases, inevitable market pressures to harmonize policies will force Canada to conform to American standards. This explains why Brian Mulroney and the Progressive Conservatives ran an anti free trade election campaign in 1984 and then pursued free trade policies once in office. The FTA represents an attempt to discipline labour and reduce the Canadian Welfare State while enhancing capital mobility — class warfare, Canadian style.33 The next chapter examines the free trade debate to reveal how the neutral discourse of neoclassical trade theory masks the non-neutral impacts of free trade.

Notes

1. John Warnock, *Free Trade and the New Right Agenda* (Vancouver: New Star Books, 1988), 69-71; Paul Phillips, *Canadian Political Economy: An Economic Introduction* (Toronto: Garamond Press, 1990), 116; Stephen Clarkson, "Disjunctions: Free Trade and the Paradox of Canadian Development," in *The New Era of Global Competition*, Daniel Drache and Meric Gertler, eds. (Montréal: McGill-Queen's University Press, 1991), 103.
2. Robert Pollen and Alexander Cockburn, "A Haunted House: Capitalism and Its Specters — the World, the Free Market, and the Left," *The Nation*, 252 (July 1991): 234; Robert Kuttner, "Forward," in *The Political Economy of North American Free Trade*, Ricardo Grinspun and Maxwell A. Cameron, eds. (New York: St.Martin's Press, 1993), xii.
3. Peter Held, "Why we must understand the competitiveness issue. Speech given to the Canadian Institute of Chartered Accountants," *Canadian Speeches*,

5 (June 1991): 53; Michael Demers, "Responding to the challenges of the global economy: the competitiveness agenda," in *How Ottawa Spends: The Politics of Competitiveness, 1992-1993*, Frances Abele, ed. (Ottawa: Carleton University Press, 1992), 151.

4. BCNI, "Canadian Trade, Competitiveness and Sovereignty: The Prospect of New Trade Agreements with the United States," (Ottawa: Unpublished Report of the BCNI, 1985), 1.
5. Michael Buroway, *The Politics of Production: Factory Regimes Under Capitalism and Socialism* (New York: Verso, 1985), 150; David Harvey, "From Space to Place and Back Again: Reflections on the Condition of Post-Modernity," in *Mapping the Futures: Local Cultures, Global Change*, Jon Bird et al., eds. (New York: Routledge, 1993), 8.
6. Immanuel Wallerstein, *The Capitalist World Economy* (Cambridge: Cambridge University Press, 1979), 31.
7. Daniel Leborgne and Alain Lipietz, "New Technologies, New Modes of Regulation: Some Spatial Implications," *Environment and Planning D: Society and Space*, 6 (1988): 263; Alain Noel, "Accumulation, Regulation, and Social Change: An Essay on French Political Economy," *International Organization*, 41 (Spring 1987): 303.
8. Michel Aglietta, *The Theory of Capitalist Regulation: The American Experience*, trans. David Fernback (New York: Verso, 1979), 68; Michael De Vroey, "A Regulation Approach Interpretation of Contemporary Crisis," *Capital and Class*, 23 (Summer 1984): 45; Alain Lipietz, *Mirages and Miracles: The Crisis of Global Fordism*, trans. David Macey (London: Verso, 1987), 32; Alain Lipietz and Jane Jenson, "Rebel Sons: The Regulation School. Jane Jenson Interviews Alain Lipietz," *French Politics and Society*, 5 (Fall 1987): 18; Robert Boyer, *The Regulation School: A Critical Introduction*, trans. Craig Charney (New York: Columbia University Press, 1990), 56; Bob Jessop, "Regulation Theories in Retrospect and Prospect," *Economy and Society*, 19 (Spring 1990): 153. Criticisms of Regulation theory can be found in Robert Brenner and Mark Glick, "The Regulation Approach: Theory and History," *New Left Review*, 188 (July/August 1991): 45; Andrew Sayer and Richard Walker, *The New Social Economy: Reworking the Division of Labor* (Cambridge, MA: Blackwell, 1992), 193-199. They criticize Regulation theory for oversimplifying the transition from Fordism to post-Fordism. Their criticisms generally ring false because their narrow focus on economic change fails to consider the manner in which Regulation theory has been used to study the changing nature of the Welfare State and society.
9. Antonio Gramsci, *An Antonio Gramsci Reader, Selected Writings: 1916-1935*, David Forgacs, ed. (New York: Shocken Books, 1988), 277.
10. David Harvey, *The Condition of Postmodernity* (Cambridge, MA: Basil Blackwell, 1989), 121; Alfred D. Chandler, *Scale and Scope: The Dynamics of Industrial Capitalism* (Cambridge, MA: Harvard University Press, 1990), 1; Bryan Palmer, *Working Class Experience: Rethinking the History of Canadian Labour, 1800- 1991, 2nd* ed. (Toronto: McClelland and Stewart, 1992), 337.
11. Harvey, *The Condition of Postmodernity*, 126.
12. Gramsci, *An Antonio Gramsci Reader*, 279.

13. Harvey, *The Condition of Postmodernity*, 126.
14. Ibid., 127.
15. Ibid., 128; Harry Braverman, *Labor and Monopoly Capital: The Degradation of work in the Twentieth Century* (New York: Monthly Review Press, 1974), 149.
16. Ernest Mandel, *Late Capitalism*, trans. Joris de Bres (New York: Verso, 1975), 130; Lipietz, *Mirages and Miracles*, 43; Harvey, The Condition of Postmodernity, 128-29.
17. Phillips, *Canadian Political Economy*, 99; Pat Armstrong, Andrew Glyn and John Harrison, *Capitalism since 1945* (New York: Basil Blackwell 1991), 12; James O'Connor, *Accumulation Crisis* (New York: Basil Blackwell 1984), 46.
18. Harvey, *The Condition of Postmodernity*, 132; Fred Block, *The Origins of International Economic Disorder: A Study of United States International Monetary Policy from World War II to the Present* (Berkeley: University of California Press, 1977), 86-92.
19. Kenneth Jackson, *Crabgrass Frontier: The Suburbanization of the United States* (New York: Oxford University Press, 1985), 190; Peter Hall, *Cities of Tomorrow: An Intellectual History of Urban Planning and Design in the Twentieth Century* (New York: Basil Blackwell, 1988), 291.
20. Warnock, *Free Trade and the New Right Agenda*, 28; David Gordon, Richard Edwards and Michael Reich, *Segmented Work, Divided Workers: The Historical Transformation of Labor in the United States* (Cambridge: Cambridge University Press, 1982), 185.
21. Gramsci, *An Antonio Gramsci Reader*, 278.
22. Michel Aglietta, "World Capitalism in the Eighties," *New Left Review*, 136 (November 1982): 8; E. A. Brett, *International Money and Capitalist Crisis: Anatomy of Global Disintegration* (Boulder: Westview Press, 1983), 8-9.
23. Gosta Esping-Anderson, *The Three Worlds of Welfare Capitalism* (Princeton: Princeton University Press, 1990), 228; Lipietz, *Mirages and Miracles*, 189.
24. Harvey, *The Condition of Postmodernity*, 142; Block, *The Origins of International Economic Disorder*, 204; Brett, *International Money and Capitalist Crisis*, 163.
25. A clarification in the terminology is required here. The term "neoconservative" has been generally used to define a particular set of economic and social beliefs that promote laissez-fair capitalism, privatization and reduced governmental intervention in the economy, monetarism and deep cuts in the Welfare State. In the United States, neoconservative has also been used to describe the beliefs of Christian conservatives exemplified in the teachings and writings of Pat Robertson and Moral Majority leader, Jerry Falwell. Some researchers distinguish the various meanings of conservative thought by using the term "neoliberal" to define the economic programme espousing reduced governmental intervention, privatization, monetarism, and personal entrepreneurship. Neoconservative has then been used to define the turn to fundamental religious beliefs as well as national chauvinism and patriarchal family values. This distinction will not be made here because it is difficult to separate the two terms in reality. In Canada and the United States, many of the same people promoting neoliberalism were also social conservatives. Hence, the term neoconservative will be used to define the economic programme typified by Reaganomics and Thatcherism, with the implicit acknow-

ledgment that the economic programme cannot be separated from the social milieu in which it was formulated and implemented. Please refer to James O'Connor, *The Meaning of Crisis: A Theoretical Introduction* (New York: Basil Blackwell, 1987), 155. As an aside, O'Connor points out contradictions within the Reagan agenda: The individualism inherent in the neoliberal agenda is in direct conflict with the social strictures espoused by the social conservatism of Christian fundamentalists.

26. Warnock, *Free Trade and the New Right Agenda*, 34; Michael Dunford, "Theories of Regulation," *Environment and Planning D: Society and Space*, 8 (1990): 297.
27. Alain Lipietz, "The Debt Problem, European Integration and the New Phase of World Crisis," *New Left Review*, 178 (November 1989): 39.
28. OECD Observer, "OECD Economic Outlook," *OECD Observer*, 161 (February/March 1991): 33; Allen Scott, "Flexible Production Systems and Regional Development," *International Journal of Urban and Regional Research*, 12 (Spring 1988): 177; Leo Panitch, "Capitalist Restructuring and Labour Strategies," *Studies in Political Economy*, 24 (Autumn 1987): 132.
29. World Bank, *World Development Report* (Oxford: Oxford University Press, 1988), 83; World Bank, *World Development Report* (Oxford: Oxford University Press, 1991), 96.
30. Mike Davis, *Prisoners of the American Dream* (New York: Verso, 1986), 136-50.
31. David A. Wolfe, "The Rise and Demise of the Keynesian Era in Canada: Economic Policy, 1930-1982," in *Readings in Canadian Social History, Volume 5: Modern Canada, 1930-1980s*, Michael Cross and Gregory Kealey, eds. (Toronto: McClelland and Stewart, 1985), 73; Phillips, *Canadian Political Economy*, 101; Clarkson, "Disjunctions: Free Trade and the Paradox of Canadian Development," 108.
32. Donald A. Macdonald, "A Leap of Faith: The Canadian Decision for Free Trade," *The American Review of Canadian Studies*, 21 (2/3 1991): 155. The fact that the Macdonald Commission supported free trade should come as no surprise. Donald Macdonald sat on the Board of Directors of the Canadian Alliance for Trade and Job Opportunities, a pro-FTA business lobby that spent millions of dollars to promote free trade.
33. Duncan Cameron, "The Dealers: We Didn't Get What We Wanted and Gave Away a Lot. So Why is Our Business Class So Happy with Free Trade?" *This Magazine*, 21 (1988): 19.

Chapter 2

Continentalism versus Nationalism: Geographic Discourse in the Debate over Free Trade

Brian Mulroney publicly rejected bilateral free trade with the United States prior to his election as Canadian prime minister in 1984. But after only one year in office, he announced that Canada and the United States were negotiating a bilateral free trade agreement. Scarce attention was paid to these developments by the general public in the United States. In Canada, however, a serious debate erupted over the merits of free trade. The debate subsided but did not end with the implementation of the FTA in 1989. After examining the discourse used in the free trade debates, it is clear that supporters and opponents of free trade differed according to whether or not geography was part of their rhetoric. Free trade boosters ignored geography by using non-spatial arguments while opponents of the FTA relied on what could be called spatial or explicitly geographic arguments.[1] Why did this dichotomy exist? By examining the discourse of free trade for its geographic content, one can determine the underlying motives of the people engaged in the free trade debate.[2] People excluded or included geographic metaphors and/or the concrete geographic implications of free trade in developing their arguments for or against free trade.

One cannot understand the implications of free trade without understanding the geography of free trade. Neoclassical theories of free trade are nothing more than strategies to achieve certain political-economic goals. Free trade can be a form of economic nationalism as Britain used it against Portugal in the eighteenth century. It can also be a form of antinationalism as it is used by Canadian supporters of free trade in the twentieth century. Free trade is not a universal economic theory but a foreign policy that is promoted by different groups of people in different places and different times.

Foucault and Discourse Theory

Canadian and American governments spent millions of dollars promoting free trade in Canada prior to 1989. In 1989, Canadian author Margaret Atwood exhorted us to ask why governments would spend so much money promoting such a controversial policy.[3] Discourse theory helps us to answer that question. Michel Foucault, a proponent of discourse theory, believes that our political task in society is to be skeptical of actors and institutions which appear to be both neutral and independent. One must penetrate beneath the level of appearances and identify the power struggles, ruptures and discourses which comprise the development of the seemingly continuous evolution of ideas and institutions within society.[4]

Foucault penetrates the neutral facade erected by particular actors or institutions by undertaking what he calls a "genealogy" of ideas and knowledge emanating from a particular institution. Foucault sees the creation of knowledge as occurring in a non-neutral manner. To understand an idea or body of knowledge is to understand how that knowledge was created to serve a particular end. A genealogy of an idea or institution therefore requires a critical study of the history of the development of that idea or institution. Foucault repudiated the traditional approach to the history of ideas which perceives the creation of knowledge as the evolutionary progress towards some immutable truth. Instead, we must uncover the complex interrelationships, discontinuities and contradictions that make up a body of knowledge. The role of the genealogy is to break apart monolithic theories in order to discover the multiplicity of discourses within a body of knowledge.[5]

A critical programme of research must expose the discourse of power and domination working behind neutral or seemingly beneficent facades. Equal attention must be paid to what is said as well as to what is left unsaid when analyzing a particular discourse. Neoclassical and Marxist theory are equally suspect because of the simplifying assumptions they make and the dominant ideologies embedded in both paradigms. Minority and oppressed voices are shut out of the debate. For oppressed and dissenting voices to be heard over the din of hegemonic discourses, Foucault advocates paying greater attention to the manner in which social scientific knowledge is presented, misrepresented, or omitted entirely. He wants us to discover who controls what questions we are allowed to ask as social scientists. When examining the regional impacts of free trade, we should therefore ask how geography is represented, misrepresented or unrepresented.[6] By answering these questions, we can uncover the intent of the supporters and opponents of free trade.

A Genealogy of Free Trade Theory

A genealogy of the discourse of neoclassical trade theory would be incomplete without tracing its roots through the discourse of mercantilist and classical trade theory. Mercantilist trade theory promoted the use of various techniques to enforce a positive balance of trade and national security. The emphasis was on the export of manufactured goods because of their higher value-added. The final goal was to maximize the flow of gold into the royal treasury. Mercantilism was really a beggar-thy-neighbor strategy employed so that a country might engage in colonialism: the granting of trade monopolies, the enforcement of unequal exchange between country and colony and ultimately war and territorial expansion in order to guarantee a positive trade balance and hence security for the State. Subtlety and understatement were alien to the discourse of mercantile trade theory. Policy-makers were concerned only with promoting policies of self-interest through economic nationalism.

In the early stages of the Industrial Revolution in the late eighteenth century, England began to experience greatly increased industrial capacity and productivity. With a surfeit of commodities, British merchants needed increased markets and a more stable world trading system than that found under mercantilism. British traders wanted a more efficient world economic system to realize the profits embedded in their surplus commodities. The question then became how to correct the errors and excesses of mercantilism and create a world economy based on stable trade while still out-competing other countries.

Two British political economists, Adam Smith and David Ricardo, solved the problems of mercantilist trade and ushered in the era of classical political economy and free trade.

The "normative" premise of the classical theory of trade was that free trade was beneficial to all trading partners. The reasons why this is so rest in the related concepts of absolute and comparative advantage. Adam Smith believed that economic specialization produced gains in productive efficiency and national income. He also believed that trade increased the consumption possibilities within a country and therefore international trade had beneficial effects on both the demand and supply sides of the economy. In the *Wealth of Nations* (1776), Adam Smith argued that economic growth was the key to national wealth and power. Economic growth was dependent upon a division of labour which was itself directly related to the scale of the market. When mercantilist countries impeded economic growth by limiting the scale of the market and by erecting barriers against the exchange of goods, it was their domestic welfare and economic growth that suffered from these protectionist strategies. Smith argued that countries should specialize in producing what they did best based upon their resource endowment and then engage in free trade with other countries in the world economy to become wealthy and powerful. Smith's trade theory was therefore based on the merits of a territorial division of labour and *absolute advantage* in production.

In his *Principles of Political Economy and Taxation* (1817), David Ricardo extended the trade theory of Adam Smith to show how trade could be mutually beneficial. His law of *comparative advantage* provided a new basis for trade theory, forming the foundation for modern neoclassical trade theory. In fact, Krugman asserts that an economist's creed would contain the affirmation: "I believe in the principle of comparative advantage."[7] Building on the ideas of Adam Smith, Ricardo established the law of comparative advantage as the fundamental rationale for free trade. Smith assumed that the wealth of two trading partners would be maximized if each country specialized in the production of goods in which it has the greatest efficiency. Consider country A and country B, both of which produce commodity P and commodity W. Country A most efficiently produces commodity P while country B is best at producing commodity W. In Smith's terminology, country A enjoys an absolute advantage in commodity P and country B enjoys an absolute advantage in commodity W. Prosperity can be maximized in both countries if they specialize in the production of the commodities in which they have an absolute advantage and then engage in free trade with each other. The basis for this absolute advantage rested entirely on the domestic endowment of factor inputs into the production process.

What happens to the country that enjoys no absolute advantage in the production of any commodity? What if, in our two-country, two-product model, country A is more efficient (has an absolute advantage) in the production of both commodities of P and W? Ricardo asserts that the countries should not regress to a situation of autarky. In his law of comparative advantage, Ricardo demonstrated that both countries should still engage in trade because the flow of goods between countries is determined by the relative, not absolute, costs of the goods produced. In our model, country A should specialize in the production of the commodity in which it is the most efficient or for which it has the greatest comparative advantage. Even though a country may have an absolute advantage in the production of every commodity, it should specialize in the production of goods in which it has the greatest comparative advantage and leave the production of other commodities to other countries. The creation of an international division of labour enables all countries to gain more from exchange. This simple yet elegant idea based on comparative advantage and the universal benefits of specialization remains a central tenet of neoclassical free trade theory.[8]

Why was Ricardo promoting this natural law of comparative advantage? According to this economic principle, universal benefits accrue to all parties involved when countries specialize in production and then trade their surplus commodities. In order to show how this could be true, Ricardo developed a model of free trade comparing England and Portugal and the production of textiles and wine. Using quantitative data, Ricardo worked out that Portugal enjoyed an absolute advantage in both the production of wine and textiles. Ricardo based his figures for this model on the labour theory of value which says that commodities produced for the market have a basic value proportional to the amount of labour time expended on their production. Ricardo then showed that Portugal possessed a comparative advantage in the production of wine and therefore England should produce and trade textiles while Portugal specialized in the production and trade of wine.

We should be careful, however, to understand the intent behind Ricardo's theory. Ricardo certainly understood that starting with the defeat of the Spanish Armada by the English in 1588, the British had clearly dominated the Iberian Peninsula. Spain and Portugal had been virtually eliminated from participating in the global expansion of capitalism during the seventeenth century by means of a series of commercial treaties culminating in the Methuen Treaty of 1703. Ricardo was well aware of England's greater efficiency in producing manufactured goods. Because there was no capital mobility or MNCs, Ricardo's work justified a policy of economic nationalism for Britain.[9] His model rationalized how logical and fair it was for the English to produce and trade textiles — a high value-added industrial product — for Portuguese wine, a much lower value agricultural product. Thus, Ricardo provided a rationalization for the exploitation of Portugal by England on the supposed natural law of comparative advantage. Free trade was presented as a natural, neutral concept, but it actually concealed the existence of unequal exchange and hid the process of technological underdevelopment. "Objective" and scientific economic discourse served to camouflage a politically-motivated justification for a particular trade policy.

Another example will reveal the political nature of the seemingly unbiased discourse of free trade and comparative advantage. Ricardo was writing during the time of the Industrial Revolution of the early nineteenth century. England, once a grain exporter, had become a net grain importer under the pressure of increasing industrialization and urbanization. During the early stages of the Industrial Revolution there was parliamentary over-representation of the landed gentry who were able to enact the Corn Laws in 1815. These laws seriously affected English society by preventing the importation of cheap grains thus raising the profits of the landed gentry. Ricardo was born into the family of a well-to-do stockbroker. He became a successful stockbroker in his own right before becoming a member of parliament. With ties to the business community, Ricardo was sympathetic to the plight of the industrialists. They had to pay higher wages because the Corn Laws increased the cost of food for labourers while providing increased profits for the landed aristocracy.

Ricardo was not writing in a vacuum. His theory was written as a polemic to counter the protectionist policies of the agrarian elite in parliament. Although Ricardo died in 1823, his theory was used to promote the 1832 Reform Bill which provided greater parliamentary representation for industrialists. Furthermore, Ricardo's theory provided the justification to gain the repeal of the Corn Laws in 1846. Therefore, the political intent of Ricardo's theory must be openly stated. Clearly, the interests of industrial capital were being served over the interests of the landed gentry and agricultural labour. Lower food prices would drive workers off the land and serve to lower the industrial wage. As the displaced farm workers migrated to the cities to find factory jobs the urban wages were driven down due to the increase in the reserve army of labour.[10] Again the political intent of the law of comparative advantage and free trade becomes apparent. The goals of one group (industrial capital) were served over the desires of other groups in society (landed gentry and labour). Despite the overtly political consequences of the law of comparative advantage, it has always been presented as a natural and therefore neutral tendency.

The classical theory of trade was based on a number of important assumptions and abstractions about reality. It omitted the cost of transportation and assumed that factors of production were domestically mobile but internationally immobile. Comparative advantage was therefore static because it was based on the endowment of natural resources which could not be transferred from one country to another. Comparative advantage as conceived by Ricardo was also based on the labour theory value and a two-country, two-product model of trade.[11]

Theories of free trade came under attack by political economists soon after the British openly promoted free trade as a foreign policy in the 1840s. Friedrich List argued in *National System of Political Economy* (1841) that the classical economic concepts of comparative advantage and free trade were not immutable laws. Rather, factor endowments and the international division of labour were a product of historical uses of economic and political power. Furthermore, List remarked that the British had relied on State intervention, protectionism and military force to weaken their trading opponents. Only after they had achieved technological and industrial supremacy did the British advocate free trade.[12]

Subsequent criticisms of the classical theory of comparative advantage and free trade have produced a number of refinements in trade theory. Neoclassical theorists have included transportation costs, assumed some factor mobility between countries and have stressed the importance of increasing returns to scale as an explanation of international trade. In the case of the Canada-United States FTA, increasing returns to scale was a crucial element in arguments made by supporters of free trade. Factors other than labour such as management and industrial organization have been added to the cost of production, thus leading to the concept of relative-factor endowment as an explanation for trade flows. The concept of labour itself has been redefined. Neoclassical economists have abandoned the labour theory of value. Instead, labour has become "human capital" and cost has become "opportunity cost."[13] Rounding out neoclassical modifications to classical theory are marginal utility theories and general equilibrium theory.

This neoclassical reformulation has become known as the Hecksher-Ohlin model of international trade after the two Swedish economists, Eli Hecksher and Bertil Ohlin who first developed it. Some credit has also been given to Paul Samuelson for further refining the neoclassical model of free trade so it is sometimes also referred to as the Hecksher-Ohlin-Samuelson (H-O-S) model — the standard neoclassical position on free trade in the 1980s and 1990s. H-O-S theory maintains that each country's comparative advantage is based on differential endowments of the factors of production. Each country will have a unique mix of capital, land, labour, management and technology which determines the products to be produced and traded.

In spite of the advances made by neoclassical trade theory over the classical ruminations of Ricardo, it is clear that it still represents a justification for unequal exchange between more-developed countries (MDCs) and less-developed countries (LDCs) due to differences in technology, wages and rates of exploitation. Adherents to the H-O-S model would explain that LDCs have an abundance of labour and MDCs have an abundance of capital and technology. Therefore, MDCs should produce and exchange capital intensive commodities such as manufactured goods while LDCs should specialize in the production and trade of labour intensive commodities.[14]

Besides continuing to conceal the non-neutral and unequal nature of free trade, neoclassical theory fails to address other macroeconomic issues. One outcome of free trade is the increased specialization of production and a narrowing of a country's economic base. Valid arguments can be made to maintain a certain level of economic diversity through the use of tariffs to reduce the impact of recessions and commodity price fluctuations. Neoclassical trade theory errs in its oversimplification of the world with its focus only on the most efficient allocation of resources to the exclusion of issues such as political security and economic survival. Furthermore, even if free trade can be shown to increase wealth, no mention is made of the distribution of newly-created wealth. Free trade and comparative advantage say nothing about distributional justice within society. Opponents to free trade argue that free trade only enhances the mobility of capital to move from high-wage to low-wage regions thus driving down wages in all regions. Far from increasing national wealth, free trade actually undermines the standard of living for workers by driving down their wages under the threat of capital mobility. For example, General Motors has threatened to abandon Canadian production sites in favor of lower-cost American sites if Canadian workers do not make concessions on wages and benefits.[15]

In fact, the most serious flaw in the concept of comparative advantage and free trade lies in the assumption of capital and labour *immobility*. In eighteenth and nineteenth-century England, industrialists invested only in Britain or the British Empire; therefore, free trade was a form of economic nationalism. The fundamental place of nationalist thinking in trade policy is illustrated by Adam Smith's proclamation that the capitalist is first and foremost a member of a national community.[16] However, in the late twentieth century, capital is much more mobile than labour. Cosmopolitan money managers and MNCs have abandoned their national communities on which the whole idea of comparative advantage was developed. In the nineteenth century an economic nationalist supported free trade. In the late twentieth century an economic nationalist is opposed to free trade. By examining the discourse of free trade, one can see that the seemingly scientific and objective law of comparative advantage is not a fixed or immutable concept but an ideology which changes to suit the purposes of the dominant fractions of capital within a particular country.

There is even a recognition amongst some neoclassical economists that the H-O-S model of international trade is becoming obsolete as a foundation for explaining current patterns of global trade. Broad agreement exists that this neoclassical model is still an appropriate theory for explaining trade between MDCs and LDCs. The problem for the neoclassical model of trade rests in its inability to explain the exchange of goods among the industrialized countries themselves. Where the H-O-S model emphasized factor endowments and perfect competition, newer approaches such as the product cycle theory and the profit cycle theory emphasize monopolistic or imperfect competition, theories of the firm and industrial organization, development of technology, the rise of intra-firm trade, the integration of international trade with foreign investment, economies of scale and the dynamic nature of comparative advantage. With the increased international spread of oligopolistic corporations and the internationalization of production, trade theory has evolved to become a theory of international industrial organization.

Striking contrasts exist between traditional trade theory and the newer approaches.[17] The emphasis of trade theory from Ricardo to the H-O-S model was on inter-industry trade. The more recent theories focus on intra-industry, intra-firm, and inter-firm trade. Classical and neoclassical theories were based on the assumption of labour and capital immobility, static comparative advantage and the trade only of finished goods. Newer theories have been developed in response to a more current reality where capital is highly mobile and products are exchanged at every step of the production process including technological knowledge, intermediate products, component parts and the final finished commodity. Intra-firm trade occupies an increasingly large proportion of global trade. Some economists estimate that up to 40 percent of international trade in manufactured goods occurs between affiliates of the same multinational corporation.[18] This development undermines the assumption of perfect competition on which neoclassical models of trade are based.

By the 1990s, it can be said that comparative advantage and the standard neoclassical theory of free trade have lost much of their relevance and predictive power. Focus on the intensity and abundance of factors of production to account for world trade patterns and free trade is of marginal use in a world of increasing intra-firm trade and rapid technological diffusion. Hecksher and Ohlin would scarcely recognize the current conception of comparative advantage. Many economists now regard comparative advantage to be a highly dynamic and arbitrary concept which is predominantly a product of corporate and State policies. As the concept of comparative advantage has lost its cogency, the argument for free trade has lost much of its efficacy.[19]

The varying patterns of global trade in the late twentieth century and the proliferation of theories to explain this trade have convinced some economists that no single or universal theory is capable of explaining the international trade of all commodities in all places at all times. The unified discourse of trade theory supporting the H-O-S model has been fragmented and replaced by a number of specific explanations for different types of commodities in different trading relations.

Despite the increased fragmentation of trade theory, it can be said that the doctrine of comparative advantage still survives. This is a testimony to the elegance and persuasive nature of the theory: that it can remain a central tenet of mainstream economics despite evidence showing its lack of relevancy. It is a tautological theory that really only applies to a world economy based on the trade of minerals and agricultural products.[20] This begs the question: why has the notion of comparative advantage and the universal benefits of free trade been used to promote the Canada-United States FTA when unified trade theory can be shown to be deficient in many ways? The answer is that the seemingly scientific and objective discourse of comparative advantage hides the intent of the corporate elite who support free trade. Their aim is to deregulate the national economies of North America in order to restore profitability by increasing capital mobility. To show how this occurred, the next section first provides the history of free trade discourse in Canada before examining the actual discourse employed most recently in Canada and the United States in support and opposition to free trade.

The Discourse of Free Trade In Canada and the United States

Historical Perspectives on Free Trade in Canada

As a British colony, Canada engaged in free trade with the United States from 1854 to 1866. Canada gained its independence in 1867 and promptly followed other late-industrializers such as Germany in adopting protectionist policies. The Tory government of Sir John A. MacDonald implemented what was called the National Policy to ensure that the Canadian economy developed independently from the American economy.[21] Canadian nationalism became manifest in a nationalist economic policy.[22] Canadian leaders who supported the National Policy believed that the natural transportation axis ran north-south between Canada and the United States. Geography was working against the creation of an independent Canada. The aim of the National Policy was to create an east-west transportation axis within Canada by constructing a transcontinental railroad and promoting the development of a domestic industrial sector through a system of tariffs and subsidized rail traffic. The basic goal was to foster a national economy based on the Canadian West as an internal colony serving the interests of commercial, financial, and industrial capital located in Southern Ontario and Québec. Free trade agreements between Canada and the United States were proposed and rejected four times between 1911 and 1948. Canadians feared that without the tariffs that maintained an east-west transportation axis, Canada could not compete with the more efficient American infrastructure. Ultimately, Canadians believed that their commercial and transportation system would be put out of business without the tariff protection.[23]

Canadian political and economic interests also feared American visions of Manifest Destiny. Many Americans resented British and Canadian support of the Confederacy during the American Civil War. Canadians believed that this resentment could be translated into American territorial expansion north of the forty-ninth parallel. As a result, Canadian officials implemented the National Policy to solidify land claims west of the Great Lakes. Furthermore, the period after the American Civil War marked the emergence of large American firms that perceived their markets as not only national, but continental. Canadian firms complained that American firms were underselling them and that they needed protection if they were to survive.

The Canadian tariff wall had a significant impact on industrial development during the first half of the twentieth century. A Canadian manufacturing sector began to develop but it had to compete with a rapidly expanding branch-plant economy. Foreign (increasingly American) companies interested in gaining access to the Canadian market were setting up branch plants to circumvent Canadian tariffs. In 1900, American investments represented 13.6 percent of total foreign investment in Canada. British foreign investment constituted 85.2 percent of total foreign investment. By 1950, American foreign investment represented 75.5 percent of total foreign investment in Canada compared to 20.1 percent for Britain. By mid-century, Canada had substituted a dependence on British capital nurtured during the era of colonialism and the British Commonwealth Preferential Tariff System for dependence on American capital.[24]

Protectionist and nationalist policies formed the backbone of Canadian economic policy up until the 1940s when the GATT negotiations began to chip away at the Canadian tariff wall. It was during the 1940s and 1950s that mainstream Canadian economists began to adopt an ideology of anti-nationalism and pro-continentalism.[25] The continentalist view was likely inspired by the close co-operation between Canada and the United States during the Second World War. An important impetus towards continentalism and free trade was the Hyde Park Declaration signed by Canada and the United States on April 20, 1941. The United States agreed to buy more military hardware from Canada and to extend credit so that England could purchase Canadian commodities on lend-lease. The Hyde Park Agreement was also designed to help Canada stabilize its balance of payments problems with the United States. A significant aspect of the Hyde Park Declaration was the decision to co-ordinate defence production programmes by producing the articles that each country was "best able to produce."[26]

The discourse of comparative advantage underpinned Canadian-American co-operation which had grown markedly during the Second World War. Canada became increasingly tied to the American economy through a growing network of joint economic committees. Studies were done to determine which nation could produce which commodities and how goods and services should be most efficiently traded across their shared border. By 1945, 37 percent of Canada's exports went to the United States and 72 percent of Canada's imports came from the United States.[27] The increased integration imposed by wartime co-operation was instrumental in promoting an anti-nationalist or even pro-continentalist viewpoint amongst mainstream economists, corporate executives, politicians, and policy think-tanks in the period following the war. The pattern was set for Canada's postwar development strategy which dictated that Canada rely on large-scale exports of resources to the United States while inflows of American capital expanded staple sectors and the branch-plant economy.[28]

One influential policy organization which helped shape Canada's postwar growth was the Canadian-American Committee (CAC) sponsored jointly by the National Planning Association of the United States and the Private Planning Association of Canada. The Private Planning Association merged with the C. D. Howe Memorial Institution in 1973 to form the C. D. Howe Institute. The CAC had been established in 1957 by Canadian and American business and labour elites. Although the CAC claimed to represent a wide range of interests, it was clear that its membership was heavily skewed toward the interests of resource and financial capital.[29] The stated goal of the CAC was to sponsor "objective [and] factual studies [by] qualified experts in both countries" in order to "serve the mutual interests of the peoples of both countries."[30] The CAC then issued policy statements couched in the terms of objective social science created for the benefit of the perceived social good. The underlying continentalist discourse of these "objective" studies reveals that North American integration was the ultimate goal of the CAC. In the introduction to some reports, the CAC claimed that it would help maintain good relations between Canada and the United States by "taking a North American approach in its search for constructive programmes."[31] Here the subtext of continental integration is subdued. However, the discourse of continental integration becomes quite explicit in other instances such as in the CAC's 1965 report entitled *A Possible Plan for a Canada-U.S. Free Trade Area.*

A more detailed analysis of this continentalist discourse reveals that Canada and the United States were not perceived as equal partners by members of the CAC. In fact, commentators such as Stephen Clarkson believe that Canada was treated with a "patronizing indulgence." The CAC claimed that "a temperate and positive Canadian nationalism is a good thing." The CAC went on to say however that Canadian "national economic aspirations can best be achieved through the mutual benefits derived from a relatively high degree of natural economic interdependence." In an earlier report, the CAC stressed that closer economic interdependence resulted from the operation of "natural economic forces operating within private enterprise systems of the two countries and stretching across the border."[32]

The discourse of *natural* laws and *objective* social science promotes the universal benefits of increased integration while hiding the intent of the CAC to weaken and defeat Canadian economic nationalism. This intent becomes more clear when it is revealed that the American National Planning Association component of the CAC receives funding from the United States government. In a similar fashion, the C. D. Howe Institute purports to provide objective analysis on issues affecting Canada. After a study is completed, the results are published in order to foster open and balanced debate over what policies need to be implemented to serve Canada's best interests. While the C. D. Howe Institute claims to take a nonpartisan approach that considers public and private, as well corporate and labour perspectives, its continentalist bias can be discerned by perusing its membership role and publications. For example, in the winter of 1989, the Canadian government paid for a four-page advertising supplement in the *New York Times.* Two staff researchers at the C. D. Howe Institute wrote the copy for this advertisement promoting Canada's new market-oriented environment after the implementation of the FTA.[33]

While the CAC and C. D. Howe Institute remained prominent voices for continental integration through the 1980s, a newer organization has taken over as the premier Canadian representative of corporate interests with a continentalist perspective. The Business Council on National Issues(BCNI) was established in 1976 and is composed of the chief executive officers of one hundred and sixty leading Canadian and foreign corporations with branch plants in Canada. The BCNI claims to be the "senior voice of business in Canada" whose purpose it is to contribute "to the shaping of national priorities."[34] The list of members includes eighteen energy giants such as Imperial Oil, Texaco, Shell Oil, Exxon, Mobile Oil, British Petroleum and Gulf Oil. Manufacturers who belong include Kodak, Ford, General Motors, Goodyear, Proctor and Gamble and Union Carbide. Financial institutions belonging to the BCNI include American Express, Merrill Lynch, International Telephone and Telegraph (ITT), the Royal Bank of Canada and Lloyds Bank. Food processing giants who belong include Cargill, Campbell Soup, General Foods, and Nabisco. The BCNI is also comprised of high technology and engineering firms such as Bechtel, Control Data, Xerox, IBM, and Honeywell.

The BCNI claims to promote Canadian national interests, but it is a national organization in name only. It represents the interests of the world's most powerful MNCs within the inner corridors of the Canadian Parliament. The BCNI was founded by a Canadian continentalist, W. O. Twaits, who was at one time the chief executive officer of Imperial Oil. His aim for the organization was to pattern it after the influential Business Round Table representing the world's 200 largest corporations in the United States. In addition to its corporate membership, the BCNI also includes influential lobbyists and former politicians. In fact, the current president of the BCNI, Thomas d'Aquino, is a specialist in international law and was an economic advisor to Prime Minister Trudeau during the 1970s. Business interests therefore have close ties to both the Progressive Conservatives and the Liberals.

It is no coincidence that the BCNI was established during the onset of the crisis of Fordism in Canada. As the crisis deepened in the 1970s, Canada experienced higher rates of inflation. Workers went on strike in many sectors of the economy as inflation eroded the value of their wage packages. To capitalist eyes, Canadian workers were unproductive when compared to workers in other industrialized countries. In addition, the Canadian corporate elite believed that the welfare state sheltered Canadian workers with an elaborate social safety net reducing labour discipline. As discussion over the economy became increasingly politicized in Canada, the Canadian corporate elite believed that it needed to present a united front in order to achieve its initial goals of cutting back the welfare state, disciplining labour in order to reduce wages and reducing inflation.[35] The BCNI successfully represented large corporate interests by persuading the Canadian government during the late 1970s and early 1980s to adopt monetarist policies that would help secure their goals.

Although the BCNI espoused an adherence to free enterprise, it remained quiet about its continentalist aims and free trade aspirations until earlier goals had largely been achieved. By 1982 however, the BCNI began to expand the number of issues on its agenda and its rhetoric took on a doctrinaire quality. Interest was expressed in deficit reduction, comprehensive tax reform and trade liberalization with the United States. It is at this point that the more diffused continentalist tendency in Canada became tied to a specific policy of promoting free trade.

A delegation of BCNI members discretely approached American officials with a free trade proposal in the fall of 1982. By 1983, d'Aquino began to publicly promote the idea of Canadian-American free trade. Starting in 1985, the BCNI and d'Aquino proselytized to Canadian and American businesses, the Canadian Parliament and the Canadian public about the virtues of free trade. In all instances, the BCNI promoted itself as an objective and "non-partisan organization dedicated to the development of public policies in the national interest."[36] The BCNI was careful to stress the universal benefits that free trade would bestow upon all Canadians regardless of their location. In particular, Canadian consumers were sure to benefit because they would pay less for imported goods when the tariffs were lowered. The BCNI obscured the continentalist intent of free trade by stressing the national benefits that would accrue to all Canadians regardless of their geographic location or class status.

Critics of the BCNI believe that this powerful lobby has managed to obscure the degree to which it has directed Canadian economic policy. The BCNI acted as though it was a shadow cabinet by first studying and then making detailed recommendations on important issues such as inflation, monetarism and free trade. D'Aquino, acting as both the BCNI president and a *de facto* cabinet minister, presented these studies as complete policy documents ready for implementation to sympathetic cabinet ministers. The BCNI was often so persuasive that Tory policy and BCNI "white papers" were nearly identical. For example, BCNI recommendations on Canada-United States trade can also be seen in the report issued by the Royal Commission on the Economic Union and Development Prospects for Canada (The Macdonald Commission).[37]

The influence of individual BCNI members on the FTA negotiations should also be mentioned. Neoclassical economists stated that free trade was about economics, not politics. The FTA was designed to allow market forces to operate in accordance with objective economic laws unfettered by outside interference. This appeal to objectivity apparently did not extend to free trade negotiations. Free trade negotiators often had vested material interests in the impact of the FTA. For example, the chief American negotiator for agriculture was Daniel Amstutz, then undersecretary of agriculture. He was also a former chief executive officer of Cargill Investor Services — a financial services subsidiary of Cargill, the American-based multinational food processing corporation. Advising the Canadian government on agricultural issues was David Gilmore, vice-president of Cargill Grain Canada. The MNCs had their best people at both sides of the negotiating table to ensure that their interests were served. The FTA can therefore be called a corporate "Bill of Rights" for a continental economy given the intimate involvement by large MNCs in the free trade negotiations.[38]

Opponents of free trade note that choice of words reflect the intent behind the apparently objective discourse used by pro-FTA organizations such as the CAC, the C. D. Howe Institute, the BCNI, and the Fraser Institute. Words with a positive connotation were used to defend the continentalist position (e.g., *free* trade, openness, universal benefits, *increasing* economies of scale, mutual growth, and security), while words that projected negative connotations were used to describe the position of opponents to increased Canadian-American integration (e.g., isolationist, autarkical, introverted, nationalist and cowardly).[39] Supporters of free trade carefully selected their words when describing people who oppose free trade. A columnist for the *New York Times* who supports the North American Free Trade Agreement blamed "protective politics" for undermining a trade deal based on "good economics."[40] In contrast to the implied scientific, mature and reasoned discourse of the free trade supporters, opponents of free trade are described as "lying," "biased," "foolishly misguided," "unprofessional" and "immature" "freaks of unreasoning passion" whose "alarmist" and "sensational myths" are characterized by "populism," "emotional irrationality" and "scaremongering." Simon Reisman, Canada's chief FTA negotiator, went so far as to say that free trade opponents were Nazis who used Goebbel's technique of "The Big Lie" to spread anti-FTA propaganda.[41]

It is not surprising to learn that organizations such as the CAC and the BCNI, with their direct transnational business affiliations, would support a continentalist agenda. What is more surprising to discover are the continentalist intentions behind supposedly neutral and publicly funded organizations such as the Institute for Research on Public Policy (IRPP) and The Economic Council of Canada (ECC). The IRPP was founded by the Canadian government in 1972 with an initial endowment of one million dollars and a promise to match an expected ten million dollar endowment over a seven year period. The IRPP claims to be Canada's first independent think tank and national organization whose "independence and autonomy are ensured" by an endowment underwritten in large part by public funds.[42] On closer examination the unbiased facade of the IRPP fades away. Many of Canada's corporate elite comprise the IRPP's board of directors. In a report weighing the pros and cons of the FTA, the IRPP published articles by seven authors, five of whom openly supported free trade, while only one article openly questioned the efficacy of free trade for Canada.[43]

The recently dismantled ECC represents a more noteworthy example of a "neutral" organization which engaged in continentalist discourse. The ECC differed from the IRPP in that the ECC was mandated by an Act of Parliament and was therefore an actual branch of the Canadian State. The ECC had a multi-million dollar budget with over one hundred research personal. It represented the single largest concentration of economists working on public policy issues in Canada. The ECC perpetuated the facade of the neutral State by making the neoclassical assumption that the market and the State can be separated for analytical purposes. Even its name reinforced the separation of the economic from the political. The underlying subtext is that economic policy does not affect political policy and vice versa.

When the ECC stated in 1975 that free trade was "the best answer to Canada's industrial concerns" and that Canada's living standards would be raised permanently if Canada entered into a free trade agreement with the United States, most Canadians accepted these pronouncements as being an objective conclusion reached through unbiased analysis.[44] Yet the biased and continentalist discourse of this branch of the Canadian State is difficult to ignore. The first report issued by the ECC in 1970 stressed that future Canadian prosperity depended on attracting more foreign direct investment and the removal of protectionist policies. In 1987, the ECC referred to the law of comparative advantage while promoting free trade. In 1989, on the eve of the implementation of the FTA, the ECC stressed that Canada needed to further deregulate financial markets.[45] The continentalist discourse of the ECC therefore spans almost two decades. During this time, the ECC was not a neutral element of the State as it would have Canadians believe, but was instead a biased advocate of a continentalist corporate agenda. Since the 1940s, the larger majority of Canadian economists and policy-makers have promoted an increasingly continentalist agenda. Corporate, political and academic influences have contributed to this transition from nationalism to continentalism.

Canadian Support for Free Trade

The single most important Canadian participant in the free trade debate was the Canadian government. The role of the ECC in promoting a continentalist perspective in the 1970s and a free trade agreement in the early and middle 1980s has been previously mentioned. As the free trade debate intensified after the 1984 election of Prime Minister Brian Mulroney, other branches of government such as External Affairs Canada and the Progressive Conservative Party increased their advertising expenditure in the promotion of free trade. An estimated Can$32 million of Canadian taxpayer's money was spent on private public relations and polling, radio and television commercials, glossy pamphlets and newspaper advertisements extolling the virtues of closer economic ties with the United States.[46] The campaign explained to Canadians how they would personally benefit from free trade. Mulroney took a lead role in the promotion of the FTA. He stated that the preservation of Canada's social programmes and cultural sovereignty depended on increased economic growth, and that the FTA would guarantee that growth by creating over 350,000 jobs in Canada by 1995.[47]

External Affairs published glossy pamphlets selling the idea of free trade to Canadians. The reduction of tariffs between Canada and the United States was predicted to help Canadian businesses gain access to a market ten times as large as the Canadian market which was too small for firms to utilize their full capacity in an efficient manner. Free trade would create a larger market allowing Canadian businesses to expand their factories to achieve economies of scale. The individual Canadian consumer would benefit because the lower production costs will translate into lower retail prices.[48] Furthermore, American commodities coming into Canada would also fall in price as tariffs are lowered. This is the standard neoclassical justification for free trade. Trade allows smaller countries to specialize and produce a few commodities at high enough levels of output to exploit the available economies of scale. Simon Reisman, the chief trade negotiator for Canada, used this argument repeatedly when he explained why Canada should engage in free trade. He also claimed that the FTA would "lower the costs of everything from food and wine to machinery and computers."[49]

Thus, according to Reisman's logic, the Canadian government promoted free trade to help Canadian firms improve their Fordist-style production systems by achieving internal economies of scale. This explanation totally ignores the fact that many productive firms are adopting flexible production techniques to increase profits through external economies of scope and scale. This explanation also ignores the nature of trade between Canada and the United States. Canada is dependent on the United States as a destination for about 70 percent of total trade and investment. About 35 percent of the value of the shipments going from Canada to the United States is generated by American subsidiaries operating in Canada. The crucial point is that 75 percent of shipments and investments by American subsidiaries is intra-firm, or between affiliates of the same multinational corporation.[50] The neoclassical conceptions of free trade, comparative advantage and increasing returns to scale rest on the assumption of perfect competition. Intra-firm trade, by definition, is most often monopolistic or oligopolistic at best.

These criticisms are tied to the broader problem of static econometric models that were used by supporters of free trade to show how Canada would benefit. The assumption of unexploited scale economies is difficult to justify given the diversity of results that the neoclassical models have produced. Econometric free trade models adhering to general equilibrium theory require restrictive and unrealistic assumptions to reach "unambiguous and elegant conclusions." Trade models based on partial equilibrium theory attempt greater realism by relaxing assumptions but achieving "indeterminate outcomes."[51] Economists have combined aspects of both general and partial equilibrium theories, however, outcomes from running these modified general equilibrium models suggest perverse and contradictory policy implications. The increasing sophistication in econometric modeling has only increased the variability of the predicted outcomes. Hazledine remarks wryly that "truth has not yet yielded to technique."[52]

According to brochures distributed by External Affairs, after tariff reduction, the establishment of fair trade guidelines represented the second selling-point of the agreement on free trade. A system was built into the FTA to settle trade disputes between Canada and the United States. In the early 1980s, American trade imbalances ignited protectionist tendencies amongst some American politicians. The FTA was promoted by the Canadian government as a strategy to guard against future American protectionism and trade sanctions.[53] By appealing to the natural law of comparative advantage and increasing economies of scale, the Canadian government was making an appeal to the Canadian sense of logic. By appealing to the fear of American protectionism, the Canadian government revealed that it was not the objective and natural laws of social science, but the realpolitik of international relations that was driving free trade.

In the service sector FTA promotional literature hailed the mutual recognition of professional credentials and certifications and the reduction of barriers for professionals wanting to do business on either side of the border.[54] This initially sounds as if there is going to be free mobility of all workers to move anywhere in North America just as there is *de facto* free mobility of finance and industrial capital. On closer scrutiny, it becomes clear that the FTA contains a class bias. Only the privileged few business managers and professionals with graduate degrees can work where they please in North America. For the working class, citizenship acts as an impediment to cross-border migration.

A second important source of support for the FTA came from Canadian economists working in academia. Canadian business schools, notably those at the University of Toronto and the University of Western Ontario have enjoyed a long working relationship with business interests in Canada. Free trade supporters were able to exploit this relationship to great effect during the FTA negotiations. Alan Rugman, a professor of business at the University of Toronto, toured Canada promoting free trade just weeks before the 1988 election. In his role as professor of international business at one of Canada's most prestigious universities, Rugman could use his university affiliation to create an aura of objectivity and detachment from the issue of free trade. Seldom mentioned was Rugman's membership in the Canadian Alliance for Trade and Job Opportunities (CATJO). This pro-business lobby represents the interests of the largest corporations in Canada. Rugman's viewpoint cannot be considered to be value-free given his corporate affiliation and sponsorship.

In addition to lobbying the Canadian public, academic economists also lobbied the Canadian Parliament. A document signed by 250 Canadian economists was submitted as testimony during a House of Commons legislative committee hearing on Bill C-130 — the act to implement the Free Trade Agreement between Canada and the United States. The document stated that Canada would benefit from free trade because it would guarantee access to the American market during a time when protectionism is a possible threat. The 250 economists agreed that the FTA would provide better investment opportunities, a higher standard of living for Canadians, lower-cost commodities for Canadians and a greater diversity of products.[55] Again the standard neoclassical argument for free trade makes an appearance. But we should ask why so many Canadian economists support free trade given the long history of political economy and staples theory in Canadian academia? One answer to this questions points to the "one-way free trade in ideas." Leading academic economists in Canada have been trained under the American paradigm of modern neoclassical economics with its assumptions of perfect competition, *homo economicus*, and the law of comparative advantage. Orthodox neoclassical economists hold to a paradigm "that is utterly unable to fathom the political." The BCNI reinforced this stereotype when they exhorted Canadians to "put economics before politics." In other words, Canadians should forget about populist rhetoric and listen to sound economic reasoning. Canadians should put their trust in the merits of free trade with the United States because "ten thousand economists can't be wrong!"[56]

The third major source of support for the FTA originated with business interests. It should be stated at the outset that not all businesses in Canada openly supported the FTA. Support from business for the FTA varied depending on the structure of the ownership, economic sector and the size of the corporation. For example, different levels of support for free trade existed between Canadians who manage branch plants of MNCs in Canada and indigenous elites. Managers of branch plants in Canada have consistently supported the FTA and also supported the earlier advocacy of increased continentalization.[57] Arguments made by multinational business interests parallel those made by the BCNI. This should come as no surprise given that membership in the BCNI includes many of the largest MNCs operating in Canada. As for indigenous Canadian business elites, their position on free trade depends on whether they are a monopoly or non-monopoly enterprise. Ironically, it was the monopolistic firms and large financial enterprises that openly supported the FTA, while non-monopoly firms advocated less dramatic trade liberalization. The irony rests in the fact that monopolistic firms were supporting a neoclassical trade theory that assumes perfect competition.

Although various justifications were made by the business community in support of free trade, four basic arguments stand out. The small Canadian market imposed restrictions on the ability of firms to produce efficiently. Canada needed to improve its comparative advantage in world markets. GATT negotiations were uncertain. The ever-present threat of American protectionism was the final justification.[58] Free trade with the United States would provide access to the larger American market and this would persuade Canadian producers to increase the scale of their production. The Investment Dealers Association stated that Alberta stood to lose Can$14 billion in resource and energy-related development if the FTA was not implemented. The president of Amoco Canada Petroleum Company Limited argued that free trade could help Canada exploit its abundant untapped petroleum resources. Many of these resources are in Canada's Far North and may cost over Can$100 billion to develop. The only way that these resources can be developed is if some of the production is exported to achieve economies of scale.[59] The FTA promised access to a larger market for scale economies to be achieved. Furthermore, the FTA would attract foreign investment capital to facilitate increased resource extraction in Canada's remote but resource-rich hinterland.

The second argument in support of free trade emphasizes the nature of Canada's comparative advantage, the increasing specialization of international trade and the need for deregulation to facilitate Canadian economic restructuring. Because of the increasingly competitive nature of global trade, Canada no longer enjoys the same comparative advantages that it had in earlier times. Canada can regain its comparative advantage by having Canadian firms increasingly specialize and trade with the United States. Increasing specialization by firms in Canada would require heavy investment and economic restructuring. Existing impediments to specialization include declining productivity, increasing production costs and excessive government regulations. Free trade is part of the strategy to deregulate North America that will help Canadian firms compete globally. The president of the Canadian Federation of Independent Business believes that "the Canada-U.S. Free Trade Agreement, the proposed North American Free Trade Agreement, the federal goods and services tax (GST) in Canada, the dismantling of inter-provincial trade barriers, the privatization of crown corporations, the restructuring of federal-provincial powers, and the drive for economic competitiveness are all necessary responses to the globalization of world economies." The president of Texaco Canada echoed these sentiments when he stated that "deregulation, competition, and trade, drive the Canadian economy." Proponents of free trade have most often promoted the FTA by alluding to greater market access and referring to neoclassical trade theory and the ineluctability of economic laws. Yet the Macdonald Commission chairman urged Canadians to take a "leap of faith" over the issue of free trade.[60]

Supporters of the FTA have also pointed to the uncertainty of the GATT negotiations as an impetus to seek a bilateral free trade agreement with the United States. Because so much of Canada's trade already goes to the United States, it seems logical to enhance the existing relationship. Attempting to develop a comprehensive multilateral agreement was deemed overly complex and unlikely to produce positive results for Canadian exporters. The BCNI neatly summarizes Canadian perspectives on GATT and the FTA by saying "multilateral trade negotiations are important ..." but "... a Canada-United States trade agreement is imperative."[61] Canadian supporters of free trade did not eschew GATT but preferred the more predictable bilateral agreement.

If the most commonly used argument supporting free trade stressed the diseconomies of scale of the small Canadian market, it was the fear of American protectionism which provided the most salient reason for promoting free trade. The U.S. Omnibus Trade Bill, passed on August 3, 1988, posed a real threat to Canadian exporters. Canadian firms needed a viable strategy to maintain access to the American market. The FTA was perceived to be the best strategy to keep American borders open to Canadian goods. This perception was misguided however, because the Omnibus Trade Bill states that the United States can impose mandatory penalties against any country it believes to be engaging in unfair trade practices.[62] The United States is the sole arbiter of what constitutes an unfair trade practice. The Omnibus Trade Bill also took precedence over the Canada-United States FTA because Article 1902 of the FTA text clearly states that each party to the trade pact can retain domestic anti-dumping and countervailing duty laws.[63] Thus, the FTA provided a false sense of security for Canadian corporate interests if they sincerely believed that the FTA would provide unimpeded access to American markets.

While the business community did not monolithically support the FTA, most of the MNCs and larger Canadian corporations vocally supported free trade. Individual corporations such as Stelco Steel and business organizations such as the Canadian National Chamber of Commerce spent an estimated Can$24.5 million promoting free trade. The Canadian Alliance for Trade and Job Opportunities (CATJO) spent Can$6 million. When a *Toronto Star* reporter attempted to identify how much each business within CATJO had contributed, he was told that the information was confidential. Critics impugned the Canadian government for spending Can$32 million promoting the FTA. Together, the Canadian government and businesses spent an estimated Can$56.5 million promoting the FTA.[64]

The large sums of money spent advertising the partisan issue of free trade begs the question of why there were no spending limits imposed during the election campaign. The answer reveals how neoconservative politics spill over into the economic sphere. The Canadian government passed Bill C-169 in the Fall of 1983. This bill was designed to impose the same spending discipline on lobby groups that applied to political parties during the official campaign period. Bill C-169 would have made it an offense to advertise in print during a campaign on behalf of a candidate or issue without the authorization of a political party or candidate. The Canadian government introduced this legislation out of fear that Canadian groups similar to those such as the Moral Majority in the United States would spend millions of dollars to buy an election through massive advertising campaigns. Although Bill C-169 became law it was almost immediately challenged in the Alberta Court of the Queen's Bench by the National Citizens' Coalition (NCC) — an Alberta-based conservative lobby reminiscent of the Moral Majority. The Alberta Court decided that Bill C-169 was unconstitutional. Thus the NCC was able to pour funds into a neoconservative advertising campaign in support of the Progressive Conservatives in 1984. The NCC promoted a pro-FTA, anti-union, anti-choice and pro-privatization agenda. To ensure that neoconservative policies continued, the NCC donated money to the Tories again in 1988. The broader significance of the NCC challenge to Bill C-169 is that while political parties cannot spend more than Can$8 million during the election period, lobby groups can spend unlimited amounts of money.[65] Corporate and neoconservative interests have a much better chance of being heard by the Canadian public during an election campaign because they have the most money to spend on advertising.

Many Canadian businessmen support the FTA despite openly acknowledging that the FTA will cause massive dislocation within Canadian society. David Culver, president of the Aluminum Company of Canada, admitted that "you can't have growth in the garden without some death ... Some flowers must die to make way for others ... Some parts of companies are in effect dying."[66] This rhetoric, in addition to the massive expenditures on pro-FTA promotion and the reluctance of large corporations to the let the public know the extent of their financial contributions, points to the broader corporate agenda behind the FTA.

On closer scrutiny, it becomes apparent that hegemonic business interests and their ideological supporters in the State are not so much interested in access to a greater market as they are in restructuring the Canadian economy along the lines of the Reagan/Thatcher agenda. The United States is a more market-oriented society than Canada. The welfare state, the Left and trade unions are much weaker in the United States than in Canada. Because of this obvious difference between the two societies, the Canadian government did not want to lose legitimacy by waging an all out war on labour while simultaneously cutting social welfare programmes. The implementation of a free trade agreement between Canada and the United States offered a more cunning approach. The Canadian government and the business elite speculated that as articulation between the two economies increased, inevitable market pressures to harmonize policies would force Canada to conform to American standards.[67] Direct confrontation with Canadians who opposed deregulation, privatization and economic restructuring could be avoided by blaming the downward spiral of wages and welfare state expenditures on the natural market forces of free trade.

American Support for Free Trade

American discourse in support of free trade between Canada and the United States started with a reaffirmation of the sanctity of the law of comparative advantage followed by the admonition that free enterprise and the reduction of trade barriers would lead to a more efficient allocation of human and natural resources.[68] How can any person evaluate the veracity of these statements? In order to judge the merits of free trade, a person would most likely turn to the print or electronic media. Herein lies a fundamental problem. The FTA debate as it played out in the media was one between economic science rooted in irrefutable laws and an entirely different logic based on ethical issues such as the public good, national interest, and the social responsibilities of corporations. People attempting to weigh the arguments of free trade, pro and con, confront a difficult task. The arguments surrounding the FTA are based on different ontologies. Without a common basis for understanding there can be no common set of scales; therefore, "the metaphor of balancing is a misleading and disguising fiction."[69]

The FTA debate is replete with rival and incompatible ideas for which the media is ill-prepared to interpret for us. Distortions in the media portrayal of the FTA arise because of the ontological interplay between the highly abstract and seemingly irrefutable logic of positivist economics and the equally detached applied ethics of objective journalism. Journalistic objectivity is based on the notions of logical positivism. Not coincidentally, neoclassical economics and free trade theory also rest on the foundation of logical positivism. It is this shared foundational principle which has kept the mainstream American and Canadian media from openly questioning the economic reasoning behind the FTA and the North American Free Trade Agreement (NAFTA).[70]

Journalists had difficulty presenting both sides of the FTA debate because they were prisoners of their own paradigm. Consider the following article on NAFTA in the *New York Times*. A front page story began with the following: "When economists *of every stripe* agree on anything, it is noteworthy ... So it is a sign of unusual accord that 300 economists ranging from conservatives like Milton Friedman to liberals including Paul Samuelson recently signed a letter to President Clinton supporting the North American Free Trade Agreement" (italics added).[71] Arguments about free trade from the Left have been excised from the debate because they are not part of the all-inclusive "every stripe." National Public Radio (NPR) also limited the range of debate on free trade. On September 20, 1993, the NPR call-in show "Talk of the Nation" invited a political writer from *Newsweek* and an economics writer from the *U.S. News and World Report* to debate free trade. Both guests supported free trade. They called opponents to free trade "emotional populists" who lacked a reasoned analysis of the potential impacts of NAFTA. The moderator, Ray Suarez and the two guests disagreed with a caller who suggested that the mainstream press and NPR did not, in fact, present a broad range of opinion on the free trade debates.

Consider also the behavior of the Canadian Broadcasting Corporation (CBC) which is editorially opposed to the FTA and to NAFTA. The CBC network framed the FTA debate to be between sentimental Canadian 'nationalists' whose preoccupation was with cultural matters, and business experts whose detached and neutral concern was with the beneficial impacts of positivist economics.[72] This debate exemplifies the scenario that confronts journalists who often depend upon positivist experts to unravel complex issues. Journalists pass on information provided by experts to a largely unwitting populace unaware, for the most part, that all experts have a bias of some sort. From this perspective, the media is partially absolved from responsibility because its pursuit of objectivity blinds journalists from the underlying bias of positivist analyses.

It is also clear that the whole story about the impact of free trade on Canada was not reported in the United States because many newspapers such as *The New York Times, The Wall Street Journal* and *The Des Moines Register* supported the FTA and NAFTA. Reasons for supporting free trade ranged from the utilitarian (*The New York Times* buys paper products from Canada), to the ideological. The *Wall Street Journal* took the position that free trade creates jobs, while the *Des Moines Register* claimed that free trade would simultaneously allow more farm exports and strengthen democracy in Mexico. *The Wall Street Journal* also editorialized that free trade was more important than health care reform.[73] Negative reporting about the FTA might have convinced Americans that NAFTA is a bad idea. The facts of the Canadian experience under the FTA could also complicate the arguments in support of NAFTA.

Academic and media discourse also served to hide the realpolitik embedded in American relations with Canada. Two basic objectives have been central to American policy towards Canada during the twentieth century. After the Second World War, American officials were anxious to ensure that Canada was tied militarily to the United States. This was achieved through a series of agreements, the most important of which was Norad (North American Aerospace Defense Command), which subordinated the Canadian military in defence of North America. Although the importance of continental defence has declined with the fragmentation of the former Soviet Union, American-Canadian co-operation in the shared defence of North America will continue to play an important role in military planning.

The second and more long standing policy objective has been to gain access to Canadian energy and other natural resources. Canada and the United States almost entered into a free trade agreement in 1911. Americans who favored this reciprocity agreement argued that free trade would provide them with greater access to Canadian resources. During World War II, the United States relied on Canada as a source of inexpensive natural resources. In 1952, the foreign policy objective of continued resource accessibility was reaffirmed in the *Report of the President's Materials Policy Commission*, commonly referred to as *The Paley Report*. It outlined how the Cold War fight against the spread of communism was depleting American reserves of strategic materials. The report concluded that Canada was the most reliable and efficient foreign source for replenishment. *The Paley Report* advised Canada to concentrate on their natural "comparative advantage" in resource export as the most efficient development strategy.[74] It further recommended that the Canadian government borrow American capital to develop an infrastructure which would facilitate the extraction and export of raw materials. The discourse of economic theory was used to mask American foreign policy goals during the height of the Cold War. In the 1990s, Canadian energy exports remain a central issue for Americans who support free trade. In 1981, the Reagan Administration was particularly opposed to Canada's National Energy Policy which impeded American access to Canadian resources. American manipulation and domination of the Canadian economy has always been underpinned by these two policies, but the crisis of Fordism brought many new issues to light.

While many Canadians had proposed free trade during the nineteenth and twentieth centuries, Ronald Reagan raised the idea of a Canada-United States free trade agreement again while campaigning to gain the GOP nomination in 1980. He proposed a continental free trade area encompassing Canada, the United States and Mexico. While Canadian business executives were intrigued by Reagan's overtures, Prime Minister Trudeau and President Lopez Portillo issued a joint statement repudiating such a proposal. American officials were not disheartened by this apparent setback. The Reagan administration took the idea of free trade to the 1983 Tokyo Round of the GATT talks. When no gains were achieved there, the Americans again reverted back to a bilateral free trade strategy. Trudeau responded more favorably this time. He recommended that Canada and the United States use the example of the Auto Pact to expand sectoral free trade.[75] Talks failed when Trudeau was defeated in the Canadian election of 1984.

Economic planners in the Reagan Administration were encouraged by this turn of events because the newly elected government of Brian Mulroney was more amenable to bilateral free trade. During the period when Americans were negotiating sectoral free trade with Trudeau, they were still hoping to achieve a sweeping free trade deal. The American ambassador to Canada, Paul Robinson, held special talks with the president of the Canadian Chamber of Commerce, Sam Hughes. Hughes took it upon himself to mobilize Canadian interest in a comprehensive trade deal. It was he who testified in favor of free trade before the Macdonald Commission. At the 1985 "Shamrock Summit" held in Québec City, Mulroney pledged his support for trade liberalization policies through GATT and a bilateral free trade agreement.[76] Even after Reagan had garnered the support of Mulroney for a bilateral free trade agreement, he was still selling the idea of a sweeping multilateral free trade agreement that would encompass all of the Americas from Alaska to Terra del Fuego.[77]

Maintaining military security and access to resources has been a longstanding goal in the twentieth century. In order to facilitate these goals, American trade negotiators wanted to secure the abolition of two nationalistic economic policies implemented by Trudeau in the 1970s that were designed to reduce Canada's dependency on the United States. The Foreign Investment Review Agency (FIRA) was established to stem the tide of foreign investment in Canada. It restricted the size and kinds of Canadian businesses, land and resources in which a foreign firm could invest. The National Energy Policy (NEP) gave the Canadian government greater control over Canadian energy resources including coal, oil, uranium and electricity. The NEP directly opposed the American policy objective of increased access to Canadian natural resources. The Reagan Administration sought to dismantle both the NEP and the FIRA through the FTA.

The Reagan Administration had one other policy objective it thought it could achieve through the FTA: tilting the Canada-United States trade balance in its favor. The United States was concerned about its growing trade imbalance with other industrialized countries. It attempted to devalue its currency during the early 1980s in order to make American commodities less costly in foreign markets. Between 1985 and 1987 the value of the American dollar dropped on world markets, but not against the Canadian dollar.[78] American officials pointed to Canada's huge deficit — larger on a per capita basis than the American deficit — as the reason for the weak Canadian dollar. The United States asserted that the low value of the Canadian dollar compared to the American dollar had increased the American trade deficit. In 1986, the U.S. National Association of Manufacturers argued that a free trade deal would be impractical unless Canada and the United States reached an agreement to reduce and stabilize the gap between the two currencies. Texas senator Lloyd Bentson suggested that Canadian and American currencies move toward parity. The Reagan Administration, including Peter Murphy, the key American trade negotiator, suggested that the two currencies move closer together in value and possibly adopt a fixed exchange rate or target zone for the Canadian dollar. American economists cheered the revaluation of the Canadian dollar during the 1985 to 1988 period.[79]

Of course the Canadian government balked at the idea of fixed exchange rates because it would totally undermine any remaining ability of the Canadian government to effect monetary policy. Canadian businesses also balked at the idea of a revalued Canadian dollar because the devalued dollar allowed Canadian goods to be sold at a lower cost in the United States. Furthermore, the devalued Canadian dollar makes it less expensive for American firms to produce in Canada. During the economic recession of 1987, the Big Three auto makers laid off 29,000 employees in the United States, but none in Canada. In addition to lower production costs, this may have been linked to the production quotas in the Auto Pact guarantying, prior to the FTA, that a certain percentage of cars sold in Canada would be produced in Canada.[80]

The issue of currency co-ordination still remains unresolved but American negotiators assured the Canadian government that eventually some form of continental monetary policy will have to be created either in a formal or informal manner. At the very least, closer consultations between money authorities in both countries would be of increasingly paramount importance. An analysis of Canada-United States exchange rates between 1986 and the early 1990s suggests that the Canadian dollar was purposely revalued before falling against the American dollar in 1994. Substantial debate surrounds the exchange rate issue — a topic revisited in later chapters.

Although some members of the U.S. Congress such as Representative Richard Gephardt (D-Missouri) expressed reservations, support for the FTA was widespread within the United States.[81] Opposition came mostly from states where the economic base consisted of timber and mining. Politicians who were opposed to the FTA were won over when it was explained that the FTA could give a push to stalled GATT negotiations. Furthermore, passage of the U.S. Omnibus Trade Bill allayed many fears by strengthening U.S. trade sanction powers which remain intact under provisions of the FTA.

At first, the most vocal support came from large transnational corporations who did business in Canada. Support was mobilized by the American Express Corporation which wanted access to the Canadian banking system, the National Association of Manufacturers, the National Chamber of Commerce, the National Foreign Trade Council and the U.S. Council for International Business who were instrumental in creating the American Coalition for Trade Expansion with Canada. In May 1987, 175 major American corporations had joined the coalition. Membership increased to 400 by August of that year. The coalition raised millions of dollars which went to Political Action Committees in Washington to persuade protectionist politicians to support the FTA when it went to the Senate for approval. Money was also spent for advertising and promoting the benefits of the FTA in the United States and Canada. By October 1987, the Reagan and Mulroney Governments had reached a basic agreement on free trade.

The only problem facing the deal was that Mulroney was elected on a platform that had repudiated bilateral free trade. To his credit, he called a federal election for November 21, 1988 to secure a mandate from the Canadian people for the FTA. However, even here we see that neoconservatives in Canada and the United States did everything in their power to ensure a Tory victory. Free trade supporters spent tens of millions of dollars simultaneously promoting the FTA and the Progressive Conservatives. American business lobbies donated an estimated Can$1.2 million to the Canadian Alliance for Trade and Job Opportunities for pro-FTA advertising. Four days prior to the election, Reagan gave a speech on the merits of free trade. Originally, Reagan wanted to devote the bulk of his speech to the Canada-United States FTA. The Tories recommended to the President that he take a more subtle approach to avoid inflaming Canadian nationalists and undermining Tory support on the eve of the election.[82] In spite of these efforts on the part of Canadian and American neoconservatives, less than half of all Canadians voted for the political party promoting free trade. Election results revealed that Mulroney won a majority of seats with only 43 percent of the popular vote.[83] After Mulroney's victory had been declared, an editorial in the *New York Times* congratulated all Canadians for "grasping the future" by choosing free trade.[84]

Canadian Opposition to Free Trade

Opponents to free trade engaged in the discourse of geographic diversity. They believed that harmonization of policies would not translate into a homogeneously high standard of living in all parts of North America. They argued that continental market forces unleashed by free trade would have regionally diverse impacts on North America, with Canada bearing more of the burden than the United States.

If neoclassical economists supported free trade on a purely theoretical and ideological basis, critics of free trade believed that geopolitics played a central role prompting Canadian neoconservatives to pursue free trade with the United States. Fears of rising U.S. protectionism, not the appeal of abstract neoclassical trade theory, explains support for free trade. Increasing American protectionism in the 1980s was directly linked to rising imports flooding the United States due to the overvalued U.S. Dollar.[85] The U.S. Dollar was overvalued because of enormous inflows of foreign capital to cover the enormous U.S. deficit. The growing deficit was directly tied to escalating military expenditures as embodied in Reagan's Strategic Defence Initiative (SDI) and the general mismanagement of the U.S. economy as exemplified in the savings and loan fiasco. Cold war geopolitics and deregulation were central elements in the expansion of the American debt and calls for increased protectionism. Canadian supporters of free trade were actually responding to fears of protectionism. Ironically, the FTA did not weaken American powers of trade retaliation toward Canada.

On a general level, Canadian economists supported, while Canadian political scientists opposed the free trade deal. Economists promoted free trade because of its theoretical basis in neoclassical economics. Political scientists opposed the free trade deal because they saw it as restricting the scope of political exchange in Canada and ultimately limiting Canadian sovereignty.[86] From a regulation theory perspective, a continental regime of accumulation would undermine a national mode of regulation. Put another way, political scientists perceived that the FTA would diminish Canada's ability to unite a geographically diverse nation. Regional development programmes and transfer payments destined for Canada's hinterland regions could be targeted as unfair. Without these programmes, regional disparity and regional antagonisms were predicted to increase as the FTA constricted the ability of the Canadian government to implement nation-building policies. A related argument points to the difference in directional bias of market forces under free trade versus that which forms the basis of the Canadian nation. Canada was built on an east-west axis by a State that consciously imposed tariffs and underwrote the construction of a transcontinental railway to connect British Columbia to Eastern Canada. The FTA and its implied policy of deregulation was predicted to enhance the north-south (i.e. cross-border) axis at the expense of the historic east-west axis that formed the backbone of the Canadian nation.

The most vocal Canadian opposition to free trade came from organized labour whose discourse problematized the geographic mobility of capital and the harmonization of standards. Union leaders recognized that the FTA would increase capital mobility thus making individual Canadian unions and their communities more susceptible to corporate whipsaw tactics. With increased geographic mobility, corporate interests would be able to restructure the balance of power in the relationship between capital, the State, and labour. In protest, the Canadian Labour Congress (CLC), the Ontario Federation of Labour (OFL), the Canadian Auto Workers (CAW), and the United Steelworkers of America spent a total of Can$2.8 million buying anti-FTA advertisements. However, the unions were no match for the organized and well funded supporters of the FTA. Furthermore, corporations with large numbers of employees adopted tactics to manipulate the workplace. Stelco first sent a small pro-FTA pamphlet home in the paycheck envelope of every employee. Next, Stelco sent a letter to the home of every employee saying that the FTA was vital to the future of the Canadian steel industry. Crown Life Insurance assembled its 400 Toronto employees and lectured them on the necessity of free trade. Loblaws, one of the largest supermarket chains in Canada, placed a seven-page pro-FTA pamphlet in the paycheck envelope of every one of its 33,000 employees. Labour was at a disadvantage because it could not control the flow of information in the workplace.

Organized labour opposed the FTA because they understood that Canadian unions were much stronger than their American counterparts. American labour lost a number of hard fought rights under the Reagan administration and were paid lower wages than their Canadian counterparts. Canadian labour leaders argued that free trade would harmonize labour practices. Because the American economy is larger than the Canadian economy, it would be the Canadian workers who would undergo the most change. The anticipated result of the harmonization was a downward spiral of wages and workers' rights in Canada to match those in the United States. In 1990, the hourly manufacturing wage in Canada was

US$16.02, compared to US$14.77 in the United States and US$1.80 in Mexico.[87] Free trade opponents believed that continental market forces would eliminate this wage differential.

Prior to the FTA, Canada had not followed the agenda of deregulation promoted by the United States. More and more however, Canadian and American businesses pressured the Canadian government to deregulate the Canadian economy. The choice of the Canadian government has been constrained by the threat that businesses could relocate where the investment guidelines are not so complex, where safety regulations are not so strictly enforced and where unions are less militant. A medium-sized and politically moderate country like Canada can expect to be "harmonized into [not] harmonized with" a large and politically reactionary United States.[88] From a Canadian perspective, it was believed that the impact of the FTA would be regionally uneven, with branch plant industries in Ontario facing the greatest pressures to compete or move to the United States. From a North American perspective, Canadian workers believed that they would have to adjust much more than their American counterparts.

Increased capital mobility brings with it the threat of plant closures and job losses. The human costs of unemployment are compounded under a neoconservative State because the social safety net has been removed from beneath the jobless worker. With lower support for the unemployed, increased pressure is placed on a community as bankruptcies, homelessness and divorces increase in the wake of plant closures. Supporters of the FTA talked coldly about short term dislocations as if everything would work out beneficially in the end. Unfortunately, layoffs take a personal toll in the form of depression, increased family violence and loss of property. In order to protect workers against the worst effects of increased capital mobility, organized labour has advocated a "charter of labour" to set minimum standards of union recognition and wages.[89] Despite their efforts, the wishes of labour to prevent social dumping were largely ignored.

Labour was not the only voice raised in opposition to free trade. Farmers, women's organizations, religious leaders, teachers and many other Canadians from diverse walks of life believed that the FTA would undermine Canadian cultural sovereignty. Many Canadians feared the increased erosion of a distinctly Canadian way of life. The argument is based on the idea that Canada was born of evolution, not the revolutionary history of the United States. While Canadians and Americans share the same continent, they do not share the same culture. Canada is a geographically distinct entity that has evolved along a different path than that of the United States. Capitalists and other denizens of the business world fail to see that Canada is a political oddity — "a socialist monarchy."[90] Canadians have created a successful Welfare State under a monarchical framework north of the forty-ninth parallel. Part of the welfare state has been given over to the support of Canadian culture. With free trade comes privatization. Some Canadians such as Robert White, former president of the Canadian Auto Workers, and Gerard Veilleux, former president of the CBC believe that the attack on the welfare state is an attack on Canadian culture.[91] Institutions such as the CBC, TV Ontario, the National Film Board, subsidized health care, the Canada Council, the national and provincial park systems and a government-funded university system, represent basic elements of Canadian culture which could be at risk. The FTA weakens the ability of these institutions to maintain the geographically distinct culture of Canada in the shadow of the United States.

Just as the railroads were built by Canada in the nineteenth century to unite eastern and western provinces, Canada first established the CBC to tie its disparate population together in the twentieth century. Later, the Canadian Radio-Television and Telecommunications Commission (CRTC) established Canadian content laws which decreed that in each 24 hour period, 30 percent of air time had to be allotted to Canadian artists. Foreign companies were also forbidden from owning majority shares in Canadian television or radio stations. Opponents protested that the FTA would emasculate these institutions and policies which were intended to protect Canadian cultural industries and to hold together a geographically distinct Canadian society.

Opponents to free trade also argued that Canada's regional development programmes were at risk because the FTA did not define the meaning of a subsidy. Canada's regional development programmes are in danger because they can be targeted as an unfair advantage under the FTA. Transfer payments have been used to ensure that the development gap between the prosperous provinces such as Ontario and the hinterland regions of Canada such as New Brunswick and Newfoundland remain within certain limits. Regional development programmes and federal transfer payments serve as nation-building and legitimation devices. These policies also underpin a broader Fordist policy of providing universal access to the resources of the State. Utilizing a Fordist development strategy, the federal government redistributed revenues to ensure that access to health care, education, job training, transportation and economic opportunity met a certain standard regardless of geographic location. The FTA threatens to undermine this policy of universality. Without subsidies, geographic differences in economic development, access to high standards of health care, educational opportunities and overall quality of life will increase.

Critics of the FTA believe that free trade is the leading edge of a post-Fordist development strategy that consciously abandons the standards of universality. They further believe that geographic and social differences will be exploited by MNCs in order to generate greater profits. Free trade opponents believe that the legitimation role of the Fordist State has been abandoned in favor of a post-Fordist State that serves corporate interests alone. The State has forsaken its mission to promote universal national development in order to serve the needs of capital through policies of deregulation, privatization and free trade.

Opponents to free trade also stressed that the FTA would force many Canadian policies to be harmonized with those of the United States. In a curious failure of logic, neoclassical supporters of free trade assume that Canada is a "price-taker" with respect to the United States because Canada's market is too small; yet they do not recognize that Canada is a "policy-taker" as well.[92] When the issue of ideological belief is factored into the examination of pro-FTA rhetoric, this failure of logic is not as paradoxical as it first seems. Many proponents of free trade truly believe in the ideas of Adam Smith, David Ricardo and salvation through market forces. John Ralston Saul, writing in the October, 1992 issue of the *Globe and Mail's Report on Business*, believes that many supporters of the FTA have a "messianic" quality based in free-market ideology. He goes on to say that "ideologies are too absolute and abstract to work. They require permanently perfect circumstances. Ideologies such as [the belief in the sanctity of] market forces are an absolute religion in the Mayan tradition. The priests live on happily, while most of the believers are marked for eventual sacrifice."[93]

The theory of free trade is not based on any inviolable law of nature but a socially constructed idea that has been used in different places during different times to suit different purposes. The FTA was promoted by supporters for its ability to stimulate economic development in Canada. Opponents of free trade worried that capital mobility and continental policy harmonization would undermine communities and overall economic growth. The next three chapters will examine which view more accurately predicted the impact of the FTA on the Canadian economy, labour and the State.

Notes

1. It could be argued that the supporters of free trade also use a geographical discourse because they assert that free trade allows manufacturers to achieve economies of scale. Issues of scale are of course inherently geographical. What this chapter attempts to argue is that supporters of free trade ignore the diversity of the economic landscape within North America by making claims that all regions within North America will benefit from free trade. The geographical nature of scale was never discussed by FTA supporters.
2. The Canada-United States Free Trade Agreement deals with tariffs, customs, quantitative restrictions, non-tariff barriers to trade, government procurement, technical standards, financial services, services, investment, temporary entry for business purposes, energy, automotive trade, agriculture, wine and distilled spirits. In addition, the FTA established a bilateral panel and dispute settlement process to mediate and adjudicate anti-dumping and countervailing duty cases. For more information about the Canada-U.S. FTA and the North American FTA please see Canada, *Elements of a Canada-United States Free Trade Agreement: Synopsis* (Ottawa: Supply and Services, 1987); Canada, *North American Free Trade Agreement* (Ottawa: Supply and Services, 1993).
3. Margaret Atwood, "Free Traders Don't Eat Quiche," *Globe and Mail*, 17 November 1988, A7.
4. Michel Foucault, *The Archeology of Knowledge and the Discourse on Language* (New York: Pantheon Books, 1972), 6.
5. Ibid., 13; Steven Best and David Kellner, *Postmodern Theory: Critical Interrogations* (New York: The Guilford Press, 1991), 43.
6. Felix Driver, "Geography's Empire: Histories of Geographical Knowledge," *Environment and Planning D: Society and Space*, 10 (1992): 35.
7. Paul Krugman, "Is Free Trade Passe?" *Economic Perspectives*, 1, no. 2 (1987): 131.
8. Robert Gilpin, *The Political Economy of International Relations* (Princeton: Princeton University Press, 1987), 172-74.
9. Guglielmo Carchedi, *Frontiers of Political Economy* (New York: Verso, 1991), 218-221; Fernand Braudel, *The Perspective of the World: Civilization and Capitalism, 15th - 18th Century*, vol. 3 (New York: Harper and Row, 1984), 48.
10. Robert Heilbroner, *The Worldly Philosophers*, 6th ed. (New York: Simon and Schuster, 1989), 98.
11. Herman Daly and John Cobb, *For the Common Good: Redirecting the Economy Toward Community, the Environment, and a Sustainable Future* (Boston: Beacon Press, 1989), 213; Gilpin, *The Political Economy of International Relations*, 175.
12. Gilpin, *The Political Economy of International Relations*, 181.
13. Ibid., 175.
14. Carchedi, *Frontiers of Political Economy*, 222-24.
15. "GM Not 'Bluffing' About Closing Plant if Concessions Not Granted," *Sault Star*, 19 June 1991, A8.
16. Adam Smith in Daly and Cobb, *For the Common Good*, 215.
17. Gilpin, *The Political Economy of International Relations*, 177.

18. Lorraine Eden, "Free Trade, Tax Reform, and Transfer Pricing," *Canadian Tax Journal*, 39, no. 1 (1991): 91.
19. Gilpin, *The Political Economy of International Relations*, 179.
20. Braudel, *The Perspective of the World*, 48.
21. A Tory was a member of the Conservative Party which was the forerunner of the present-day Progressive Conservative Party in Canada. The Progressive Conservatives are still called Tories by many Canadians.
22. Craig Brown, "The Nationalism of the National Policy," in *Nationalism in Canada*, Peter Russell, ed. (Toronto: McGraw-Hill, 1966), 155.
23. Paul Phillips, "The National Policy Revisited," *Journal of Canadian Studies*, 14, no. 3 (1979): 3; Paul Krugman, *Geography and Trade* (Cambridge, MA: MIT Press, 1991), 91.
24. Edelgard Mahant and Graeme S. Mount, *An Introduction to Canadian-American Relations* (Toronto: Methuen, 1984), 272; Robert Bothwell, *Canada and the United States: The Politics of Partnership* (New York: Twayne Publishers, 1992), 20.
25. Stephen Clarkson, "Anti-nationalism in Canada: The Ideology of Mainstream Economics," *Canadian Review of Studies in Nationalism*, 5, no. 1 (1978): 50.
26. Canada, *The Hyde Park Declaration*, in Mahant and Mount, *An Introduction to Canadian-American Relations*, 153; J. L. Granatstein, "Free Trade: The History of an Issue," in *The Future on the Table: Canada and the Free Trade Issue*, Michael Henderson, ed.(North York: Masterpress, 1987), 19.
27. Mahant and Mount, *An Introduction to Canadian-American Relations*, 153.
28. Alan Ernst, "From Liberal Continentalism to Neoconservatism: North American Free Trade and the Politics of the C. D. Howe Institute," *Studies in Political Economy*, 39 (Autumn 1992): 114.
29. Wallace Clement, *The Canadian Corporate Elite: An Analysis of Economic Power* (Toronto: McClelland and Stewart, 1975), 256.
30. Canadian-American Committee, *Cooperative Development of the Columbia River Basin* (Washington, DC: Canadian-American Committee of the National Planning Association and the Private Planning Association of Canada, 1959), v.
31. Clarkson, "Anti-nationalism in Canada," 50; Canadian- American Committee, *A Possible Plan for a Canada-U.S. Free Trade Area* (Montréal: Canadian-American Committee of the National Planning Association and the Private Planning Association of Canada, 1965), v; Canadian-American Committee, *Toward a More Realistic Appraisal of the Automotive Agreement* (Washington, DC: Canadian-American Committee of the National Planning Association and the Private Planning Association of Canada, 1970), i.
32. Clarkson, "Anti-nationalism in Canada," 51; Canadian- American Committee, *The Perspective of Canadian-American Relations* ((Washington, DC: Canadian-American Committee of the National Planning Association and the Private Planning Association of Canada, 1962), 5-9; Canadian-American Committee, *Cooperative Development of the Columbia River Basin*, 1.
33. Richard Lipsey and Robert York, "U.S.-Canada Free Trade Agreement: Handshake Across the Border," *New York Times*, 27 February 1989, 29-32.
34. BCNI, "Economic Priorities and the National Agenda," (Ottawa: Unpublished Report of the BCNI, 1986), i.

35. Ibid., 3; David Langille, "The Business Council on National Issues and the Canadian State," *Studies in Political Economy*, 24 (Autumn 1987): 49-57; BCNI, "Social Policy Reform and the National Agenda," (Ottawa: Unpublished Report of the BCNI, 1986), i; BCNI, "A Business Perspective on the Reform of the Unemployment Insurance Program. Notes for a Presentation of the House of Commons Standing Committee on Labour, Employment and Immigration," (Ottawa: Unpublished Report of the BCNI, 1987), 1; BCNI, "The Canada-United States Free Trade Agreement: Submission to the House of Commons Standing Committee on External Affairs and International Trade," (Ottawa: Unpublished Report of the BCNI, 1987), 1
36. Thomas d'Aquino and John Bulloch, "The Canada-United States Trade Initiative: A Joint Statement by the President of the BCNI and the President of the Canadian Federation of Independent Business," (Ottawa: News Conference Press Release, 1986), 1; BCNI, "Economic Priorities for Canada," (Toronto: Unpublished Report of the BCNI, 1988), i.
37. BCNI, "The Canada-United States Free Trade Agreement: Submission to the Ontario Select Committee on Economic Affairs," (Toronto: Unpublished Report of the BCNI, 1988), i; Murray Dobbin, "Thomas d'Aquino: The Defacto PM," *Canadian Forum*, 71 (November 1992): 8-9; Donald Macdonald, "A Leap of Faith: the Canadian Decision for Free Trade," *The American Review of Canadian Studies*, 21, no. 2/3 (1991): 155.
38. David Orchard, "What They Don't Want Us to Know About Free Trade," *NeWest Review*, 14, no. 2 (1989): 8-14.
39. Clarkson, "Anti-nationalism in Canada," 48; Atwood, "Free Traders Don't Eat Quiche," A7.
40. David Rosenbaum, "Good Economics Meets Protective Politics," *New York Times*, 19 September 1993, 5E.
41. Clarkson, "Anti-nationalism in Canada," 48; Richard Lipsey, "The Economics of a Canadian-American Free Trade Association," in *The Future on the Table: Canada and the Free Trade Issue*, Michael Henderson, ed. (North York: Masterpress, 1987), 46; John Burns, "Canadians Urged to Accept Pact," *New York Times*, 10 November 1988, 53; John Crispo, "Conclusion," in *Free Trade: The Real Story* (Toronto: Gage Educational Publishing, 1988), 190; John Crosby, "International Trade Minister's Remarks from Debate in the House of Commons, August 29," *Canadian Speeches*, 2, Special Supplement (August/September 1988): 22; Alan Rugman, "Free Trade Opponents have 'Mickey Mouse' Criticism," *Halifax Chronicle-Herald*, 7 November 1988, 7; Robert Sheppard, "Wilson Calls Turner Liar, Coward, Defends National Sales Tax Plan," *Globe and Mail*, 11 November 1988, A16; Earle Gray, "Maude Barlow, Hobgoblin of Little Minds, and Terrors of Free Trade," *Canadian Speeches*, 6, no. 3 (1992): 66; Paul Krugman, "The Uncomfortable Truth About NAFTA. It's Foreign Policy Stupid," *Foreign Affairs*, 72, no. 5 (1993): 13; Orchard, *NeWest Review*, 9.
42. Clement, *The Canadian Corporate Elite*, 256; Alvin R. Riggs and Tom Velk, eds., "The Institute for Research on Public Policy," in *Canadian-American Free Trade: Historical, Political and Economic Dimensions* (Halifax: The IRPP, 1987), i.
43. Riggs and Velk, *Canadian-American Free Trade*, 65-158.

44. Clarkson, "Anti-nationalism in Canada," 52.
45. Clarkson, "Anti-nationalism in Canada," 53; ECC, *First Annual Review, Economic Goals for Canada to 1970: A Statement by the Economic Council of Canada* (Ottawa: Supply and Services, 1970), 204; ECC, *Reaching Outward: A Statement by the Economic Council of Canada* (Ottawa: Supply and Services, 1987), 5; ECC, *A New Frontier: Globalization and Canada's Financial Markets* (Ottawa: Supply and Services, 1989), 24.
46. Nick Fillmore, "The Big Oink: How Business Won the Free Trade Battle," *This Magazine*, 23 (March 1989): 19.
47. Brian Mulroney, "Social and Cultural Goals Underlie Canada's Pursuit of Freer Trade. Speech to the Chambre de Commerce de la Rive-Sud, Longueuil, Québec," *Canadian Speeches*, 2, Special Supplement (1987): 9.
48. External Affairs Canada, *Canada's New Free Trade Agreement: How It Benefits Women* (Ottawa: Supply and Services, 1988), 1; External Affairs Canada, *Canada's New Free Trade Agreement: Key Benefits* (Ottawa: Supply and Services, 1988), 1.
49. Simon Reisman, "Free Trade Will Strengthen Canada's Ability to Survive as a Strong, Free Nation. Speech Given to the Canadian Club of Toronto," *Canadian Speeches*, 1, no. 7 (1987): 3.
50. Warnock, *Free Trade and the New Right Agenda*, 131; Eden, "Free Trade, Tax Reform, and Transfer Pricing," 91.
51. Kieran Furlong and Douglas Moggach, "Efficiency, Competition, and Full Employment in Canadian Free Trade Literature," *Studies in Political Economy*, 33 (Autumn 1990): 141.
52. Tim Hazledine, "Canada U.S. Free Trade? Not So Elementary, Watson," *Canadian Public Policy*, 14, no. 2 (1988): 205.
53. External Affairs Canada, *Trade Negotiations: Securing Canada's Future* (Ottawa: Supply and Services, 1987), 4.
54. External Affairs Canada, *Canada's New Free Trade Agreement: Key Benefits*, 2; John Richard and Richard Dearden, *The Canada-U.S. Free Trade Agreement: Final Text and Analysis* (Toronto: Commerce Clearing House Canadian Limited, 1988), 47, 254.
55. Rodrigue Tremblay, "250 Economists Say Its Our Best Option. Excerpts From an Address to the House of Commons Legislative Committee on Bill C-130, A Bill to Enact the Canada- U.S. Free Trade Agreement," *Canadian Speeches*, 2, Special Supplement (August/September 1988): 5.
56. Tim Hazledine, "What Do Economists Know About Free Trade?" in *Canadian-American Free Trade: Historical, Political and Economic Dimensions*, Alvin Riggs and Tom Velk, eds.(Halifax: The IRPP, 1987), 152; Mel Watkins, "Forum," *Queen's Quarterly*, 98, no. 2 (1991): 495; BCNI, "National Economic Priorities: Challenges and Opportunities," (Ottawa: Unpublished Report of the BCNI, 1991), 7; Peyton Lyon, "CUFTA and Canadian Independence," in *Canadian-American Free Trade: Historical, Political and Economic Dimensions*, Alvin Riggs and Tom Velk, eds. (Halifax: The IRPP, 1987), 197.
57. Francois Rocher, "Canadian Business, Free Trade and the Rhetoric of Economic Continentalization," *Studies in Political Economy*, 35 (Summer 1991): 140.
58. Ibid., 141.

59. Drew Fagan, "Alberta May Lose $14 Billion in Projects: IDA," *Globe and Mail*, 11 November 1988, B6.
60. John Bulloch, "Restructuring of Canada Driven by Global Economy. Speech Given to the Sales and Marketing Executives of Vancouver," *Canadian Speeches*, 5, no. 5 (1991): 17: Peter Bijur, "Deregulation, Competition and Trade Drive Canadian Economy. Address Given to the Empire Club of Canada," *Canadian Speeches*, 1, no. 9 (1988): 11; Macdonald, American Review of Canadian Studies, 155.
61. BCNI, "Economic Priorities and the National Agenda," 10-11.
62. Marjorie Bowker, *On Guard for Thee: An Independent Review of the Free Trade Agreement* (Ottawa: Voyageur Publishing, 1988), 22.
63. Richard and Dearden, *The Canada-U.S. Free Trade Agreement*, 290.
64. Fillmore, "The Big Oink: How Business Won the Free Trade Battle," 19; Warnock, *Free Trade and the New Right Agenda*, 114; Atwood, "Free Traders Don't Eat Quiche," A7; Bowker, *On Guard for Thee*, 22.
65. Palmer, *Working Class Experience*, 403; Mary Gooderham, "Election Officials' Hands Tied on Flood of Late Ads," *Globe and Mail*, 17 November 1988, A10.
66. Judy MacDonald, "Talkin' Trade," *This Magazine*, 23 (May 1989): 42.
67. Daniel Drache, "The Systematic Search for Flexibility: National Competitiveness and New Work Relations," in *The New Era of Global Competition: State Policy and Market Power*, Daniel Drache and Meric Gertler, eds. (Montréal: McGill-Queen's University Press, 1991), 258.
68. Paul Wonnacott and Roderick Hill, *Canadian and U.S. Adjustment Policies in a Bilateral Trade Agreement* (Washington, DC: Canadian-American Committee Representing the C. D. Howe Institute and the National Planning Association, 1987), vii; Ronald Reagan, "An Historic Step Toward World Economic Renewal. Speech Given to the Canadian House of Commons," *Canadian Speeches*, 1, no. 7 (1987): 12; Peter Morici, "The Environment for Free Trade," in *Making Free Trade Work: The Canada-U.S. Agreement*, Peter Morici, ed. (New York: Council on Foreign Relations, 1990), 3; Gary Hufbauer and Jeffrey Schott, *North American Free Trade: Issues and Recommendations* (Washington, DC: Institute for International Economics, 1992), 11; Sylvia Naser, "A Primer: Why Economists Favor Free Trade Agreements," *New York Times*, 17 September 1993, A1, C4.
69. Stephen Block, "Free Trade on Television: The Triumph of Business Rhetoric," *Canadian Journal of Communications*, 17 (1992): 75.
70. Ibid., 77.
71. Naser, "Why Economists Favor Free Trade Agreements," A1.
72. Block, "Free Trade on Television: The Triumph of Business Rhetoric," 77.
73. "Canada Grasps the Future," *New York Times*, 23 November 1988, 22; "What's the Point of NAFTA?" *Des Moines Register*, 17 August 1993, 6A; "Nafta before health," *Wall Street Journal*, 18 August, A10.
74. Warnock, *Free Trade and the New Right Agenda*, 86; Bothwell, *Canada and the United States: The Politics of Partnership*, 59.
75. Bruce Doern and Brian Tomlin, *Faith and Fear: The Free Trade Story* (Toronto: Stoddart Publishing Company, 1991), 5; The Auto Pact was actually a managed

trade agreement between Canada and the United States that was implemented in 1965. It helped expand the Canadian automobile manufacturing sector by stipulating that the number of cars produced in Canada was linked to the number of cars sold in Canada. This ensured that a minimum number of jobs would always be available for Canadian workers. Please see chapter three for more details.

76. Warnock, *Free Trade and the New Right Agenda*, 95; Doern and Tomlin, *Faith and Fear*, 6; Mulroney and Reagan called their meeting the "Shamrock Summit" because both leaders claim to have descended from Irish settlers. This label implies the idea of shared ideological as well as ethnic background.
77. Reagan, "An Historic Step Toward World Economic Renewal," 11.
78. Juliet Schor, "The Great Trade Debates," in *Creating a New World Economy: Forces of Change and Plans for Action*, Gerald Epstein, Julie Graham and Jessica Nembhard, eds. (Philadelphia: Temple University Press, 1993), 281; Federal Reserve Bank of St. Louis, *International Economic Conditions*, May (1992): 11.
79. Warnock, *Free Trade and the New Right Agenda*, 99: Mel Hurtig, *The Betrayal of Canada*, 2nd ed. (Toronto: Stoddart Publishing, 1992), 14.
80. John Holmes, "Industrial Restructuring in a Period of Crisis: An Analysis of the Canadian Automobile Industry," *Antipode*, 20, no. 1 (1988): 35-37.
81. "Foreign Trade Legislation: Forward," *The Congressional Digest*, 65, no. 8/9 (1986): 193.
82. Fillmore, "The Big Oink: How Business Won the Free Trade Battle," 7; Bob Hepburn, "Reagan Promises 'co-operation' of Free Trade," *Toronto Star*, 18 November 1988, A3.
83. Chief Electoral Officer, *Report of the Chief Electoral Officer of the Thirty-Fourth General Election in Canada* (Ottawa: Chief Electoral Officer and Supply and Services, 1988), 20.
84. "Canada Grasps the Future," *New York Times*, 22.
85. Stephen Cohen, "Geo-economics and America's Mistakes," in *The New Global Economy in the Information Age: Reflections on Our Changing World*, Martin Carnoy et al., eds. (University Park: Pennsylvania State University Press, 1993), 126.
86. R. A. Young, "Political Scientists, Economists, and the Canada-U.S. Free Trade Agreement," *Canadian Public Policy*, 15, no. 1 (1989): 49.
87. Dan O'Hagen, "Free Trade, Our Canada or Theirs: Workers Confront the Corporate Blueprint," *Canadian Labour* (September, 1986): 17; CLC, "Submission by the CLC on the North American Free Trade Agreement to the Subcommittee on International Trade of the Standing Committee on External Affairs and International Trade of the Canadian House of Commons," 26 January 1993, 29.
88. Mel Watkins, "Ten Good Reasons to Oppose Free Trade," *This Magazine*, 20 (April, 1986): 15.
89. James McCambly, "North American Free Trade Demands a Charter of Labour. Speech Given by the President of the Canadian Federation of Labour to the Americas Society in New York." *Canadian Speeches*, 4, no. 10 (1991): 47.
90. Robertson Davies, "Signing Away Canada's Soul: Culture, Identity, and the Free Trade Agreement," *Harper's*, January 1989, 45.

91. Robert White, "Control of Canada is Free Trade Issue," *Canadian Speeches*, 2, no. 1 (1988): 18; Gerard Veilleux, "Do We Need and Can We Afford the CBC?" *Canadian Speeches*, 5, no. 1 (1991): 54.
92. Hazledine, "What Do Economists Know About Free Trade," 152.
93. Dobbin, "Thomas d'Aquino: The Defacto PM," 11.

Chapter 3

The Canadian Economy and Free Trade

Canada's Permeable Fordism

Canadian political economists have a difficult question to answer.[1] Why would Canada agree to continental integration in the 1980s after vacillating for a century between cultivating and eschewing closer political and economic ties with the United States? This question is particularly vexing because Canada acceded to continental integration just when American world hegemony was on the wane and institutions of the Canadian State had reached their most advanced stage of Fordist development. In seeking and negotiating the Canada-United States Free Trade Agreement (FTA), the Progressive Conservatives initiated a process whereby Canadians voluntarily surrendered broad powers to control their economy, maintain the Welfare State and promote cultural sovereignty without gaining commensurate supranational power at a continental level. The FTA opened up the less efficient Canadian private sector to possible takeover by American competitors. Free trade also initiated a process whereby Canadian economic and social policy could be harmonized with that of the United States. How was it that the Canadian model of national development came to be undermined by the continental regime of accumulation embodied in the FTA? In order to answer this question it is necessary to examine the development that occurred in Canada in the post-World War II era. This model of development has been called Canada's "permeable Fordism."[2]

In the aftermath of World War II, the United States emerged as the world's hegemonic power. Canadian development must be seen in the shadow of American domination. The Canadian and American economy and military-industrial complex became closely integrated under the Hyde Park Agreement. The United States also served as an expanded market for Canadian natural resources such as petroleum and agricultural products. After the war, Canada attempted to embark upon an independent development strategy. In order to perpetuate the Canadian Fordist economy based in heavy investments in fixed capital and assembly line labour, the Canadian State developed a mode of regulation at the federal and provincial levels of government that combined Keynesian macroeconomic policies with labour-management relations, recognizing workers' right to strike and to share in the prosperity they helped to create. A modest expansion of the Welfare State was also part of this post-war Fordist development.

Canadian economic development was therefore based on a national mode of regulation and a permeable yet national regime of accumulation. This statement runs counter to the inaccurate claim that Canada had a continental regime of accumulation with a national mode of regulation.[3] After World War II, Canada increasingly turned to the United States as a market for goods because Great Britain was unable to resume its historical role as an imperial market for Canadian staple commodities. Despite attempts at independent development, Canada also became increasingly integrated into the military-industrial complex of the United States. Canada had attempted to follow the Fordist model of development by maintaining an independent national technological and productive capacity in military aviation and other leading-edge technologies. This strategy ended with the controversial abandonment of the Avro Arrow military aircraft programme in 1959. The cancellation of this programme lead to the demise of one of the most important segments of Canadian high technology research and development as well as the elimination of over 15,000 aviation industry jobs. As a result, Canadian national development was hindered as many of Canada's leading engineers and technicians found employment with such American aviation giants as Boeing and McDonnell-Douglas. Instead of relying on a domestically produced technology, Canada signed a defense production-sharing agreement with the United States, creating a managed trade zone in military production and procurement. American branch plants in Canada secured many contracts for military production. These branch plants were an important part of the American military-industrial complex. Integration of military production only intensified Canadian links to the United States that had been created with the establishment of the North American Aerospace Defense Command (Norad) in 1957.

Further continental integration occurred in 1965 with the creation of the Canada-United States Auto Pact. This sectoral free trade agreement in automobiles and auto parts created a continental managed free trade zone for Ford, General Motors, Chrysler and American Motors as well as for their respective Canadian assembly branch plants. The Auto Pact was a free trade agreement in that virtually all tariffs were removed from automobiles and auto parts shipped across the Canada-United States boundary. For example, Ford could produce cars in Windsor, Ontario that were destined for the American market while cars produced in

Flint, Michigan could be sold in the Canadian market without a tariff surcharge. It was a managed trade agreement in that content rules applied to cars sold within Canada to ensure that a certain number of Canadian jobs existed regardless of the condition of the North American automobile market. Canada's permeable Fordist economy also relied more heavily on foreign trade and investment than other industrialized countries. As a result, the Canadian government pressed the United States to increase their purchases of Canadian petroleum, natural gas and hydroelectric surpluses.

If this brief review of Canadian economic development ended here, it would appear that Canadian economic growth relied primarily upon a continental regime of accumulation. It would, however, be an incomplete view. It is true that much of the industry within Canada relied on American markets and American capital investment. On closer examination however, it can be shown that it was primarily American branch plants that relied on not just the Canadian, but North American market. Many Canadian-owned firms and Canadian politicians were interested in promoting a Fordist model of development where the foundation of economic growth and prosperity depended upon the deepening of the domestic market, not on the expansion of international trade. Countering the continentalist push was a growing economic, political and cultural nationalism and a vociferous questioning of foreign control over the Canadian economy and polity.[4]

In the immediate post-war era, the Canadian government explicitly outlined elements of a Fordist model of development. In 1945, the Canadian government planted the seeds for a Canadian Welfare State with the *White Paper on Employment and Income.* Specific goals of this White Paper included the expansion of social programmes, the implementation of the Fordist policy of maintaining high levels of employment through government intervention and the linkage of wage increases to productivity increases.

Overt economic nationalism began to emerge in Canada during the late 1950s. The year 1957 "lies like a fault line" across the road to Canadian national development.[5] The continentalist pretensions of Prime Minister Mackenzie King had long since passed with his defeat in 1948. He had advocated a free trade agreement between Canada and the United States immediately after World War II. In 1957, Lester B. Pearson won the Nobel Peace Prize instilling a sense of pride amongst Canadians. The Canada Council was finally instituted to promote Canadian culture. Prime Minister Diefenbaker was elected and Canadian economic nationalism became an acknowledged goal.

Since World War II, Canada had balanced its current account deficit with the United States by attracting American investment capital, hence the permeable nature of Canada's Fordism. In 1958, the Government of Canada sponsored the Royal Commission on Canada's Economic Prospects. The study produced by the Commission, entitled the *Gordon Report* after its chairperson Walter Gordon, emphasized the extent to which Canadian industry was foreign-owned and controlled. Gordon concluded that Canadian development was being hindered by its excessive reliance on foreign capital, limiting opportunities for Canadian entrepreneurs. The report concluded that Canada needed to secure greater control over its economy.[6] By 1959, American interests controlled about 44 percent of all Canadian manufacturing including 55 percent of all mining, 90 percent of the automobile industry and two-thirds of capital invested in natural gas and petroleum extraction and refining.[7]

Despite these warnings against over-reliance on foreign-controlled branch plants, the Canadian government did not immediately implement any radical policies to limit the repatriation of profits or to screen foreign investment. It was difficult to be an economic nationalist when the ability to maintain a manageable balance of payments was tied to securing American investment. In fact, Canada's balance of payments with the United States deteriorated so much in the early 1960s that the Canadian government was forced to secure loans from the International Monetary Fund (IMF). Prime Minister Diefenbaker was only able to put in place a few significant nationalist policies. He established the National Energy Board to manage oil exports and created the National Energy Policy, blocking Canadian oil imports from going past the Ottawa River Valley. This created a guaranteed Canadian market for domestic oil production. Diefenbaker also imposed a 15 percent withholding tax on dividends repatriated outside Canada in 1961.

In 1963, Lester B. Pearson became Canada's new prime minister. Despite the increasing pitch of nationalist rhetoric, Pearson was not able to accomplish much more than Diefenbaker in promoting a nationalist economic agenda. Early in his tenure, Pearson approved a national budget proposed by finance minister Walter Gordon levying a 30 percent tax on foreign takeovers of Canadian firms and a 15 percent tax on profits repatriated outside of Canada. These and other policies suggested by Gordon were either watered down or retracted under the influence of the Canadian business community who feared American retaliation and a downturn in the major Canadian stock markets. Chief amongst the opponents to new nationalist policies was Eric Kierans, president of the Montréal Stock Exchange.

Although many events combined to inspire the Canadian government to promote nationalist economic policies, the foreign ownership issue and continuing balance of payments problems were most influential. In 1963, Citibank of New York purchased controlling interest of a Dutch-owned bank in Canada. Citibank's directors failed to notify Gordon, the Canadian minister of finance, despite being advised to do so by the governor of the Bank of Canada. The Canadian government placed an injunction on the deal. Negotiations persisted until 1967 when the Canadian government passed The Bank Act, originally intended to limit foreign ownership of any bank in Canada to 25 percent. After lengthy negotiations, Citibank gained control over the bank but it had to comply with more stringent Canadian regulations.

The real significance of The Bank Act was the attention it drew to foreign ownership in Canada among the Canadian populace. This particular foreign ownership case attracted attention for two reasons.[8] First, it involved a bank. This was important because financial capitalists have always played an important role in Canadian economic development by financing the extraction of Canada's resources. So important have bankers been to Canada's staple economy that they have been called Canada's "fiscal father-confessors."[9] The second factor was that James S. Rockefeller represented the interests of Citibank when he appeared before the House of Commons finance committee in January of 1967. Canadians learned from his testimony that he honestly did not see any difference between Canada and the United States. According to Rockefeller, the fact that no real differences separated the two countries meant that there should be no problem in Citibank holding controlling interests in a bank located in Canada. The fact that a Rockefeller, a member of one of most influential families in the United States, could so blithely disregard Canada's aspirations for independent development shocked many Canadians.

A more important issue for symbolic as well as practical reasons was the nagging problem of Canada's balance of payment problems with the United States. Ever since its 1962 loan from the IMF, Canada had gotten special treatment from the United States so that it could balance its accounts in a timely manner. However, the United States had also been running balance of payments deficits since 1958. By the late 1960s, the United States was finding the situation unmanageable. Specific problems confronting the United States included the economic resurgence of Europe and Japan, massive expenditures on the Vietnam War and President Johnson's Great Society social welfare programmes. Canadians had long relied on a special relationship with the United States based on "exceptionalism" and "exemptionalism."[10] Canada expected to be treated as an exception to American policy and to be given special exemptions as a result. Canada assumed that American balance of payments problems would not affect the importation of American investment capital, essential for Canada's balance of payments with the United States.

By 1971, capital outflow from the United States was so severe that President Nixon implemented radical policies to stop the hemorrhaging of capital. At the beginning of 1971 the United States had gold reserves to cover 32 percent of foreign dollar holdings. By the end of 1971, the United States could only muster enough gold to cover 18 percent of foreign dollar holdings. On August 15, 1971, Nixon declared that the American dollar would no longer be convertible to gold which meant the abandonment of fixed currency exchange rates. Nixon also announced that the American tariffs were to be increased by 10 percent to discourage imports to the United States. Finally, Nixon instituted the Domestic International Sales Corporation (DISC) which gave tax concessions to American MNCs that exported from their United States sites rather than their foreign branch plants. Canadian officials were genuinely surprised to discover that Canada would not be exempted from the DISC policy. As it turned out, Nixon's policy had a limited impact on Canadian trade because it lasted for only four months. A more profound impact was felt by Canadian policy-makers who realized that the United States was treating Canada just like any other trading partner. The combined effects of the election of Prime Minister Pierre Trudeau in 1968 and the actions of President Nixon in 1971 marked another important juncture in Canadian economic nationalism and Fordist development.

With American hegemony in abeyance, Canada was able to put a more thoroughly national model of development in place. For much of his life, Pierre Trudeau had been a staunch anti-nationalist. As an intellectual in Québec, he had written anti-nationalist articles in *Cité Libre*, a French language magazine based in Montréal. However, flourishing cultural and political nationalism converged with a burgeoning economic nationalism to alter Trudeau's conception of Canadian development. A new cultural nationalism was reflected in the writings of such authors as Northrop Frye and Margaret Atwood.[11] Politically, a nationalist ideology was promoted by an unusual group of Leftist political strategists called The Waffle. In 1969, this splinter group from the New Democratic Party (NDP) issued a manifesto that proclaimed as its purpose the creation of an independent socialist Canada. This manifesto, written by Jim Laxer, research director of the NDP and Mel Watkins, a political economist from the University of Toronto, advocated nationalization of the means of production in Canada to more equitably distribute wealth to Canadians.[12] The irony here of course is that traditionally, Leftists had been staunchly anti-nationalist as a matter of principle. Nationalism was a form of false consciousness impeding the development of an international class consciousness. This tradition was reinforced by the fact that the major unions in Canada allied to the NDP were international, that is, branches of American unions. Although the Waffle was eventually silenced by the mainstream of the NDP, the influence of these Leftist nationalists could be seen in later NDP policies and ultimately in the development of Canadian Fordism during the late 1960s and 1970s.

The Waffle was not alone in attempting to recapture control of the Canadian economy. Between 1968 and 1972, three major reports were released by the Canadian government, all of which concluded that there was a need to monitor foreign investment in Canada. In 1968, the Canadian government issued the *Report of the Task Force on the Structure of Canadian Industry*. Also known as the *Watkins Report* after its chairperson, it recommended the creation of an agency to screen foreign investment as well as a Canadian Development Corporation to provide incentives for Canadian entrepreneurs. In 1970, the Canadian government's Standing Committee on External Affairs and National Defence issued the eleventh *Report of the Committee Respecting Canada-U.S. Relations*. Also known as the *Wahn Report* after its chairperson, it concluded that there be a Canadian Ownership and Control Bureau to limit access by foreign MNCs to Canadian resources and corporations. In 1972, the Canadian government issued the most comprehensive report to date, *Foreign Direct Investment in Canada*. Also known as the *Gray Report*, it recommended that Canada increase regulations governing foreign investment to reduce its dependence on a foreign-dominated branch plant economy. The report stated that Canada was being dominated by an increasing number of "truncated firms" that did not carry out their own research, product development or strategic planning in Canada.[13]

By the early 1970s, Trudeau had implemented a series of overtly nationalist economic policies that closely resembled recommendations proposed by the *Waffle Manifesto, Watkins Report, Wahn Report* and *Gray Report*. Paradoxically, Fordism was being reinforced in Canada at a time when conditions perpetuating Fordism in the American and global economy were beginning to deteriorate. Mitchell Sharp, Canada's minister of external affairs, referred to Canada's attempt to reduce its economic vulnerability as the "third option." Sharp had evaluated Canada's treatment by the United States in the late 1960s, publishing his results in a 1972 report entitled *Canada-U.S. Relations: Options for the Future.* The options available fell into three categories. First, Canada could maintain the status quo by vacillating between nationalism and continentalism as it had for decades. Second, Canada could abandon its nationalist pretensions and embrace the notion of closer integration with the United States. The third option recommended that Canada develop a more comprehensive industrial and social policy and reduce its dependence on the United States by increasing trade ties with other countries. It gave "doctrinal coherence" to Canada's industrial and trade policy in the 1970s and early 1980s.[14] The third option was based on Fordist policies promoting full employment, a guaranteed annual income and increased governmental intervention to reclaim control over the Canadian economy.

In 1973, Trudeau announced the creation of a new National Oil Policy. The Canadian government wanted to establish a State-owned, vertically integrated, petroleum products corporation responsible for all aspects of resource development including extraction, refining, distribution and marketing to the Canadian public. Trudeau started to build this crown corporation in 1975 by purchasing the energy-based subsidiaries of several foreign MNCs. Petrofina of Belgium sold oil, gas, and coal rights in Western Canada, an oil refinery in Montréal, and 1,100 service stations in Eastern Canada to the Canadian government. Other foreign subsidiaries purchased by the Canadian government included the American and French-owned Hudson Bay Oil and Gas Company and Gulf Oil of Canada which was actually owned in part by Chevron Oil of the United States.[15] This policy, based on resource exploitation, represents only one facet of Trudeau's nation-building strategy. A State-financed holding company called the Canadian Development Corporation (CDC) was established to funnel Canadian capital into domestically-owned enterprises. Although the CDC was only marginally successful, the aim of the CDC was to lower the level of foreign ownership of industry in Canada and to promote the growth of high paying, high skilled jobs in Canadian-owned industry.

A controversial institution established during this period was the Foreign Investment Review Agency (FIRA) which had been recommended in the *Watkins Report.* Foreign investors had to demonstrate to FIRA how they were going to help Canada by creating jobs for Canadians and by doing research and development in Canada. Although FIRA received mixed reviews in its ability to screen foreign investments, it represented a bold attempt by the Canadian government to regain control of its domestic economy.

Canada's industrial policy was greatly influenced by the increase in world oil prices in the 1970s. Despite signs that the Fordist blueprint for development was beginning to show its weakness in the United States and in Canada, oil price increases convinced Canadian planners that a social-democratic economic strategy could be implemented. In 1979, the Organization of Petroleum Exporting Countries (OPEC) doubled oil prices for a second time. Canada shaped its industrial strategy for the early 1980s based on the assumption of continued high and increasing oil prices. In 1980, Trudeau established the National Energy Program (NEP) in order to redistribute oil rents from Alberta's productive oil fields. Based on the assumption of increased tax revenues from oil proceeds, governmental planners wanted to build a series of massive energy and natural resource projects to promote regional development. Ultimately, backward linkages forged between central Canadian industry and regional energy projects were to comprise Canada's industrial strategy.[16] With the promise of new revenues from these planned energy projects, Trudeau's government promised to expand the Canadian industrial base, the Canada Pension Plan and to increase spending in other social programmes. It can therefore be said that Canada had Fordist aspirations up until the early 1980s, even though the underpinnings of Fordist development had begun to decay almost a decade earlier. As the world price of petroleum leveled and then dropped, the Canadian government had to modify its nationalistic accumulation strategy. This involved the abandonment of its attempts to link historic dependence on staple products with a balanced industrial policy.[17] Plans for an expanded array of social programmes also had to be shelved.

It is not enough, however, to blame fluctuating world energy prices in the demise of Fordism in Canada. A complete view of how Canadian Fordism became moribund can only be attained by considering the actions of Canadian and American corporate interests. As the United States attempted to reverse its economic decline in the late 1970s, the Carter Administration was sensitive to problems in Canada including rising Québec separatism, oil price fluctuations, and high Canadian unemployment. In the late 1970s, Canada and the United States broached their bilateral problems with a high degree of mutual understanding. In 1980, Carter was voted out of office in part due to his inability to spark economic growth in the face of the crisis of Fordism. Ronald Reagan was elected based on a platform of monetarism, privatization and the unleashing of market forces to cure the malaise that had besieged the American and world economy. As for Canada, the Reagan Administration looked upon the NEP, FIRA and Trudeau's attempt to expand social spending with contempt. American resource-oriented MNCs in Canada vociferously complained to the sympathetic American government about Canadian restrictions on investment. American entrepreneurs and financiers warned Reagan about the "socialist government" in Ottawa that was blocking the repatriation of profits.[18] Canadian governmental intervention in its economy ran against the tenets of the *laissez-faire* capitalism that formed the basis of the post-Fordist economic policy under Ronald Reagan.

The Reagan Administration wanted to implement an economic, political and military programme that would restore the United States to its former hegemonic status without the previous levels of government intervention. Specific policies included cuts in social spending and tax reforms favoring corporate interests. Solutions to the worsening American trade deficit and balance of payments problem were based on increased protectionism at home and coupled with a call for reduced protectionism by other countries. Canada was soon to become a test case for Reaganomic trade policy.[19] From 1981 onward, Trudeau's Fordist agenda came under relentless pressure from Washington, American Business and American media.

Initial protest came from U.S. Secretary of State Alexander Haig, who complained about Canadian protectionism. Federal ministers received official letters from their American counterparts berating them for the NEP, FIRA and overall trade policy. The American Ambassador to Canada Paul Robinson, openly stated that the NEP was one of the worst Canadian policies in recent history. Both the *Wall Street Journal* and the *New York Times* ran editorials excoriating Canadian energy and trade policy for their inherent "xenophobic nationalism."[20] Pressure applied from Washington heartened Canadian opponents to Trudeau's policies. Resource-dependent provinces such as Alberta that wanted greater freedom to manage resources, business lobbies such as the Business Council on National Issues(BCNI), and corporate-influenced media such as the Toronto-based *Globe and Mail*, renewed their attempts to derail Canada's Fordist model of development.

Attempts at Fordist development slowed after the presentation of the Canadian federal budget in November 1981. Despite increasing evidence that the Canadian economy was in a deep recession, the budget called for increased social spending. The most controversial aspect of Trudeau's budget was his attempt to achieve social equity through radical tax reform. So many tax loopholes were closed that outcries of indignation came from labour and capital alike. The pursuit of Fordism was discredited as the recession intensified during the period from 1981 to 1983.

Room for economic maneuvering in Canada was constrained by the monetarist policy of high interest rates that formed the basis of Reaganomics. Canada followed the American lead in using high interest rates as a weapon against high inflation. Although inflation was corralled by this strategy, interest rates in excess of 20 percent exacerbated the recession in Canada by increasing business bankruptcies and raising the unemployment rate to 12 percent by 1982.[21]

While the Trudeau Government was attempting to maintain and extend Fordism into the 1980s, the Canadian business community was bridling at high corporate taxes, governmental regulations, powerful unions, high wages and nationalist constraints on their continentalist aspirations.[22] Their constant complaints paid off in 1982, when Trudeau shuffled his Cabinet and replaced the nationalist Herb Gray with the continentalist Edward Lumley as minister for industry, trade and commerce. Trudeau also placed his most respected minister, Marc Lalonde, in charge of the ministry of finance in order to more competently respond to the needs of the business community. Lalonde had been the architect of the NEP, a basic element for Canadian Fordism in the 1980s. After this shuffle, Lalonde went from being a paragon of Fordist social democratic ideals to being a promoter of neoconservative policies. The placement of Lumley and Lalonde in powerful cabinet positions signified that "a decisive watershed had been crossed."[23] Canada was shifting from a national to a continental model of development. Policy statements of the BCNI received increasing attention from Trudeau and his reorganized Cabinet. Greater governmental attentiveness to the corporate agenda can be seen in the aforementioned Macdonald Commission. The stated purpose of this nonpartisan commission was to travel across Canada soliciting ideas from a cross-section of Canadians on how to create prosperity and equity. It was clear from the final recommendations of the Macdonald Commission that priority had been given to business interests.[24]

The pace of Canada's march to continentalism accelerated after the Canadian federal election of September 1984. Despite Trudeau's increasing embrace of neoconservative policies, the Liberals were voted out of office. While the Liberal Party was in power during the early 1980s, the disaffected business community represented by the BCNI had cultivated a close relationship with the Progressive Conservative Party whose ideology was more thoroughgoing pro-business. Party leader Brian Mulroney, cultivated support amongst the Canadian business elite, particularly natural resource and oil company executives in Western Canada who disliked the NEP. Support from the business community, coupled with Trudeau's policy debacles, ensured victory for

Mulroney's Progressive Conservatives in the 1984 federal election. Mulroney's vision for Canada crystallized with the release of the final report of the Macdonald Commission which concluded that Canada could prosper by engaging in free trade with the United States. Mulroney now had validation for a programme that was implicit in his speech to the Economic Club of New York where he stated that "Canada is open for business again."[25] With support from a purportedly nonpartisan source, Mulroney could openly promote the Tory neoconservative agenda.

Despite their best efforts, the Progressive Conservatives were not able to implement their neoconservative policies with the same vigor that Ronald Reagan or Margaret Thatcher did in the United States or Britain. The dismantling of the Welfare State, privatization, deregulation and the disciplining of labour could not be easily achieved because of the strong social democratic tradition in Canada. The difference between Canada and the United States in this regard is striking. Free trade was seen as the central mechanism by which social-democratic institutions in Canada could be restructured or eliminated. For economic integration to be feasible, participating countries must share similar objectives in economic development, taxation, currency exchange, social spending and income distribution.[26] If harmonization is not done voluntarily in anticipation of a free trade agreement, market pressures will force the standardization of policies between free trade partners.[27] Free trade can therefore be used to justify social change long before free trade as a policy is implemented.

Free Trade Related Restructuring In Canada, 1984-89

Two free trade related changes occurred within months of the Tory electoral victory in 1984. The first was the dismantling of FIRA in December 1984 and the second was the elimination of the NEP in April 1985. FIRA embodied both Fordist and nationalist ideals. It served a nation-building role by screening all foreign investment greater than Can$50 thousand to ensure that MNCs met performance requirements such as providing jobs for Canadians and conducting research and development in Canada. It also symbolized to Canadians that they could stand up to the demands of foreign capital by actually turning down some foreign investments. However, FIRA was only a partial success because its inefficient bureaucracy did not apply standards in a consistent manner.

Although FIRA achieved only limited success, it angered American investors who did not like the imposition of investment restrictions or performance requirements, however haphazardly these regulations may have been applied. In response, Mulroney dismantled the FIRA and replaced it with an agency called Investment Canada. The mandate of this new agency was to screen foreign investment, but only if it was greater than Can$5 million. Furthermore, the standards for approval were far less stringent than those set forth by FIRA. Between 1985 and 1989, Investment Canada screened 696 applications and denied none of them.[28] In a later complement to investment deregulation, Canada implemented a two-stage tax reform to harmonize its tax structure with that of the U.S. Tax Reform Act of 1986. In effect, Canadian tax reforms involved reducing the corporate tax burden. Eric Owen, taxation consultant for the Canadian Manufacturers' Association, said Canadian businesses needed the tax reforms to restore competitiveness.[29]

The spring of 1985 witnessed the demise of the NEP. If American investors were unhappy with FIRA, they were outraged by the NEP. During the postwar period, foreign multinational energy corporations controlled an increasingly large share of Canada's resources. The NEP was established in 1980 in order to repatriate control over domestic energy resources through buy-outs and performance requirements. Trudeau planned to use the increased profits from energy as a basis for expanding the Welfare State and Canadian Fordist development. Between 1980 and 1985, the NEP was instrumental in increasing Canadian control over energy resources in Canada from 40 percent to 48 percent.[30] The Reagan Administration, the *New York Times* and the *Wall Street Journal* viewed the NEP as an extremely restrictive and nationalist policy that could set an unhealthy precedent for other countries to follow.[31] Given the long-standing American view that Canada represents the most dependable foreign source of strategic energy and mineral resources, it is not surprising that the United States would condemn any policy which impeded American access to Canadian resources.

When the Tories won the election in 1984, the NEP did not stand a chance of survival. While the NEP would most likely have been gutted on the grounds that it impeded market forces in Canada, it is arguable that the largest factor prompting the Tories to dismantle the NEP and FIRA was their need to curry American favor in order to secure a free trade deal. It was no coincidence then that Mulroney announced Canada's abandonment of the NEP in the United States.[32] By the summer of 1989, Canadian control over its own resources had dropped from a high of 48 percent achieved around 1984 to 42 percent.[33]

The demise of FIRA and the NEP coupled with the Tory policy of deregulation reversed the trend of increased Canadian control over Canadian industry, triggering a spate of mergers and takeovers. Businesses justified these mergers by arguing that they needed to increase their size in order to compete in the larger economy created by the imminent FTA. Companies achieving the most success under the FTA planned for the new trade regime long in advance of its implementation. In the years leading up to the FTA, hundreds of the largest corporations in Canada and the United States either began merger discussions with other firms or actually completed the merger process. Consider actions taken by Dominion Textiles. Two years prior to the FTA, this Canadian textile giant went on a merger and acquisition spree to increase its presence in the North American market. In 1987 Dominion Textiles purchased a denim manufacturer named Erin Mills Incorporated of North Carolina for Can$274 million. In 1989, WaynTex, a Virginia-based woven fabrics manufacturer, was acquired for Can$170 million. In 1989 Dominion Textiles became North America's largest producer of bath towels when it purchased C. S. Brooks of New York City.[34]

Many firms initiated merger plans after the FTA negotiations began but did not announce the completion of mergers or acquisitions until the first weeks after the FTA came into effect on January, 1 1989.[35] On January 18, 1989, Elders IXL Limited of Australia, brewers of Foster beer and the parent company of Carling O'Keefe Brewers in Canada, purchased Molson's Brewing Company at a cost of Can$1.6 billion. During the same week, Wardair Canada, Canada's largest charter airline service was purchased by PWA Limited, the parent company of Canadian Airlines International for a purchase price of Can$248 million. On January 20, 1989, Imperial Oil of Canada (owned by Exxon) purchased controlling interests in Texaco Canada for Can$4.9 billion. On January 26, 1989, Consolidated Bathurst, a huge Canadian forest products corporation, was purchased by the Chicago-based Stone Container Company for Can$2.6 billion. Later that same day, Southam Incorporated, a major Canadian newspaper publisher laid off hundreds of workers to thwart a takeover bid.[36] Each of these maneuvers were initiated long in advance of the implementation of the FTA in order to complete the necessary research and legal work.

According to a recent Statistics Canada survey, concentration of ownership has been accelerating in Canada since the mid-1980s.[37] While some firms became more competitive, mergers have had many deleterious effects. First, layoffs are inevitable because merging companies cannot afford to duplicate all functions and jobs. Over 2,000 employees lost their jobs in the Dominion Textile mergers. In the case of the Wardair-PWA merger, approximately 4,500 employees lost their jobs. Over 400 workers were permanently laid off at Southam Incorporated. In the Molson's-Carling O'Keefe merger, over 1,400 employees lost their jobs at Molson's least efficient plants in St. John's, Montréal, Toronto, Winnipeg, Saskatoon, Lethbridge, and Vancouver.[38]

A second impact of the mergers has been an increase in price. Theoretically, mergers and deregulation should allow prices to drop due to increased reliance on market forces and economies of scale created by the new larger firms. However, increased mergers mean fewer firms operating in a market. With less competition, there is reduced incentive to drop prices. Consider the Canadian beer industry. The merger of O'Keefe Breweries with Molson Breweries creates a company which controls 53 percent of the market. Labatt Breweries already controlled approximately 43 percent of the market. After the FTA, two companies controlled over 90 percent of the Canadian market. Free trade has not promoted competition but has instead created an oligopoly.

A third impact of mergers is a reduction in choice as fewer firms operate in a particular market. Free trade was touted as a mechanism to provide a greater variety of less expensive and higher quality goods for the North American consumer. In some sectors(i.e. brewing), prices have risen while choice and quality have actually dropped due to deregulation, mergers and free trade. Ironically, as Canadian author Douglas Coupland noted, "economy of scale is ruining choice."[39]

In 1989, Calvin Goldman, director of Canada's federal Bureau of Competition Policy, stated that increased mergers in Canada were part of a global trend where businesses are simply trying to adapt to increased international competition. However, Goldman qualified that statement by noting that "at least companies are using that argument to try to justify proceeding with a merger."[40] He also admitted that he was very surprised to see the dramatic increase in mergers immediately after the signing of the FTA. Analysts also speculate that many firms postponed mergers until after the FTA had been officially implemented to avoid jeopardizing the fate of the trade pact.

Other impacts of mergers prompted by the impending FTA included expanded sales for Canadian companies and the relocation of production from Canadian and American firms to the United States in order to prepare for continental free trade. The majority of companies moving out of Canada prior to 1989 were foreign multinationals, however, hundreds were also small to medium-sized Canadian firms that located to upstate New York and other cross-border locations. Several large Canadian firms expanded sales and production into the United States. As early as 1985, John Labatt's Brewers greatly expanded their marketing efforts in the United States in preparation for the FTA.

Securing a free trade agreement with the United States was the single most important foreign policy issue for Mulroney after 1984. In order to achieve this policy objective, the Tories had to convince the Reagan administration that free trade was a good idea. Evidence suggests that Canada made several concessions to the United States in order to secure a free trade agreement. During the early and mid-1980s, Canada enjoyed a huge trade surplus with the United States. Before many prominent American politicians would approve of free trade with Canada, something had to be done about the low value of the Canadian dollar. Lloyd Bentson, then Democratic senator from Texas, Senator Max Baucus (D-Montana) and Congressman Richard Gephardt (D-Missouri), with the support of prominent business lobbies such as the National Manufacturers Association, expressed serious doubts about the viability of a free trade agreement with an undervalued Canadian dollar. Although no formal agreement was ever reached on Canada-U.S. currency exchange this much is known: between 1985 and 1989 the Canadian dollar appreciated against the U.S. dollar more than any other currency in the industrialized world.[41] Some would say that this revaluation was done to persuade the United States to sign the FTA.[42]

In another concession that angered much of the Canadian arts community, the Mulroney Government reneged on film distribution legislation that would have reserved 15 percent of the Canadian movie market for Canadian films. Prior to this, Canadian film-makers could only gain access to about three percent of the Canadian movie market because American movie companies controlled film distribution in Canada. Frank Valenti of the Motion Picture Association of America (MPAA) — the chief lobby for the American movie industry — asked Reagan to intercede on behalf of the MPAA in order to get Canada to back off. Valenti believed that Canada was setting a bad example. Other countries might also decide to regulate film distribution. The message Valenti wanted to send to Canadians was that the United States would not sign a free trade deal if Canada engaged in protectionist cultural practices. Valenti carried enough clout that he was able to persuade Reagan to discuss the matter personally with Mulroney. Furthermore, Valenti flew to Ottawa to have a personal conference with Flora MacDonald, who was then Canadian minister of communications and who had also written the proposed film distribution bill. Valenti was also able to convince the U.S. Senate and House of Representatives to pass resolutions condemning Canadian cultural practices as protectionist. These resolutions were then sent to Mulroney. Senator Alan Cranston exclaimed that if Canada persisted in passing its film distribution bill he and other senators would not ratify the FTA.[43] By 1988, it was apparent that the pressure tactics used by the MPAA and Valenti were successful. Legislation to allow Canadians greater access to their own films died in committee without being considered by Parliament. Canada was prevented from developing its movie industry because of continental market forces and American political pressure.

A third concession made by Canada concerned Canadian softwood exports to the United States in the 1980s. Canadian forest product companies cut trees on public land. In order to do this, they must pay the Canadian government "stumpage fees." American timber companies operate under a similar system in the Western United States. Problems arose when American timber companies complained that Canadian stumpage fees were too low. In effect, American corporations and the American government accused the Canadian government of subsidizing the Canadian wood products industry by charging too little to cut trees on public land. In retaliation, the American government levied a tax on Canadian softwood imports. Canadians protested the American actions but could do little if they wanted free trade talks to continue. American free trade negotiators used the softwood issue to force Canadian negotiators, as the party pursing the negotiations, to play the role of *demandeur.*[44] Canadians were outmaneuvered at the bargaining table. In order to salvage what he could, Mulroney asked Canadian forest product companies to pay an export tax on softwood products destined for the United States instead of paying an import tax to U.S. Customs. The Canadian export tax would convince the Americans that softwood exporters were paying adequate production costs while simultaneously keeping free trade talks alive. At the same time, the money paid in taxes would stay in Canada instead of being paid to American customs officials. As a result of this concession to secure free trade, the Canadian share of the U.S. softwood market dropped from 33 percent in 1987 to 26.7 percent in 1990. An estimated 50,000 Canadian jobs were jeopardized as exports declined.[45]

Alterations to Canadian generic pharmaceutical production represents a fourth concession made to gain a free trade deal with the United States. One of the pillars of the Canadian health care system is the ready supply of inexpensive generic drugs. The Canadian government had long decreed that Canadian pharmaceutical companies could produce inexpensive versions of more expensive brand-name prescriptions. Royalties were paid to the owners of the patent but not to the satisfaction of many large American pharmaceutical companies. The powerful American pharmaceutical lobby pressed the American trade negotiators to strengthen intellectual property rights in the FTA. In order to appease the American drug lobbyists, the Canadian government lengthened the time that a drug patent and production monopoly would be recognized in Canada. Generic drug companies now had to wait longer before they could produce inexpensive versions of the brand name pharmaceuticals. The Canadian government conceded greater profits to American drug companies and higher costs for the Canadian health care system in order to receive the vaunted benefits of an FTA.

Between 1985 and 1989, Canada pursued a free trade agreement with the United States. In order to convince the Americans that Canada was serious about free market economics, the Tories embarked on a programme of deregulation and privatization. The dismantling of the NEP and FIRA were not just concessions to secure free trade with the United States, their demise marked the beginning of the end of the remaining vestiges of Fordism. Concessions, tax reform, deregulation policies, privatization and currency appreciation were all initiated to prepare the ground for a continental economy in Canada.

The Canadian Economy After Six Years of Free Trade

Canadian Perceptions About Free Trade

Before looking at actual data on Canadian economic performance, it is worth examining how Canadian views about free trade varied temporally and geographically. As the following polling data shows, Canadian support for the FTA has dropped precipitously since the 1988 federal election. In that election, only 43 percent of Canadians gave their approval to the Tory policy of free trade. However, despite an overall national distaste for free trade, there is wide regional variation in support for the FTA. Figure 3 shows that some regions were openly supportive of the FTA while others were very much opposed. Over 50 percent of Albertans believed that the FTA would bring greater prosperity for the resource-rich provinces while trimming the power of Ottawa to regulate the Canadian resource industry. In provinces such as Ontario, a majority of the people polled opposed the FTA because they believed that free trade would eliminate manufacturing jobs in southern Ontario.[46]

According to a *Maclean's*/Decima poll of 1 500 Canadian residents, one year after the implementation of the FTA a majority of Canadians believed that it was bad for Canada. In fact, 52 percent of Canadians blamed the FTA for job losses, plant closures and poor overall economic performance in Canada.[47] Prior to 1989, the federal ministry of finance

Figure 3
Regional Variation in Canadian Support for the FTA (%)

Region of FTA	Favour FTA	Oppose FTA	Unsure
National	39	51	11
Atlantic	38	45	17
Québec	47	42	11
Ontario	32	60	8
Manitoba	38	48	14
Saskatoon	39	58	13
Alberta	56	32	12
British Columbia	31	50	10
Western Provinces	40	48	12

Source: Michael Adams, Donna Dasko, and James Matsui, "Polls Say Canadians Want to Renegotiate, Not Rip Up Trade Deal," *Globe and Mail* 11 November 1988, p. A1.

predicted that the positive benefits of free trade would be felt in Canada shortly after the implementation of the FTA. After one year, the ministry of finance was so desperate to point out the success of the FTA that they paid Can$40 thousand to Infometrica, a Canadian public relations firm, to devise a strategy to convince Canadians that the FTA had helped Canada.[48]

Two years after the FTA was implemented, Canadians still had a distaste for the FTA. In a 1990 *Maclean's*/Decima poll of 1,500 people, the following question was asked: "As you know, Canada entered into a free trade agreement with the United States almost two years ago. As part of the agreement, either side can get out of the deal with six months' notice. At this point, do you personally think Canada should use the clause to get out of the deal?" Fifty-five percent of the respondents said that Canada should abrogate the FTA, 40 percent said no, while 5 percent had no opinion.[49] Further analyses reveals that wide geographic variation still existed in support of the FTA. The lowest levels of opposition to the FTA came from Québec where 44 percent opposed the deal after two years,

British Columbia with a 47 percent disapproval rating and Alberta where 51 percent of the population wanted to end the FTA. On a national basis, only 15 percent of Canadians believed that Canada should remain in the existing FTA and also push ahead with negotiations for the North American Free Trade Agreement (NAFTA).[50] In a poll conducted by the Canadian Federation of Independent Business in 1991, small Canadian business is more worried about NAFTA than about the FTA. Almost 22 percent of small business owners opposed NAFTA while only 16 percent opposed the FTA. Small businesses had a better understanding of how free trade and the threat of competition from low-wage Mexican labour would affect them.[51]

The Tories spent over Can$1.4 million of tax-payer's money to mail a pro-FTA tabloid to 10 million Canadian households in an attempt to document how Canada had benefited from free trade and sell the proposed NAFTA. They also spent Can$1.8 million on a series of radio commercials telling Canadians how they were better off after two years of free trade. Highlights of this media barrage included the following contentions: the Canadian recession would have worsened without free trade; Canada was winning the trade war with the United States; Canada gained a bigger share of the U.S. market; Tory expenditures for job retraining were large and growing; and that a small country like Canada would continue to benefit from engaging in free trade.[52] The media campaign did not convince many Canadians because many of the Tory claims were easily refuted. For example, while Canada did gain greater access to the American market from 1989 to 1991, Australia and other countries actually expanded their trade with the U.S. more rapidly than Canada during the same period.

In spite of spending Can$60 million dollars promoting free trade during the 1988 election campaign and another Can$3 million documenting gains from free trade after two years, Mulroney had not yet convinced a majority of Canadians to support free trade. Figure 4 contains the responses to a number of questions asked of 2,000 Canadians before the 1988 election, after the Tory electoral victory, and again at the end of 1990 after the impact of free trade had been felt in Canada for two years. The data reveals that Canadians believed more in 1990 than in 1988 that the FTA has had a direct and negative impact on Canadian economic growth, employment opportunities and social programmes. Respondents also became more certain about their answers over time. In each case, the percent of people unsure about their feelings either diminished or remained that same. Overall, this poll shows that Canadians have become

Figure 4
Percentage of Canadians Who Support or Oppose the FTA

Statement Presented by Pollster to Respondent:	1988 Pre-FTA	1989 Post-FTA	1990 Post FTA
1. The FTA ensures Canada's future prosperity.			
Agree with statement:	36%	46%	28%
Disagree with statement:	48%	42%	65%
Don't know:	16%	13%	8%
2. The FTA threatens Canada's political independence.			
Agree with statement:	44%	39%	54%
Disagree with statement:	44%	52%	41%
Don't know:	11%	9%	5%
3. Economically, the FTA helps some industries but hurts others.			
Agree with statement:	31%	37%	23%
Disagree with statement:	57%	54%	70%
Don't know:	12%	9%	7%
4. The FTA threatens Canadian culture.			
Agree with statement:	37%	33%	42%
Disagree with statement:	48%	55%	48%
Don't know:	15%	13%	11%
5. The FTA benefits all of Canada, not just certain regions or provinces.			
Agree with statement:	31%	37%	23%
Disagree with statement:	57%	54%	70%
Don't know:	12%	9%	7%
6. The FTA could threaten social programs such as health care and unemployment insurance.			
Agree with statement:	not asked	41%	57%
Disagree with statement:	not asked	48%	33%
Don't know:	not asked	11%	10%
7. Overall, are you in favor of the FTA or opposed to it?			
In favor:	39%	50%	35%
Opposed:	45%	40%	57%
Don't know:	16%	10%	10%

Source: Harold Clarke and Allen Kornberg, "Support for the Canadian Federal Progressive Conservative Party Since 1988: The Impact of Economic Evaluations and Economic Issues," *Canadian Journal of Political Science* 25, no. 1 (1992): 42.

increasingly unhappy with the FTA despite the costly campaign launched by the Progressive Conservatives to promote free trade.

Even after four years, a majority of Canadians were not convinced that the FTA was beneficial. A poll was conducted in April 1992 by Angus Reid and Southam Newspapers to determine how Canadians and Americans viewed bilateral free trade. The poll posed the following question to an American and then a Canadian sample: "What is your opinion of the U.S.-Canada Free Trade Agreement?" In the American sample, 78 percent supported the FTA, while only 9 percent opposed it. Only 32 percent of the Canadians supported it, while 66 percent opposed it.[53] The poll then asked Americans and Canadians to respond to the following question: "How would you assess the impact of the Free Trade Agreement on your country?" To this question, 34 percent of the Americans responded that the FTA was beneficial while 7 percent believed it to be harmful. Only 6 percent of the Canadians believed that the FTA was beneficial. On the other hand, 73 percent of Canadians believed that the FTA had a harmful impact on Canada. What do these polls tell us about how a majority of Canadians view the FTA? Simply that Canadians view the FTA as a bad policy that has hurt the economy, cost Canadian workers their jobs and undermined the Canadian Welfare State. The next section examines whether Canadian misgivings about free trade are grounded in reality.

Indicators of Canadian Economic Performance

Evaluating the impact of the FTA is not a simple process. The FTA must be situated within the overall conservative agenda of privatization, deregulation, and the disciplining of labour. According to Bruce Campbell, the various components of Tory economic strategy "act upon and reinforce one another and their effect is cumulative," while the effects of free trade "ripple through a complex economic and social structure."[54] In theory, the FTA was supposed to encourage restructuring on the basis of comparative advantage. Firms would become more efficient through specialization. Increased specialization, scale economies and efficiency would increase overall output while reducing per unit costs of production. As output increased, workers would move from lower value-added jobs to higher ones. The FTA would therefore result in increased investment in productive capacity, increased production, increased jobs for Canadians, increased trade with the United States, lower-cost goods for consumers and overall growth in the Canadian economy. These predictions were based on the following four assumptions: Canada would gain secure access to the U.S. market; full employment existed in Canada and the United States; capital is relatively immobile beyond national borders; and trade takes place between independent firms in a competitive marketplace.[55] As Canada's poor economic performance reveals, none of these four assumptions hold in the real world.

Supporters of the FTA contend that it is still too early to pass judgment on the impact of free trade because there is still a certain element of the "fog of war" where dust has not settled. High interest rates and the revalued Canadian dollar of the late 1980s complicate analyses.[56] The Macdonald Commission concluded that free trade requires a "leap of faith" from Canadians. Free trade proponents continue to claim that free trade was and remains a necessary "leap of faith" and any clear-cut and systematic evaluation of the FTA is impossible given the complexity of the economy. *Maclean's* writer Diane Francis noted that the FTA's impact can only be analyzed "anecdotally."[57] This statement confounds logic given that it was made by a free trade proponent who has promoted the FTA elsewhere on its sound scientific basis.[58]

There is abundant data available to systematically evaluate the FTA. Consider first the growth of the Canadian economy during the period from 1989 to 1994. An appropriate measure of overall economic performance would be the annual growth in the real gross domestic product (real GDP). The real GDP represents the total output of goods and services produced within a national economy with no deductions for depreciation and not counting the earnings of assets owned abroad. Before the FTA, Canadian economic growth paralleled that of the United States. Studies conducted by the Economic Council of Canada (ECC) predicted that over the first ten year period, free trade would increase Canadian output by 2.5 percent and create a net increase of 250,000 jobs.[59]

This conservative estimate pales before the more optimistic predictions of External Affairs which claimed that the FTA would generate a 3.6 percent growth in output while creating over 370,000 new jobs.[60] An interim estimate for growth over the first five years of free trade based on ECC figures would be a 3 percent output increase and a net job increase of about 310,000. Mulroney and Reagan touted the FTA because it was supposed to promote growth in both countries. Figure 5 shows the performance of Canada's real GDP before and after free trade. Despite an increase in the real GDP during the 1980s, it decreased after the implementation of the FTA before showing modest recovery in 1993. Taking into account the North American-wide recession, Figure 5 also compares Canadian economic performance to that of the United States before and after free trade. This figure reveals that since the FTA has been in effect,

Figure 5
Canadian and American Real GDP Growth

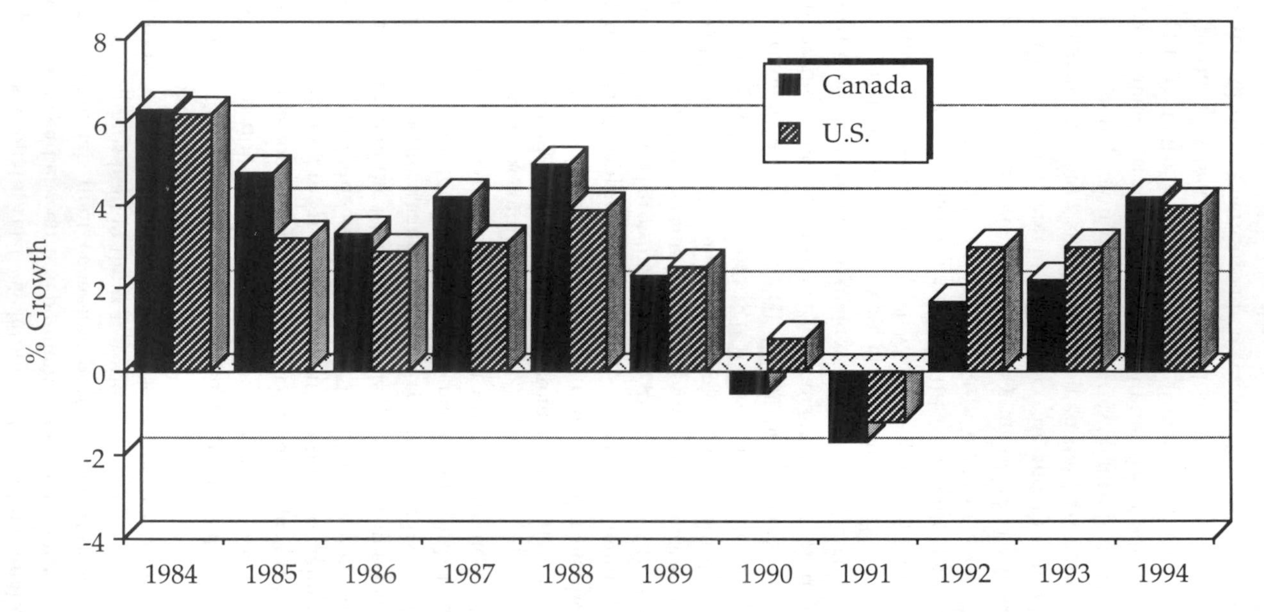

Source: Statistics Canada, Canadian Economic Observer (Ottawa: Supply and Services, 1991), 5.116; Statistics Canada, Canadian Economic Observer (Ottawa: Supply and Services, 1995), 65-67.

the Canadian economic experience has not paralleled that of the United States. Canada suffered more during the recession than did its neighbor to the south. Why is this so? Supporters of free trade such as trade minister Michael Wilson argue that without free trade, the recession in Canada would have been even worse.[61] Yet the Tories were so embarrassed by plant closures, layoffs and recent polls reflecting the unpopularity of free trade that they hired a public relations firm to put a positive spin on Canadian economic conditions. When asked about the lack of economic growth or new jobs, the Tories responded that it was too soon to see the impacts of freer trade. When asked about job relocations and mergers, free trade supporters responded that they would have happened anyway.

Businessman James Pattison believes that the FTA will benefit Canada over the long run. He admits that the FTA is bound to create some business dislocations but he says free trade "is like castor oil — you have to get it over with. The Canada-U.S. border is an imaginary border."[62] According to Pattison's perspective, the FTA will cause some short-term pain in exchange for long-term prosperity.

Many Canadians do not share this sanguine view of the hardships created by free trade. Starting with free trade negotiations and accelerating after the implementation of the FTA, the Canadian industrial base has been eroded. In nearly every sector, companies are curtailing their operations, abandoning or relocating production outside of Canada as well as converting manufacturing sites into regional distribution centres and storage facilities The immediate effect of the FTA has been the accelerated deindustrialization of Canada. American repatriation of production and global restructuring are the official justifications of the fleeing branch plant managers. As the pressures of free trade dismantle Canada's engine of economic growth, Canada is being transformed from a developed to an underdeveloped nation. In 1986, The Science Council of Japan dubbed Canada a third world nation with an artificially high standard of living. Canada's accelerated loss of its manufacturing base since the implementation of the FTA underscores this assessment.[63]

Changes in real GDP growth do not fully reveal how Canadian manufacturing has fared under free trade. A more convincing indicator would be to examine the increase in manufacturing and total industrial output which was predicted by FTA supporters. As illustrated in Figure 6, prior to the FTA, Canadian growth in total industrial and manufacturing production equaled or exceeded the rates of growth in the United States and other OECD countries.[64] Before the FTA, the Canadian total industrial output paralleled that of the United States, diverging after 1989. Figure 7 provides an index of manufacturing growth in OECD countries. Here again, the Canadian experience resembles that of the United States and OECD states but then slows after 1989. Another way to reveal the impact of free trade on the Canadian economy is to examine the number of new jobs created since its implementation. Time and again, the FTA was promoted for its ability to create more jobs. The Canadian government vowed that new jobs would be high-skill and high-wage jobs created for men and women.[65] Figure 8 reveals that during the mid-1980s, Canada experienced net job growth. However, this figure also shows that job growth slowed in 1989, the year that the FTA was implemented. From 1990 to 1992, Canada actually experienced a net job decrease. Figure 9 provides evidence that net job creation in the manufacturing sector has also declined since the implementation of free trade in contradistinction to the U.S. and OECD countries.

It has been widely noted that net job creation in the manufacturing sector has been a losing proposition over the past several decades.[66] What Figure 9 reveals is that after a period of sporadic growth and decline, 1989 brought a sudden and persistent drop in the net number of manufacturing jobs available to Canadians. Figure 10 provides a closer look at the industrial sectors where job losses have occurred. The data presented in Figure 10 was part of Canadian Labour Congress (CLC) testimony given to the Canadian Parliament stating that NAFTA would accelerate the job losses that had occurred under the FTA.[67]

Canada also suffered a precipitous drop from 18 to 2 percent per year in domestic investment as well as experiencing a steep increase in bankruptcies. The rapid decline in investment and concomitant increase in deindustrialization is particularly apparent in Canada's beleaguered steel industry, the foundation for Canada's manufacturing sector. Canada's largest steel producers lost hundreds of millions of dollars, laid off tens of thousands of workers and have been perilously close to bankruptcy. Initially, the managers of Canadian steel producing companies supported the idea of free trade. After four years of free trade, Canadian steel producers have performed poorly. Mismanagement, U.S. protectionism (despite the FTA) and the high value of the Canadian dollar have been blamed. Three of the largest steel producers have appealed to the Canadian government to obtain monetary assistance, however, this strategy was disallowed as an unfair subsidy under the FTA. All that the FTA has done is to limit the options available to the plant managers.

The threat of bankruptcy does not confront the steel industry alone. In 1991, bankruptcies soared to a record level in Canada. The Canadian

Figure 6
Growth Index of Total Industrial Production

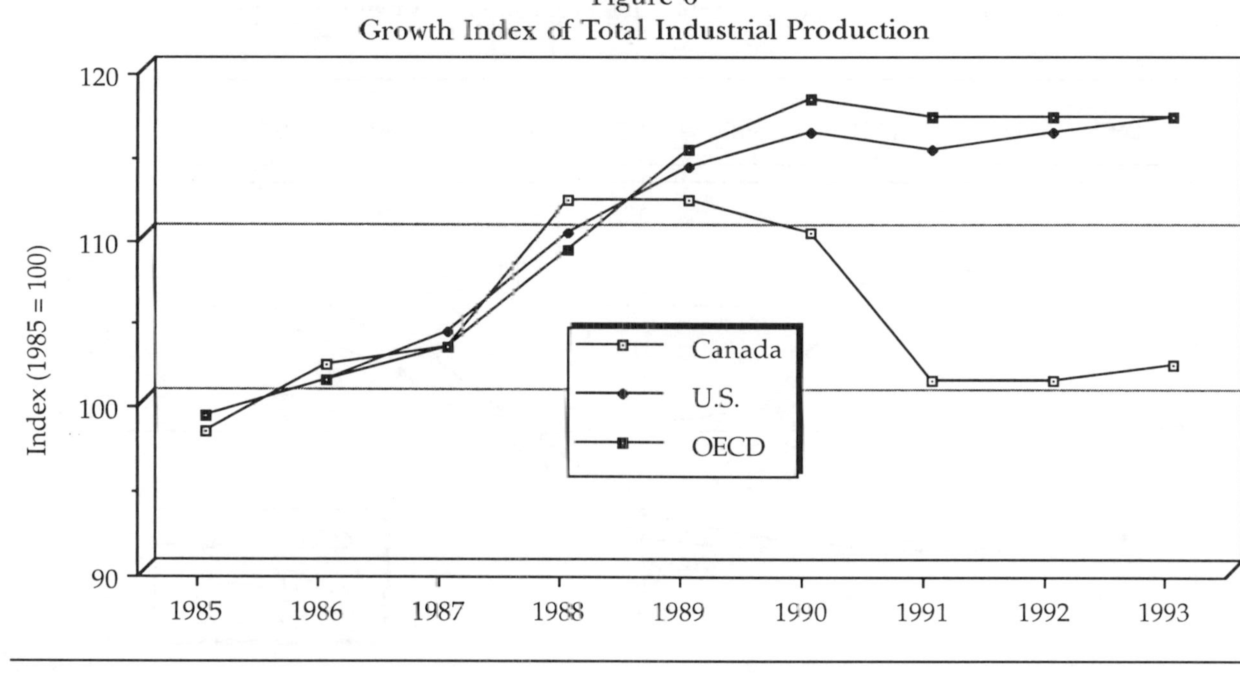

Source: Statistics Canada, Canadian Economic Observer (Ottawa: Supply and Services, 1993).

Figure 7
Growth Index of Manufacturing Production

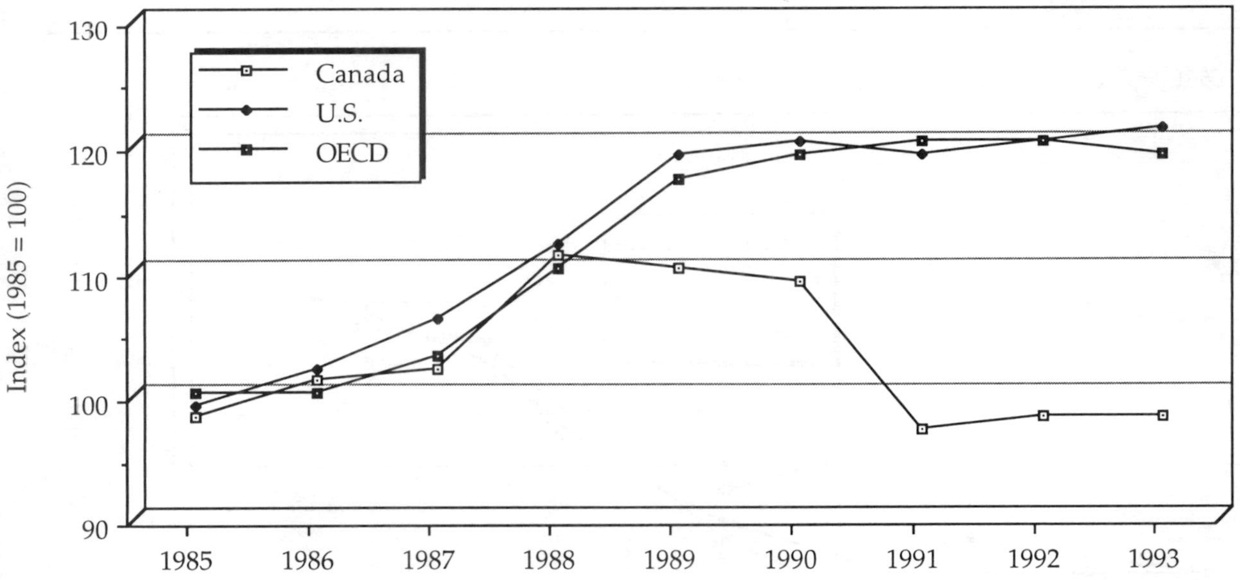

Source: Statistics Canada, Canadian Economic Observer (Ottawa: Supply and Services, 1993).

Figure 8
Net Job Creation in Canada

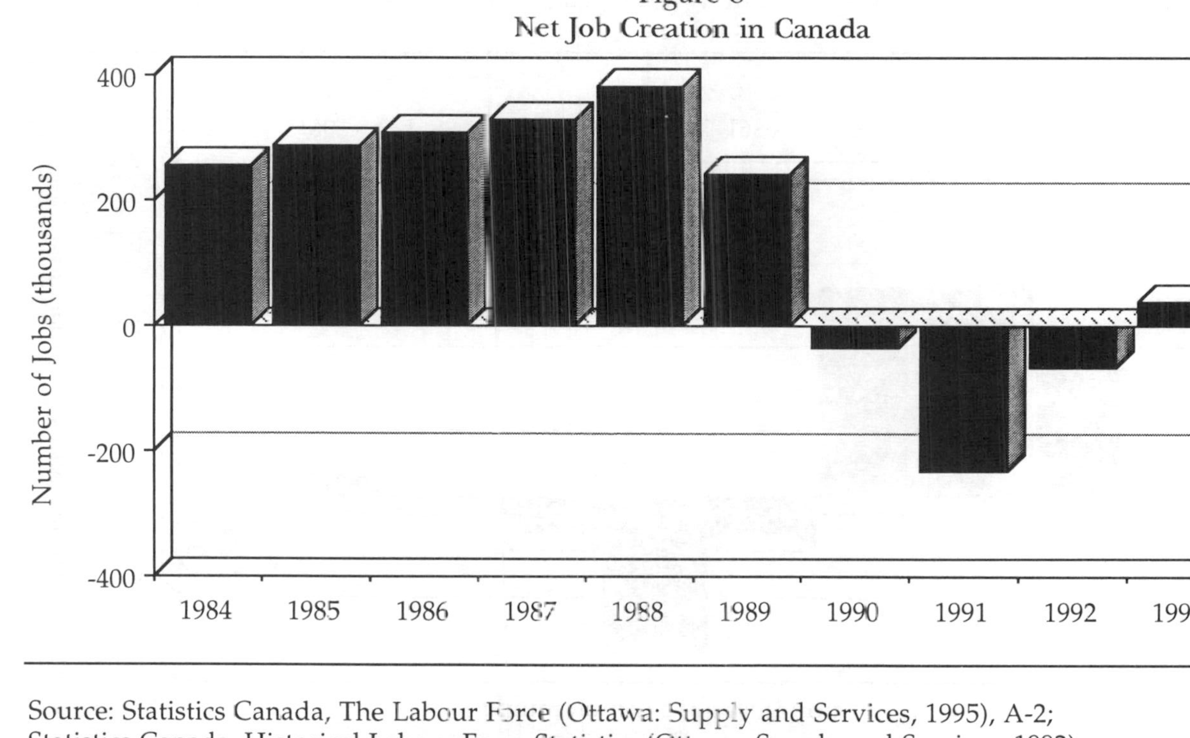

Source: Statistics Canada, The Labour Force (Ottawa: Supply and Services, 1995), A-2; Statistics Canada, Historical Labour Force Statistics (Ottawa: Supply and Services, 1992).

Figure 9
Net Manufacturing Job Creation in Canada

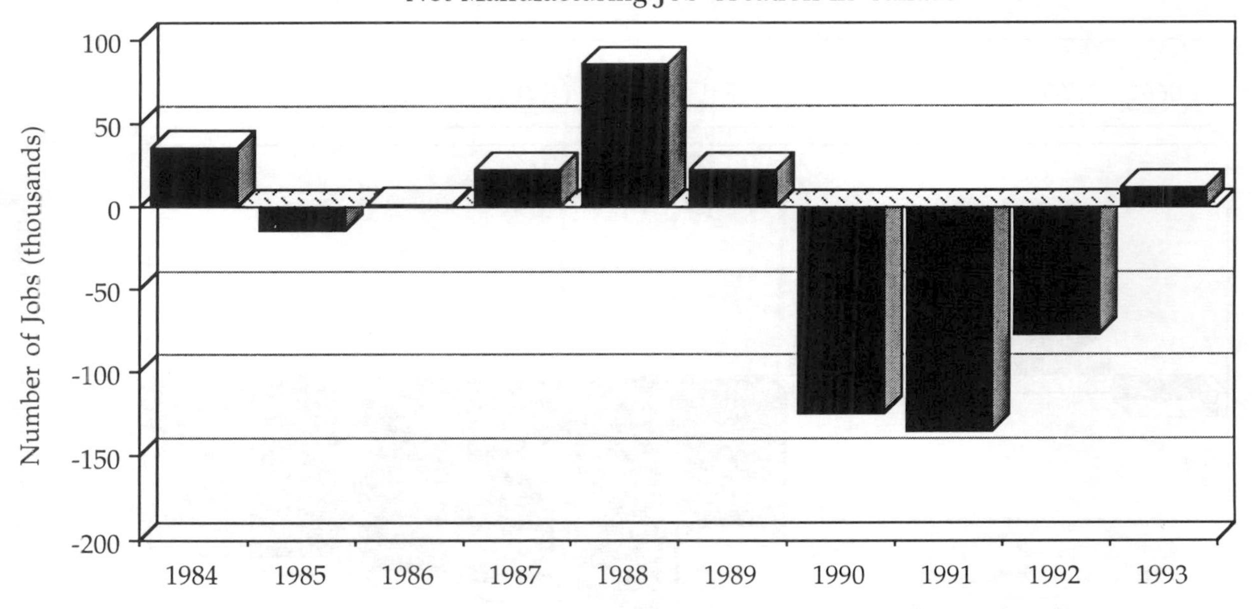

Source: Statistics Canada, The Labour Force (Ottawa: Supply and Services, 1995); Statistics Canada, Historical Labour Force Statistics (Ottawa: Supply and Services, 1992).

Figure 10
Manufacturing Job Losses in Canada (thousands)

Sector	Jobs in 1989	Jobs in 1992	Change	% Change
Aircraft/Aircraft Parts	43.7	42.0	-1.7	-3.9
Chemicals	97.5	87.4	-10.1	-10.4
Clothing	94.7	61.6	-33.1	-35.0
Electrical Products	129.0	100.4	-28.6	-22.2
Food and Beverage	224.1	191.5	-33.1	-14.5
Furniture and Fixtures	63.1	41.4	-21.7	-34.4
Machinery	100.4	77.2	-23.2	-23.1
Metal Fabrications	160.4	120.0	-39.6	-25.2
Motor Vehicles/Parts	128.5	104.2	-24.3	-18.9
Non-metallic Minerals	49.1	39.8	-9.3	-18.9
Petroleum and Coal	19.4	22.3	+2.9	+14.9
Primary Metals	99.4	80.8	-18.6	-18.7
Printing and Publishing	142.0	114.0	-28.0	-19.7
Pulp and Paper	125.5	108.7	-16.8	-13.4
Rubber and Plastics	81.0	55.7	-25.3	-32.2
Textiles	66.7	46.9	-19.8	-29.7
Wood Industries	109.2	75.1	-34.1	-31.2
Total	1,900.9	1,493.3	-407.6	-21.4

Source: Canadian Labour Congress, "Submission by the Canadian Labour Congress on the North American Free Trade Agreement to the Sub-committee on International Trade of the Standing Committee on External Affairs and International Trade of the House of Commons, January 26," (Ottawa: Unpublished Document of the CLC, 1993), 4.

Office of the Superintendent of Bankruptcy stated that 75 773 Canadian businesses and consumers went under. That figure is up from 54 424 bankruptcies in 1990 which was also a record year. In addition, analysts projected 66,000 bankruptcies in 1994. In order to evaluate whether these insolvencies are linked to free trade or just the recession, a comparison can be made with 41,000 business and consumer bankruptcies that occurred during the depths of economic recession in 1982.[68] The recession has certainly played an important role causing economic hardship but free trade cannot be discounted as the central factor causing bankruptcies and job losses after 1989. The situation was so bad that the Canadian National Advisory Board on Science and Technology criticized the Tories for not understanding the ramifications of the FTA and for failing to follow through with the appropriate policies. This advisory board warned that Canada will suffer further deindustrialization under the FTA without assistance to struggling Canadian manufacturers coupled with appropriate fiscal and monetary policies.

Free trade was also promoted for its ability to allocate resources more efficiently through specialization in production. In theory, free trade is able to encourage this because it provides a manufacturer with access to a bigger market. With a bigger market, a firm can increase its production by utilizing more of, or expanding its existing capacity. Figure 11 compares Canadian and American capacity utilization before and after free trade began. Prior to 1989, Canada used more of its productive capacity than the United States. After 1989, recession effects show up as capacity utilization drops in both countries while usage of productive capacity by Canadian industry fell far below that of the United States. Even after five years of the FTA, Canada still lags behind the United States in its utilization efficiency.

What Figure 11 does not show is that Canada permanently lost some of its productive capacity and manufacturing jobs after 1989. Although Canada was in a recession by 1990, productive capacity decline and job loss were linked to free trade. Again compare the current recession to that of 1981-82. During that time, many jobs were lost, but most were eventually hired back. In 1990, the situation was different. A significant proportion of Canadian industry permanently closed down or shifted production to the United States. According to the CLC, analyses of Canadian manufacturing did not significantly decline during the 1980s when output and productivity increases were used as measures. They go on to note that the FTA has created a "crisis [in] Canadian manufacturing," especially when Canada's economic performance prior to free trade is compared with its performance after free trade.[69]

Figure 11
Productive Capacity Utilization in Canada and the United States

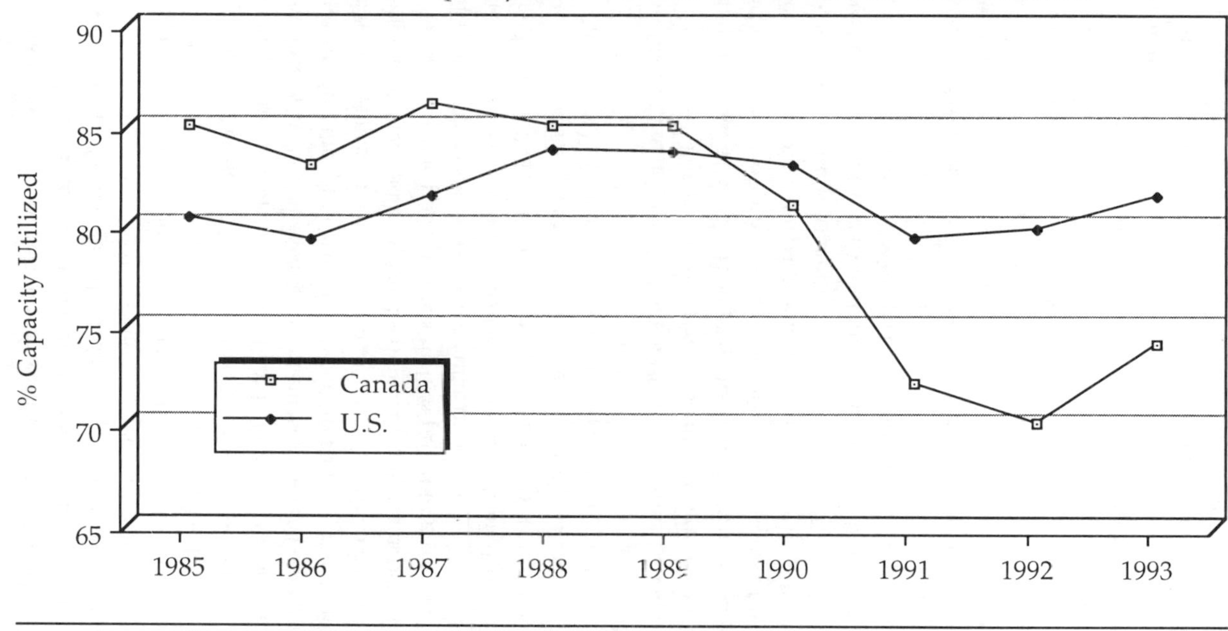

Source: Council of Economic Advisors, Economic Indicators (Washington, DC: U.S. Government Printing Office, 1994).

Figures show strong correlation between production decline and free trade. The challenge is to identify the factors and causal mechanisms within free trade that accelerated deindustrialization, restructuring and job loss within Canada. One factor was the promise of free trade which prompted an increase in mergers and acquisitions prior to 1989. The FTA entrenched the foreign investment guidelines that Mulroney had initiated by dismantling FIRA. Article 1602 of the FTA text says that Canada can no longer screen or regulate American investment less than Can$150 million. By 1993, foreign investment reviews by the Canadian government were phased out entirely. Furthermore, under the principal of national treatment, the FTA requires Canada to treat American companies the same as Canadian companies. Canada cannot implement policies that discriminate against American firms even if they do so for public policy reasons such as promoting regional development or protecting jobs in less efficient industries.

The FTA also hurts the Canadian economy through the "right of non-establishment" clause. This right gives American firms the ability to trade services cross-border without having to establish a presence in Canada.[70] Under FIRA, foreign MNCs were required to provide a certain number of jobs, to conduct some research and development, and to leave some profits in Canada. Article 1603 of the FTA forbids Canada from imposing these kinds of performance requirements on American companies operating in Canada. Article 1606 prevents Canada from placing restrictions on the transfer of profits out of Canada. Furthermore, the FTA forbids certification procedures, licensing schemes and other non-tariff barriers to trade and investment.

The link between the FTA and increased mergers in Canada is made in figures showing more foreign takeovers and mergers in the first six months of free trade than in the previous three years combined. Mergers increased after free trade despite the fact that the three years leading up to 1989 exhibited far greater economic growth than after 1989.[71] Canadian firms were bought out by foreign investors because so many of them were undervalued due to poor economic performance. Foreign investors were also attracted by lay offs, streamlined production and Tory reductions in corporate tax burdens. Those firms that did not go bankrupt were anticipated to be profitable enterprises.

A concrete example of how free trade induced increased merger activity can be seen in the case the Canadian subsidiary of Connecticut Chemical Limited. CCL Canada completed nine acquisitions since 1989 to become one of the largest firms in its sector within the North American market. Wayne McLeod, president of CCL Canada, declared that the

FTA forced him to expand the operations of CCL or be forced out of business by larger operations.[72] The merger trend has even affected some law firms which have merged in order to be large enough to handle the intricacies of cross-border trade.

Free trade can be tied to the merger increases in two other ways. First, managers believe that they have to expand in order to compete in the continental market. Second, free trade is directly implicated because none of the mergers could have occurred without the elimination of investment restrictions in the FTA. As restrictions were lowered, investors rushed in to take advantage of the new deregulated environment. Between 1988 and 1990, a record 1 403 Canadian companies were taken over at a price of Can$35.5 billion. In the first year of free trade, 460 Canadian-controlled firms were taken over by foreign (mainly U.S.) interests, while only 136 firms were taken over by Canadian investors.[73] A mere 10 percent of this expenditure was actually new investment. The upswing in mergers and foreign investment increased foreign control over the Canadian economy, reversing a ten-year positive trend in Canadian control. The FTA prevents the Canadian government from regulating how and where this investment takes place.

An equally important aspect of these mergers is that takeovers translate into job loss for Canadian workers. For every billion dollars of profit made by Canadian firms in Canada, 765 jobs are created. For every billion dollars of profit made by American firms operating in Canada, 17 jobs are created. An American takeover of a Canadian firm can therefore be considered as an indirect job loss of 748 jobs for every Can$1 billion in American profits from Canadian subsidiaries. The justification for increased merger activity is that only world-scale corporations can compete successfully in international trade. Such justifications, even if valid, apply only to a narrow range of exports.[74] The disappearance of Wardair, Texaco Canada and Consolidated Bathurst will not boost Canadian production, job growth or balance of trade. Justification for mergers has come from the seemingly detached and objective rhetoric of international trade theory that economies of scale will be achieved and all interests will be served.

The reality is that most mergers and takeovers benefit only the majority stockholders of the winning company and the stock *arbitrageurs* who have correctly anticipated the move in stock prices.[75] Communities lose out when the new owner of the local factory closes it down and moves production elsewhere. With a dwindling industrial base, the evaporation of the municipal tax base results in reduced spending on streets, schools and local social services. The real losers include employees who lose their jobs and consumers who lose freedom of choice. As ownership in each industry becomes more concentrated, incentive to innovate is reduced and the drive to produce better goods and services disappears. Eventually prices no longer reflect supply and demand but are set by the logic of monopoly pricing.

Why has merger activity increased so much in the late 1980s and 1990s? High interest rates purportedly set to combat a perceived Canadian inflation problem made it cheaper to buy than to build assets. High profits earned from 1983 to 1989 made dominant Canadian and American firms cash-rich. In Canada, a dormant stock market left many firms undervalued. Instead of developing new production techniques and investing in new production facilities, companies were attempting to expand their corporate assets through mergers. The FTA acted as a factor forcing mergers by cleared away impeding regulations and serving as an explanatory justification.[76] It is difficult to separate out the various ways that the FTA increased merger activity, however the end result is that FTA-induced mergers have accelerated the deindustrialization of Canada.

The FTA also accelerated deindustrialization through tariff reduction. By its very definition, free trade requires that tariffs be eliminated. Figure 12 provides the tariff schedule which applied to trade between Canada and the U.S. prior to 1989 according to the Tokyo Round of the GATT. The FTA dictates that these tariffs be lowered incrementally over a ten year period starting in 1989. As tariffs began to drop after 1989, many Canadian industries or branch plants of American MNCs either went south, restructured or closed down entirely. Either way, Canada lost some of its industrial base, tax revenues and jobs in order to achieve a continentally efficient allocation of resources.

According to neoclassical trade theory, restructuring of this sort is an expected and desired outcome as production is rationalized between the trading partners. Canada should have expected a "large reallocation of its resources relative to the United States, but it will also get proportionately much larger benefits in the form of productivity increases due to greater economies of scale."[77] However, this ignores the fact that tariff elimination would provide greater benefits to American exporters and that Canadian tariffs were higher on average then those imposed by the United States. In addition, tariff reduction gave American firms greater access to the Canadian market while allowing firms to leave Canada with the intention of serving the Canadian market from the United States.

Has the impact of tariff reduction on the Canadian economy been

Figure 12
The GATT Tariff Schedule for Trade Between Canada and the United States

Economic Sector	Canadian Tariff (% of import value)	US Tariff (% ofimport value)
Chemicals	7.5	2.4
Electrical Machinery	5.8	4.4
Footwear	21.9	8.8
Furniture and Fixtures	14.3	4.1
Glass and Glass Products	7.2	6.2
Iron and Steel	5.4	3.6
Leather Products	6.3	4.2
Metal Products	8.5	4.8
Miscellaneous Manufactures	5.4	4.2
Non-electrical Machinery	4.5	3.3
Nonferrous Metals	2.0	0.7
Nonmetal Mineral Products	6.4	5.3
Printing and Publishing	1.0	0.7
Pulp and Paper	6.7	0.2
Rubber Products	6.7	2.5
Textiles	16.7	9.2
Transportation Equipment	1.6	2.5
Wood Products	3.2	1.7
All Industry	5.2	4.3

Source: CLC, *The Crisis of Canadian Manufacturing* (Ottawa: CLC, 1991), 11.

overstated when over 75 percent of the goods and services traded between Canada and the United States crossed the border tariff-free prior to 1989? Certainly, tariffs were very low or nonexistent for a majority of goods. However, there was significant protection in a few select sectors. In particular, the Canadian government used relatively high tariffs to protect the textile, clothing, footwear, furniture and fixtures sectors. Tariffs on some goods were scheduled to be phased out over ten years. Tariffs on furniture, chemicals, machinery and most other manufactured goods were scheduled for elimination over five years. Tariffs on remaining manufactured goods were entirely phased out on January 1, 1989. Furthermore, the FTA was not even one year old when the United States and Canada decided to lower tariffs earlier than planned. In March 1991, Canada and the United States decided a second time to accelerate tariff reductions.[78] Under these amendments to the tariff elimination schedule, 250 tariffs on over 400 products affecting Can$6 billion in trade were dropped earlier than planned. Some tariffs that were supposed to remain in place for ten years disappeared in 1994. Canada and the United States have managed the FTA using a flexible approach to suit the needs of corporate interests. As tariffs dropped at an accelerated pace, continental competition increased. Previously protected industries such as furniture manufacturers, electrical machine firms and garment manufacturers either sought out new low-cost production regions outside Canada, merged with other corporations or closed down. Only a few Canadian firms have been able to compete.

Consider the plight of the Canadian garment industry which has fared badly since 1989. Some pundits blamed the recession for the current state of the Canadian garment and textiles industry. A better explanation can be found by more closely considering the impact of free trade. Even the C. D. Howe Institute willingly admits that free trade has hurt Canadian garment manufacturers.[79] Lowered tariffs have permitted American garment exports to Canada to increase 32 percent from 1989 to 1990. Fred Abramovitch, former chief executive officer of the now-bankrupt T.A.G. Apparel Group, says that over half of Canadian garment manufacturers could go bankrupt or leave Canada before the FTA-induced restructuring is complete. Free trade has affected Canadian garment companies through lowered tariffs, the Goods and Services Tax (GST), and cross-border shopping. Lower tariffs allow larger American firms to out-compete smaller Canadian firms. The GST hurts sales by making clothing more expensive in Canada, encouraging Canadians who live close to the border to purchase items in the United States.[80]

In response to the pressures unleashed by the FTA, many garment manufacturers have moved their production to low-cost regions of the United States and Southeast Asia. Firms that remained in Canada merged with others or adopted new strategies such as abandoning low-margin, high-volume mass production and specializing in higher quality clothing destined for niche markets. Although some Canadian garment manufacturers are doing well under free trade, a majority are not. One garment manufacturer, Peter Nygard, once avidly promoted the FTA. He has since changed his mind as his company, Nygard International, has had to compete with less expensive American imports and higher Canadian tariffs on textile imports from outside North America. Nygard has since moved 20 percent of his 1,500 employee operation to the garment district of southern California to exploit the lower-cost production and tariff environment.[81]

The final point about tariffs has as much to do with sovereignty as with economic performance. Under the FTA, Canada and the United States retain the right to raise tariffs against third parties as long as they are in accordance with GATT guidelines. Supporters of free trade point to the ability of Canada to retain high third party tariffs as an example of how Canada has not lost sovereignty under the FTA.[82] However evidence is mounting that Canada is already feeling the pressure to harmonize its third-party tariff schedule with that of the United States. Nygard moved some of his garment production out of Canada partly in response to Canada's high third-party tariffs. In 1989, Japanese Consul General in Canada Yasuo Noguchi stated in the *Financial Post* that the gap between Canadian and American tariffs on third-party imports could potentially divert Japanese investment from Canada to the United States.[83] Noguchi recommended that Canada lower its tariffs to be equal to those of the United States, thus avoiding the diversion of third-party investment. With harmonized third-party tariffs, Canada and the United States will have evolved from a free trade area to a full-fledged customs union. However, even if Canada does harmonize its third-party tariffs with the United States, the threat of American protectionism will continue to divert trade and investment from Canada.

American Protectionism and Free Trade

Canadian negotiators pursued the FTA to circumvent American protectionism. Exporters feared that the United States would continue to target Canadian "hogs, logs, suds, and spuds," as well as cars made in Canada, unless something was done to guarantee secure access to the U.S. market.[84] The Tories stated that an important goal of the FTA was to maintain a permanent exemption from U.S. "fair trading laws." This was an ambitious goal. The compromise that emerged — a bilateral panel with power to settle disputes — looked meager to most Canadians. Supporters of free trade claimed that the dispute settlement provisions within the FTA would reduce trade disagreements while putting a check on American protectionism.[85] To the contrary, the FTA text revealed that the FTA did not dramatically alter the dispute settlement environment between Canada and the United States. Article 1902 of the FTA stated that Canada was still subject to United States trade sanctions as detailed in the U.S. Omnibus Trade Act. Furthermore, the United States retained the right to change or modify trade sanction laws.

The preservation of U.S. "fair trade laws" was a primary goal of American negotiators. Clayton Yeutter, a U.S. Trade Representative (USTR) under Reagan, confirmed that the United States had retained its trade sanction powers in an interpretation of the FTA he had presented to Senator Dennis DeConcini (D-Arizona).[86] The final repudiation of the notion that the FTA would guarantee Canadian access to the U.S. market was contained in a report issued by Carla Hills, the primary USTR under President George Bush. Hills explained that according to Resolution "Super 301" of the 1988 Omnibus Trade Bill, the USTR must submit a list to Congress of countries considered to have unfair barriers to U.S. exports by May 30 of each year. If the named countries do not remedy their trade practices, they are then subject to possible U.S. retaliation. In 1989, Japan, the entire European Community, South Korea, Brazil and Canada were listed as unfair traders.[87] Ultimately Canada was dropped from the list, but the United States continued to levy trade sanctions against Canadian exporters. Canada was placed on the "Super 301" list of unfair traders again in 1990 and 1991, however this time they were not removed. The message was very clear: The FTA does not exempt Canada from any U.S. trade laws. Furthermore, section 409 of the American FTA implementing legislation actually makes it easier for U.S. firms or trade organizations to request that U.S. trade remedy laws be used against Canadian imports. Prior to the FTA, evidence of unfair trade practices had to accompany a complaint to the International Trade Commission (ITC). Now the USTR was obligated to investigate complaints even if no proof exists that Canada has engaged in unfair practices.[88]

After six years of free trade, Canadian exporters now take Yeutter and Hills at their word. Canada is clearly liable under U.S trade laws. Furthermore, Canadian exporters understand that U.S. trade laws supersede FTA guidelines. How do they know this to be true? Since 1989, trade disputes have continued to flair up in sectors that were problematic prior to the FTA. Furthermore, the FTA has not caused the United States to change the way it operates with regard to protectionism and dispute settlement. In fact, American treatment of Canadian exporters had gotten so bad by 1992 that Canada's chief free trade negotiator Simon Reisman and his deputy Gordon Ritchie felt obliged to speak out against the FTA.

Prior to 1989, Reisman and Ritchie tirelessly promoted the benefits of free trade to the Canadian electorate.[89] Their confidence in the FTA was shattered after the United States persisted in levying countervailing duties on Canadian softwood exports and auditing Honda cars made in Canada for their North American market. Reisman fumed that the Americans were "behaving like real thugs in promoting their interests." Ritchie condemned "the highly aggressive American protectionism" which "[called] into question the fundamental basis of the Canada-U.S. Free Trade Agreement."[90] Disparaging remarks made by Canada's two highest ranking trade negotiators provide a clear indictment of the FTA as the root of many of Canada's economic problems. Despite these outbursts from high-ranking and previously pro-FTA Canadian officials, the United States maintained its adversarial stance towards Canada. With no prospect for change, many Canadian commentators view the continued harassment of exporters and the lack of a binding trade dispute mechanism to be a significant failure of the FTA which has not been remedied by NAFTA.[91]

Canadian jobs and investment are at stake because of American protectionism. Canadian firms and manufacturers from third countries located in Canada are becoming increasingly frustrated by American attempts to impede exports from Canada. The easy solution is to relocate production from Canada to the United States. American trade sanctions working in tandem with lowered tariffs represents yet another way that the FTA contributes to the economic problems of Canada. The remainder of this section will consider several Canadian economic sectors which reveal how American protectionism coupled with weak dispute-settlement mechanisms has disrupted the Canadian economy.

Consider the forest product sector which includes the pulp and paper, logging, and forest services industries. More Canadians work in the forest products industry then in any other. High sectoral employment rates reveal the importance of this staple product to the Canadian economy. The forest products industry provides the economic base for some 300 single-industry localities in Canada. Depending on the year, wood and paper products also contribute the most to the total value-added in Canadian manufacturing. As the world's largest exporter of forest products, Canada has accounted for up to 22 percent of all forest product trade in the world market.[92] The United

States has repeatedly used trade remedy laws before and after the FTA to challenge Canadian forest product exports. More importantly, the United States has used coercive trade remedy laws to provide greater access for American companies to Canada's vast forest resources. In 1986, the United States placed a 35 percent import duty on cedar shakes entering from Canada. To show that the FTA did not supersede U.S. trade remedy law, USTR Clayton Yeutter announced in 1988 that this punitive surcharge would remain in effect until 1991, although it was lowered from 35 to 10 percent.

The year 1986 also marked the beginning of an even more bitter trade dispute involving Canadian softwood exports to the United States. In 1986, the ITC declared that Canada's low "stumpage fees" constituted an unfair advantage to Canadian softwood lumber exports.[93] The Canadian government was accused of subsidizing softwood exporters by charging them too little for cutting trees on public land. In response, the ITC threatened to levy a 15 percent surcharge on Canadian softwood imports. The Canadian government acquiesced to American trade law by levying their own 15 percent export tax on Canadian softwood products destined for the U.S. market. Between 1986 and 1991, the share of Canadian softwood exports in the U.S. dropped from 35 percent to 27 percent. In 1991, Canadian finance minister Don Mazankowski declared that the Canadian softwood industry would no longer have to pay the export tax because Canada's currency had revalued by over 15 percent against the American dollar since 1986. The 15 percent Canadian currency revaluation combined with the 15 percent export tax created a 30 percent export tax on Canadian softwood products. Angered by this unilateral Canadian decision, American legislators then asked Canadians to post a provisional 14.48 percent bond on lumber exports while the ITC investigated Canadian softwood exporters for unfair subsidization. If the ITC decided that Canada was trading in a fair manner according to U.S. (not FTA) trade rules, then the bonds would be repaid with interest.

The United States decided that Canada was still an unfair trader. The ITC levied a 6.51 percent countervailing duty on all Canadian softwood exports. However the ITC decided that Canadians could avoid paying the countervailing duties if they agreed to harmonize their forest management and tree cutting system with that of the United States. Under the U.S. system of forest cutting, logging companies bid for timber cutting rights. Under the Canadian system, companies avoid bidding at auctions by paying set rates for the wood they cut. In addition, Canada bans the export of uncut logs to conserve forests and to ensure that the Canadian economy benefits from the value-added processing.[94] In order for Canada to avoid paying the American softwood import surcharges, Canada would have to adopt the American-style bidding system and abolish the export ban on uncut logs. The U.S. Commerce Department ruled that the 6.51 percent levy was justified due to the price-depressing effect created by the ban on log exports, artificially lowering costs to Canadian lumber producers.

It becomes clear that Canada was not simply being punished for its unfair subsidies. Rather, U.S. trade sanctions can be seen as part of a strategy to pry open Canadian forests to American logging companies. The United States forest industry has been hampered by a high level of uncut log exports and forest protection measures. According to Frank Oberle, Canadian forestry minister, American politicians have been trying to gain access to Canadian logs in order to bolster their sagging industry which has been squeezed by mismanagement.[95] The United States cynically used the countervailing duty as a lever to force open the Canadian market to American firms. The U.S. attempt to eliminate Canada's ban on uncut logs was seen as a blatant grab for Canadian natural resources.

Although the provisional duty had been lowered from 14.48 percent to 6.51 percent, Canadian officials were angered that it had been kept at all. Premier Mike Harcourt of British Columbia and Tom Buell, chairman of the Canadian Forestry Institute, claimed that the Americans were able to impose duties because the FTA fails to spell out the definition of a subsidy. As a result, Canada is the target of constant harassment from office-seeking senators and congressmen who think duties on Canadian lumber play well in U.S. election campaigns. Canada has paid a high price in the wake of U.S. trade sanctions. Court costs for appeals in the softwood dispute have risen above Can$10 million for Canada. This figure pales in comparison to the economic and social costs affecting hundreds of small Canadian lumber communities which have been devastated by job losses and company bankruptcies. In the end, Canada appealed the U.S. trade sanctions to the bilateral dispute settlement panel instituted by the FTA. In July of 1993, the panel agreed with Canada that the U.S. had no basis for imposing the countervailing duties on Canadian softwood exports.[96] Supporters of free trade have stated that the Canadian victory in the softwood dispute shows that the FTA is a success because the dispute mechanism works. A more realistic interpretation is that the FTA has failed Canadians because it lacks a definition of a subsidy. Without a subsidy definition, the United States can easily launch trade complaints. While trade disputes increase, the dispute settlement process takes far too long. Companies have gone out of business waiting for decisions by the bilateral panel.

American protectionism has also had a devastating impact on the Canadian steel industry. Prior to 1989, Canadian steel producers supported the FTA because they believed that it would guarantee access to the American market. Canadian steel producers were concerned about U.S. protectionism because they were a primary target in the increasing number of U.S. trade actions against Canada. Despite strong initial support some analysts within the Canadian steel sector doubted the efficacy of the FTA to protect the Canadian steel industry. Daniel Romanko, managing director of the Canadian Steel Producers' Association, believed that U.S. actions in 1988 against Algoma Steel Corporation of Sault Ste. Marie, Ontario and the Sydney Steel Corporation (SYSCO) of Sydney, Nova Scotia were just the tip of the iceberg. The FTA would not change anything despite governmental rhetoric to the contrary.[97] Romanko was correct. U.S. actions against Canadian steel producers have not decreased under the FTA. Don Belch, director of governmental relations for Stelco Steel in Hamilton, Ontario stated that even though tariffs dropped under the FTA, Canada has never gained secure access to the U.S. market. Americans perceive that Canadian steel producers have been unfairly subsidized and that they have dumped steel in the U.S. market. In response, the United States levied dumping charges and imposed quotas on Canadian steel exports several times since 1989. In 1993, the U.S. Customs Service hit Canadian steel producers with levies varying from 1.5 to 68 percent, depending on the steel product or company involved.[98]

How can these restrictive and punitive measures be imposed under the FTA? Very easily because Article 1902 of the FTA and Section 309 of U.S. Trade Bill 5090 show that most protectionist policy tools remained unaltered under the FTA. Article 1902 of the FTA confirms that domestic anti-dumping and countervailing duty laws have been retained. Although this provision applies to both Canada and the United States, the nature of trade between them favors the U.S. This inequality can be directly linked to Canada's largely one-sided trade dependence on the United States. In 1992, 73 percent of Canada's exports went to the United States while only 22 percent of American exports went to Canada. Section 309 of U.S. Trade Bill 5090 concerning steel products ensures that voluntary restraint agreements and U.S. import quotas on steel are perfectly legitimate under the FTA. Americans have used their trade laws to punish Canada for unfairly subsidizing steel production. Canadian steel producers are angry about this accusation because American steel makers have also received subsidies worth US$30 billion from 1980 to 1990.[99] The FTA is flawed because it put off the definition of an unfair subsidy until 1996.

American trade complaints and the lack of a subsidy definition have had a devastating impact on the flagging Canadian steel industry. Canadian steel had already lost its competitiveness in U.S. markets as the Canadian dollar appreciated in the late 1980s. The placement of a punitive tariff upwards of 70 percent on some Canadian steel exports further crippled the Canadian steel sector. Companies such as Algoma Steel and SYSCO Steel were devastated by these tariffs and were on the verge of bankruptcy. Although it was not clearly stated in the FTA, Canadian officials believed that a government bail out of these two beleaguered steel plants would also be attacked as an unfair subsidy. In order to restructure the debt at Algoma steel, managers have resorted to long-term bank loans and an employee ownership programme. The Government of Nova Scotia, owner of SYSCO Steel, attempted to sell the Cape Breton steel firm to Kohlberg and Co. of New York City. The American firm backed out on the deal when it realized the extent to which U.S. trade actions had destabilized the Canadian steel industry. On the other hand, Canadian steel firms with capital to invest have been prompted by the uncertainty of the Canadian market to invest in the United States. Dofasco Steel of Hamilton, Ontario plans on spending Can$375 million to build a new mini-mill in the United States. IPSCO steel of Regina is building a new US$360 million steel plant in Iowa. The threat of American trade sanctions is hurting the Canadian steel industry while driving new investment out of Canada.

The FTA is linked to the crisis of the Canadian steel industry in yet another way. The lack of domestic demand for Canadian steel is caused in part by the fact that, since the beginning of the FTA, 300 manufacturers in Canada who formerly purchased domestic steel have relocated to the United States. Furthermore, some American buyers of Canadian steel fear that the dumping charges could disrupt the steel production process in Canada. Therefore, some American factories have abandoned their Canadian suppliers just on the threat that Canadian firms will be hit with duties. As demand drops, workers lose their jobs and Canadian steel companies must cope with the threat of insolvency. After five years of U.S. harassment, the steel producers now want to pull the steel sector out of the FTA. In its place, the Canadian steel producers are promoting the creation of a "Steel Pact" modeled along the lines of the Auto Pact. Such a managed bilateral trade system would provide for a more strict subsidy definition, a less arbitrary dispute arbitration process and a guaranteed minimum production limit for Canada steel mills.[100] American officials and most American steel producers want no part of this Canadian proposal.

American intimidation of Canadian agricultural exporters provides yet another example of how the FTA fails to protect Canada from U.S. protectionism. The U.S. believes that Canada's pork producers receive unfair subsidies. The U.S. Customs service, under orders from the ITC, levied punitive tariffs on Canadian pork entering the United States. By April 1991, Can$17 million in extra duties had been collected. Canadian pork producers protested and asked the bilateral FTA dispute settlement panel to adjudicate the dispute. The FTA panel ruled in Canada's favor and ordered the ITC to stop collecting the punitive duties and to repay the Can$17 million to Canadian pork producers. The USTR appealed the decision under the "extraordinary challenge" provision of Annex 1904.13 of the FTA.[101] The appeal was turned down again by the FTA panel. Canadians were angered by U.S. actions because the appeal to the extraordinary challenge clause implied that Canada had consciously engaged in grossly unfair trading practices. Appealing to the panel without just cause showed to Canadians that the United States was not bargaining or trading in good faith.

Canadian exporters prevailed in the softwood and pork disputes. On the surface, it appears that Canada has benefited from the dispute settlement process. On closer examination it is evident that the pork victory took more than twice as long as a GATT decision would have taken. Furthermore, the GATT decision would have come at no cost to Canadians. Decisions made by the bilateral FTA panel cost Canadians millions of dollars and only reinstated the pre-FTA status quo for Canadian pork exporters. Increasingly, Canadians saw themselves as mere pawns in the broader geopolitical trade strategy of the United States.

Finally, an examination of the FTA and U.S. protectionism would not be complete without considering their combined effect on the Canadian automobile industry and the Auto Pact. The Auto Pact was established in 1965 as a sectoral managed trade agreement between Canada and the United States. It was the culmination of a half century of automobile production in Canada. The Canadian automobile industry was established in the early twentieth century behind a high tariff wall. High tariffs forced the major U.S. auto manufacturers to build branch plants in Canada if they wanted to sell cars north of the border. By the late 1950s, Canadian policy-makers became concerned about the effect of high tariffs on the structure of the Canadian automobile industry. Canadian tariffs were supposed to protect the nascent Canadian auto industry until it could compete in a lower-tariff environment. Efficiency gains never developed to the degree deemed necessary.

As late as 1964, Ford was producing sixty different models of five distinct lines in its single Canadian plant. The existence of high tariffs on autos and auto parts had resulted in the creation of a small replica of the U.S. Industry within Canada. Of course the Canadian market was too small to take full advantage of potential increases in productivity. Because Canada's market was so small, production runs were short and unit costs of production were high. A report by the Royal Commission on the Automobile Industry in 1960 recommended policies which were embodied in the Automobile Products Trade Act of 1965 — more commonly known as the Auto Pact. The stated goal of the Auto Pact was to increase productivity in the Canadian automotive manufacturing industry by creating a larger market for automotive products within which economies of scale could be achieved.[102] Access to the larger market was achieved by lowering Canadian tariffs and specializing in production for a continental market. This was done on the condition that auto production in Canada was roughly proportional to total automobile sales in Canada.

The Auto Pact was not a true sectoral free trade agreement. Rather it was a managed trade agreement that guaranteed Canada a certain proportion of jobs and production in the North American market. The Auto Pact did this by mandating that all cars sold in Canada have at least 60 percent Canadian content. Failure to ensure this minimum level of production would provide Canada with grounds to levy a 9.2 percent punitive duty on automobile exports from the United States. The Auto Pact has been a success for Canada. As productivity rose dramatically in Canadian plants, employment grew and auto exports to the south increased dramatically. By 1988, automotive exports to the United States comprised 7 percent of Canada's GDP.

Canadian prosperity derived from the Auto Pact angered American public officials and businessmen alike. Canadian automotive export growth was viewed as a zero-sum game by American manufacturers and workers. Growth in the Canadian automotive industry meant less investment in Michigan or Ohio. As negotiations over the FTA progressed, many pondered the fate of the Auto Pact. Most Americans hoped it would be eliminated by the FTA. Marc Santucci, a trade advisor for the state of Michigan, said that his office would spearhead a drive to dismantle the Auto Pact if the FTA was not implemented.[103] Michigan officials believed that the elimination of the Auto Pact would dissuade Asian automobile manufacturers from investing in Canada, diverting new investment to the United States. American labour leaders and managers also resented high levels of investment by American car manufacturers during the 1980s, that now far exceeded minimum requirements set forth by the Auto Pact.

Most Canadians hoped that the FTA would leave the Auto Pact unaffected. The pro-FTA lobby attempted to assuage Canadian fears by proclaiming that the FTA left the Auto Pact fundamentally intact.[104] What the supporters of free trade failed to mention was that the 9.2 percent punitive duty was to be eliminated along with all other tariffs. As the 9.2 percent tariff was phased out, the Auto Pact remained but Canada lost its only available weapon for enforcing terms of trade. In addition, the FTA removed the 60 percent Canadian-content guidelines and replaced it with a 50 percent North American content rule. The penalty for not meeting the assembly-to-sales ratio is not based on what you bring in from the United States, but what you bring in from offshore. The elimination of the 9.2 percent tariff and Canadian content rules decreased the power of the Canadian government to attract investment to Canada. The FTA eliminated all the negative incentives that the Canadian government used to lure American and Asian automobile manufacturers to Canada. In addition, the threat of American harassment of Canadian car exports deflected investment and production in Canada. The content audit by American Customs officials of Hondas made in Canada verifies these assertions.

Just days after Canada won a bilateral settlement on pork requiring the United States to repay Canadian pork producers US$20 million, the United States accused Honda Canada of not having the required 50 percent North American content. Change is desired by U.S. manufacturers who must have 60 percent North American content to sell in Canada compared to only 50 percent for Asian cars. This trade dispute was initiated by the U.S. during NAFTA talks and was perceived by Canadian officials as a broader campaign to change auto trade policy, diverting investment from Canada. Trade diversion is also an underlying motive of U.S. officials. Patrick Lavelle, a former deputy minister of trade in Ontario, remarked that the USTR was sending a message that if the Japanese build new automotive plants in North America, they had better be in the United States.[105]

The specific strategy of the U.S. Customs Service is to perform audits (sometimes retroactively) on Asian cars produced in Canada for the U.S. market to ensure that they have the requisite North American content. The U.S. audit concluded that Honda Canada produced cars during 1989-90 with only 38 percent North American content for export to the U.S. The U.S. Customs service levied a 2.5 percent punitive duty on Hondas produced in Canada entering into the United States amounting to approximately US$200 per car. Honda Canada's total fine was estimated to be US$20 million in retroactive duties. In addition, the U.S. Customs Service also performed audits on Suzuki, Hyundai and Toyota of Canada, fueling further resentment amongst Canadian officials who saw this as harassment to force the renegotiation of the auto provisions of the FTA and persuade Asian auto makers to produce their cars in the U.S. Canadian fears were heightened when Democratic House Majority leader, Richard Gephardt (D-Missouri) called for sweeping investigations of all foreign cars made in Canada destined for the United States. Canadian fears about broader U.S. intentions were confirmed when the Honda Canada audit was announced in a press release. Ordinarily, these audits are not newsworthy. However, given the trade climate created by NAFTA talks and American dissatisfaction with the status quo, officials in the Canadian trade minister's office believed that the release of the audit results was a ploy to put pressure on Canadian trade negotiators.

Canadian officials agreed with William Safire, columnist for the *New York Times*, who commented that the U.S. "kicked [Canada] in the teeth on lumber and Canadian-assembled cars."[106] Gordon Ritchie, former deputy chief Canadian trade negotiator, openly accused the U.S. Customs service of using the audit tactic to send a message to Asian car manufacturers who were planning to expand production in Canada. Faced with the prospect of constant harassment from U.S. Customs officials, Asian manufacturers would be more likely to invest in the United States before expanding capacity in Canada.

This type of harassment discourages investment in Canada because companies are assumed guilty until proven innocent. The exporter must post a bond equivalent to the punitive duty in order to gain access to the U.S. market while the dispute is examined by the bilateral panel where it takes upwards of two years to get a dispute settled. If found innocent, the bond is returned in full plus interest, but foreign investors perceive that the time and money spent fending off U.S. charges exceeds any benefits derived from locating in Canada. By this point the United States has achieved its policy objective. From the American perspective, the actual money collected in punitive tariffs is secondary to the more important goal of diverting investment and changing automobile trade policy in Canada.

American harassment has had the intended effect on Canada and automobile trade. First, Asian investment in Canada has not grown the way Canadian officials had expected that it would. Second, the trading provisions agreed to under the FTA have been altered under NAFTA as it currently stands. Compare the size of Asian car manufacturing in Canada with that of Asian car manufacturing in the United States. Factories such as the Honda plant in Alliston, Ontario, the Toyota plant in Kitchener, Ontario and the Hyundai plant in Bromont, Québec are much smaller in scale than their American counterparts in Tennessee, Ohio and Kentucky. The plants in Canada produce between 50,000 and 200,000 vehicles per year compared to plants in the United States which produce upwards of 300,000 per year. If there is a continental market, why does this difference exist? Asian firms have been threatened by the U.S. Customs Service thus creating doubts about Canada as a viable platform for export to the United States. Even the recent expansion at the Toyota Plant in Kitchener came long after Toyota expanded production at their plants in California and Kentucky.[107]

The United States also achieved most of the policy changes it wanted in automobile trade. In the realm of North American content (or rules of origin as it is sometimes called), Canadians hoped that NAFTA would not alter the 50 percent North American content provision that was established under the FTA. The United States declared at the outset of the NAFTA negotiations that it wanted tighter "rules of origin," meaning that the North American content rules should be raised from 50 to 70 or 80 percent. By the end of NAFTA talks, Canada had agreed to a 62.5 percent North American content rule. The raised North American content requirements are a ploy to fence out Japanese and other cars imported from Canada.[108] Automobile trade to the United States represents a large component of Canadian exports. Tighter rules of origin discourage Asian investment in Canada concomitantly reducing Canadian trade to the United States. NAFTA also contains the FTA provision that gradually phases out Canada's right to impose penalties on vehicles or parts manufactured in the United States. Under the FTA and NAFTA, car companies can no longer be forced to build cars in Canada in order to gain tariff-free access to the Canadian market.

What do all these disputes have in common? In all cases, it was the retention of U.S. trade remedy laws and the lack of a clear subsidy definition that allowed the United States to launch as many trade grievances as they have. Some domestic subsidies are allowed under GATT rules, but countervailing duties may be levied if a company perceives that the imported products of a foreign competitor have been unfairly subsidized. The critical point is to define what constitutes a countervailable subsidy. The development of a workable definition has been complicated because subsidies can take various forms such as grants, interest-free loans, loan guarantees, tax credits and utility concessions. Chapter nineteen of the FTA text commits Canada and the

U.S. to agree on what constitutes an unfair subsidy by 1996 but so far no progress has been made.

Because of this ambiguity in the FTA, the U.S. targeted Canadian pork, autos, forest products and any other Canadian industries that posed a competitive threat to American producers. Canadians railed against American accusations, pointing out that the U.S. subsidized production to the same or greater extent but in a less visible manner. William Cavitt, director of the U.S. commerce department's Canadian Affairs Office, acknowledged in the original draft of a paper released in August 1989 that American subsidy programmes are less visible than those in Canada, but the benefits are no less real. The commerce department excoriated Cavitt for his candor, retracted his report and submitted a second draft that made no such admissions. According to the deputy director of the U.S. Commerce Office in Canada, Cavitt's original report does not exist.[109] Some analysts claim that failure to resolve the subsidy definition issue did not hamper the FTA and that it will be resolved eventually under NAFTA.[110]

In contrast to the sanguine view held by American trade theorists, the CLC reads sinister intent on the part of American negotiators to avoid resolving the subsidy issue.[111] They claim that the ambiguity in subsidy definition permits greater flexibility for the ITC to target Canadian industry with countervailing duties. The CLC buttresses this claim by pointing out how NAFTA does not contain any statement obliging the signatories to define an unfair subsidy as well as weakening the dispute settlement mechanism established under the FTA.

The CLC believes that NAFTA frees the United States from its commitments under the FTA, showing that the United States is resolved to never commit to a subsidy code with Canada or Mexico. To further prove their point, the CLC notes that the NAFTA text incorporates large sections of resolutions from the Uruguay Round of GATT where it is coincident with U.S. goals (for example in intellectual property rights and trade in services). However, the U.S. did not want to include the GATT subsidy code in NAFTA. The CLC notes that the GATT subsidy definitions are imperfect but better than nothing. Under NAFTA, there is no general definition of a subsidy. This means that the U.S. has preserved its power to define countervailable subsidies according to its own trade laws. Because the U.S. has resorted to using its trade laws in an unpredictable fashion, Canada does not know what will be targeted as an unfair subsidy. The long term effect of such uncertainty is that Canada will be reluctant to engage in farm price supports or regional development programmes

Figure 13
Canada's Trade Balance with the United States

	1984	1986	1988	1990	1992	1994
A. Merchandise Trade (C$billions)						
Exports	84.8	93.3	102.6	110.5	122.3	179.5
Imports	65.8	76.4	88.8	93.7	104.6	151.2
Balance	19.0	16.9	13.8	16.7	17.7	28.3
B. Non-merchandise (Services) Trade (C$billions)						
Exports	14.2	16.6	21.7	19.6	20.1	24.8
Imports	27.6	28.6	34.5	39.0	40.4	47.7
Balance	-13.4	-12.0	-12.8	-19.4	-20.3	-22.9

Source: Statistics Canada, *Canada's Balance of International Payments* (Ottawa: Supply and Services, 1995), 66-67.

for fear of retaliation. Furthermore, the fear of U.S. trade sanctions dampens enthusiasm for foreign investment in Canada. Was it crucial for Canada to enter into an FTA rife with ambiguity? An economist with the Northeast-Midwest Institute believes that trade between Canada and the U.S. would have grown with or without the FTA.[112]

Canada's Trade Balance with the United States

By 1991, Canadian Trade Minister Michael Wilson was celebrating the fact that Canada was setting records for the amount of goods it was exporting to the United States. Free trade proponents in the media and academia also chimed in by documenting Canada's increased exports to the United States.[113] Figure 13 verifies that trade has increased between Canada and the United States. However, it is not clear that the FTA is responsible for this growth given that comparable annual increases in trade between Canada and the United States occurred prior to the FTA in 1983

(Figure 14). Theoretically, there should be an upward point of inflection in Figure 14 during 1989 when a large proportion of the tariffs had been eliminated. This did not happen. In fact, growth in Canadian exports to the United States from 1989 to 1991 was the slowest three years of growth since the early 1960s.[114] When trade growth did occur in 1994, it appeared to be driven by a devalued Canadian dollar rather than free trade. While overall trade has increased between Canada and the United States, Canada has lost domestic market share to American goods in almost every sector (Figure 15).

Admittedly, Canada's market share grew in the United States, but the U.S. market shares of Australia, Mexico and South Africa grew even faster than that of Canada. Furthermore, the CMA announced that 44 percent of Canadian firms have lost domestic market share since 1989.[115] Even if trade has increased, FTA supporters seem to be advocating increased trade as an end in itself. The whole argument for free trade was that it would increase the volume of trade which in turn was supposed to increase investment, production and jobs in Canada. Evidence shows that by the end of 1994, unemployment was still above 10 percent and bankruptcies continued at high rates.[116]

An important aspect of the Canada-United States trading relationship revolves around the fluctuating trade balance. Prior to the FTA, Canada had a huge trade surplus with the U.S. due primarily to the low value of the Canadian dollar. As Figures 13, 16, 17 and 18 reveal, Canada experienced a trade deficit with the U.S. before showing a trade surplus in 1994. Even though Canada is exporting more goods to the United States, it is increasing its imports of services. Critics of the FTA predicted this would happen because the U.S. had a trade surplus in services even before the FTA. With special provisions for services in the FTA and NAFTA, it is not surprising to see the trade in services deficit increase dramatically.

Both supporters and opponents of the FTA say that the single greatest factor creating Canada's trade deficit with the U.S. was the dramatic revaluation of the Canadian dollar between 1986 and 1992.[117] Figure 18 shows the relationship between the revaluation of the Canadian dollar and the development of Canada's current account deficit. The figure shows a direct relationship between the increasing size of the Canadian current account deficit and the rising value of the Canadian dollar in U.S. terms. Analysts of the FTA have asked why the Canadian dollar was allowed to revalue so much in so short a time. It was imprudent to allow the dollar to revalue because the resultant trade deficit damaged the Canadian economy by increasing bankruptcies,

Figure 14
Growth of Canadian Exports to the United States

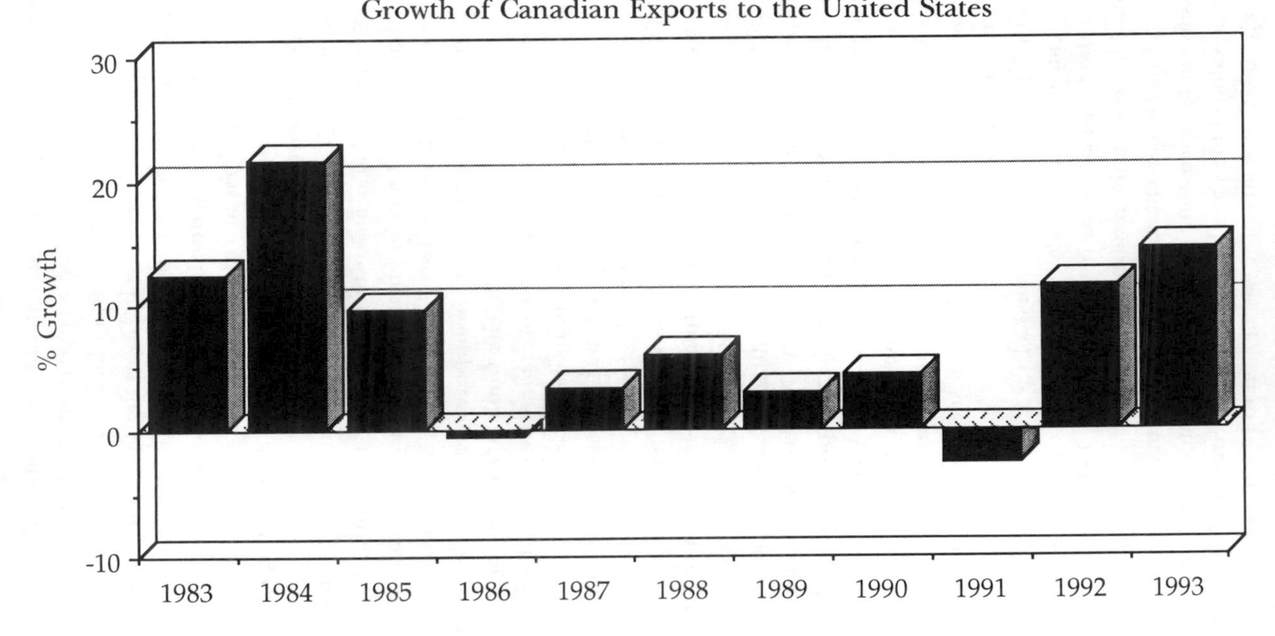

Source: Statistics Canada, Canada's Balance of International Payments (Ottawa: Supply and Services, 1995).

Figure 15
Share of American Products in the Canadian Market (%)

Industry	U.S. Share 1985-87	U.S. Share 1991	Change 1987-91
Beverage Industries	1.0	1.7	+0.7
Chemicals	21.9	26.9	+5.0
Clothing	1.3	3.2	+1.9
Electrical/Electronic Equipment	39.6	44.1	+4.5
Fabricated Metal Products	13.7	19.4	+5.7
Food Industries	5.1	8.0	+2.9
Furniture	5.9	26.4	+20.5
Leather Products	4.3	7.5	+3.2
Machinery	49.1	51.2	+2.1
Non-metallic Mineral Products	11.5	19.1	+7.6
Paper Products	10.2	20.3	+10.1
Plastics	19.4	25.5	+6.1
Primary Metals	18.7	25.7	+7.0
Primary Textiles	15.1	22.7	+7.5
Printing and Publishing	11.1	13.4	+2.3
Refined Petroleum and Coal	4.9	5.9	+1.0
Rubber Products	21.8	37.9	+16.1
Textile Products	9.1	19.5	+10.4
Transportation Equipment	71.6	55.3	-16.3

Source: CLC, "Submission by the CLC on the NAFTA to the Sub-committee on International Trade of the Standing Committee on External Affairs and International Trade of the Canadian House of Commons," (Ottawa: Unpublished Report of the CLC, 1993), 10.

Figure 16
Canada's Current Account Balance with the United States

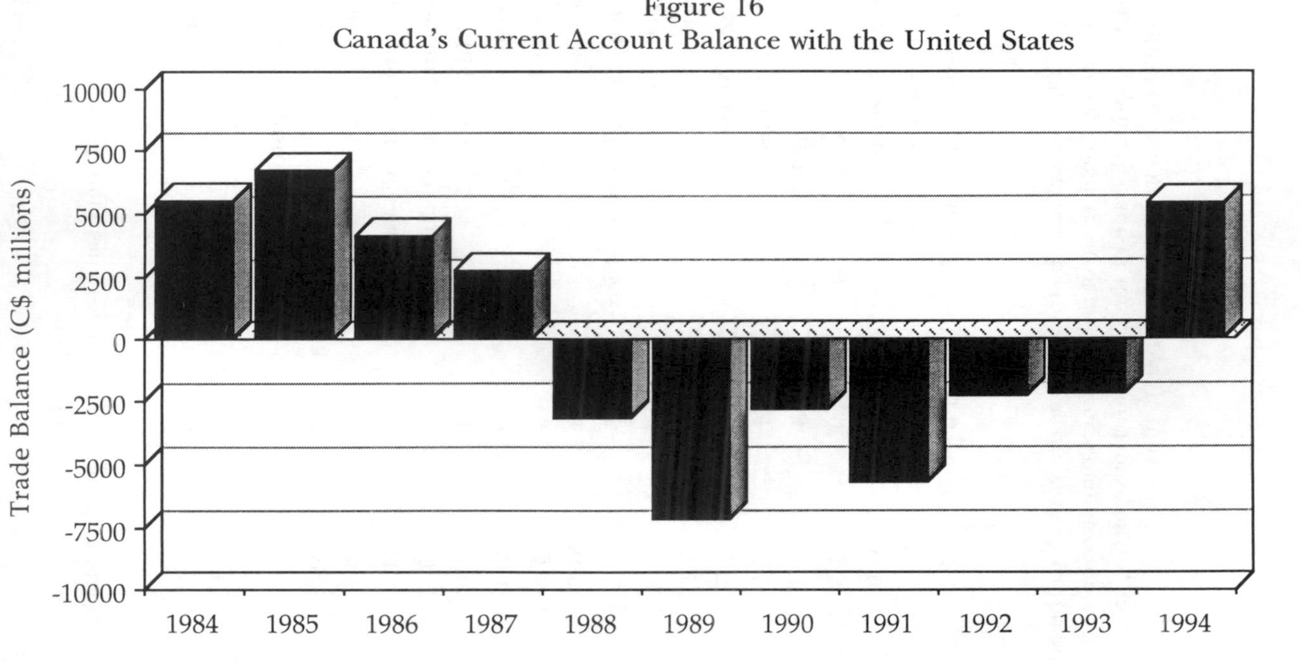

Source: Statistics Canada, Canada's Balance of International Payments (Ottawa: Supply and Services, 1995)

Figure 17
Canadian Merchandise and Non-merchandise Trade Balance with the United States

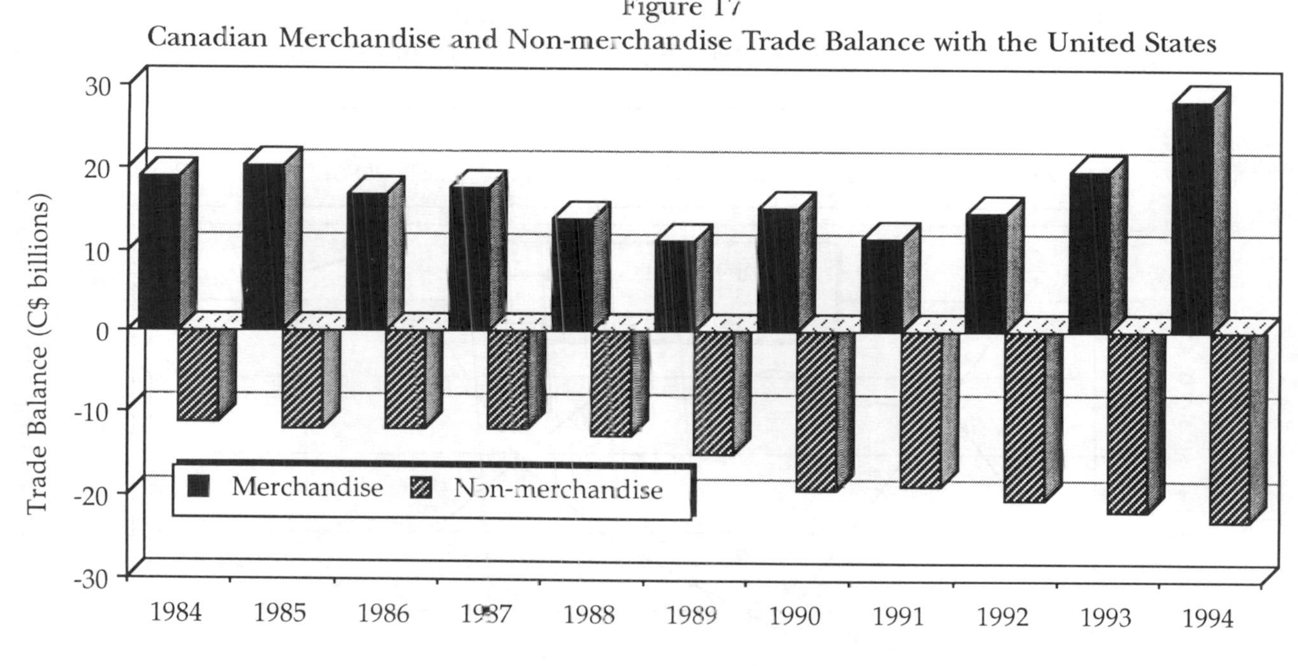

Source: Statistics Canada, Canada's Balance of International Payments (Ottawa: Supply and Services, 1995).

Figure 18
Exchange Rates and the Canadian Current Account Balance with the United States

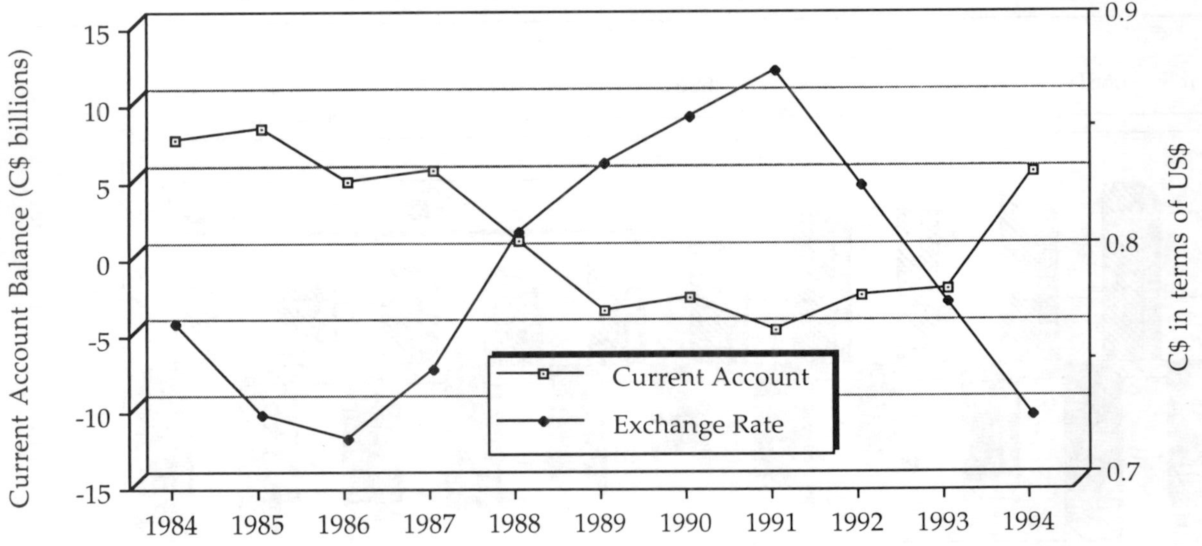

Source: Statistics Canada, Canadian Economic Observer (Ottawa: Supply and Services, 1995), 52; Statistics Canada, Canada's Balance of International Payments (Ottawa: Supply and Services, 1995), 66.

plant relocations and unemployment.[118] Explanations for this currency revaluation fall into three categories: Revaluation was a pure side-effect of anti-inflation measures adopted by the Bank of Canada and is unrelated to the FTA. Modest revaluation was an expected by-product of closer economic integration although the magnitude of the currency appreciation may have been more than anticipated. And finally, revaluation could have been the direct outcome of an informal agreement acquiesced to by Canada in order to secure the FTA with the United States.

The first argument says that the increasing value of the Canadian dollar is just a side-effect of higher interest rates that are themselves part of a larger monetarist policy implemented by the Bank of Canada to fight inflation.[119] The price of goods, and hence inflation, tends to rise faster when consumer expenditure rises. In order to slow down the circulation of capital and price increases, central banks raise interest rates in order to make borrowing money from banks or purchasing on credit less desirable. As consumer spending drops, inflation would be expected to drop. However, policies in Canada that raise interest rates tend to cause the Canadian dollar to appreciate. This happens because of the close links between the financial markets of the industrialized countries. Investors are constantly comparing interest rates between countries to determine where the greatest returns can be obtained. Literally billions of dollars, marks, francs, pounds and trillions of yen worth of "hot money" owned by banks, corporations, wealthy governments and individuals circulate the globe in search of the highest returns.

When considering the investment relationship between Canada and the United States, it is the interest rate differential which determines the volume and direction of investment capital. If Canadian interest rates rise relative to the U.S. rate, then U.S. investors will want to hold more Canadian bonds and fewer U.S. bonds. To effect this transaction, investors will sell their U.S. bonds, exchange U.S. dollars they receive for Canadian dollars and use them to buy the higher-yield Canadian bonds. The increased demand for Canadian dollars will drive up their exchange rate value. In short, inflation is the disease, higher interest rates are the cure, and the revaluation of the Canadian dollar is just an inevitable, if nasty, side-effect. This explanation is made by the Canadian government and free trade supporters who deny any connection between the revaluation of the Canadian currency and the FTA.[120] John Crow, the governor of the Bank of Canada between 1987 and 1993, stated that Canada's inflation rate must be equal to that of the United States in order for Canadians to prosper. As a result, he promised to keep Canadian interest rates high until he forced harmonization between Canadian and

American inflation rates. For waging such a vigorous anti-inflation war, Crow has been dubbed a hero by the international business media.[121]

Some analysts also identify another explanation for high interest rates unrelated to the FTA. Interest rates are high in Canada because of events occurring in the broader global economy. Canada has a balance-of-payments problem which the Canadian government attempts to solve by keeping foreign investment flowing into Canada. It attracts investment by keeping interest rates higher than most other industrialized countries. However, inflationary pressures have forced Japan, Germany and the United States to also raise their interest rates in the late 1980s. In the summer of 1990, Canada's central bank discount rate was four points higher than that of the U.S. In order to prevent this gap from narrowing, Canada was forced to raise their rate to attract investment.[122] If the gap narrows, investors will flock to other industrialized countries and Canada will face a balance of payments crisis. Canada has become increasingly dependent on the sale of government securities to stabilize their balance of payments. From this perspective, the increased value of the Canadian dollar is a side-effect of the higher interest rates needed to attract foreign investment.

A second explanation, supported by neoclassical theorists and free trade proponents, states that Canadians should expect a modest appreciation in the value of the Canadian dollar due in some measure to the FTA. Countries that integrate their production markets but do not establish a monetary union will find it desirable to co-ordinate or harmonize their monetary policies to some extent in order that payments difficulties or exchange rate volatility do not impede the operation the new free trade area. Furthermore, Paul Volker, former chairman of the U.S. Federal Reserve, says that stable exchange rates are helpful to trade and he would not be surprised to eventually see a fixed exchange rate between the Canadian and U.S. dollars, and eventually with the Mexican Peso once NAFTA is implemented. If Canada does not enter into a formal currency union, the Canadian dollar should be allowed to stay revalued through an informally pegged exchange rate to create a stable currency zone.[123] Of course this explanation no longer seems reasonable given the rapid devaluation of both the Canadian dollar and the Mexican Peso after the implementation of NAFTA.

Some analysts see the revaluation of the Canadian dollar arising from the favorable response of the international community to the FTA. With the signing of the FTA in 1987, foreign investors in Europe and Asia perceived that Canada's economic future looked bright and it was therefore a good place to make new investments. As more foreign investments poured into Canada, the Canadian dollar was forced upwards.[124] Currency revaluation is therefore not due to any formal agreement in the FTA but is rather a natural response to the perception that Canada was a good place for foreign investments in the late 1980s as a result of the prospect of free trade.

Still other supporters and opponents of free trade argued that the revalued Canadian dollar is part of the Tory competitiveness agenda to drive out inefficiencies in the Canadian economy. A low-valued Canadian dollar allowed many large Canadian firms to become complacent in the knowledge that their products were competitive in the world market due to the undervalued Canadian currency and not because of their efficient production methods. Canadian firms were in a state of corporate denial, believing that they were competing well in the global economy. The revalued Canadian dollar is therefore part of the Tory strategy to restructure the Canadian economy by plunging corporate Canada into the cold bath of continental competition.[125] Companies are being forced to make tough choices — to become competitive through production efficiency, not exchange rate policy. Many companies would not survive the restructuring process, but the Tories and neoclassical economists believed that those that did would be successful in the new trade environment.

The high interest rate was also part of the strategy to discipline labour whose wage demands were putting inflationary pressures on the Canadian economy. Furthermore, lower-cost labour helps Canadian firms to compete with firms in lower-wage regions of the United States.[126] This explanation is embodied in a report issued by Wood Gundy, a Canadian accounting and investment firm. Prior to the FTA, free trade supporters argued that if Canadian wages and social standards caused Canadian firms to be uncompetitive, then the exchange rate would depreciate to compensate. Wood Gundy's April 1989 *Monthly Indicators Bulletin* explains to the contrary why the Canadian dollar appreciated when pre-FTA predictions said that it should fall:

> Rather than allow the exchange rate to adjust to higher unit labour costs, the Bank of Canada is more likely to force domestic costs to adjust to a higher valued dollar. If Canadian workers are to compete effectively for jobs in an increasingly integrated North American market, wage gains in Canada (negative in real terms from 1983-89) must be constrained to even more austere settlements in U.S. industries. Unfortunately, domestic wage adjustments are unlikely to occur without higher unemployment. By maintaining [the Canadian dollar] in the US$0.80 range, the Bank of Canada will let rising unemployment

> in export-sensitive sectors in the economy discipline wage growth, eventually bringing labour costs in line with those in the United States.[127]

The Canadian dollar actually flirted with the US$0.90 mark, almost ten cents higher than Wood Gundy predicted, before dropping below the US$0.75 mark in 1994.

Virulent monetarism was also more than many free trade supporters had expected. Excessively high interest rates were criticized by some former supporters of free trade because the cost of doing business became too expensive. Corporations that planned to expand to compete in the continental market found that, as interest rates skyrocketed, the credit needed to increase production had become prohibitively expensive. Canadian exporters also found that the increased value of the Canadian dollar decreased their competitiveness in the U.S. market. Robert Blair, chairman of the oil-producing Nova Corporation, stated that his firm suffers a 3 percent reduction in profit for every one cent increase of the Canadian dollar in U.S. terms. Some firms, such as Outboard Marine Canada, relocated from Canada to the United States in part because of the lower interest rates in the United States.[128] Supporters of free trade said that any benefits that Canada might have enjoyed from the FTA were destroyed by the recession created by an over-zealous attempt to fight inflation. The implication drawn is that the impacts of the FTA and the recession are two completely separate events with independent effects on the Canadian economy. Supporters of the FTA talk about a "made-in-Canada" recession created by high interest rates.[129] No mention was made of the recession also affecting the United States and the interplay between the recession and the FTA.

An alternative explanation shows that free trade and the recession may have had separate origins but came to reinforce one another. Free trade may have even precipitated the onset of recession. Consider the fact that Canada lost, comparatively speaking, four times as many manufacturing jobs as the United States between 1989 and 1994. Job losses would be about the same if they were just artifacts of the recession. During the 1982 recession, 24 percent of job losses were permanent. From 1989 to 1992, the figure is 65 percent.[130] The recession has certainly affected both Canada and the United States, but evidence reveals that the FTA has combined with the recession to hobble the Canadian economy. If this explanation is the most plausible, the Tories were guilty of mismanaging the Canadian economy during the implementation of free trade.

Opponents to free trade, who see nothing well-intentioned in the activities of the Progressive Conservatives and the Bank of Canada, offer the third explanation for currency revaluation. Bank of Canada policy openly advocated a goal of "zero inflation" by pushing up the cost of borrowing money (interest rates) to reduce overall spending.[131] When consumer spending drops, the circulation of capital slows down thereby reducing the upward pressure on prices. Although John Crow vowed that inflation-rate management is the only reason why interest rates and the Canadian dollar are so high, critics of the FTA believe otherwise.[132] They argue that Canadian inflation has not been a major problem because it did not vary from inflation in the United States by more than two percentage points during the 1980s (Figure 19).

Inflation, as measured by changes in the Canadian consumer price index (CPI), was relatively stable during the 1980s. Inflationary pressures that did exist often came from Tory policies. From 1989 to 1992, the average annual inflation in Canada was 3.8 percent for all goods and services. Food items in the CPI increased by only 2.8 percent. Housing increased 3.5 percent. Clothing costs rose 3.8 percent. Above average price increases occurred in health care at 4.1 percent, and tobacco and alcohol at 8.0 percent.[133] Where prices rose above the norm, increases are linked to government policies. Clothing price increases are linked to the introduction of the GST. Health care costs rose due to legislation which gave pharmaceutical companies longer drug patents. This effectively pushed generic drug companies out of the market thereby forcing Canadians to pay more for their prescriptions. There is also regional variation in the inflation rate. In 1992, the overall inflation rate was 1.5 percent. Yet consumers in British Columbia faced a 2.7 percent rise in prices while residents of Newfoundland confronted only a 1 percent increase. Thus, it is apparent that a federal policy on inflation management affects different sectors and regions in different ways.

A more fundamental question asks whether a high interest rate policy actually works at all to bring down inflation. Conventional economic theory suggests that a high interest rate is justified to cool an overheated economy caused by increased consumer spending and full employment occurring when plants and equipment are being used very close to full capacity. Higher interest rates will slow consumer spending by raising the price of consumer credit. As previous figures have shown, Canada has not been in any danger of overheating. The Canadian unemployment rate has been above 10 percent since 1991. As well, capacity utilization dropped well below 80 percent. None of the conditions hold for interest

Figure 19
Inflation Rates in Canada and the United States

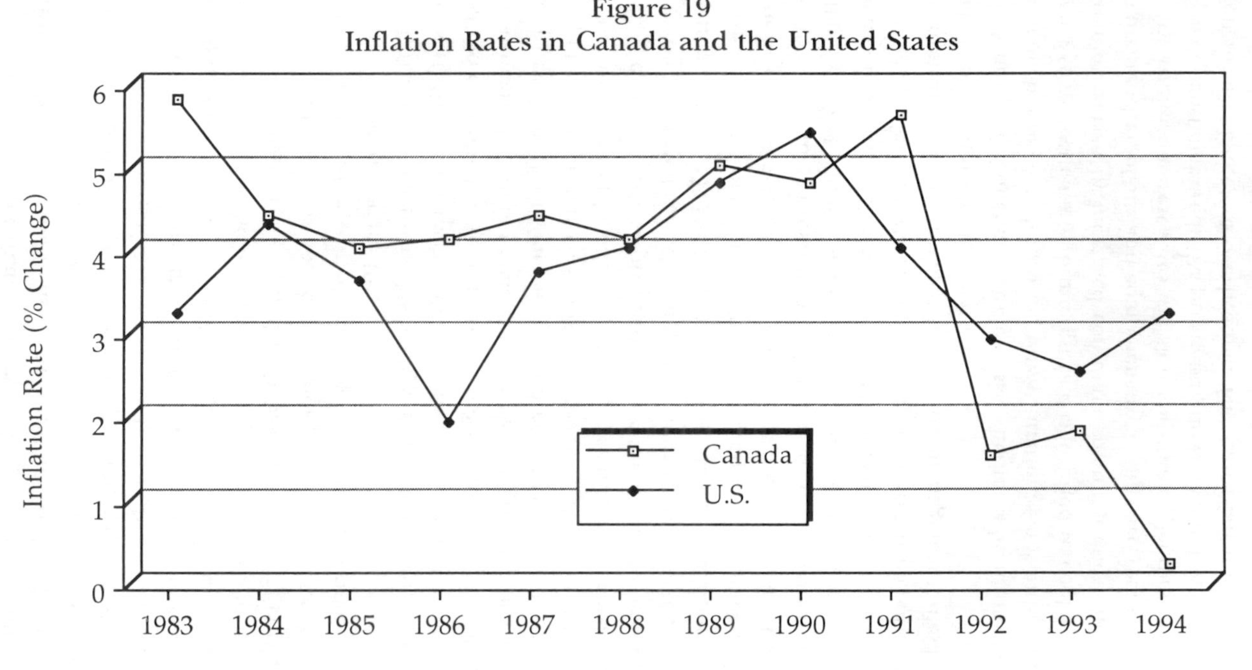

Source: Statistics Canada, Canadian Economic Observer (Ottawa: Supply and Services, 1995), 65.

rate manipulation to be used for fighting inflation. Although Crow's ostensible goal of zero inflation is admirable, his high interest rate had such negative impacts as to make the remedy worse than the alleged malady. In the short term, interest rates fuel inflation by driving up the costs of goods that are components in the cost of living index such as housing and durable goods. Manufacturers undertaking new investment in plants and equipment pass on higher credit costs to the consumer. In the longer term, higher interest rates choke off new investment and purchases of big ticket items such as homes and automobiles. High interest rates have made Canadian exports more expensive in the United States, costing thousands of Canadian jobs.

Instead of blaming inflation for driving up Canadian interest rates, fault can be placed on market forces unleashed by the FTA. Prior to the FTA, FIRA was eliminated and replaced by Investment Canada which only screened foreign investment over Can$5 million. After the FTA, the screening guideline rose to Can$150 million before being phased out altogether. The United States and Canadian capital markets, already closely linked, became even more integrated. Foreign investors looked at the value of Canadian stocks compared to American stocks and decided that Canadian companies were undervalued. Acquisitions accelerated under the FTA with 376 foreign takeovers worth Can$12.6 billion in the first 18 months of the FTA.[134] These takeovers often hurt the Canadian economy as they were often leveraged buyouts where the purchaser borrows against the value of the newly acquired asset. Rationalization quickly ensued leading to plant closures, downsizing, layoffs and the reselling of assets in order to finance the cost of buying Canadian property. American dollars and other foreign currencies poured into Canada sustaining the rise of the Canadian dollar. This investment spree coupled with the high Canadian interest rate drove up the value of the Canadian currency.

Historically, the spread between the Canadian interest rate and the U.S. Federal Reserve rate has varied between 2 and 3 points.[135] The Canadian rate has usually been higher than the American rate in order to attract foreign capital to finance its current account deficit. At the end of 1987, the gap was 2.75 points (Figure 20). Crow then widened the gap far beyond its traditional size until it had reached over 6 points by 1990. For a brief period during 1990, the gap actually reached 7 points. The size of the gap made Canadian paper assets very attractive. Treasury bills were paying the buyer 5 or 6 percentage points more than a comparable U.S. bill. Foreign holdings of new Canadian government and corporate securities increased by Can$20 million in 1989 and again in 1990.[136] High interest rates attracted foreign investors.

Figure 20
Gap Between Central Bank Discount Rates in Canada and the United States and Exchange Rate Fluctuation

Year	Canadian Rate (%)	American Rate (%)	Spread (%)	Can$ in terms of US$
1983	9.6	8.5	1.1	.81
1984	11.3	8.8	2.5	.77
1985	9.7	7.7	2.0	.73
1986	9.2	6.3	2.9	.71
1987	8.4	5.7	2.7	.75
1988	9.7	6.2	3.5	.81
1989	12.3	6.9	5.4	.84
1990	13.1	7.0	6.1	.86
1991	9.0	5.5	3.5	.87
1992	6.8	3.3	3.5	.83
1993	5.6	3.0	2.6	.76
1994	5.8	7.0	1.2	.73

Source: Statistics Canada, *Canadian Economic Observer* (Ottawa: Supply and Services, 1995), 68; Statistics Canada, *Canadian Economic Observer* (Ottawa: Supply and Services, 1990), 5.119.

As more foreign investors purchased Canadian securities, demand for the Canadian dollar forced its value upwards. As the Canadian dollar revalued, Canadian goods became more expensive in the United States market and American products became more attractive in the Canadian market. From 1988 on, the Canadian trade-in-goods surplus began to diminish because currency revaluation was equivalent to a 20 percent across-the-board surtax on Canadian goods.

Canada was now set on a vicious cycle that lasted close to five years. High interest rates attracted investment and pushed up the Canadian dollar, lowering Canada's trade-in-goods surplus. This in turn pushed Canada's balance of payments (including interest payments and service costs) deeper into deficit. The rising payments deficit forced Canada to increase its borrowing abroad. The money needed to pay international bills was flowing in due to the high interest rates and because foreigners were purchasing Canadian companies. As the dollar rose, the balance-in-goods trade worsened. This triggered the need for more foreign money. Interest rates rose to attract the requisite money, which in turn forced the Canadian dollar to rise. This cycle occurred repeatedly before and after the FTA. By 1992, the discontented murmuring of corporations and consumers alike had grown into a rancorous tumult. The economic landscape was littered with personal and corporate bankruptcies. Crow lowered the Canadian bank rate but proclaimed that he had done so because inflation had been vanquished, not because his policies had devastated the Canadian economy.[137]

What started Canada's vicious cycle of rising interest rates, revalued currency and growing current account deficit? Was Crow's monetarist policy misguided but well-intentioned? James Coyne, the Bank of Canada's governor from 1955 to 1961, fits this model.[138] Coyne's high interest rates were well-intentioned, but they were so unpopular that he was forced to resign under the threat of being removed through a legislative order.

A second view held by Canadian labour leaders and Left intelligentsia suggests that Bank of Canada policy is linked to an informal currency agreement between Canada and the United States. The evidence for such an agreement is purely circumstantial. In 1985, the five largest industrialized countries (the U.S., West Germany, France, United Kingdom, and Japan) sent their finance ministers and commerce secretaries to meet at the Plaza Hotel in New York City. The so-called G-5 countries convened this meeting because exchange rate volatility and the threat of U.S. protectionism sparked by the growing United States trade deficit was destabilizing world trade. The G-5 countries agreed to have their central banks sell U.S. dollars to drive down the value of the American currency in world markets. The formal agreement that prompted the G-5 countries to take these actions came to be known as the Plaza Accords. Subsequently, Italy and Canada were brought into this coterie to form the G-7 and have been party to subsequent reforms. On May 22, 1986, both the *Toronto Star* and *Globe and Mail* quoted U.S. Treasury Secretary James Baker saying that Canada would have to raise the value of its currency versus the U.S. dollar as a price of admission to the G-7.[139]

In 1985, U.S. Commerce Secretary Malcolm Baldridge told former Canadian minister of industry Sinclair Stevens that a revalued Canadian dollar was the key to securing an agreement on free trade. It was suggested that the Canadian dollar appreciate to between US$0.80 and

Figure 21
Link Between the Bank of Canada Rate, the Canadian CPI and the Real Interest Rate in Canada (%)

Year	Bank of Canada Rate	CPI Inflation	Real Interest Rate Column 1-Column 2
1984	11.3	4.4	6.9
1985	9.6	4.0	5.6
1986	9.2	4.1	5.1
1987	8.4	4.4	4.0
1988	9.7	4.1	5.6
1989	12.3	5.0	7.3
1990	13.6	4.8	8.8
1991	9.0	5.6	3.4
1992	6.8	1.5	5.3
1993	5.6	1.8	3.8
1994	5.8	0.2	5.6

Source: Statistics Canada, *Canadian Social Trends* 36 (Spring 1995): 35; Statistics Canada, *Canadian Economic Observer* (Ottawa: Supply and Services, 1995), 52.

US$0.90 from its late 1985 value of US$0.71.[140] Baldridge and Secretary Baker, the architect of the U.S. negotiating strategy, openly agreed with the U.S. National Manufacturers' Association and other lobby groups who believed that the undervalued Canadian dollar unfairly subsidized Canadian exports to the United States.[141] USTR Peter Murphy said that exchange rate adjustment was one of six major objectives in the FTA talks and that exchange relations were an inextricable part of the free trade pact.

The timing of interest rate and inflation increases comprise the final bit of circumstantial evidence. The Progressive Conservatives claimed that interest rates were raised in Canada as a response to inflationary pressures. This assertion can be refuted by looking at the difference between the real interest rate and Bank of Canada rate to show that interest rates were raised long before inflation took hold in Canada.[142] The real interest rate is the difference between the CPI and the Bank of Canada rate. By looking at the data in Figure 21, it is apparent that the real interest rate rose long before inflation (CPI) did. The real interest rate was raised in 1987 when inflation was about 4.4 percent per year. The next year inflation dropped to 4.1 percent but the interest rate continued to rise. It is important to get the causal direction correct: increased interest rates caused the inflation and not vice versa. When Crow increased the traditional bank rate differential from 2 points to over 6 points, the real interest rate skyrocketed, the Canadian dollar revalued and economic crisis ensued.

The real interest rate increased when it did because the FTA talks had broken down and Mulroney had to show the United States that he was bargaining in good faith.[143] Currency revaluation was therefore the price of admission to the G-7 as well as to the FTA. Of course, most supporters of the FTA scoff at the suggestion that currency revaluation was tied to the FTA.[144] Whether or not there was an informal agreement to peg the dollar upwards, the revaluation of the Canadian dollar was responsible for the loss of hundreds of thousands of Canadian jobs, billions of dollars in lost investment and Canada's merchandise trade surplus with the United States.

The only point left in question is whether the Tories were well-intentioned incompetents who misunderstood the link between exchange rates and interest rates or shrewd neoconservatives who would do anything to secure a free trade agreement with the United States. The answer to this question might become more clear after the next chapter which examines the impact of free trade on Canadian workers.

Notes

1. Clarkson, "Disjunctions: Free Trade and the Paradox of Canadian Development," 103.
2. Jane Jenson, "'Different' but not 'Exceptional': Canada's Permeable Fordism," *Canadian Review of Sociology and Anthropology*, 26, no. 1 (1989): 69.
3. Clarkson, "Disjunctions: Free Trade and the Paradox of Canadian Development," 104.
4. See for example: Andrew Lamorie, *How They Sold Our Canada to the U.S.A.* (Gravenhurst, ON: Northern Books, 1964); Stephen Hymer, "Direct Foreign Investment and the National Economic Interest," in *Nationalism in Canada*, Peter Russell, ed. (Toronto: McGraw-Hill, 1966); Kari Levitt, *Silent Surrender* (Toronto: Macmillan, 1970); Ian Lumsden, ed., *Close the 49th Parallel Etc.: The*

Americanization of Canada (Toronto: University of Toronto Press, 1970); Abraham Rotstein and Gary Lax, eds., *Independence: The Canadian Challenge* (Toronto: Committee for an Independent Canada, 1972).

5. Richard Gwyn, *The 49th Paradox: Canada in North America* (Toronto: Totem Books, 1986), 57.
6. Canada, *Royal Commission on Canada's Economic Prospects* (Ottawa: Queen's Printer, 1958); Morton, *The Canadian Identity*, 130.
7. Mahant and Mount, *An Introduction to Canadian-American Relations,* 203.
8. Gwyn, *The 49th Paradox,* 70.
9. Peter Newman quoted in Gwyn, *The 49th Paradox,* 70.
10. Robert Chodos, Rae Murphy and Eric Hamovitch, *The Unmaking of Canada: The Hidden Theme in Canadian History Since 1945* (Toronto: James Lorimer, 1991), 54.
11. See for example: Gwyn, *The 49th Paradox,* 76; NorthropFrye, *The Bush Garden* (Toronto: Anansi, 1971); Margaret Atwood, *Survival: A Thematic Guide to Canadian Literature* (Toronto: Anansi, 1972).
12. Gwyn, *The 49th Paradox,* 78.
13. Abraham Rotstein, "Foreign Control of the Economy: A Screening and Ownership Policy," in *Getting It Back: A Program for Canadian Independence,* Abraham Rotstein and Gary Lax, eds. (Toronto: Clarke, Irwin and Company, 1974), 25; Canada, *Foreign Direct Investment in Canada* (Ottawa: Information Canada, 1972), 405.
14. Clarkson, "Disjunctions: Free Trade and the Paradox of Canadian Development," 107.
15. Diane Francis, *Controlling Interest: Who Owns Canada?* (Toronto: McClelland-Bantam, 1987), 221.
16. David A. Wolfe, "The Rise and Demise of the Keynesian Era in Canada: Economic Policy, 1930-1980s," in *Readings in Canadian Social ;History, Volume 5: Modern Canada, 1930-1980s,* Michael Cross and Gregory Kealey, eds. (Toronto: McClelland and Stewart, 1984; reprint 1985), 75.
17. Clarkson, "Disjunctions: Free Trade and the Paradox of Canadian Development," 110.
18. Ibid., 111.
19. Ibid., 111.
20. Gwyn, *The 49th Paradox,* 98-99.
21. Statistics Canada, *Canadian Social Trends,* 24 (Summer 1992): 30.
22. BCNI, "Economic Priorities and the National Issues," 2.
23. Clarkson, "Disjunctions: Free Trade and the Paradox of Canadian Development," 114.
24. Richard Simeon, "Inside the MacDonald Commission," *Studies in Political Economy,* 22 (Spring 1987): 177; Duncan Cameron and Daniel Drache, "Outside the Macdonald Commission: Reply to Richard Simeon," *Studies in Political Economy,* 26 (Summer 1988): 173.
25. Gwyn, *The 49th Paradox,* 309; Doern and Tomlin, *Faith and Fear,* 275.
26. Ronald J. Wonnacott and Paul Wonnacott, *Free Trade Between the United States*

and Canada: The Potential Economic Effects (Cambridge, MA: Harvard University Press, 1967), 213
27. Daly and Cobb, *For the Common Good*, 219.
28. John DeMont, "Spreading the Net Widely," *Maclean's*, 3 July 1989, 76.
29. Christopher Story, "The Canadian Dollar," *International Currency Review*, 20, no. 1 (1989): 135.
30. John DeMont, "Takeover Fever," *Maclean's*, 28 August 1989, 36.
31. Gwyn, *The 49th Paradox*, 99; Andre Plourde, "The NEP Meets the FTA," *Canadian Public Policy*, 17, no. 1 (1991): 22.
32. John Honderich, "A Leap of Faith Not Worth Taking," *Toronto Star* 19 November 1988, D2; Maude Barlow, *Parcel of Rogues: How Free Trade is Failing Canada* (Toronto: Key Porter Books, 1990), 131.
33. DeMont, "Takeover Fever," 36.
34. Ibid., 36; DeMont, "Spreading the Net Widely," 76.
35. D'Arcy Jenish, John Daly and Bruce Wallace, "Takeover Fever Hits Canada," *Maclean's*, 19 September 1989, 30.
36. D'Arcy Jenish, "Merger Wave Rolls On," *Maclean's*, 6 February 1989, 28-30.
37. Jenish, Daly and Wallace, "Takeover Fever Hits Canada," 30.
38. Barry Came, "In Search of the Bigger Gulp," *Maclean's*, 30 January 1989, 36.
39. Douglas Coupland, *Generation X: Tales for an Accelerated Culture* (New York: St. Martin's Press, 1991), 80.
40. Bruce Wallace, "A Warning From Ottawa: Regulating the Merger Wave," *Maclean's*, 30 January 1989, 38.
41. Federal Reserve Bank of St. Louis, *International Economic Conditions*, 42.
42. Hurtig, *The Betrayal of Canada*, 14; William McGaughey, *A U.S.-Mexico-Canada Free Trade Agreement: Do We Just Say No?* (Minneapolis, MN: Thistlerose Publications, 1992), 73.
43. Manjunath Pendakur, *Canadian Dreams and American Control: The Political Economy of the Canadian Film Industry* (Detroit: Wayne State University Press, 1990), 271-72.
44. Doern and Tomlin, *Faith and Fear*, 157; To play the role of the *demandeur* implies that concessions must be given first in order to achieve a certain goal or gain access. It connotes anunequal and subservient role where the *demandeur* is a supplicant who must give much in order to receive only a fraction in return. In the case of Canada, many free trade analysts believed that Canada gave up far too much for free trade. Cedric Ritchie, chairman of the Bank of Nova Scotia, commented that Canada had "given up most of its bargaining chips" without making "adequate progress towards our principal goal of secure access to the U.S. market" (quoted in Hurtig 1992, 11).
45. Hurtig, *Betrayal of Canada*, 343.
46. Shirley Carr, "Why Canadian Labour Opposes Free Trade," *Canadian Speeches*, 1, no. 10 (1988): 5.
47. Tom Fennell, et al., "A Free Trade Anniversary," *Maclean's*, 18 December 1989, 44.
48. Duncan Cameron, "Free Trade Looks Good — For the Americans," *Canadian Dimension*, 69 (February 1990): 2.

49. *Maclean's*/Decima, "Sex, Politics, and Dreams: the Poll Texts," *Maclean's*, 19 September 1991, 35.
50. Brenda Dalglish, "Free Trade: A Cutthroat?" *Maclean's*, 7 January 1991, 28.
51. "Small Business Not So Sure About Trilateral Trade Deal Survey Says," *Sault Star*, 10 October 1991, A10.
52. Bruce Campbell, *A Critique of 'The Global Trade Challenge.' A Tory Trade Tabloid* (Ottawa: Canadian Centre for Policy Alternatives, 1992), 11.
53. Gavin Scott, "Free-for-all," *Time*, 18 May 1992, 37.
54. Bruce Campbell, "Beggar Thy Neighbour," *The American Review of Canadian Studies*, 21, no. 2/3 (1991): 25.
55. Naser, "Why Economists Favor Free Trade Agreements," C4.
56. Patricia Chisholm, "The Winners and Losers," *Maclean's*, 18 December 1989, 49.
57. Diane Francis, "Myths about the Free Trade Agreement," *Maclean's*, 29 January 1990, 15.
58. Diane Francis, "Opposing Free Trade is like Opposing Gravity," *Maclean's*, 27 April 1992, 13.
59. ECC, *Venturing Forth: An Assessment of the Canada-U.S. Trade Agreement* (Ottawa: Supply and Services, 1988), 22.
60. External Affairs Canada, *Trade Negotiations*, 5.
61. "Wilson Credits FTA for Gained Share of U.S. Markets," *Sault Star*, 16 April 1992, A6.
62. James Pattison, "Paradise Postponed," *Maclean's*, 3 December 1989, 56.
63. Peter C. Newman, "Sliding Down the Path to Third World Status," *Maclean's*, 25 February 1991, 36.
64. Jack McArthur, "Compared to Global Statistics, We've Been in a Long Slump," *Toronto Star*, 18 June 1991, B2.
65. External Affairs Canada, *Canada's New Free Trade Agreement: Key Benefits*, 3; ECC, *Venturing Forth*, 18.
66. Barry Bluestone and Bennett Harrison, *The Deindustrialization of America: Plant Closings, Community Abandonment, and the Dismantling of Basic Industry* (New York: Basic Books, 1982), 3; Doreen Massey, *Spatial Divisions of Labour: Social Structures and the Geography of Production* (London: Macmillan, 1984), 2.
67. CLC, "Submission by the CLC on the North American Free Trade Agreement to the Sub-committee on International Trade of the Standing Committee on External Affairs and International Trade of the Canadian House of Commons," (Ottawa: Unpublished Document of the CLC, 1993), 4.
68. "Bankruptcies Hit Record," *Sault Star*, 4 February 1992, B16. "Bankruptcies Down," *Maclean's*, 15 August 1994, 29.
69. CLC, The Crisis of Canadian Manufacturing (Ottawa: CLC, 1991), 1.
70. Congress, House of Representatives, Committee on Energy and Commerce, *U.S.-Canada Free Trade Agreement: Hearing before the Subcommittee on Consumer Protection, and Competitiveness*, 100th Cong., 2nd Sess., 22 March 1988, 243.
71. Fennell, et al., "A Free Trade Anniversary," 47.
72. Deirdre McMurdy, "Packaged for Growth," *Maclean's*, 12 August 1991, 31.
73. Barlow, *Parcel of Rogues*, 165.

74. Peter Newman, "The Dark Side of Merger Mania," *Maclean's*, 6 February 1989, 31.
75. Ibid.
76. Ibid.
77. Richard Caves, Jeffrey Frankel and Ronald Jones, *World Trade and Payments: An Introduction* (Glenview, IL: Scott, Foresman and Company, 1990), 326.
78. Clyde Farnsworth, "U.S. and Canada Decide to speed cuts in Tariffs," *New York Times*, 21 March 1991, C6.
79. Bruce Little, "Howe Study Finds Free-trade Winners," *Globe and Mail*, 20 October 1992, B1.
80. The GST is directly linked to the FTA because it replaces the vanishing tariffs as a revenue raising device for the Canadian government. The FTA was supposed to have brought less expensive and more abundant goods and services to Canada. It can be shown that neither has happened. In fact, the GST is so costly that millions of Canadians shopped in American border communities for items that they would have previously purchased at home. Only after the value of the Canadian dollar dropped in 1993 did Canadians reduce their cross-border shopping. Cross-border shopping is not a new phenomenon, but the impact of free trade and the GST has increased the number of Canadians shopping in the United States (Merrett 1991, 35). Barbara Wickens and John Daly, "Riches to Rags," *Maclean's*, 23 September 1991, 55.
81. Wickens and Daly, "Riches to Rags," 55.
82. Richard Lipsey and Robert York, *Evaluating the Free Trade Deal* (Toronto: C.D. Howe Institute, 1988), 31; Hufbauer and Schott, *North American Free Trade*, 6.
83. Judy MacDonald, "Talkin' Trade," *This Magazine*, 23 (December 1989): 42.
84. Jennifer Lewington, "It Began as a Case of Self-Defence," *Globe and Mail*, 12 November 1988, D1.
85. Canadian Alliance for Trade and Job Opportunities, "Straight Talk on Free Trade," *Maclean's*, (Advertising Supplement) 21 November 1988, 24; Peter Cook, "Free Trade Fears: Zap, Zap, Zap You're Frozen," *Globe and Mail*, 11 November 1988, B2.
86. "We Can Impose Import Laws with the Deal - U.S.," *Sault Star*, 17 November 1988, A6.
87. D'Arcy Jenish, "A New Hard Line on Trade," *Maclean's*, 22 May 1989, 31; In 1992, the Canadian government listed 47 U.S. barriers to trade in response to the list the U.S. issues every year. American barriers to trade from a Canadian perspective included subsidies to defense and NASA contractors; handouts to American grain and oilseed farmers which depress export prices for Canadian grains (this was a major complaint made by many countries against American farm subsidies in the current GATT negotiations); tight sugar quotas which hamper Canadian exports of corn syrup and other industrial sweeteners; delays and unfair procedures under U.S. trade remedy laws; the Buy America Act which limits the purchase of Canadian goods by the U.S. government; and laws impeding the access of Canadian banks to the American securities and insurance markets.

88. Hurtig, *The Betrayal of Canada*, 374; Trade disputes that occur under the FTA and NAFTA are handled much the same way they were handled prior to the FTA. If a Canadian firm believes that it has been hurt by American firms that have been dumping goods in Canada or produce goods using unfair subsidies, the Canadian firm can seek redress through Revenue Canada which will then launch an investigation. In the U.S., an American firm would approach the commerce department with its complaint. Revenue Canada decisions are appealed to the Canadian International Trade Tribunal. Commerce department decisions are reviewed by the United States International Trade Commission. The FTA just adds to this process of dispute settlement a final court of appeal in the guise of a bilateral (now trilateral) dispute settlement panel. Decisions made by this panel are not binding as later evidence will show. Furthermore, the dispute settlement process often takes a year or more for each decision. During this time, the targeted company must pay the surcharge or import duty. If the bilateral panel finds that the targeted firm or sector has been trading fairly and the aggrieved party adheres to the panel's decision, the surcharge payments will be returned to the exporter(s) in question. The routine however, is that the firm is presumed guilty until found innocent. For example, if an accused Canadian company wants to continue to export into the United States, it must first post the bond before its goods can cross into the United States.
89. Simon Reisman, "Free Trade Will Strengthen Canada's Ability to Survive as a Strong Free Nation," *Canadian Speeches*, 1, no. 7 (1987): 2; Gordon Ritchie, "The Negotiating Process," In *Free Trade: The Real Story*, John Crispo ed. (Toronto: Gage Educational Publishing, 1988), 16.
90. John Ferguson, "Reisman Accuses Americans of Thuggery in Trade Dealings," *Sault Star*, 18 January 1992, B16; Gordon Ritchie, "The Free Trade Agreement Revisited," *The American Review of Canadian Studies*, 21, no. 2/3 (1991): 212.
91. Keith Damsell and Peter Morton, "Open Trade Door, Maclaren Warns," *Financial Post*, 24 September 1994, 1.
92. Statistics Canada, *Employment Earnings and Hours* (Ottawa: Supply and Services, 1993), 32; Statistics Canada, *Canada: A Portrait* (Ottawa: Supply and Services, 1989), 199.
93. Lynne Olver, "MP Hails End of 'Devastating' Lumber Tax," *Sault Star*, 4 September 1991, A6.
94. Eduardo Lachica, "U.S. Issues Rule Against Canada Lumber Imports," *Wall Street Journal*, 18 May 1992, A2.
95. "Foresters Chop Down U.S. Softwood Proposal," *Sault Star*, 8 April 1992, A6.
96. Ken Bradsher, "U.S. Told to Review Lumber Duty," *New York Times*, 27 July 1993, C5; Kelly McParland, "Cross-border TradeIssues Unresolved," *Financial Post*, 24 December 1993, C5.
97. Ken Romain, "Steel Industry Under Pressure From U.S. Actions," *Globe and Mail*, 11 November 1988, B1.
98. Barbara Wickens, "Hammered By Trade Laws, Canadian Steel Producers Face U.S. Penalties," *Maclean's*, 5 July 1993, 21
99. "Stelco finds trade deal not working," *Sault Star*, 26 January 1991, A7.

100. Clyde Farnsworth, "Canadians Seek Freer Trade in Steel," *New York Times*, 20 July 1992, C5.
101. "Panel Rejects Ruling of Unfair Subsidies for Canadian Hogs," *Wall Street Journal*, 20 May 1992, B3; Eric Beauchesne, "Joint Committee Will Settle Port Standoff - Crosbie," *Sault Star*, 16 April 1991, A1.
102. Holmes, "Industrial Restructuring in a Period of Crisis," 35.
103. James Daw, "Michigan to Resume Fight If Deal Dies," *Toronto Star*, 18 November 1988, C1.
104. ECC, *Venturing Forth*, 10; External Affairs Canada, Canada's New Free Trade Agreement: Key Benefits, 9; Paul Wonnacott, "The Auto Pact: Plus or Minus," in *Free Trade: The Real Story*, John Crispo, ed. (Toronto: Gage Educational Publishing, 1988), 65.
105. Ross Laver, "A Collision Course," *Maclean's*, 1 July 1992, 84-85.
106. William Safire, "Canada's Comeback Kid," *New York Times*, 23 March 1992, A13.
107. Tony Wohlfarth, "Honda: What's at Stake?" *Action Canada Network Dossier*, 36 (March 1992). 4; Susan Smith, "Toyota's Canadian Strategy," *Financial Post*, 8 April 1995, 16.
108. Mark Hallman, "No Special Deal in Cars," *Financial Post*, 30 October 1991, 3; Clyde Farnsworth, "U.S. Trade Pact a Spur to Canada," *New York Times*, 22 July 1992, C1; Kenneth Bacon, "Quick Reaction: Trade Pact is Likely to Step Up Business Even Before Approval," *Wall Street Journal*, 13 August 1992, A1, A10.
109. Tom Fennell,et al., "A Free Trade Anniversary," 44.
110. Hufbauer and Schott, *North American Free Trade*, 29-39.
111. CLC, "Briefing Notes on the North American Free Trade Agreement," (Ottawa: Unpublished Document from the CLC, 1992), 9.
112. "Canadian Elections Hinge on Trade Pact," *Des Moines Register*, 19 August 1988, 8S.
113. Jonathon Lemco, Richard Belons and Laura Subrin, "The Free Trade Agreement: Initial Winners and Losers," *Canada-U.S. Outlook*, 2, no. 1 (1990): 10.
114. Statistics Canada, *Canada's Balance of International Payments* (Ottawa: Supply and Services, 1993), 78.
115. Campbell, *A Critique of "The Global Trade Challenge,"* 10.
116. "Bankruptcies Hit Record," *Sault Star*, 30 January 1992, B16; Statistics Canada, *Employment Earnings and Hours*, 1; "Bankruptcies Down," *Maclean's*, 15 August 1994, 29; Federal Reserve Bank of St. Louis, *International Economic Conditions*, February (1995): 11.
117. John Crispo, *Making Canada Work: Competing in the Global Economy* (Toronto: Random House, 1992), 64; McGaughey, *A U.S.-Mexico-Canada Free Trade Agreement*, 73.
118. Chris Wood, "A Distrust of Government," *Maclean's*, 1 January 1990, 23; Hurtig, *Betrayal of Canada*, 13.
119. The Bank of Canada was established to be an independent branch of the State that reports to and provides independent advice to the Department of Finance on issues of monetary policy. The Bank of Canada utilizes interest rates, exchange rates and public statements influencing private expectations to shape economic development in Canada.

120. Canadian Manufacturers' Association, The Canadian Chamber of Commerce, and The BCNI, "Joint Statement on the National Economy" (Ottawa: Unpublished Press Release, 1990); Crispo, *Making Canada Work*, 64.
121. Bernard Simon, "Bank Governor is Hero After Fall in Inflation," *Financial Times*, 9 December 1992, 24.
122. Madelaine Drohan, "U.S. Cuts Rates, Canada Doesn't: Wilson Sees Problems in Following the U.S. Lead," *Globe and Mail*, 14 July 1990, B1.
123. John Berry, "Economists Say Blocs May Block Free Trade, Regional Accords Seen As Troubling," *Washington Post*, 4 September 1991.
124. Story, "The Canadian Dollar," 48; Marian Stinson, "Dollar Zooms to a 7-year High as Buying Clamor Hits Markets," *Globe and Mail*, 1 December 1988, B1.
125. Deirdre McMurdy, "A Show of Strength," *Maclean's*, 28 October 1991, 40; G. Norcliffe, "Regional Labour Market Adjustments in a Period of Structural Transformations: An Assessment of the Canadian Case," *The Canadian Geographer*, 38, no. 1 (1994): 7.
126. Canada, *Inflation and the Canadian Economy: A Report by the Department of Finance* (Ottawa: Supply and Services, 1991), 3.
127. CLC, *CLC Free Trade Briefing Document* 2 (July 1989): 22.
128. James Daw, "Interest Rate Strategy 'Crude' Executive Says," *Toronto Star*, 8 June 1990, F1; John Daly, "A Triple Threat," *Maclean's*, 8 October 1990, 48.
129. Shawn McCarthy, "Economists See 'Glimmer' in the Gloom," *Toronto Star*, 1 June 1991, C1; Crispo, *Making Canada Work*, 64.
130. Dobbin, "Thomas d'Aquino: The De Facto PM," 9.
131. John Crow, "Monetary Policy Must Aim for Zero Inflation," *Canadian Speeches*, 3 no. 9 (1990): 23.
132. Duncan Cameron, "Crow Rates," *Canadian Forum*, 69 (September 1990): 11; CLC, *CLC Free Trade Briefing Document*, 7 (January 1991): 1.
133. Errol Black and Guy Landry, "Guess Who Wants High Interest Rates," *Canadian Dimension*, 23, no. 3 (1989): 17.
134. Cameron, "Crow Rates," 11.
135. Ibid.
136. Ibid.
137. Charlene Lee, "Canadian Dollar Falls to 28-month Low on Signs Ottawa May Seek Cut in Rates," *Wall Street Journal*, 12 May 1992, C15.
138. Black and Landry, "Guess Who Wants High Interest Rates?" 16.
139. CLC, *CLC Free Trade Briefing Document*, 7 (January 1991): 2.
140. Ibid.
141. Clyde Farnsworth, "Economic Spur Set by U.S. and Canada in New Pact," *New York Times*, 5 October 1987, A1.
142. Andrew Jackson, *Job Losses in Canadian Manufacturing: 1989-1991* (Ottawa: CLC, 1991), 1.
143. CLC, *CLC Free Trade Briefing Document*, 7 (January 1991): 2.
144. Tony Van Alphen, "Dollar, Trade Pact at Odds, Lougheed Says," *Toronto Star*, 1 January 1991, B1.

Chapter 4

Canadian Labour and Free Trade

For much of the twentieth century, Canada followed the American lead in labour relations. In the first three decades of the twentieth century, Canadian managers emulated American managers who were using the scientific management methods proposed by F. W. Taylor. After the Second World War, there was further convergence as Canadian corporations adopted the Fordist model of labour relations first established by the Roosevelt Administration during the Depression. By the late 1960s however, American workers began to lose ground while Canadian workers retained many of the gains made during the rise of Fordism. After three decades of convergence in labour relations under Fordism, American workers witnessed the erosion of their hard-won rights while Canadian workers managed to solidify and even advance the cause of workers' rights along the Fordist model. This divergence between workers' rights in Canada and the United States was tolerated until the economic crisis of the 1980s. Fordist labour relations were perceived by corporate interests in Canada to be blocking the necessary restructuring that would lead to renewed corporate profitability. The problem confronting corporate interests was how to dismantle the edifice of Fordist labour relations without losing legitimacy in the eyes of the Canadian populace. This chapter argues that the FTA was the corporate solution to the labour problem. The market pressures created by a post-Fordist continental model of development would be able to force a reconvergence between Canadian and American wages, labour relations and practices.

The Rise and Demise of Fordist Labour Relations in Canada.

While Fordist labour relations existed in the 1930s and still exist today, they reached their zenith in the postwar period leading up to the crisis of Fordism in the 1970s. Canadian Fordist labour relations evolved as a palliative to growing labour militancy and management intransigence prior to World War Two. In 1911, prior to the era of Fordism, production in the industrialized world was influenced by the research of Frederick W. Taylor and his scientific management methods. Efficiency experts came onto the shop floor with note pads and stop watches in order to eliminate superfluous worker movement, standardize worker tasks, minimize worker autonomy, and increase overall worker output while increasing management control over production. In Canada, the principles of scientific management had their greatest impact in the industrial heartland of Canada: the nascent automotive industry, textiles and new industrial staples such as ore smelting and pulp and paper processing. Taylor's handpicked disciple, Henry Gantt, reorganized the locomotive repair facilities of the Canadian Pacific Railroad in Montréal along the lines proposed by his mentor.[1]

Of course, there was wide regional variation in the ability of factory owners in Canada to implement the principles of scientific management. The success of Taylor's principles in the heartland of southern Ontario and Québec contrasted starkly with the dismal failure of Taylorism in the mines, on the docks or in the lumber camps of the Canadian hinterland. Taylorist practices were therefore not universally applicable and were regionally concentrated in central Canada where mass production, innovation and expanding markets were increasingly important. Despite this regionalized application of scientific management, Taylor's concern for increasing worker efficiency had an ideological impact that extended across Canada regardless of region or economic sector. As management attempted to increase worker efficiency, labour relations became increasingly adversarial. Canadian labour leaders attempted to organize workers to protect wages and worker control but attempts to foster union growth fell on fallow ground.

During the first three decades of the twentieth century, the Canadian economy was increasingly dominated by monopoly capital which ushered in new patterns of investment, corporate organization and banking practices. Heavy investments were made in Canada by American corporations who wanted to avoid the tariffs imposed by the British Empire. Canadian union organizers met with little success in this era of increasing corporate concentration and rapid industrialization. Management used a two-pronged strategy to counter the organizing efforts of Canadian labour leaders. Factory owners first resorted to a strategy of paternalism to dampen worker militancy. Factory beautification programmes, profit sharing plans, industrial councils that "smothered unionism in a suffocating rhetoric of worker-employer cooperation," and leisure activities such as company picnics and recreation programmes were used to reduce the effectiveness of union organizing efforts.[2] If paternalism failed to quell labour unrest, managers resorted to the tried-and-true methods of worker control such as union busting, blacklisting, firing of militant labour leaders and overt violence. Authoritarian actions taken during the Winnipeg

General Strike of 1919 epitomized the attitude taken by capital and the State towards Canadian unions during this period.[3]

The 1930s witnessed continued capital concentration and retrenchment in the Canadian economy. As British capital withdrew from Canada during the Depression, American capital gained a greater foothold in the Canadian economy. Economic upheaval in the Depression prompted the Canadian government to launch the Royal Commission on Price Spreads. This commission concluded that while many small firms where going bankrupt, well-established firms intensified their hold on core industries. Canadian monopolies fared well during this period earning rates of return of 12 percent annually, while firms in competitive sectors were losing money. The largest of the successful firms, such as those in the automotive and the electrical products industries, were American-owned branch plants. American firms were persuaded to invest in Canada by a combination of the protectionist effects of the U.S. Smoot-Hawley Tariffs of 1930 and the British Imperial Preference Tariffs of 1932 of which Canada was a participant. Resource exports, a cornerstone of the Canadian economy, collapsed as protectionism increased in the global economy. Industries reliant upon exports such as the pulp and paper industry only operated at 53 percent capacity while mineral exports dropped by 60 percent between 1929 and 1939.[4] Because the hinterland regions of the Prairies and Maritimes depended upon resource exports, workers in these regions suffered more than workers in the industrial heartland of central Canada which was increasingly being dominated by branch plants from America. Despite attempts to organize during the 1930s by such groups as the Workers' Unity League, unions in the hinterland were devastated by the economic collapse of the Depression.

By the mid-1930s, the centre of Canadian strike activity had shifted from the hinterland to the cities of the industrial heartland such as Toronto and Hamilton where unions struggled for recognition in the burgeoning steel, automobile, meat packing and textile industries. The Depression dramatically altered the socioeconomic landscape of Canada. The Depression disabused Canadians of the notion that unemployed workers could solve their problems by relocating to an agricultural or resource frontier. The rise of industry in central Canada demonstrated the superior incomes and stability of industrial employment. While better than the resource-based jobs of the hinterland, workers still had to struggle to gain representation through industrial unions. The rise of "Big Labour" came late to Canada, trailing the development of "Big Business" and "Big Government."[5] On the eve of

World War Two, the percentage of nonagricultural workers represented by unions was the same as it was in 1914.

This scenario changed as the concentration of Canadian industry into fewer, more centrally located companies in the industrial heartland facilitated the growth of industrial unions in Canada. Many of the new Canadian industrial unions were organized to bargain with the managers of U.S. branch plants. The Canadian unions themselves were often just extensions of the American unions. Union leadership from the United States was welcomed by Canadian union organizers because American unions had the necessary start-up funds and organizing expertise. The legitimacy of American unions in Canada was bolstered in 1935 when President Roosevelt implemented the National Labor Relations Act. Also called the Wagner Act, this legislation guaranteed the right of American workers to bargain collectively through representatives of their own choosing. The momentum gained by American workers spilled over into Canada. In the late 1930s, Canadian workers, heartened by the success of American unions, called a number of unionization and recognition strikes. The Canadian State attempted to counter the renewed vigor of the Canadian labour movement through the War Measures Act of 1939. Using the excuse of the Second World War which Canada had just entered, this legislation attempted to repress union activity. However, workers were in short supply. Unions were able to use this fact as a lever to wrest concessions out of the Canadian government.

A series of strikes and provincial labour reforms in 1942 and 1943 culminated in new Canadian federal legislation in 1944 which was modeled after the U.S. Wagner Act. The official name of this legislation was Order-in-Council PC 1003, but Canadian union leaders called it the Magna Carta of Canadian labour law because of the sweeping changes it brought to Canadian labour relations.[6] PC 1003 granted new freedoms to Canadian workers such as the right to organize, the certification of collective bargaining units, and compulsory collective bargaining rights in exchange for a truce on the shop floor.

Seeds planted by union leaders in the late 1930s were beginning to germinate as Fordist labour relations took root in industrial Canada in the 1940s. By following the Wagner model, Fordist labour relations in Canada became tied to a regulated and delimited form of adversarialism. This approach to industrial relations differed from the corporatist co-determination models adopted by Sweden and Austria. In these and other Western European countries, structures of a more thorough-going industrial democracy such as workers' councils and employee representation on corporate boards allowed employees to participate in managerial decisions directly affecting the plight of unions. Under the Wagner model adopted in the United States and then Canada, labour and management recognized each other as legitimate adversaries. Conflict between them was to be regulated through agreed upon rules and structures which both sides were expected to "respect in good faith."[7] The role of the State was to enforce adherence to these rules and act as an impartial arbiter when disputes could not be resolved through negotiation. In Canada, the State intruded into the sphere of industrial relations primarily through labour relations boards which had been set up at the federal level and in all ten provinces. The Wagner model had diffused throughout Canada by the 1960s. Even the public sector had gained the right to strike. This broke with the long-standing British and Canadian tradition that "the crown [did] not bargain" with workers.[8]

The diffusion of Fordist labour relations throughout Canada was no mean feat. Workers had to struggle in the postwar period to extend the Fordist model beyond its modest beginnings in southern Ontario. The onset of peace worried union leaders who believed that returning soldiers would increase the reserve army of labour. Increasing unemployment could undermine worker solidarity that had been nurtured during the war. If workers were not united, the recognition of unions and the right to strike gained on paper in PC 1003 would not help workers in practice. Furthermore, unions had never managed to impose a "closed shop" in the mills and factories of Canada. Union leaders believed that the closed shop would enhance worker solidarity and provide the necessary resources to bargain effectively with management.[9]

The first test of peacetime labour relations came in 1945 with a strike at the Windsor, Ontario Ford plant. The union, which represented the 17,000 workers at the Windsor facility, insisted on a closed shop to stabilize union membership and finances. The Windsor strike was settled by what was called the Rand Formula. The Canadian government assigned Justice Ivan Rand to arbitrate the labour-management stalemate that had brought car production in Windsor to a standstill. He decreed that all workers in a unionized shop have an automatic check-off on their paychecks to provide unions with sufficient resources to bargain with management. Justice Rand had provided Canadian workers with the union shop, the next best thing to the closed shop desired by labour leaders. The Rand Formula also restricted the shop floor tyranny of the foreman by imposing a litany of impersonal rules and grievance procedures.

The Canadian government further codified workers' rights by grafting the wartime PC 1003 policy onto the peacetime Industrial Disputes Investigations Act in 1948. This amended legislation came to be called the Industrial Relations and Dispute Investigation Act (IRDI Act). The IRDI Act was the single most important piece of labour legislation in the postwar period because it ensured that gains made by labour during wartime were not lost as returning soldiers flooded the labour market. After the federal government promulgated the IRDI Act, the provinces without comprehensive labour laws adopted laws modeled after the IRDI Act. Organized labour in Canada was gaining the legitimacy that it had longed for. By 1950, 90 percent of Canadian unions had secured the Rand Formula as a model for industrial relations. Furthermore, union membership rose from 16 percent of the labour force in 1940 to 29 percent in 1949. The Canadian Welfare State also expanded in the immediate postwar period to meet the demands of labour and an expanding population. New programmes included the Unemployment Insurance Commission, the Department of Health and Welfare and the Central Mortgage and Housing Corporation. These programmes stimulated effective demand by helping employed workers to purchase new suburban houses filled with consumer durables and by helping unemployed workers maintain consumption patterns adopted when they had jobs.

During the 1950s, Canadian unions continued to follow trends originating in the United States. In 1947, the United States government modified many of the pro-labour provisions of the Wagner Act. The Labor-Management Relations Act of 1947, also called the Taft-Hartley Act, outlawed the closed shop, required union officials to sign affidavits condemning communism and curtailed many workers' rights gained in the 1930s.[10] Anti-communism and anti-unionism running rampant in the United States affected labour relations and politics in Canada as well. During the same period, Canadian unions had won a forty-hour work week, paid holidays, expanded pensions and medical benefits, strict job classifications to protect skill levels and guarantees of equal pay for equal work. However, Cold War politics cast a pall over the radical elements of Canadian labour and leftist political parties. The Communist Party of Canada withered away during the 1950s under pressure from outside and even from within organized labour.[11]

In the 1940s, Canadian workers found a stalwart ally in the Canadian Commonwealth Federation (CCF), the forerunner to the New Democratic Party (NDP). Many CCF candidates were elected to provincial legislatures in British Columbia, Alberta, Saskatchewan, Ontario and Nova Scotia on a platform advocating universal health care and increased worker rights. In 1944 the CCF won 47 of 52 seats in the Saskatchewan provincial election while winning enough seats in British Columbia to become the official opposition in the provincial legislature. By the early 1950s, the CCF had dropped its socialist rhetoric under the pressure of red-baiting and the pacifying effect of Fordist labour relations. The death-blow for radical worker politics in Canada was delivered during the 1958 federal election when the CCF only garnered 10 percent of the popular vote.[12] The CCF was resurrected in 1961 as the New Democratic Party, but it had been shorn of the radical doctrines of its predecessor, entering mainstream Canadian politics as a more centrist social democratic entity. Just as the radical elements had been purged from American organized labour and politics during McCarthyism, the radical Left had been eliminated from the Canadian political scene. Canadian labour established the more modest goal of maintaining legitimacy within capitalism rather than transforming capitalism.

Convergence between Canadian and American labour practices and organization increased during the 1950s in other ways as well. In the United States, the Congress of Industrial Organizations (CIO) was moving far to the right and had basically converted to business unionism. In 1955, the CIO merged with the American Federation of Labor (AFL) to form the AFL-CIO. In Canada, the Canadian Labour Congress (CLC) had so many ties to American unions that it was perceived to be "largely a northern echo" of the AFL-CIO.[13] Canadian unions mirrored the development of their southern counterparts because nearly 70 percent of organized workers in English-speaking Canada were members of international unions headquartered in the United States. The CLC retained its more radical bent because of its ties to the CCF, but it adopted many of the labour demands, negotiating strategies and leadership practices of the AFL-CIO.

By the middle of the 1950s, the development of Canada's permeable Fordism could be seen in full outline. As mentioned, the permeable nature of Canada's Fordist model of development came first from American investment in Canada and Canadian reliance on the United States as a market for resource exports. The permeable nature of Canadian Fordism was reinforced through the dominance of Canadian workers by their American-based unions.[14] Some of the largest Canadian unions were actually affiliated with such American union giants as the United Auto Workers (UAW) and the United Steel Workers of America. In both the United States and Canada, the Fordist regulation of labour relations had become focused on the private sector with the State playing a supporting role in the mediation of industrial relations. It should be stated however, that the State played a much greater role in Canadian Fordist labour relations than it did in the United States. For example, the Canadian federal industrial relations legislation of the 1940s and 1950s such as the Rand Formula and the IRDI Act set basic guidelines for collective bargaining in Canada. Like the United States, Canada is a federal system that allowed provincial variations in union rights. Unlike the United States, Canada did not allow the creation of Canadian provincial equivalents of the right-to-work states where the open shop could undermine union strength.

It is in this regard that one can start to see how Canadian and American union movements began to diverge in the 1950s and 1960s with regard to the maintenance of labour reforms won in earlier times. Canada had closely followed the American model of industrial relations through the first half of the twentieth century. The Wagner Act of 1935 represented the crowning achievement of the American labour movement because it legitimated the right to organize and the right to strike for higher wages. Canadian workers envied those achievements to such an extent that they struggled through the Second World War to secure a labour accord similar to the Wagner Act. Despite these pioneering efforts, American unions have been in retreat since the late 1950s while Canadian unions forged ahead before losing ground in the 1980s. In 1961, union density (union membership as a percent of all wage and salary earners) stood at about 31 percent in both Canada and the United States. By 1985, overall union density had dropped to 18 percent in the United States but had risen to 37 percent in Canada (Figure 22). The divergence in labour movement success between Canada and the U.S. can also be seen by comparing union density in particular economic sectors (Figure 23).

How was it that American unions faltered in the 1960s while Canadian unions made progress until the 1980s? The decline of American labour can be attributed to the lack of a social democratic party in the United States.[15] In Canada, the NDP has managed to protect many labour freedoms because even when it has lacked influence in Ottawa, it has exerted a continuous influence at the provincial level since World War Two. In 1994, after a decade of neoconservative politics in Canada, the NDP became the ruling party in Ontario, Canada's industrial heartland and most populous province. In the United States, unions do not have a comparable pro-labour ally in the State because even the Democratic Party has a corporate or neoconservative bias. Without a dependable pro-labour political party, the American labour accord that established the Wagner model in the 1930s began to weaken in the 1950s,

Figure 22
Union Density in the United States and Canada

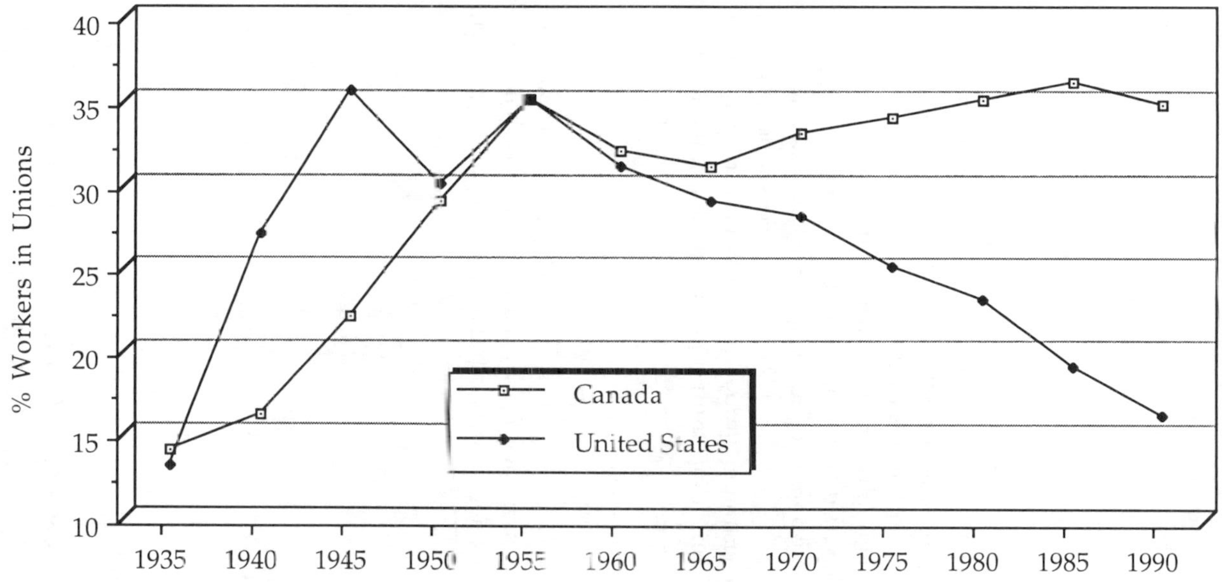

Source: Mike Davis, Prisoners of the American Dream (New York: Verso, 1986), 146; Statistics Canada, Canadian Economic Observer (Ottawa: Supply and Services, 1995), 35.

Figure 23
Canadian and American Union Density in 1984 by Sector (%)

Economic Sector	Unionized In Canada	Unionized In the U.S.
Manufacturing	45.0	26.0
Mining	32.8	17.7
Transportation	54.9	37.7
Services	38.1	7.3
Government	66.6	35.8
Retail	12.4	7.8

Source: Rianne Mahon, "Post-Fordism: Some Issues for Labour," In *The New Era of Global Competition*, ed. Daniel Drache and Meric Gertler (Montreal: McGill-Queen's, 1991), 326.

and eventually unraveled in the crisis of Fordism during the 1970s. As the Fordist labour accord disintegrated, American industrial relations became increasingly adversarial.

Management replaced good faith bargaining with explicit policies of union decertification. Some employers used arcane provisions within existing labour law to delay the recognition and certification of newly organized unions. In some cases, firms resisted attempts by their workers to unionize by deliberately flouting labour laws. Penalties for illegally resisting workers in this way have been either light or nonexistent. The success rate for union certification elections in the United States declined from 80 percent in 1949 to 50 percent in 1980.[16]

Apart from overt attempts to abrogate the labour accord, management also attempted to rework it by subverting the adversarial and rigid nature of Fordist labour relations. In placc of the Fordist Wagner model — with its strict definitions of managerial prerogatives and union rights — management attempted to introduce more flexible approaches. Borrowing from the "co-operative strategies" employed by the Japanese, the new post-Fordist, post-Wagner American model of labour relations emphasized flexible job descriptions, informal dispute settlement procedures and the explicit recognition of a segmented labour force. Managers wanted to separate a small group of highly-trained core employees with good job security from a much larger group of peripheral employees who could be hired and fired depending on market conditions. While scholars have debated how pervasive these reforms have been in the United States, it is safe to say that workers in the United States have been under increasing pressure since the 1970s to adopt new forms of flexible production.[17] This pressure, rooted in the crisis of Fordism, ushered in an era of economic and labour market restructuring not seen in the United States since the Depression.

Developments in the United States have had profound implications for workers in Canada. It is true that Canadian workers had accomplished much between the 1940s and 1970s. They prospered during the Fordist era as union membership increased from 15 percent of the labour force in 1940 to 35 percent in 1970. Fordist labour relations had helped workers to quadruple their wages and to double their purchasing power. Canadian workers benefited from an expanded Canada Pension Plan and Unemployment Insurance Plan. Union leaders could look back on thirty years of progress, but the crisis of Fordism threatened to undo much that had been won. Inflation posed the greatest challenge to labour during this period. Inflation ate into wages making life increasingly difficult for the average worker. Inflation prompted non-unionized workers to seek representation in order to keep wage increases tied to inflation. This was a futile tactic because even some of the strongest unions failed to receive wage increases proportional to cost of living increases. Unemployment and wage figures began to show that many working families were being left behind.[18] The Fordist ideals of full employment and universal access to social welfare programmes proved to be illusory for an increasing number of Canadians. Strike activity burgeoned in the early 1970s due to increasing worker frustrations. The level of frustration can be measured in the fact that 25 percent of all strike activity between 1900 and 1975 occurred between 1971 and 1975.[19] Canadian businesses were growing tired of the adversarial Wagner model which had led to even more confrontations during the spate of strikes of the early 1970s. Canadian managers, in co-operation with the State, looked to the United States for new strategies that could reduce worker militancy while restoring corporate profitability.

The economic malaise of the early 1980s revealed the fundamental weaknesses of the Canadian model of development with its dependence on resource exports and branch plant manufacturing. The first corporate strategy prompted by these weaknesses entailed replacing militant workers with automated production facilities. Throughout the nineteenth and twentieth centuries, management has tried to make resource extraction and export a more capital intensive endeavor. Primary industries such as mining operations are not as mobile as other industries because the inputs have to be extracted from a particular point under the surface of the earth. Immobility makes resource-based firms more susceptible to the demands of militant labour. Increased automation during the 1970s offset the vulnerability of resource-based firms by decreasing labour requirements. Herein lies an important source of hinterland unemployment and labour unrest. Canadian branch plants also experienced increased labour militancy. Their American managers suggested that worker unrest could be reduced through a judicious use of capital investment, worker replacement and labour force restructuring.

The Canadian State also helped ameliorate the impact of economic crisis on profitability. As inflation increased, managers demanded higher profits while workers demanded higher wages to offset price increases. Employers responded by laying off workers in ever-increasing numbers. Government programmes were stretched to the limit as unemployment benefits and job retraining vouchers were automatically distributed at an ever-increasing pace. Public sector deficits soon increased dramatically in response to rising unemployment. In the face of rising unemployment, 14 percent inflation and a fiscal crisis, the Canadian minister of finance implemented a wage and price control programme in 1975 to corral out-of-control State expenditures. The three-year programme managed by the Anti-Inflation Board restricted wage and price increases to 10 percent in the first year, 8 percent in the second year and 6 percent in the final year. A study performed by the Conference Board of Canada concluded that the wage and price controls were more effective at constraining wage increases than price increases, concluding that wage earners suffered disproportionately during this time.[20]

The crisis of Fordism prompted private and public employers to use strategies to drive down wages beyond those accomplished by the Anti-Inflation Board. From 1975 until 1987, the minimum wage in Canada fell 20 percent when compared to the average industrial wage.[21] This erosion occurred as firms hired more part-time and temporary workers. Part-time and temporary workers are an inexpensive alternative to permanent full-time employees because they usually have no union representation and companies seldom pay for health care or retirement benefits. Labour force segmentation during the 1970s and 1980s led to a situation where an ever decreasing proportion of workers held full-time high-paying jobs while an increasing proportion earned minimum wages. Even the Economic Council of Canada (ECC) noted that the Canadian labour force was becoming polarized. In 1981, 56 percent of the Canadian paid labour force was employed on a full-time basis. By 1987, that figure had dropped to 50 percent.[22]

In Canada, the State employs a large number of workers at minimum wage levels. By doing so, the State sends a powerful message to the private sector that workers do not have to be adequately compensated when there is an increasingly large reserve of labour desperate to work.[23] In helping to drive down wages, the Canadian State was emulating the policy used by the United States to discipline labour. In the United States, minimum wage legislation has been used extensively to reshape the labour market and wage structure during the 1970s and 1980s. So successful was this strategy during the Reagan years that the Joint Economic Committee of Congress reported that from 1980 to 1987, eight of the thirteen million jobs created in the United States paid less than Can$8,000 per year and half of the thirteen million jobs have kept families below the poverty line.[24] The Canadian State understood that Canadian unions had survived the neoconservative onslaught better than American unions. The Canadian State also saw that minimum wage legislation had worked against the American unions so the Tories adopted this policy in Canada. Here was an attempt to create a continent-wide, low-wage economy even before the FTA was implemented.

The importation of Reagan's brand of neoconservatism spelled trouble for Canadian workers during the 1980s. Probably the most famous anti-worker action taken by Reagan was the firing of air traffic controllers who went on strike in August of 1981. Reagan went on national TV and warned the Professional Air Traffic Controllers Organization (PATCO) that if they did not return to work in 48 hours, they would be fired. When the air traffic controllers did not return as ordered, Reagan fired the federal employees in order to break the strike and eventually the PATCO union. The president was sending a clear message to both business and labour: the Reagan Administration had embarked on a mission to transform labour relations in America. Expect a pro-business environment to be promoted at the expense of labour. Canadian business organizations such as the BCNI picked up on this message and relayed it to the Canadian government. The Canadian corporate message was that labour relations had become intractable and the Welfare State had become unwieldy. Greater flexibility in the Canadian labour force was pivotal if higher profits were going to be achieved.

The Canadian State obliged the business agenda in manifold ways. First of all, labour rights were circumscribed at the provincial and federal level in response to corporate demands. In 1979, the Nova Scotia legislature, controlled by the Progressive Conservatives, made it more difficult for workers to certify a new union. The new law said that a union had to obtain the support of a majority of the workers at all locations where an employer carried on business rather than on a shop-by-shop basis. The Canadian press called this the Michelin Bill because Michelin Tire said that it would leave Nova Scotia unless restraints were placed on unions. During 1982, the Trudeau government restricted the ability of government employees to strike and imposed another set of wage controls on government workers. Provincial governments from the right-wing Social Credit Party of British Columbia to the left-wing Parti Québecois followed with similar restraints on provincial employees. British Columbia implemented the most aggressive anti-union legislation in 1987. The Social Credit Party passed Bill 19 which restricted picketing, facilitated decertification and constrained strikes under certain circumstances in order to attract investment to British Columbia.

By establishing an overtly pro-business environment, the Canadian government was creating the conditions where businesses in Canada could more easily implement flexible or post-Fordist production and management techniques. Business managers believed that flexible specialization improved upon Fordist production in a number of ways. Flexible specialization was promoted for its purported greater reliance on skilled workers, increased employee participation in the workplace, and its emphasis on a "worker trained to be more like a self-motivated artisan than a classic proletarian.[25] Skeptics doubted that flexible specialization could improve the conditions for the average worker when this reorganization was done primarily to boost productivity.

In order to understand how post-Fordist production negatively affects the worker, one must consider what flexibility really means. Three types of flexibility in post-Fordist production can be identified: financial, functional and numerical.[26] Financial flexibility cuts costs by rationalizing the labour force. Smokestack industries in decline often rely on this form of flexibility which cuts costs by firing workers. Functional flexibility requires that managers make more efficient use of permanent full-time employees by reorganizing production on the shop floor. Strict job classifications are abolished and workers are asked to adopt the "team concept" or "management-by-stress" techniques developed by the Japanese. The Wagner model of labour relations is replaced by a nonunion or open shop environment with informal grievance procedures. Numerical flexibility is achieved by more closely tailoring the size of the work force to the needs of the company. This flexibility can only be attained by segmenting the labour force into a small core of permanent employees and a large number of part-time and temporary workers who can be hired and fired according to economic conditions.

All three flexibility strategies attempt to increase profits by controlling labour costs. Of course other strategies can also increase profits but monitoring labour costs remains a central preoccupation because it is the principle way to maintain discipline on the shop floor. The rhetoric of flexibility hides the intentions of managers who want to exert greater control over the production process. Canadian workers have faced increasing difficulties negotiating the pace of technological change and hence their autonomy on the shop floor. Few unions have contracts that provide protection against layoffs or other changes brought about by new technology. A survey conducted by the ECC found that 80 percent of the managers polled believed that the introduction of new production technology does not require consultation with workers. Canadian companies and MNCs in Canada have rejected the idea that managers and labour leaders should co-operate at the planning and policy level as changes occur on the post-Fordist shop floor. Instead, corporate interests have lobbied the federal government to make Canada internationally competitive by adopting American standards with respect to unemployment insurance, tax structure, the Welfare State, labour laws and macroeconomic policy. During the 1980s, the BCNI and CMA repeatedly complained to the Liberals under Trudeau and then the Tories under Mulroney that Canada's massive social programmes and the coddling of workers have hurt their competitiveness.

Despite the fact that Canadian unions had been hurt by neoconservative reforms during the 1980s, even British Columbia with its right-wing Social Credit Party remained a bastion of Fordist labour relations in North America. The resilience of the Canadian union movement can be attributed in part to the legacy of social democratic political parties at the provincial level. Canadian workers also launched their own strategy to resist changes imposed upon them by union bosses from the United States. Between 1972 and 1986, thirteen Canadian unions broke away from their American parent unions. These secessions involved more than 300,000 Canadian workers. Canadian union leaders perceived that the American parent unions were rolling over too easily to corporate demands for wage concessions, flexible production techniques and less rigid work rules. Canadian unions defected from the American international unions because the Canadian leaders believed that they had better legal standing to resist changes.

The 136,000-member Canadian wing of the UAW expressed its dissatisfaction with the UAW leadership who were perceived to have acquiesced to plant closures and changes in production technology which displaced workers.[27] In 1986, the Canadian wing of the UAW defected to become the independent Canadian Auto Workers (CAW). Canadian unions had been beaten down during the 1980s but the actions of such unions as the CAW revealed that the Canadian union movement could not be ignored. The BCNI and CMA clamored for greater flexibility and less adversarial labour relations but they could not force these issues on Canadian workers without losing legitimacy. In their testimony to the Macdonald Commission, representatives from BCNI were very careful to emphasize the continuing legitimacy of organized labour.[28] It was clear to corporate interests that their agenda could not be fully attained by directly confronting the Canadian union movement. Instead, corporate interests used the more subtle strategy of embedding their agenda in the Macdonald Commission with its facade of objectivity and value-neutrality.

The Macdonald Commission catered to the neoconservative agenda by recommending new and lower benchmarks for job remuneration and social assistance. By cutting unemployment benefits, the State saves money while sending a message to all workers that conditions are getting worse for the unemployed. People should be content with their current position because the Welfare State will no longer provide a satisfactory standard of living. By increasing the sense of insecurity, workers would be more willing to make concessions in order to hold on to their existing jobs. The problem was how to convince workers that their jobs were really at risk unless they accepted flexible production techniques and wage concessions. The Macdonald Commission provided an answer when it recommended that Canada enter into a free trade agreement with the U.S. Despite rollbacks of labour rights by Canadian and American neoconservatives during the 1980s, Canadian workers continued to fare better than their American counterparts. Free trade was pursued by corporate interests because it would permit companies to use the threat of relocation as a mechanism to drive down Canadian wages, to create a more flexible Canadian labour market, and to facilitate the implementation of flexible production techniques over the wishes of workers.

From Fordist To Flexible Labour Relations

Job Loss and Labour Market Restructuring

A pro-business lobby called the Canadian Alliance for Trade and Job Opportunities (CATJO) proclaimed that there would be "more jobs, better jobs" resulting from the FTA. The ECC estimated that the FTA would

Figure 24
Persons Employed in the Canadian Economy (thousands)

Year	Total Employed	Manufacturing Sector	Trade Sector
1984	11,000	1,968	1,929
1985	11,311	1,981	2,001
1986	11,634	2,015	2,082
1987	11,861	2,018	2,097
1988	12,244	2,104	2,168
1989	12,486	2,126	2,186
1990	12,572	2,001	2,247
1991	12,340	1,865	2,169
1992	12,240	1,879	2,155
1993	12,383	1,893	2,138
1994	12,644	1,949	2,199

Source: Statistics Canada, *Canadian Social Trends* 36 (Spring 1995): 35; Statistics Canada, *Canadian Economic Observer* (Ottawa: Supply and Services, 1995), 17.

create three new jobs for every one job lost. The ECC also predicted that the FTA would generate 250,000 new jobs for Canadians between 1989 and 1998. More conservatively, an economist at the University of Wisconsin, stated that the worst-case scenario for Canada would be a 0.2 percent job loss in manufacturing employment.[29]

The reality for the Canadian worker has been quite different. One year after the implementation of free trade, Canada experienced a net loss of over 125,000 jobs.[30] Figure 24 reveals that job growth in Canada has stagnated while the number of manufacturing jobs available to Canadians has dropped. The FTA could not even generate a surplus of jobs in the trade and commerce sector which was supposed to benefit the most under free trade. Figure 25 compares the ECC econometric predictions for job gains and the actual job losses in 1992 for particular sectors in Canada. These specious predictions were used by the Canadian government to justify entering into the FTA.

Figure 25
The Canadian Job Creation Potential of the FTA (%)

Economic Sector	Change Predicted by the ECC in 1988	Actual Change by 1992
Chemicals	-0.1	-4.5
Clothing	+0.7	-25.0
Electrical Products	-1.4	-14.9
Food and Beverage	+0.8	-4.0
Furniture and Fixtures	+0.4	-30.8
Machinery	+0.3	-22.6
Metal Fabrications	+0.4	-25.5
Motor Vehicles / Parts	+0.1	-11.5
Non-metallic Minerals	+0.4	-21.3
Petroleum and Coal	+0.3	-12.5
Primary Metals	+1.2	-17.8
Printing and Publishing	+2.4	-8.5
Pulp and Paper	+0.2	-12.5
Rubber and Plastics	-0.7	-8.9
Textiles	-0.8	-22.0
Wood Industries	+0.4	-16.5

Source: Calculated from ECC, *Venturing Forth*; Statistics Canada, *Manufacturing Industries of Canada: National and Provincial Areas, 1989* (Ottawa: Industry, Science and Technology, 1992); Statistics Canada, *Manufacturing Industries of Canada: National and Provincial Areas, 1991-1992* (Ottawa: Industry, Science and Technology, 1995).

Figure 26
Unemployment Rates in Canada, the United States and the OECD

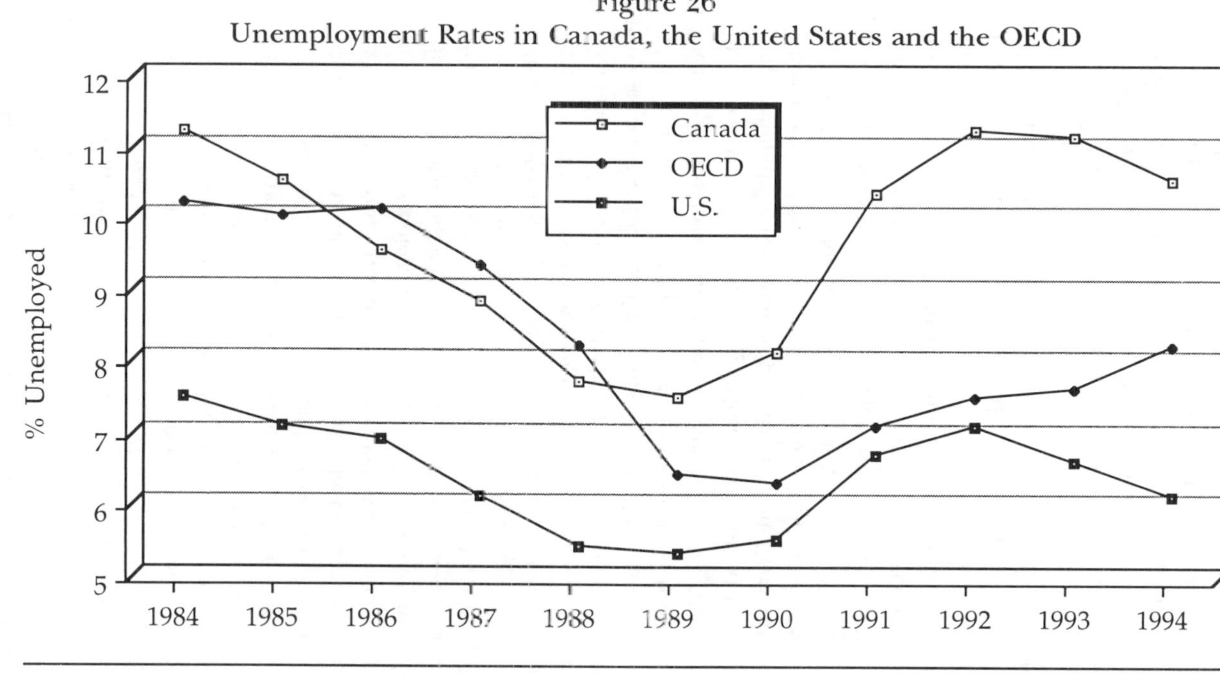

Source: Statistics Canada, Canadian Economic Observer (Ottawa: Supply and Services, 1995), 67; "Economic Outlook," OECD Observer 163 (February 1993).

Unemployment figures confirm that the Canadian labour force has not fared well since the implementation of the FTA. Figure 26 shows that the Canadian unemployment rate dropped steadily during the 1980s until it was about 7 percent in 1989. By mid-1993, over 11 percent of the Canadian labour force was out of work. Of course the recession affecting much of the industrialized world can be blamed for causing some of the job losses in Canada. However, supporters of the FTA such as Canadian trade minister Wilson said that all the job losses were due to the recession.[31] In order to counter these assertions, Figure 26 also compares the Canadian unemployment rate with that of the United States and the other OECD countries. The Canadian unemployment rate was lower than the OECD average during the mid-1980s but then rose dramatically after 1989. While Figure 26 shows a recession effect on unemployment in the United States and the OECD countries, the dramatic upswing in the Canadian unemployment rate reveals that something else is going on besides a recession. The FTA is the primary suspect for causing this increase. Statistics Canada Labour Force Survey data from 1981 to 1990 shows that most of the manufacturing jobs lost during the 1981-82 recession had been regained by 1988. Canada only lost 0.9 percent of its manufacturing employment during the early and mid-1980s. From June 1989 to the end of 1990, Canada lost 6.9 percent of its manufacturing jobs.[32] The job losses in the post-FTA period are therefore of a structural nature and not due to a cyclical downturn in the economy.

In the early 1980s, many people lost their jobs. Most workers were eventually rehired by the company that had laid them off in the first place because the companies did not close down. Only 22 percent of workers lost their jobs due to plant closures during this time. Rising unemployment was mostly due to cyclical job losses.[33] After 1989, 65 percent of all layoffs were due to plant closures. These plants will not be rehiring. Structural job losses are responsible for driving up the unemployment rate after 1989.[34]

The recession can be downplayed as contributing to job loss for other reasons as well. Job losses in Canada amounted to 150,000 even before the official onset of the recession in Canada during the second quarter of 1990.[35] Many Canadian firms and MNCs in Canada went on a merger and acquisitions spree in 1988 and in every year since the FTA was implemented to compete in the larger continental market. Mergers have the unfortunate side-effect of eliminating redundant jobs. Over 10,000 workers lost their jobs in FTA-related mergers and consolidations by such firms as Molson's, Gillette Canada, GM Canada, Jarman Incorporated, and Pittsburgh Paint and Glass.[36] Trimming the payroll has been a central corporate goal during this restructuring period initiated by the FTA. In October 1989, a private agency called the Canadian Institute held seminars instructing senior executives how to best approach the firing of surplus workers. The theme for the seminar was that firing workers is a necessity "when companies merge or restructure in response to free trade and global economic pressures."[37]

The monetary policy adopted by the Bank of Canada has also had a profound impact on the structure of the Canadian labour market. The high interest rate policy affected Canadian workers in two related ways. First, it sparked the appreciation of the Canadian dollar against the United States dollar. The revaluation of the dollar made Canadian exports to the United States more expensive. As the cost of Canadian goods rose south of the border, Americans were less likely to purchase Canadian products. With demand falling in Canada's largest export market, Canadian companies that relied on that market were forced to lay off workers until surplus production was sold off. Particularly hard hit during this time were those who worked in garment industries and resource industries such as logging, forestry and mining (Figure 25).

Second, Canadian workers were directly affected by the impact of high interest rates in the Canadian economy. The governor of the Bank of Canada claims to have adopted high interest rates as an anti-inflation policy. The Canadian Department of Finance stated that although it appears that inflation is not a problem on the surface, the Bank of Canada must continue to treat "the underlying pressures" which are continuing to contribute to inflation. The Department of Finance also claimed that "the most important source of upward pressure on future prices is the price of labour which represents 60 percent of business costs." Labour is being blamed for inflation. High interest rates were implemented to slow down the economy and increase unemployment in order to discipline labour. The monetary policy of the Bank of Canada, by its own admission, was designed to discipline labour and "curb inflationary pressures" such as wages.[38] This policy is in accordance with the wishes of BCNI and other business lobbies concerned that new wage settlements were increasing too fast.

Labour was also targeted when the Department of Finance claimed that government spending was out of control.[39] Excessive spending at all levels of government were blamed for exacerbating the existing inflation problem. Pay increases given to government employees had to be minimized because workers in the private sector would seek similar pay hikes. Therefore, the Canadian government reduced wage pressures and the bargaining position of organized labour by increasing the unemployment rate. The Canadian government also trimmed expenditures by reducing its payroll. Over 10,000 employees lost their jobs as the government rationalized or privatized such Canadian institutions as the CBC, Air Canada, Petro-Canada, the National Film Board and Via Rail. Meanwhile, the Bank of Canada said in a study of Canada's UI programme that high unemployment would help to dampen wage demands.[40]

Economists at the Bank of Nova Scotia have stated that Canada has not suffered from high inflation or a serious recession.[41] High interest rates were implemented to harmonize Canada-U.S. wages and labour practices. Blaming inflationary pressures for the high interest rates is a ruse. The strategy of using increased unemployment to drive down wages and create a more flexible labour force has been a central part of the competitiveness strategy of the supporters of the FTA.

Hard-won labour rights are being undermined and wages are being driven down because Canadian business leaders continue to adhere to the classic notion that increased competitiveness comes mainly by lowering labour costs. The Tories increased unemployment as a strategy to drive down wages when they publicly promoted the FTA for its ability to create jobs and increase wages. Finance minister Wilson argued that the FTA was a success because it has increased exports and created jobs.[42] The value of Canada's exports to the United States has indeed increased since 1989, but wage and job growth has stagnated and even gotten worse (Figs. 27 and 28). Canada's unemployment rate has remained consistently above 10 percent since 1989, rising to 11.4 percent by the middle of 1993. Canadian workers have seen corporate profits in export sectors increase while their wages have stagnated or even fallen. The average Canadian worker is worse off now under the FTA than he was prior to 1989 despite the dramatic increase in trade.

The decline in labour income growth points to the broader strategy embedded in the FTA. Neoconservatives want to generate profits by segmenting the labour force. The FTA was designed to create renewed profitability by increasing social inequality. Free trade was promoted for its ability to boost competitiveness and efficiency so that Canadian firms could compete continentally and globally. Opponents to free trade predicted that the FTA would undermine wage levels and social programmes in Canada. Both sides of the debate may be correct. The goal of increased corporate profitability may occur in conjunction with greater social polarization. Standard economic theory predicts both "gains from trade" meaning higher income and more efficient production, and "trade adjustments" including job losses and salary cuts.[43]

Figure 27
Relationship Between Trade Growth, Unemployment and Wages

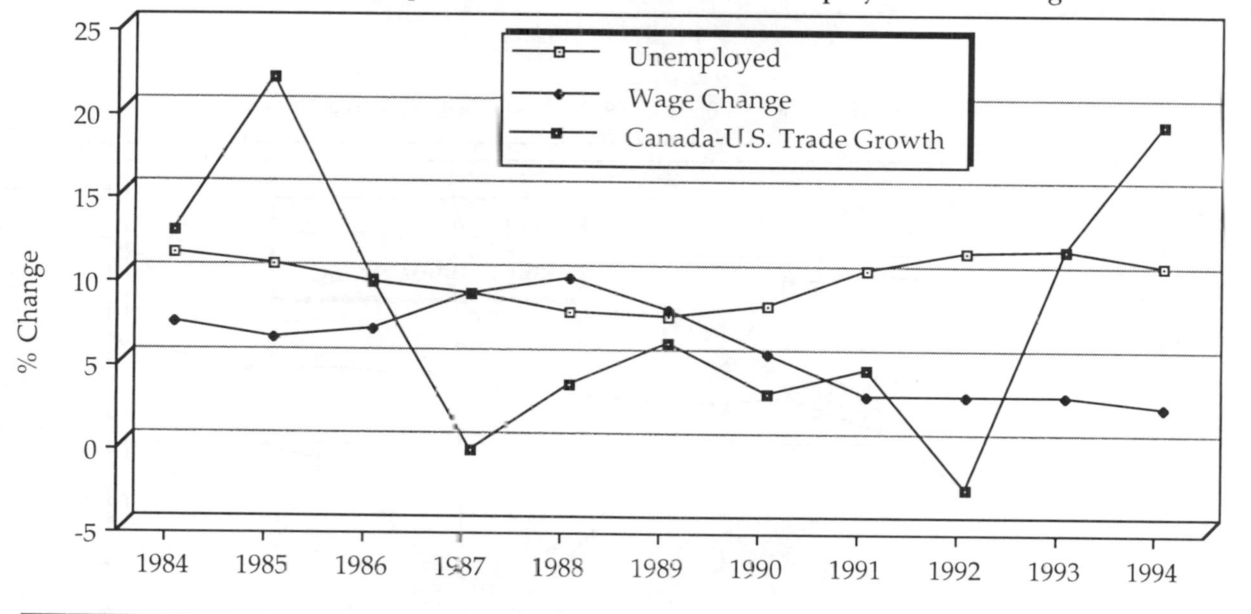

Source: Statistics Canada, Canadian Economic Observer (Ottawa: Supply and Services, 1990); Statistics Canada, Canadian Economic Observer (Ottawa: Supply and Services, 1995).

Figure 28

The Value of Canadian Exports to the United States and Wage Growth in Canada

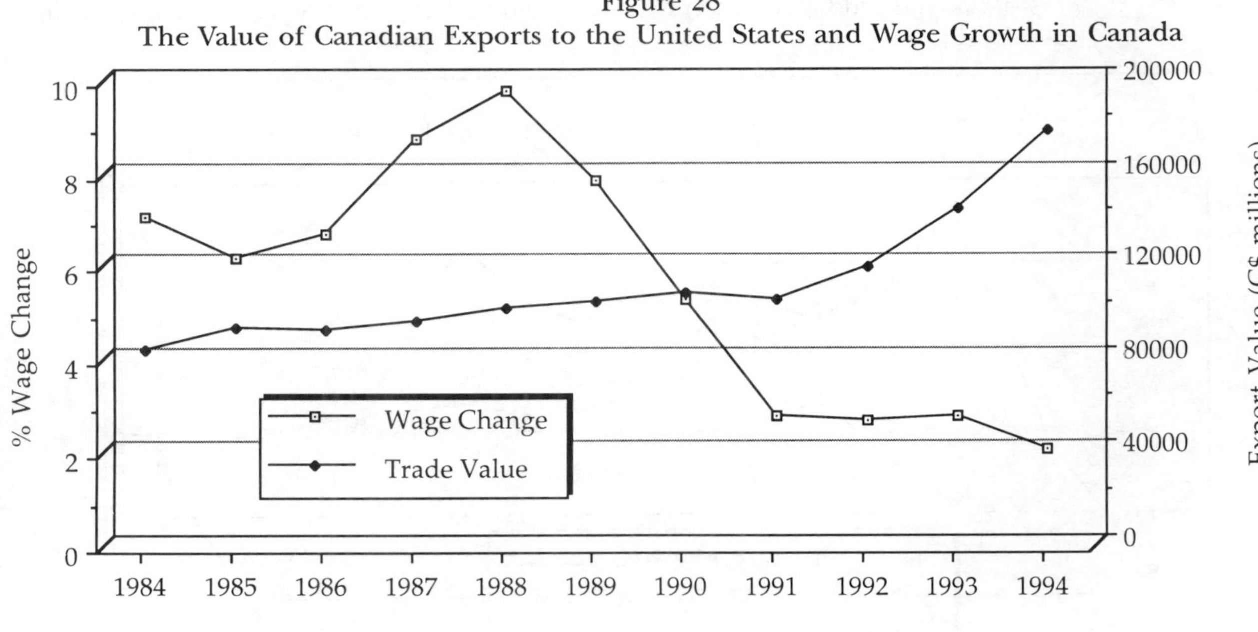

Source: Statistics Canada, Canada's Balance of International Payments (Ottawa: Supply and Services, 1995); Statistics Canada, Canadian Economic Observer (Ottawa: Supply and Services, 1995).

Many economists hesitate to admit this, but trade adjustments can permanently affect localities and large numbers of working families.[44] Economists have the ability to see that more national income derived from trade has the potential to yield greater utility. The problem is that economic theory has not led to the creation of a public policy that can redistribute the gains from trade to those who have been hurt most by it. So it is quite possible that national income might increase over the long run, but there is a great risk that polarization will increase between skilled and unskilled workers.

During the final days of the FTA debate, the Canadian government finally admitted that Canada would experience some labour market restructuring and unemployment directly related to the FTA. Supporters of free trade such as CATJO and the Tories stated that this restructuring would be made relatively painless through the implementation of a free trade adjustment programme for workers.[45] Mulroney proposed that workers' needs could be met with the Can$1.4 billion Canadian Jobs Strategy designed to retrain workers who lost their jobs as a result of the impact of free trade. In addition to the job retraining programme, Mulroney proposed that a Can$125 million fund be established to supplement the incomes of displaced workers who could not find work. Finally, the Progressive Conservatives promised to appoint the Advisory Council on Adjustment (ACA) to determine what help might be given to labour and business during the FTA restructuring period.[46]

Despite the promises made by business interests and the Canadian government that a special job retraining programme would be established, nothing has been done. The pledge to help workers displaced by free trade was nothing more than a campaign promise made to assuage the fears of working-class Canadians. Judith Maxwell of the ECC acknowledged that some firms would suffer during a brief restructuring period, but she believed that it would be too difficult to distinguish between workers who lost their jobs due to the FTA and workers who lost their jobs due to other factors. She recommended to the Canadian government that their proposed free trade adjustment programme be shelved because it would be unworkable. Maxwell concluded that existing job retraining programmes were sufficient to handle any workers thrown out of work by the impact of free trade.[47] In fact, programmes were deemed to be too generous. As a result, Can$100 million was cut from Canadian job retraining programmes that had been established long before the FTA was ever implemented.

Mulroney did follow through on his promise to commission the ACA to study the free-trade restructuring process in Canada. He appointed Jean de Grandpré to chair the ACA. It is noteworthy that de Grandpré is a prominent Canadian businessman and an executive member of the BCNI. After soliciting opinions from "the construction industry, community colleges, high-tech companies, [politicians in] single industry towns, textile unions, native organizations" and other interested parties, the ACA concluded that nothing needed to be done. In its report entitled *Adjusting to Win,* the ACA concluded that the FTA would not create any noticeable adjustment problems because "millions of Canadians change jobs annually."[48] According to the ACA, Canadian workers adjust almost effortlessly to technological change, increased competition and changing consumer tastes. Because there are close to 400 federal and provincial programmes of adjustment already in place, the ACA concluded that a special adjustment programme for victims of free trade would be a waste of resources.

It is worth examining the language used here. The ACA states that "millions of Canadians change jobs annually."[49] This consciously ignores the fact that people were not so much changing as losing their jobs. Between 1989 and 1994, manufacturing jobs have declined from 2.1 million to 1.9 million workers. Figure 24 emphasizes the fact that Canadians have been losing their jobs by the tens of thousands since 1989. To make matters worse for workers, the Canadian government plans to spend Can$27 million between 1993 and 1997 helping Canadian businesses to adapt to the North America Free Trade Agreement (NAFTA).[50] The Canadian government plans to establish a Canadian Business Centre in Mexico City where seminars will be held to show Canadian managers how to profit from North American free trade. The Canadian government established a free trade adjustment programme for corporate interests but not for workers.

By reneging on their promise to implement an adjustment policy soon after winning the 1988 election, the Tories have shown that they have embarked upon a policy of promoting economic growth through labour force segmentation and social inequality. In 1988, the Tories promised a free trade adjustment programme and then failed to implement it. In 1990, the Tories ensured that the Canadian labour force would become segmented and then harmonized with that of the United States when it restructured the Canadian unemployment insurance programme. Unemployment insurance (UI) reform confirms that the Tories were promoting economic growth through labour force polarization, inequality and the continental harmonization of labour standards.

Prior to the FTA, the differences between the Canadian and American unemployment insurance programmes were enormous. In 1987, 70 percent of unemployed Canadians received 60 percent of their former wages. In contrast, 32 percent of unemployed Americans received benefits covering only 35 percent of their former wages. A full 70 percent of unemployed Americans received no benefits. Business leaders recommended by 1987 that Canada needed sweeping UI reform if Canadian firms were to compete in a continental free trade area. Suggested reforms included increasing the minimum length of time that an employee had to work in order to qualify for unemployment benefits and reducing UI benefits from 60 to 50 percent of the former wage level.[51] The ACA agreed with the BCNI by recommending that cuts be made to UI benefits provided to unemployed workers. Labour leaders were angered by this pro-business recommendation from a supposedly neutral commission. Not only did the ACA fail to acknowledge that free trade would force many Canadian workers to lose their livelihood, it was recommending that the jobless have their existing benefits cut. The commission, purportedly established to study ways that workers could be helped, was actually suggesting ways that the Canadian labour force could be made more flexible under free trade. Neoconservatives who complained about the generous Canadian UI programme were able to take solace in the ability of the FTA to harmonize Canadian UI standards with those of the United States.

Trade minister John Crosbie emphatically denied that the Tories had plans for UI reform.[52] Despite assurances made during the 1988 election campaign, the Tories presented proposals for the fundamental restructuring of Canada's UI system in 1989, just four months after the implementation of the FTA. It was no coincidence that Bill C-21 proposing UI reforms was presented so soon after the implementation of FTA. Barbara McDougall, Canadian minister of employment, linked UI reforms with free trade when she stated in the House of Commons on June 6, 1989, that legislation to cut federal funding of the UI programme was essential in order for Canada to be globally competitive. She further linked UI reforms to the FTA when she said that "privatization, deregulation, tax reform and free trade are all parts of the same agenda [as the UI cuts] for revitalizing the Canadian economy."[53]

Bill C-21, a radical transformation of the Unemployment Insurance Act of 1941, was implemented in October 1990. This controversial legislation cut Can$1.3 billion from the Can$13 billion annual UI budget by enacting several changes.[54] First, the legislation eliminated the federal government's contribution to the UI programme. Only workers and their employers now supported the UI system. To make up for the funding shortfall, Canadian workers saw their UI paycheck deductions increase from Can$1.95 to Can$2.25 for every Can$100 of insurable earnings.[55] Employer contributions per Can$100 of worker earnings also increased from Can$2.73 to Can$3.15. These increases did not make up for the lack of federal government contributions. Bill C-21 also increased the minimum amount of time a person has to work in order to collect UI benefits from 10 to 12 weeks. The length of time that a worker can receive benefits was reduced and the federal government also reduced the weekly amount of benefits each unemployed worker receives. The Tories simultaneously privatized the Canadian UI programme while cutting its benefits. The United States is the only other industrial democracy to have done this. Bill C-21 included many of the recommendations made by BCNI and the ACA. More importantly, Bill C-21 also fits the logic of an integrated continental economy because it creates the conditions necessary to harmonize Canadian UI and wage standards with those of the United States.

Canadian UI reforms in 1990 mirror those undertaken by the United States during the 1980s. American UI reforms have included: a freeze or reduction in the level of maximum benefits; an increase in the time a jobless worker must wait between applying for benefits and receiving benefits; an increase in the minimum criteria necessary to qualify for benefits; and the elimination of federal government funding of the American UI programme. Bill C-21, including the withdrawal of federal funding, creates conditions in Canada that have already been put in place in the United States. More fundamentally, Bill C-21 dismantled a cornerstone of Fordist social and labour relations which were designed to promote worker equality and prosperity.

In 1935, Prime Minister Bennett introduced the Employment and Social Insurance Act in the Canadian House of Commons. He was prompted to do this because the Depression had caused widespread unemployment in Canada. Local municipal governments which had traditionally cared for the jobless were no longer able to provide benefits. Because Bennett's proposed legislation impinged upon provincial jurisdiction over labour and social welfare programmes, a constitutional amendment was needed to give the federal government legal responsibility for imposing a national unemployment programme upon the provinces. After a five-year ratification process, the constitutional issues were resolved, allowing the Unemployment Insurance Act of 1941 to be passed. In the short term, the UI programme was instituted to help Canadians who were suffering at that moment by providing them with a living wage. But the Canadian government really wanted to stress the insurance aspect of the UI Act over the long term. The new UI programme required funding from three parties: workers, employers and the State. The programme was national in nature in order to provide an incentive for the federal government to work towards the Fordist ideal of full employment. With a fully employed labour force, no UI benefits would have to be paid by the federal government.[56] The national structure of the programme also allowed the risk of unemployment to be pooled across the whole population regardless of region or current level of prosperity. This built-in equalization feature made Canada's UI system a "truly *social* insurance scheme, unlike commercial insurance which emphasizes high risk categories and forces those at highest risk to pay the highest premiums."[57]

The UI system operating in the United States was designed according to a different set of prerogatives. In the United States, each State sets its own standards for the State UI tax, eligibility rules and benefit payment rates. By giving the States primary responsibility for UI, there is no national pooling of unemployment risk. In 1988, the United States with ten times Canada's population, paid just over Can$15 billion in UI benefits and administrative costs. In the same year, Canada spent Can$12 billion.[58] How is it that Canada spent 80 percent of the U.S. total with only 10 percent of the population? In 1988, Canada had an unemployment rate of about 7 percent which was not much higher than the 6 percent unemployment rate in the United States. Thus, vastly differing unemployment rates is not the answer. The explanation lies in the fact that the United States federal government did not contribute to the American UI programme. Furthermore, only about 32 percent of the American jobless were eligible for benefits compared to the 70 percent of Canadian workers, prior to Canadian UI reforms. Without national standards, UI benefits vary dramatically by State. In sixteen States, less than 25 percent of unemployed workers receive UI payments. In Texas and Florida, only 20 percent of the unemployed are deemed eligible to receive UI benefits.[59] States are economically pitted against each other to drive down UI benefits in order to create a "positive business environment."[60]

The fragmentation of the American UI system presaged what is happening in Canada as a result of Bill C-21 and the FTA. Now that the federal government no longer contributes to the UI system, provinces will compete more against each other and UI benefits will shrink under the FTA-driven whipsaw process where a company can use the threat of relocation to force concessions out of a union, locality or province. As competition has heightened under the

FTA, Canadian corporations have already asked to have their UI contributions reduced from the levels outlined by Bill C-21. The federal government, which still manages the UI programme, has obliged corporate interests by forcing workers to increase their contributions to the Canadian UI plan while cutting back on the distribution of UI payments.[61]

Even though the Canadian UI system has been substantially rationalized, corporate interests continue to clamour for more reductions. When the Tories were voted out of office in 1993, Canadians believed that the new Liberal Leadership under Prime Minister Jean Chretien would be less neoconservative in its approach to social policy. The Liberal Party in the 1960s had been responsible for much of the expansion of Canada's Welfare State. Many Canadians voted for the Liberals in 1993 in the belief that the Liberals would return to social democratic policies that had been abandoned by the Tories. Liberal proposals to reform UI in 1994 and 1995 undermined this belief.[62] Human resources minister Lloyd Axworthy, has proposed further reforms to UI. Axworthy has proposed that UI claimants work 15 instead of 12 weeks to qualify for benefits, that they only receive 55 percent of insured earnings and that they be permitted to stay on UI for only 40 instead of 50 weeks.[63] UI reforms initiated by the Tories but extended by the Liberals have combined with the market forces of the FTA and NAFTA to harmonize Canadian labour standards with those of the United States. UI reforms and free trade have helped to eliminate Fordist tendencies in the Canadian labour force. Workers are more likely to accept technological change or make wage concessions knowing that UI benefits have been dramatically cut.

There are 200,000 fewer Canadian manufacturing jobs in 1994 than in 1989. Overall wage growth has stagnated since the implementation of the FTA (Figure 24). The long-term impact of a job restructuring of this magnitude is that it creates a more flexible labour force that will work harder for lower wages. Increased unemployment and decreased UI benefits have combined to keep wage increases in check. Companies have also kept wages down by implementing numerical flexibility. Temporary and part-time workers have been a staple of the office environment for years but are now found increasingly on the shop floor of factories.[64] Because most temporary and part-time workers lack union representation, they can be hired and fired easily according to the needs of existing market conditions. Besides enhancing the flexibility of a firm, temporary and part-time workers start at two to three dollars less per hour than a permanent worker and do not have to be paid health or retirement benefits.[65]

Since the implementation of the FTA in 1989, Canadian firms have restructured their work forces to rely upon temporary and part-time workers to a much greater extent. The number of full-time jobs has stagnated at about 10.6 million between 1988 and 1994. During the same time, the number of part-time and temporary employees increased by 21 percent from 1.9 million to 2.3 million.[66] Figure 29 compares the rate of growth for part-time and full-time employment in Canada. Canada's labour force has been restructured under the continental market pressures of the FTA. Firms are cutting costs by hiring part-time and temporary workers who must find work to supplement decreasing UI benefits. If a firm performs well during a particular quarter, managers are opting to pay more overtime rather than hire new permanent workers to meet increased consumer demand.

Besides restructuring the labour force along the part-time/full-time axis, free trade and related reforms have restructured the Canadian labour force along a service sector/manufacturing sector axis. It is a maxim within the social sciences to talk about the increasing importance of the service sector within the information economy or post-industrial society.[67] The proportion of manufacturing jobs in industrialized societies has declined over several decades. Yet, the degree to which the Canadian labour force has come to rely on the service sector for job growth after 1989 is no mere continuation of a pre-existing trend. As the point of inflection in Figure 30 shows, job growth in the goods-producing sector stagnated while it continued unabated in the service sector. Not only has job growth slowed in the goods-producing sector since 1989, employment dropped in absolute numbers for four straight years.[68] Costly unionized manufacturing labour has been replaced by more machinery and less expensive nonunion service sector workers.

In 1992, Canada increased manufacturing output while eliminating manufacturing jobs.[69] What is wrong with increasing service sector employment and the information economy if manufacturing productivity continues to increase? Some commentators have embraced the increasing importance of the service sector by claiming that it will create high-paying jobs.[70] Economic development strategies can therefore be designed around the service sector and the burgeoning information economy.[71]

The problem is that service-sector jobs pay far less on average than a job in the goods-producing sector. In 1988, the average Canadian worker in the goods-producing sector earned Can$3.73 more per hour than a service sector employee. By 1994, that gap had expanded to Can$4.21 per hour.[72] Workers in the service sector include highly-paid lawyers, accountants, data

Figure 29
Growth Index for Part-time and Full-time Employment in Canada

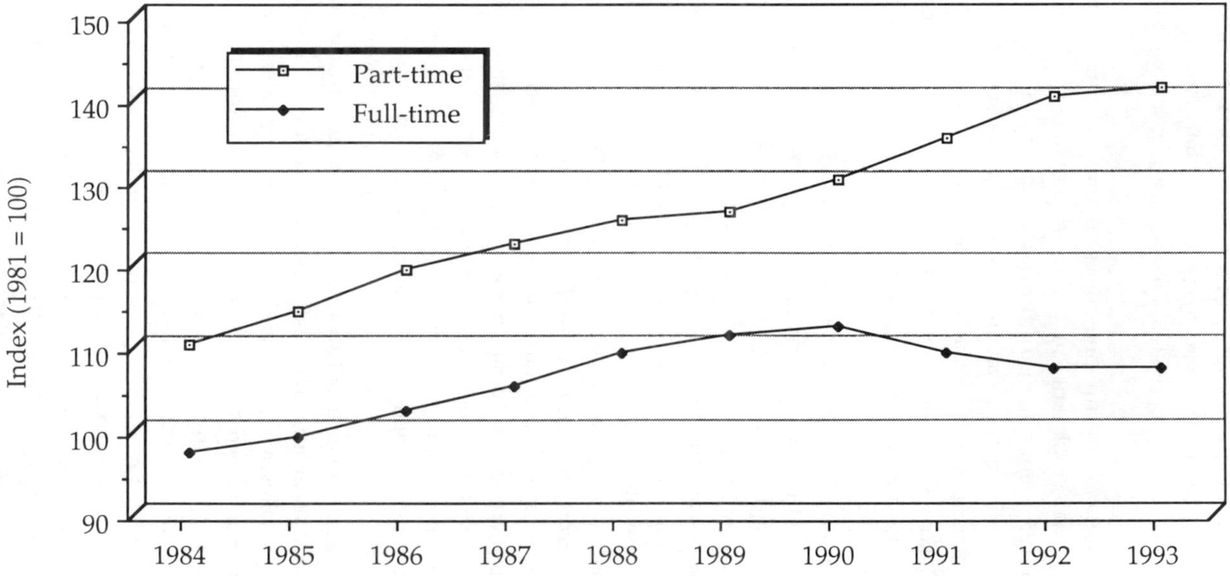

Index (1981 = 100)

150
140
130
120
110
100
90

Part-time
Full-time

1984 1985 1986 1987 1988 1989 1990 1991 1992 1993

Source: Statistics Canada, The Labour Force (Ottawa: Supply and Services, 1995);
Statistics Canada, Historical Labour Force Statistics, 1991 (Ottawa: Supply and Services, 1992)

Figure 30
Growth Index for Employment in the Services and Goods Producing Sectors in Canada

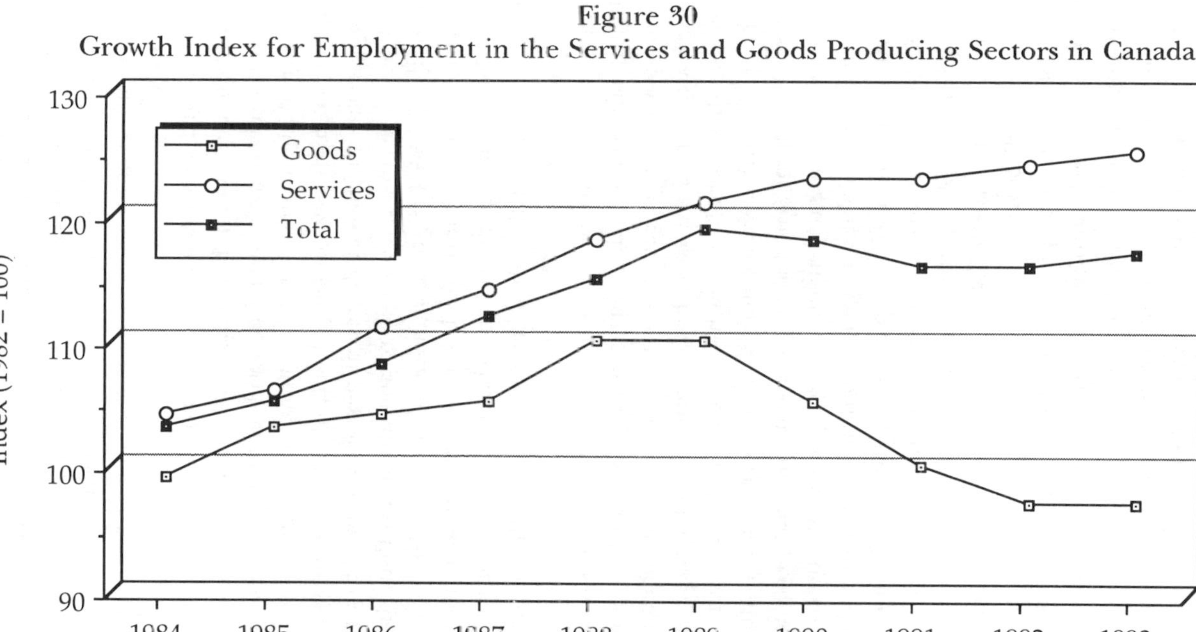

Source: Statistics Canada, Canadian Social Trends 29 (Summer 1993); Statistics Canada, Canadian Social Trends 36 (Summer 1995).

managers, computer programmers, engineers and economic forecasters. However, a much larger proportion of the service sector is comprised of underpaid workers such as retail sales clerks, data entry computer operators, office clerical staff, food service and accommodations staff, truck drivers, and other members of the distribution network who deliver manufactured goods to market.[73]

A partial explanation for why service sector workers are paid so poorly can be found in Figure 23 which shows that workers in the service and retail sector have the lowest levels of union representation in North America. Without union representation, workers are unable to bargain effectively for higher wages and job security. As it is, companies have come to appreciate the higher degree of flexibility afforded by the non-unionized service sector. That is one reason why it has flourished in the post-Fordist era. Women and minorities comprise an increasingly large proportion of the poorly paid service sector because they are the most easily exploited members of the work force.[74] Women are vulnerable to the polarization of the labour force because of the gender bias existent even under Fordism. Under a post-Fordist environment where all pretensions of equality are being abandoned, gender bias is being used to further enhance profitability. One only has to see the rise of female workers in low-paying service-sector jobs that used to be provided for by the Welfare State such as day care, health care and elder care. In addition, the fact that these social services have been privatized means that Canadian workers are further segmented between those who can afford to pay and those who cannot. The Canadian labour force has become polarized because of increasing dependence on temporary, part-time and service sector workers combined with gender and racial discrimination.

Another reason to be skeptical of development propelled by the service sector is that manufacturing jobs still matter. The proportion of manufacturing jobs in the Canadian labour force remained fairly constant during the 1980s before dropping after 1989. The proportion of Canada's GDP provided by manufacturing remained stable throughout the 1980s at about 20 percent before dropping to 18 percent by 1994.[75] Manufacturing jobs also matter because their job multiplier effect on a community is between three and four times greater than a service sector job. Manufacturing jobs simply generate more income and secondary jobs for a community than do service-sector jobs.[76] Where a manufacturing job may spin off three secondary jobs, the service sector job may only generate one.

To a very large extent the service sector exists to provide information about, or manage aspects of, the manufacturing sector. To celebrate the rise of the information economy without keeping an eye on the condition of the goods-producing sector is naive and possibly perilous. The privatization of services usually provided by the Welfare State is contributing in a substantial way to the rise of the service sector. Day care, elder care, health care and education are increasingly operated by profit-seeking enterprises. This situation further impoverishes and polarizes Canadian workers between those who can afford to pay and those who cannot. The privatization of social services also allows for disparities to emerge across regions because the federal government is no longer imposing a national standard for services.

The FTA has prompted Canadian firms to rely more upon service sector and part-time employees. This macroscale restructuring of the national labour market has eroded the resolve of unions, making it easier to implement flexible specialization at the microscale of the factory shop floor. The adoption of flexible specialization is just one more way that companies have exploited worker segmentation and inequality in order to increase profitability. The challenge at hand is to identify the nature of these flexible production techniques and explain why Canadian firms have been so eager to adopt them.

Flexible Specialization and Free Trade

In the wake of free trade, Fordist manufacturers in Canada believed that they had to restructure in order to compete with larger American firms that had greater economies of scale, less expensive labour, lower infrastructural costs and fewer taxes. Many American companies had adopted flexible production techniques because they were either subsidiaries or competitors of Japanese corporations. Cutting labour costs has become a fetish for Canadian businesses since the implementation of the FTA. Post-Fordist techniques have been praised by business leaders around the world for their ability to increase productivity while cutting labour costs. As a result, Canadian firms have been adopting the flexible production technique known as *kanban* at an increasing pace.[77]

How does the flexible *kanban* system differ from traditional Fordist assembly-line production? Consider a Fordist manufacturer of household appliances. The Fordist manufacturer relies upon the mass production of goods on an assembly line. The amount of goods produced is planned in advance based on 120-day projections of sales, economic conditions and housing starts. The Fordist plant relies on heavy investments in fixed capital and a massive inventory system. A manufacturer using the *kanban* system is very unlike its Fordist predecessor which pushes goods through the factory based on a predetermined schedule. Flexible production is designed to react quickly to the marketplace by pulling the goods through the factory in response to current consumer demand, not in response to what plant managers predict demand will be 120 days in the future. The chain reaction of events starts when a customer buys a product. That purchase electronically signals the factory to replace the product (*kanban* is the Japanese word for signal). To avoid waste and excessive inventory costs, parts are sent to the factory for assembly only when signaled to do so. Managers refer to this as the "just-in-time" inventory system.[78] The need to be more competitive under free trade has been a central factor causing Canadian firms to transform their production and supply systems.

Besides transforming production, the adoption of the *kanban* system has transformed labour relations and organization on the shop floor. One might say that the FTA has accelerated the transformation of "factory regimes" in Canada.[79] A factory regime describes the way that production is organized on the shop floor, the type of relationships among workers and between labour and management, and the political apparatuses which regulate production on the shop floor. Factory regimes under Fordist production were based on each factory having a linear input-output assembly line with strict job classifications, rigid work rules, regimented tasks, fixed grievance procedures, a closed or union shop, and a regulated but adversarial relationship between workers and management.

In order to maximize productivity under the flexible production system, rigid Fordist factory regimes had to be transformed. Other names for the new factory regimes accompanying flexible specialization include: "labour-management participation programs" (LMPPs), "total quality management," "employee involvement programs," or "quality of work life."[80] In order to implement a flexible work system such as an LMPP, management had to be aware that it consists of two components: the co-operation apparatus (CA), and the management-by-stress (MBS) system of work management. One can utilize regulation theory to think of the CA as a mode of regulation for the shop floor. It consists of the events away from the actual production process which help to foster worker co-operation, loyalty and acquiescence. Specific components of the CA include labour-management committees and quality circles where workers meet with facilitators, co-ordinators, trainers and other representatives from management to discuss quality control, co-operation and productivity issues. The end goal of the CA is to introduce the flexible MBS system and then maintain it against worker unrest.

The MBS system could be described as a shop floor equivalent of a regime of accumulation. The MBS system describes the actual production system operating on the shop floor. Other names for the MBS system include: the "lean production system," "Toyotaism," "Japanese production methods," "synchronous production," or the "team concept."[81] Specific aspects of this system clearly differentiate it from Fordism. The MBS system relies on increasing the level of Taylorism on the shop floor. This entails standardizing and speeding up the work so that employees are forced to work more for the same or even less pay. The just-in-time inventory system cuts costs by reducing the size of the inventory a company has to manage. The MBS system dramatically cuts labour costs by eliminating job classifications, using nonunion subcontractors for part of the production process, replacing workers by using computerized machine tools and robotics, and relying on a segmented labour force.

The whole MBS approach operates by keeping the entire production system stressed for tighter management control. Managers can more readily identify the points that frequently break in the production chain (not enough resources) and those points that never break (too many resources).[82] Fewer managers are needed because the MBS system monitors itself to a certain extent. However, the fact that the whole system is kept under constant stress means that new labour control problems develop. The team concept was designed to address that problem by eliminating job classifications. Rigid job classifications are replaced with a team of interchangeable workers who can spell each other off. Incentives are built into the team concept by giving each worker in a team a base salary and then bonuses are given to an employee based on team productivity. In other words, the MBS system relies upon peer pressure to increase worker performance levels.

Corporations promote the team concept because it is supposed to give workers more autonomy and promote better labour-management cooperation. A UAW survey of 2,400 workers at the Mazda plant at Flat Rock, Michigan, tells another story.[83] According to the MBS system design and the team concept, workers are supposed to have equal opportunity to work at all tasks assigned to their team in order to avoid burnout. When the Mazda employees were asked if they rotated job assignments fairly, 50 percent responded no. The MBS system is supposed to give the worker greater autonomy. The survey asked the workers how often their worksheet (the step-by-step instructions for doing a job) was changed by management without their consultation? Only 19 percent reported that this had never happened. Three quarters of the respondents said that their worksheet had been changed "several/many times." Under a Fordist labour agreement, union workers would have the protection of their job classification in which the nature and pace of their work is spelled out. With the MBS system, the nature and pace of the job can and has been changed or accelerated without labour-management consultation. When workers were asked how the changes in their worksheet affected their job, 6 percent said their job was now easier while 67 percent said their job had become more difficult. The final question asked workers if they believed that they could stay healthy until retirement at their present work intensity. Only 20 percent responded in the affirmative. Plant managers have used flexible specialization to regain control over the shop floor that had been lost through Fordist work rules. Unions desperately want to abolish this system despite claims made by management that flexible production has helped both labour and management.

In Canada, businesses have stepped up their attempts to implement flexible production systems. In their presentation to the Macdonald Commission, the CMA openly stated that Canadian manufacturers wanted to "accelerate the adoption of a flexible production system and reap the benefits that our highly educated work force can provide."[84] Now that free trade is a reality, that acceleration has begun. Firms that have adopted flexible production techniques in Canada include appliance manufacturers such as Camio (which produces goods for General Electric) and car manufacturers such as the Chrysler plant in Bramelea, Ontario. Sam Gindin, union research director for the CAW, says that Canadian unions will fight the team concept and the broader flexible production system in which it is embedded because they are being used to weaken labour.[85]

Canadian workers are being displaced by robotics and machine tools. Productivity gains are achieved by stifling worker's rights. Managers are able to impose extra work requirements on employees who have no formal work contract, no job classification and often no formal grievance procedures. The use of peer pressure in the team concept paradoxically breaks down worker solidarity by pitting team against team and worker against worker. This undermines union strength — one of the goals of the MBS system. The current search for flexibility in the workplace is a euphemism for dismantling existing entitlements. The use of a non-unionized and segmented labour force is a rejection of the central Fordist tenet that wage earners have their wage increases tied to productivity increases. Corporate interests have adopted flexible production techniques because they allow wages to be pushed down while increasing productivity. The flexible model of development promotes economic growth based on increased worker exploitation.

From a development standpoint, it is not clear that promoting economic growth by increasing social inequality is a viable strategy.[86] In the case of Canada, the increasing reliance on service sector economic growth and flexible specialization reveals the "poverty" of *laissez-faire* economics and free trade. The invisible hand of the unregulated marketplace is supposed to promote prosperity for all participants. Capitalists are exhorted to selfishly adopt what is best for their own firm without concern for other businesses. If all capitalists engage in this self-interested strategy, the economy as a whole and the individuals within it are all predicted to prosper. In a test of this theory, individual firms in Canada have cut their payrolls in a self-interested way by adopting flexible specialization and relying more on service sector growth to compete in a free trade environment. This is a poor recipe for long term economic growth because manufacturing jobs generate more secondary and spin-off jobs than any other type of job. The Economic Policy Institute published a report entitled *Employment Multipliers in the United States Economy*. It concluded that the average manufacturing job generates 4.5 times more secondary jobs as the average retail job and three times as many jobs as those in the personal or business sector.[87] Canada is making a mistake by promoting growth on the backs of poorly paid service sector workers whose labour does not help to stimulate job growth in an effective manner. Free trade has therefore initiated a downward spiral where the increasing reliance on growth in the service sector and flexible specialization in the manufacturing sector increases the polarization of the Canadian labour force.

Free trade was promoted as a long-term development strategy which would create more jobs with higher wages. Precisely the opposite has happened. Free trade has been used by corporate interests to reorganize the North American economy by reducing the checks and balances once provided by unions, social movements and the State. By polarizing the Canadian labour force through free trade, neoconservatives have been able to roll back fifty years of State controls and labour laws that had regulated business practices in the interests of the majority of the people.[88] Of course, this statement begs the following question: by what means has free trade polarized and fragmented the Canadian labour force? The next section shows how the threat of plant relocations has been used by firms to restructure the Canadian labour force.

The Whipsaw Process and Job Relocation

Continental hypermobility has given business the "trump card" when dealing with workers and communities.[89] The "whipsaw process" has been a primary tactic used by corporate interests to force concessions out of workers by threatening to relocate. The whipsaw is used when a manufacturer exploits geographical differences in the economic landscape by forcing localities and workers into a bidding war over the location of investment. The factory owner can pressure local unions to accept a particular wage offer under the threat that production will be moved to another more flexible locality. Localities and regional governments such as provinces and states also bid against each other for investment by offering potential investors tax breaks, low-cost infrastructure, low-wage labour and even labour reforms. Free trade enhances the power of the whipsaw for Canadian firms by giving them access to a continental market where much larger regional differences exist with regard to union strength and wage levels. Businesses can threaten to move to right-to-work states or Mexico if Canadian workers refuse to make wage concessions or to adopt new flexible production techniques.

This is in direct opposition to pro-FTA rhetoric which promised significant improvements in job quantity and quality for Canadians as industrial production expanded within Canada under the stimulus of free trade. Optimistic predictions were based on econometric models and mathematical simulations conducted by agencies of the Canadian government such as the ECC, economists at Canadian universities, economic forecasters working for private corporations such as the Royal Bank of Canada, and economic forecasters working for private think-tanks such as the C.D. Howe Institute.[90] The ECC made the following statement about econometric models predicting job increases and economic growth resulting from free trade: "Mathematics cannot fully capture reality; nor can today's forecast foretell the future in all its complexity. Nevertheless, the [mathematical] simulations tell a consistent story. The implementation of the free-trade agreement will encourage increased economic growth and employment in Canada."[91] One reason that economists at the ECC and elsewhere predicted job increases when jobs have actually been lost by the tens of thousands in Canada is that they did so based on an array of faulty assumptions. Models were particularly flawed when they assumed that Canadian firms and the branch plants of MNCs in Canada would remain in Canada after the implementation of the FTA.[92]

The dependence of models on untenable assumptions goes to the very problem of economics as a scientific discourse. Models are only as good as their assumptions. In general, neoclassical economists assume that unemployment is a short-term effect of recessions. According to

James Stanford, an economist at the New School for Social Research, the Canadian free trade model assumed full employment and a fixed volume of investment in both the United States and Canada.[93] Under this assumption, corporations would not widely shut down their factories and or move production to the United States. Capital would move to more productive activities and regions within Canada. In the first place, the assumption of full employment was wrong because Canada had an official unemployment rate of 8 percent in 1988 when most econometric models were conducted. By 1993, the Canadian unemployment rate had risen to 11.4 percent. More importantly, economists failed to make the most important assumption of all: that geography matters. Economists ignored geography by assuming firms would not relocate outside of Canada under free trade.

The ECC said that "there is little evidence to support the idea that the agreement will lead to the 'de-industrialization' of Canada or to the exodus of manufacturing and other jobs from this country."[94] The problem with this assertion is that evidence for job loss cannot be found if the possibility of job loss is not included as an assumption in the econometric model in the first place. The FTA created a continental market, yet economists modeled the impact of the FTA on a national basis. The implications of Canadian workers having to compete against workers in low-wage regions in the United States and Mexico were ignored. On the other hand, an econometric model that acknowledged the importance of geography would assume that firms would exploit the differences in the variegated economic landscape of North America, not just Canada, in order to maximize profits.

Companies have long used the threat of relocation and geographical differences within a country to secure lower-cost production sites. This strategy works particularly well in a country such as the United States where there are wide regional disparities in wages, union strength and labour laws. Conditions in low-wage regions can be used to threaten unions in high-wage regions into making concessions on wages, benefits, technological change or work rules. A recent example of this occurred in 1992 when General Motors extracted concessions from their employees in Ypsilanti, Michigan, playing them off against GM workers in Arlington, Texas.[95] Business interests can also use the whipsaw against the local state to gain concessions. Again, GM threatened to leave Michigan unless it was given Can$250 million in tax abatements by the Ypsilanti Township from 1984 to 1988.

During the Fordist era, the whipsaw was not used to any great extent in Canada because there were and still are no provincial equivalents to American right-to-work states. That is not to say that Canada does not have regional disparities of income or union strength. They do, however the disparities are not as great as those in the United States. During the crisis of Fordism, conditions began to change for Canadian labour. The whipsaw became part of the Canadian labour experience in 1979 when the Nova Scotia legislature made it more difficult to organize workers within individual factories. This action came in response to the threat of Michelin Tire Corporation leaving Nova Scotia unless something was done about union activity. In 1984, the Social Credit Party of British Columbia made changes to that province's labour code which were opposed by unions. In 1987, the Grocery Products Manufacturers of Canada (GPMC) undertook an impact analysis of the FTA, concluding that some producers in Canada would not be able to compete with American corporations if free trade became a reality. American companies were less unionized which meant that American wages were lower and American management had greater flexibility in dealing with the labour force. The GPMC recommended that some "fundamental realignments in legislated benefits, income expectations, programmes and labour union organizations" had to occur in order to allow Canadian firms to be competitive in a free trade area.[96]

The neoconservative message was clear. Canadian companies could only become competitive with American companies at the expense of labour. Canadian workers should expect the FTA to place great pressure on Canadian wages and labour laws to be harmonized with those of the United States. Economists operating in the theoretical world discounted these fears. Corporate leaders operating in the real world validated them. Ray Verdon, president of Nabisco Brands, said that "nothing clears the mind so much as the specter of being hung in the morning [and that managers should] use free trade as a catalyst to mobilize employees to cut costs."[97] Many executives in Canada have taken his advice to heart. In 1990, Blue Bell Canada, a clothing manufacturer in Ontario, used the whipsaw on its 165 unionized employees. They were asked to accept an 18 percent reduction in wages and benefits. Bob Silver, president of Blue Bell Canada, said that he would move production elsewhere if the union did not make wage concessions.[98]

The threat of relocation has also been used to cut short legal strikes. The contract had expired for workers at Bowie Manufacturing in Lindsay, Ontario. The Bowie management threatened that jobs would be transferred to Mexico if the union went on strike.[99] General Motors has now expanded their use of the whipsaw from the national to the continental scale. General Motors used the whipsaw to begin the harmonization of wages, work rules and benefits of Canadian GM employees in Oshawa, Ontario, with those of GM workers in the United States. General Motors sent a letter to the CAW which stated that they were "not bluffing" about closing the plant down if concessions were not made.[100] In theory, the Auto Pact is supposed to be exempt from the FTA, making it difficult for firms to use the threat of relocation to bid down wages. In fact, the Auto Pact was already affected when the 9.2 percent punitive tariff ensuring a certain proportion of cars are made in Canada was removed under the provisions of the FTA. American car manufacturers are supposed to continue to adhere to the Auto Pact provisions, but there is no longer any penalty for failing to doing so. Therefore, the FTA makes it much easier for firms in the automotive industry to use the whipsaw to drive wages down to U.S. standards.

Other automotive industry firms have also used the threat of relocation to force concessions out of their workers. Uniroyal Canada threatened to leave its Kitchener, Ontario location unless its workers agreed to new schedules. The Akron-based tire and rubber products manufacturer said that 2,000 jobs would be shifted to the United States unless the Canadian workers agreed to adopt a seven-day work schedule. Electro-Wire Canada Incorporated is an auto parts firm with plants in Canada, the United States, and the *maquiladora* region of Mexico. In 1991, they used the whipsaw on their employees at their plant in Owen Sound, Ontario. Union leaders believed that Electro-Wire Incorporated was serious about their threat to move production south so they agreed to make the concessions demanded by management. David Ondrack, professor of organizational behavior at the University of Toronto, says that the FTA has allowed American and Canadian CEOs to rethink their current locations.[101] Ondrack believes that wage concessions will be even greater under NAFTA.

The largest corporations in Canada have also used the whipsaw to block labour law reforms proposed by the NDP party of Ontario. Premier Bob Rae and his NDP party attempted to reinforce workers' rights in Canada's industrial heartland. They proposed Bill 40 which was designed to raise the Ontario minimum wage, to make it even more difficult for companies to use replacement workers during strikes, to make it easier for workers to unionize, and to make chief executive officers liable when a factory closes down without providing workers adequate severance pay. Corporate interests were united in their negative response to the NDP proposals.[102]

Critics of the labour reforms included the 40,000-member Council of Ontario Construction Associations, the CMA, the Mining Association of Canada, and numerous local Chambers of Commerce. Two business organizations, Project Economic Growth and the More Jobs Coalition, representing more than one hundred firms, complained that the NDP was anti-business, arguing that Bill 40 gave too much power to unions. The Toronto Board of Trade accused the NDP of scaring off foreign investment. The Human Resources Professionals Association of Ontario went even further and said that the proposed NDP labour reforms would make Ontario the most "left-wing, pro-union, [and] anti-business" region in North America. Businesses threatened the NDP that if the reforms were put in place, they were going to leave Ontario.[103]

General Motors, Ford Motor Company and Chrysler explained to the NDP that labour reforms could force them to close or relocate to the United States because the reforms would place Canadian automobile factories at a disadvantage compared to car plants in the United States.[104] The NDP understood the seriousness of this threat because tens of thousands of jobs in the automobile industry had already been shifted south. Hayes-Dana Incorporated said that it postponed the expansion of its auto parts factory in St. Catherines, Ontario, because of NDP labour reforms. Criticism was so widespread and the threats so serious that the NDP backed off on certain provisions within Bill 40.

In a further bid to appease the business community, the NDP passed Bill 48 which was designed to keep the Ontario government deficit below Can$10 billion. This deficit reduction strategy consisted of three parts. First, the NDP raised individual income taxes while leaving corporate taxes unchanged. The second part was an expenditure control plan to trim Can$4 billion by cutting social services and eliminating 11,000 public sector jobs. The third element included a Can$2 billion annual reduction in government expenditures between 1993 and 1996 by adopting a "social contract" with public sector employees.[105] The social contract was originally designed to be a voluntary negotiation between the 900,000 provincial employees and the NDP to accept a three-year wage freeze, restrictions on collective bargaining and an additional twelve days of unpaid leave. When unions rejected the social contract, the NDP imposed their plan through Bill 48. In passing Bill 48, the NDP managed to alienate hundreds of thousands of workers in Ontario. As a result, it was no surprise when the NDP and Bob Rae lost to Michael Harris and the Ontario Progressive Conservatives in the 1995 election. Disaffected workers abandoned the NDP which had, in turn, abandoned workers under pressure from corporate interests. The provincial Tories gained power in

Ontario on a neoconservative platform that promised to eliminate the vestiges of Bill 40 and the "damage" done by the NDP.[106]

The NDP leadership in Ontario is not the only provincial government to succumb to multinational corporate pressure. Consider the case of British Columbia and the corporate response to provincial NDP labour reforms. The NDP attempted to regain some of the ground that unions lost to the neoconservative reforms of the Social Credit Party in 1987. The NDP raised the corporate capital investment tax and made it easier to organize a union. These reforms prompted many firms to abandon British Columbia in favor of Washington State. David Bell is the director of the Fourth Corner Economic Development Group in Bellingham, Washington. This is a government agency that is designed to attract investment to the city of Bellingham and the surrounding Whatcom County using a combination of private and public development funds. Bell has been traveling to Vancouver, British Columbia, where he has held numerous seminars aimed at attracting Canadian manufacturers to the Whatcom County area. When he took over the development agency in 1990, there were 17 Canadian companies in Whatcom County. By 1993, there were over 100 Canadian companies employing over 1,600 employees and representing Can$82 million in investments.[107] Bell believes that his success has been due to free trade and the tax and labour reforms in British Columbia. The elimination of tariffs has permitted these firms to shift production to Whatcom County where they can serve their Canadian market while enjoying the benefits of the lower-wage, lower-tax environment of the United States.

What actions do businesses take when unions do not acquiesce to corporate demands? Businesses adopt the same strategy against unions that they did against pro-labour governments. When a union does not succumb to the corporate threat of relocation, many firms have actually shifted production in order to secure a low-wage labour force. Consider this letter sent by management to 26 legally striking production workers at the Hartz Canada plant in St. Thomas, Ontario:

> As a result of the passage of the free-trade agreement, we now have the opportunity of sourcing products produced in the U.S. without incurring any duty. In the event of work stoppage ... replenishment stock will be provided by Hartz U.S. Once products are sourced outside our St. Thomas facility, the likelihood of [the production of] these products returning here after the work stoppage is very remote.[108]

The workers continued to strike and Hartz permanently moved production to the United States. Hartz Canada is not the only company to follow through on the threat of relocation. It can be documented that many thousands of jobs have been shifted to the United States when a Canadian union or state agency would not make concessions. Many firms also shifted production out of Canada without even negotiating with Canadian workers or agents of the Canadian State. Production costs were so low in other parts of North America that some companies simply closed their doors in Canada and moved south.

Other factors have influenced where a firm relocates after leaving Canada. The question remains: have Canadian companies moved to upstate New York or northwestern Washington to remain close to the Canadian market, or have companies moved all the way to Mexico or a right-to-work state in order to take advantage of lower wages and tax rates? What impact has American recruitment of Canadian firms had on plant relocation? The rest of this section will be devoted to documenting how and where over forty-two thousand jobs have been shifted from Canada to the United States or Mexico since the implementation of the FTA. As the Appendix and Figures 31, 32 and 33 reveal, firms have shifted production and jobs from Canada to four basic regions within North America: American border-states close to the Canadian market, states in the industrial heartland, right-to-work states in the southeast and central United States, and the *maquiladora* region of Mexico.

Many Canadian firms shifted production and jobs from Canada to border-states such as Washington, Montana, Minnesota, New York, Vermont, New Hampshire, and Maine. The kind of firm that generally relocated from Canada to a border state was a small Canadian-owned firm that was not a branch plant of a multinational corporation.[109] The most often cited reason for moving production was to take advantage of lower production costs in the United States while remaining close to the Canadian market. As Figures 31, 32 and 33 show, the border-states attracted the most firms but the fewest jobs of the four regions. This reflects the small scale and local focus of these predominantly Canadian-owned firms which had grown tired of high Canadian wages and taxes.

It should be pointed out, however, that Figures 31, 32 and 33 contain conservative estimates of job relocation. The actual number of job relocations is most certainly higher than these figures reflect. Data was difficult to collect because no central Canadian or American State agency or labour organization has been concentrating on this issue in great detail. Parties interested in job shifts have focused on national movements from Canada to the United States and Mexico without being overly concerned about regional location within the United States or Mexico.

Figure 31
Jobs and Firms that Shifted from Canada

Region	Jobs Shifted	Firms Shifted	Job/Firm Shifted
Border States	4,359	122	36
Right-to-work States	5,336	32	167
Industrial Heartland States	12,844	62	207
Mexico	19,523	68	287

Source: Calculated from Data in Appendix

How do we know that these figures underestimate job shifts from Canada to border-states? The evidence which shows that job losses have been even greater than stated comes from reports on the activities of American state and local agencies which have spent millions of dollars recruiting Canadian investment since 1989. The case of David Bell and his success in attracting Canadian production to the state of Washington has already been recounted. A similar situation has been developing in upstate New York in the Buffalo-Niagara Falls region.

In the 1980s, Buffalo lost many jobs when industries such as Bethlehem Steel closed their doors. Since that time, business and political leaders have expended a great deal of energy attempting to recruit new industries to the Buffalo area. The passage of the FTA has made this task considerably more rewarding. The Greater Buffalo Chamber of Commerce, the Buffalo Enterprise Development Corporation and the Lackawanna Development Zone have aggressively recruited Canadian investment since the implementation of the FTA. Public and private agencies from New York State have advertised in Canadian newspapers and held seminars in Canada extolling the virtues of relocation to the Empire State. New York State has established a business office in downtown Toronto to field inquiries from managers in Canada who are interested in shifting production to the Buffalo region.[110] Government officials from New York State and Buffalo have co-ordinated their efforts

Figure 32
Location of Job Shifts from Canada to United States and Mexico

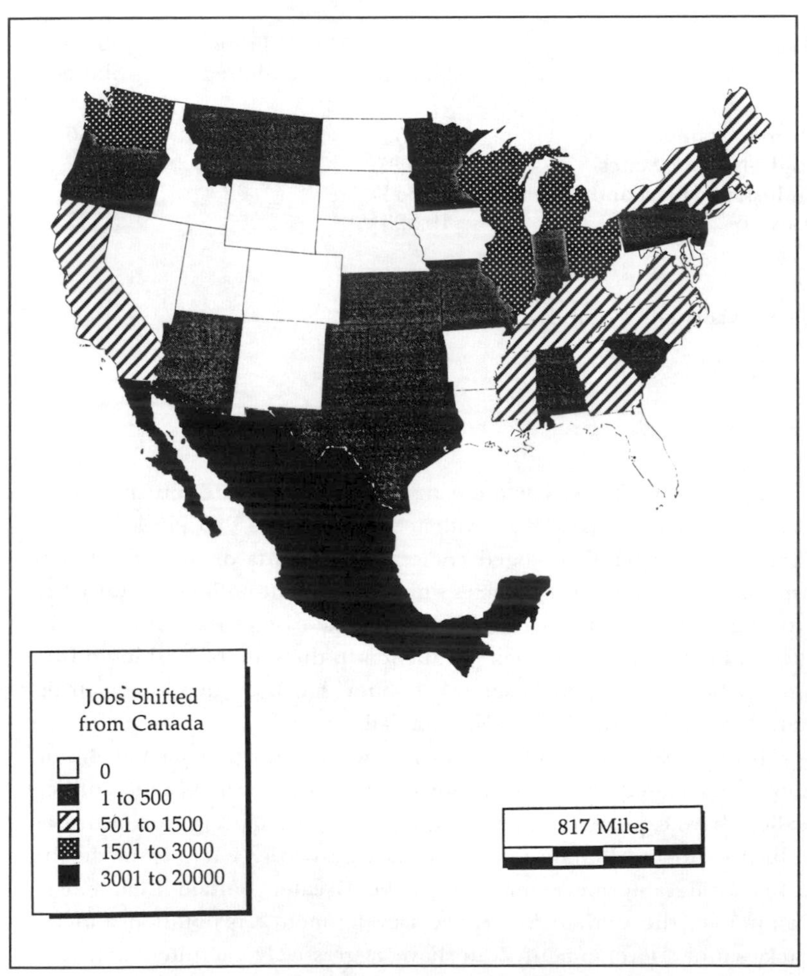

Source: Appendix

Figure 33
Jobs Relocated from Canada to the United States and Mexico

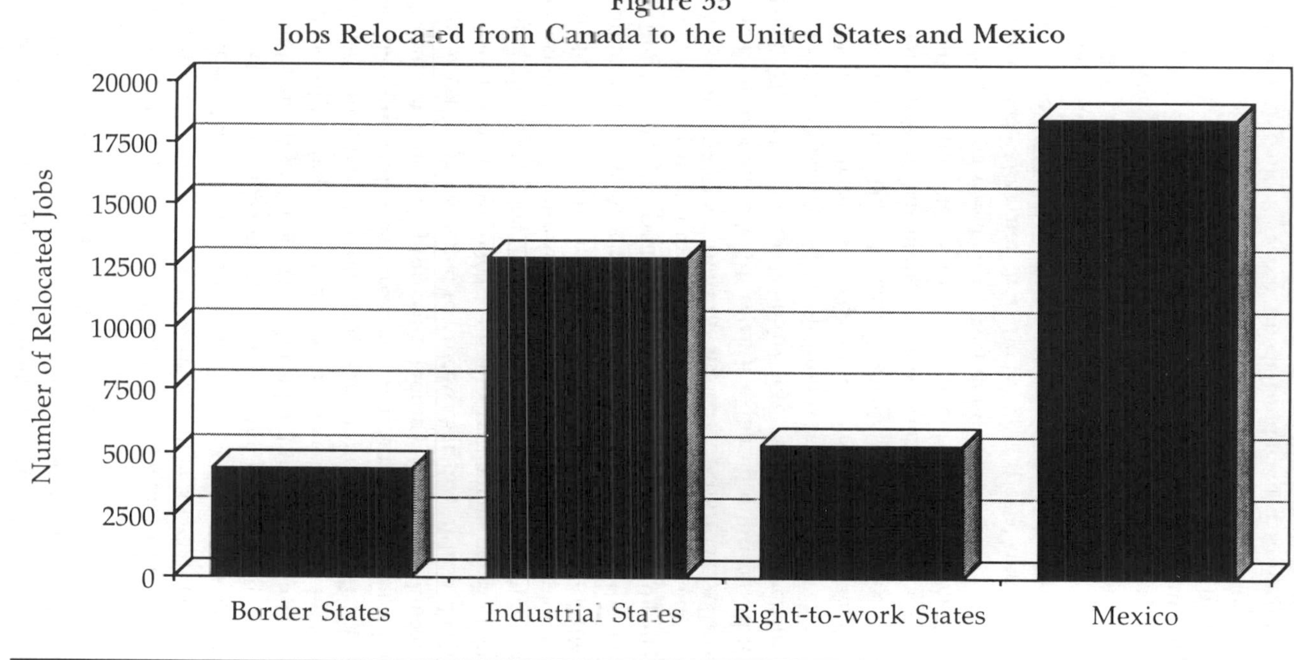

Source: Appendix

to offer an array of incentives to attract firms from Canada including employee retraining programmes, seven-year property tax deferments, lower taxes and lower wages. The recruiting efforts have successfully attracted 91 Canadian firms to relocate or expand production in the Buffalo area.[111] Canadian firms have long recognized that the FTA would allow them to relocate. A 1991 survey of the Canadian Federation of Independent Business found that about 33 percent of its 44,000 members were actively investigating relocation to the United States or Mexico.

Jobs and production have also shifted from Canada to border-states because of the impact of the FTA on Canada's fishing industry. Canada has had a long-term ban on the export of unprocessed fish as a conservation measure, and to ensure that Canadian workers contributed to the value-added. The fish processing industry from New England and the State of Washington wanted to process Canadian fish so they launched a protest to GATT. The GATT dispute settlement panel sided with the United States declaring that Canada could not impose an outright ban on the export of unprocessed fish. However, the GATT panel did permit Canada to impose an export tax which would accomplish the same goal as an outright ban. Article 349 of the FTA text changed this situation, forbidding the imposition of any tax, duty or other charge on an export that is not also levied on the product when sold in the domestic market. In other words, the FTA forbids the use of an export tax. As a result, up to 25 percent of Canada's fish catch is exported unprocessed to American plants. The FTA effectively shifted over 900 fish processing jobs from Nova Scotia to Maine and Massachusetts.[112]

Many jobs have also been shifted from Canada to the industrial heartland of the United States.[113] Again, aggressive recruiting by state and local officials has attracted many firms from Canada after the implementation of the FTA. State development agencies from Illinois, Michigan and Ohio have established recruiting offices in Toronto. The Council of Great Lakes Governors has also set up a special trade office in downtown Toronto. The managers of these offices have said that high taxes and wages in Canada are the most commonly stated reasons why Canadian plant managers inquire about possible relocation to the United States. When asked why American firms are not relocating to Canada, the manager from the Illinois office said that Canadian unions and high wages act as disincentives to American manufacturers. This statement was corroborated by Richard Freeman of Harvard University's National Bureau of Economic Research which conducted a study for the ECC.[114] Freeman concluded that American firms that sell goods in Canada would be more likely to locate production in the United States in order to avoid Canadian unions.

The industrial heartland has attracted very large firms from Canada on average when compared to firms that shifted to border-states (Figure 31). A large proportion of these firms were branch plants of large American MNCs. The factories were built in Canada to avoid the high tariffs at the Canadian border. Promoters of free trade said that these branch plants would remain in Canada after the implementation of the FTA reorganizing their production to specialize as an export platform. The FTA ultimately had the opposite effect, prompting the out-migration of dozens of branch plants from Canada to the United States.[115] As the tariffs dropped under the FTA, MNCs moved production back to the United States where costs were less. The FTA makes it easier for firms to organize production, locate investment, source inputs and determine prices according to corporate rather than social priorities. Canadian content or performance requirements no longer act as barriers to trade or capital mobility. This explains why the Canadian subsidiaries of General Tire, BF Goodrich and United Technologies were closed and production was moved back to the industrial heartland where wages are lower and the State is less intrusive.

What factors have attracted production from Canada to relocate in the right-to-work states? Recruiting has again played an important role in the movement of production out of Canada. Officials from North Carolina visited 27 Canadian companies in the summer of 1992 to lure them south with promises of subsidized worker retraining, right-to-work laws where unions are weak, cheap real estate and low taxes. Dallas Hardenbrock, international development representative for the state of North Carolina, stated that it is unfair to say that his organization is raiding the jobs of another country. He responds that he cannot help it if Ontario's pro-union stance and high wages force companies out. Moving to North Carolina can save a company from Canada a lot of money. By the end of 1994, the recruiting strategy had paid off. Over 60 Canadian firms had relocated to North Carolina.[116] With only 4.8 percent of the labour force represented by a union, workers in North Carolina cannot bargain effectively for higher wages. In 1990, the average Canadian wage was Can$16.02 per hour. The average American wage was only Can$14.77 per hour while the average wage in North Carolina was even lower at Can$12.00 per hour. On labour costs alone, a firm that shifts production from Canada to a right-to-work state like North Carolina can save 25 percent. Although the right-to-work states had the lowest production costs in the United States, they did not attract the most investment from Canada. That honor goes to northern Mexico.

More jobs moved from Canada to the *maquiladora* region of Mexico than all the other three regions combined. The firms that shifted production to Mexico were also larger than those that relocated to the other three regions (Figure 31). Generally speaking, the firms that relocated to Mexico were branch plants of large American MNCs from the automotive and other manufacturing and high-technology sectors (see Appendix). This was not supposed to happen for several reasons. First of all, jobs and production moved from Canada under the impetus of the Canada-U.S. FTA, not NAFTA. Mexico was not supposed to be part of the 1989 free trade agreement. Furthermore, Mexico is supposed to be an industrial backwater with low productivity, poor infrastructure, unskilled workers, high tariffs and unco-operative bureaucrats. If the theory behind the law of comparative advantage is valid, then Mexico should not have been able to attract high-technology or manufacturing investment in the first place. Its comparative advantages should be in those industries which utilize labour-intensive, low-wage and low-skill assembly workers. How then, can the outflow of manufacturing jobs and production from Canada to Mexico be explained? It can be explained by considering the nature of North American trade, economic development in Mexico and the nature of the firms and jobs that moved there.

More than 90 percent of North American trade is carried out by a small number of MNCs such as General Motors, Ford, IBM, Xerox, Kodak, Goodyear, Proctor and Gamble, and Union Carbide.[117] The bulk of these economic exchanges are not governed by the laws of supply and demand operating in a competitive market. More than 75 percent of all trade in manufactured goods is intra-firm, that is, between branch plants of the same MNC. Because these transactions are intra-firm, the prices at which these intermediate goods trade are often determined by nonmarket considerations such as the reduction of regulatory costs imposed by national or subnational jurisdictions. The creation of an integrated North American market reduces the importance of national boundaries, thus providing MNCs more freedom to organize production in the most efficient manner possible. The FTA was therefore supported by most large MNCs because it allowed them to leave Canada in search of a less-regulated, lower-wage environment. But why move to Mexico? The right-to-work states appear to offer all the advantages of Mexico with the political stability of the United States. Mexico has been able to attract so much investment from Canada because of the virtues of the export processing zone Mexico created along its northern border which provides even lower-cost labour than a right-to-work state.

In 1965, Mexico instituted the Border Industrialization Program which opened up a 12 mile strip along its northern border to labour-intensive, export-oriented assembly plants. These plants are commonly called *maquiladoras*.[118] The Mexican government hoped to stimulate industrialization in northern Mexico by matching foreign capital with low-cost Mexico labour. In 1990, the average Mexican *maquiladora* worker earned US$1.40 per hour — only a tenth of what an American worker earns.[119] Foreign investors were also attracted to the *maquiladora* region because there were no restrictions on foreign ownership and no taxes were levied on the importation of raw materials and production equipment. Since 1972, *maquiladora* production has been allowed throughout Mexico but 80 percent of *maquiladora* production still occurs along the border in five cities: Tijuana, Mexicali, Nogales, Ciudad Juarez and Matamoros. Since 1980, the number of *maquiladoras* has quadrupled rising to over 2,000 plants which employed more than 450,000 workers. *Maquiladora* production provides Mexico with US$3.5 billion in foreign exchange, which is second only to the amount provided to Mexico by oil exports. The value-added by *maquiladora* production represents 1.5 percent of Mexico's GDP, 13 percent of total exports and 24 percent of manufacturing exports. Exports from the *maquiladora* region account for 60 percent of Mexico's non-oil exports to the United States. Foreign companies that produce goods in the *maquiladora* region are allowed to sell as much as 50 percent of those goods in Mexico, but as of 1990, 95 percent of goods were exported to the United States and elsewhere either as intermediate or finished products.

The *maquiladora* region was originally set up to exploit Mexico's comparative advantage in abundant, low-wage, low-skill labour.[120] In the 1960s and 1970s, unsophisticated assembly plants employed mainly Mexican women who would partially or completely assemble toys, garments and other consumer goods for export back to the United States. It was this image of Mexico that supporters of NAFTA have used to discount Canadian and American fears of job shifts to Mexico. The BCNI argued that low-wage workers in Mexico would not compete against Canadian workers for jobs. Furthermore, Mexico could not attract a large number of firms because productivity is so low in the *maquiladoras*. In addressing the fears of American workers, the U.S. Department of Commerce has made the same argument that Mexican workers are unproductive despite their low wages.[121]

The problem is that this argument is wrong. The *maquiladora* region of Mexico became "the newest American industrial belt" by the early

1990s.[122] Production in the border region of Mexico was once low-tech and labour-intensive. In the 1980s and 1990s, it became increasingly automated and high-tech with a good infrastructure. The technology and productivity gap that was supposed to dissuade firms from relocating to Mexico has virtually disappeared. Harley Shaiken, a labour economist at the University of California at San Diego, says that northern Mexico is now "almost a fifty-first state in terms of production."[123] Using this argument, northern Mexico could also be called the twenty-first right-to-work state. Mexican workers, with the help of imported American and Japanese technology, have increased their productivity levels. Current estimates place productivity levels of Mexican workers at about 70 percent of those achieved by the American labour force.[124] In certain sectors, Mexicans have the capacity to produce automobiles, computers and other electronic equipment at the same quality and productivity levels as the very best American or Japanese factories.[125] Sony produces colour televisions in Tijuana using sophisticated state-of-the-art circuit board technology. Ford Motor Company operates an assembly plant in Hermosillo that produced Mercury Tracers judged to be the second-highest quality subcompact in the United States. The problem for Canadian and American workers is that Mexican workers are matching their level of productivity while being paid only a fraction of the Canadian or American wage. Firms are shifting so much production to Mexico from Canada for the simple reason that the infrastructure is vastly improved, the wages are low and the unions are nonfunctional.[126]

A potential problem existed for companies that shifted production from Canada to Mexico. Because Mexico was not part of the FTA, companies could not export products made in Mexico directly to Canada without paying tariffs. This problem has been circumvented in three ways. The first strategy by MNCs was to use a regional "shell game" approach. American MNCs shifted branch plant production from Canada to Mexico. Goods produced in the *maquiladora* region were then exported to the American market. Goods produced in a plant in the United States were then redirected from the American market to serve the Canadian market. The second strategy is used in rare instances by MNCs who rely on Mexican labour only for the assembly of goods which are then sold in Canada. Firms can get away with this because the only value-added by Mexicans is the actual labour which is difficult to trace in the inventory of a MNC. The third strategy involved the implementation of NAFTA on January 1, 1994. NAFTA makes the first two strategies unnecessary because it eliminates all trade barriers between Canada, the United States and Mexico.

Canadian firms have been anticipating NAFTA for several years.[127] Some firms shifted production to Mexico in anticipation of NAFTA while others shifted production after the implementation of NAFTA. While it is not clear how many firms will leave Canada as a result of NAFTA, it is clear that as a result it is even easier to use the whipsaw to drive down Canadian wages or to serve the Canadian market from a Mexican or American production site.[128] Mexico launched an aggressive promotional and recruiting campaign in Canada and the United States detailing the advantages to Canadian and American firms who shift jobs and production to northern Mexico. David Conklin of the University of Western Ontario conducted a survey of large Canadian MNCs and found that most firms had considered shifting at least part of their production to Mexico or the United States. Many Canadian plant managers referred to the "psychological impact" of the FTA and NAFTA prompting them to think about the benefits of adopting a continental strategy.[129]

In January 1991, the president of the Automotive Parts Manufacturers Association of Canada (APMAC) led a trade mission of 18 automotive parts executives to Mexico. Ostensibly the mission was sent to Mexico to promote Canadian exports. However, the president of APMAC admitted that all the executives on the trade mission were actually scouting opportunities to shift Canadian production to Mexico. Prior to the FTA and NAFTA, managers had operated on the basis of a Canadian strategy. Under a continental strategy, corporations were now free to move production anywhere in North America. Only a skeleton crew of sales and warehouse staff is needed in Canada to serve the Canadian market.

Plant managers have justified their departure from Canada in three ways. First, companies have to cut costs in order to survive in the increasingly competitive global economy. The easiest way to control costs is to use the least expensive labour that can be found. If firms did not relocate to the United States or Mexico, they would have gone to East Asia. Mexico or the southern United States is closer and therefore more desirable for North American executives and workers. Many made the argument that people should not complain because the jobs were going to leave sooner or later anyway.[130] Free trade allows firms to move sooner rather than later, and at least the company is producing goods somewhere on the North American continent.

The second justification comes from plant managers who blame the Canadian unions and government regulations for forcing companies out. Paul Davidson, the president of Tridon Limited which moved from Ontario to Tennessee, blames Canadians for job relocations out of Canada.

He says that Canadians are at least partially to blame because they have failed to modify their high wages, exorbitant taxes and expensive social programmes in the face of international competition.[131] James Pattison, a Canadian entrepreneur and former chairman of Vancouver's Expo '86, agrees that Canadians are to blame for job losses. He went on to say that if he is not able to get his production costs down in Canada he will move his remaining Canadian assets to Seattle and Atlanta where he has already shifted some of his production. A CMA survey found that Davidson and Pattison are far from isolated examples. Of 2,500 companies surveyed, 313 had investigated the possibility of shifting production out of Canada. Of those, 237 concluded that it would be less expensive to produce in the United States. Furthermore, 156 firms revealed that they had been approached by U.S. state and local government officials trying to help them to relocate.[132]

The third way that managers justified relocations is to point out that they represent only a small fraction of the total Canadian labour force and that this small job loss is necessary for Canada to restructure its economy to compete in a free trade environment. David Culver, president of Alcan Aluminum, rationalized the southward migration of Canadian jobs by saying that "workers who suffer under free trade are like flowers that die so that other flowers can grow."[133] The business elite expect Canadians to accept southward migration of production and the concomitant loss of jobs as the unavoidable costs of preparing Canada for competition in the continental economy.

Are Canadian job losses a small but necessary price to pay? Let's consider the statement that job losses due to relocation are small in comparison to the total Canadian labour force. Over 42,062 jobs shifted from Canada to the United States and Mexico between 1988 and 1994 (see Appendix). When a mill shuts down and moves production out of Canada, the plant closure creates a ripple effect through the whole community that was abandoned. A plant closure sends a series of secondary shocks into the surrounding business community by affecting suppliers and contractors who used to conduct business with the firm before it moved production. A series of tertiary shocks affects the community as the newly-unemployed workers are not able to shop as much in local stores, the tax base is reduced and the demand for social services is increased.

Economists talk about indirect job losses in terms of employment multipliers. Several values have been suggested for the (un)employment multiplier or factor by which a plant relocation causes job loss in the broader community. The U.S. Department of Labor has pegged an unemployment multiplier for the closing of an automobile or auto parts plant at between 2.4 and 3.[134] The job loss multiplier is used in the following way. Assume the unemployment multiplier for this hypothetical example has a value of 2.4. This means that for every 100 workers that lose their jobs directly because of a plant relocation, another 140 lose their jobs indirectly in the broader community. The total job loss with a factor of 2.4 is 240 workers when 100 workers initially lost their jobs.

Lets reconsider the impact of plant relocations on Canadian job losses using the unemployment multiplier. The number of jobs lost directly because of plant relocation is estimated to be 42,062. The value of the multiplier ranges from 2.4 to 3.0 with an average value of 2.7. Using the average value, the estimated total job loss due to plant relocations alone is about 113,567 Canadian jobs. This figure does not include the estimated net loss of 350,000 manufacturing jobs that disappeared because of the rationalization process.[135] Adding up these two job loss estimates, Canada lost about 463,000 jobs due to the relocation of production and plant closures. The total number of Canadians employed in 1992 was estimated to be 12.2 million people. This means that the FTA eliminated 4 percent of the jobs in Canada. Canadian losses have far exceeded the worst-case scenario predicted by the professor from the University of Wisconsin who advised the ECC that Canada would lose at most 0.2 percent of its jobs.[136] Massive job losses have come in addition to the increasingly segmented work force and declining real wages.

The implementation of a continental model of development turns out to be a prescription for growth through social inequality. The FTA and now NAFTA ushers in a model of social polarization with islands of prosperity surrounded by a sea of poverty.[137] Corporations can either use the whipsaw to drive down wages *in situ* or move to low-cost production regions. Either way, jobs are lost and profits are increased. Despite the increase in volume of trade, Canada's unemployment rate has risen to 11 percent after five years of free trade. With increased unemployment comes increased demands on the Welfare State which in turn mean increased demand for government spending. Neoconservatives object to increased government expenditures because the higher taxes required to support the expenditures hurts their competitiveness.

Canadian workers are now faced with a situation where UI benefits are being cut just when they need them the most. Rising unemployment combined with a shrinking Welfare State represents the new model of development in North America. In the Fordist era, the mode of regulation was based on a Canadian Welfare State which generated social consensus and the perception of universality and equality. In the post-Fordist era of free trade, the pretensions of social equality have been abandoned. The State no longer poses as an impartial arbiter between labour and management. The post-Fordist State promotes a supranational model of development based on capital mobility and social inequality. The next chapter explains how the Canadian State came to adopt this role.

Notes

1. Palmer, *Working Class Experience*, 161.
2. Ibid., 217.
3. Harold Chorney, "Amnesia, Integration and Repression: the roots of Canadian Urban Culture," in *Urbanization and Urban Planning in Capitalist Society, Michael* Dear and Allen Scott, eds. (New York: Methuen, 1981), 547.
4. Wallace Clement, "Canada's Social Structure: Capital, Labour, and the State," in *Readings in Canadian History, Volume 5: Modern Canada*, Michael Cross and Gregory Kealey, eds. (Toronto: McClelland and Stewart, 1984), 87; Wayne Roberts and John Bullen, "A Heritage of Hope and Struggle: Workers, Unions, and Politics in Canada," in *Readings in Canadian History, Volume 5: Modern Canada*, Michael Cross and Gregory Kealey, eds. (Toronto: McClelland and Stewart, 1984), 107.
5. John Finlay and Douglas Sprague, *The Structure of Canadian History*, 2nd ed. (Scarborough, ON: Prentice-Hall, 1984), 446.
6. Roberts and Bullen, "A Heritage of Hope and Struggle," 117. Anne Forest, "Labour Legacy in Question," *Canadian Dimension*, 29 (February 1995): 29; American workers have similarly referred to the Wagner Act of 1935 as the Magna Carta of American labour law. In Both the United States and Canada, these labour reforms often only helped men, ignoring the plight of women in the workplace.
7. Carolyn Tuohy, *Policy and Politics in Canada: Institutionalized Ambivalence* (Philadelphia: Temple University Press, 1992), 164.
8. Ibid., 165.
9. A closed shop refers to a plant that agrees to hire only those persons who already belong to the union representing workers in that particular factory. In the United States, the closed shop was outlawed by the Taft-Hartley Act of 1947. In its place the union shop arose to permit a firm to hire a nonunion worker as long as the new employee agrees to join the union within a specified time. Unions would prefer a closed or union shop but twenty American states have implemented "right to work" legislation which permits an open shop to exist. Under an open shop, workers never have to join the union in order to work in a particular shop or to enjoy the benefits bargained for by union representatives in that shop.
10. Palmer, *Working Class Experience*, 292.

11. Ibid., 297.
12. Roberts and Bullen, "A Heritage of Hope and Struggle," 126.
13. Finlay and Sprague, *The Structure of Canadian History,* 448.
14. Rianne Mahon, "Post-Fordism: Some Issues for Labour," in *The New Era of Global Competition: State Policy and Market Power,* Daniel Drache and Meric Gertler, eds. (Montréal: McGill-Queen's University Press, 1991), 325.
15. Davis, *Prisoners of the American Dream,* ix; Kim Moody, *An Injury to All: The Decline of American Unionism* (New York: Verso, 1988), 140.
16. Bluestone and Harrison, *The Deindustrialization of America,* 136; Martin Morand, "Canada: Our Model," *Monthly Review* 42, no. 2 (1990): 47; Tuohy, *Policy and Politics in Canada,* 169.
17. Charles Sabel and Jonathon Zeitlin, "Historical Alternatives to Mass Production: Politics, Markets and Technology in Nineteenth-Century Industrialization," *Past and Present* 108 (August 1985): 133; Allen Scott, "Flexible Production Systems and Regional Development," *International Journal of Urban and Regional Research,* 12, no. 2 (1988): 171; John Lovering, "Fordism's Unknown Successor: A Comment on Scott's Theory of Flexible Accumulation and the Re-emergence of Regional Economies," *International Journal of Urban and Regional Research,* 14, no. 1 (1990): 159.
18. Statistics Canada, *Historical Labour Force Statistics,* (Ottawa: Supply and Services, 1992), 236.
19. Roberts and Bullen, "A Heritage of Hope and Struggle," 131.
20. Wolfe, "The Rise and Demise of the Keynesian Era in Canada," 73.
21. Drache, "The Systematic Search for Flexibility," 259.
22. Ibid., 256.
23. Ibid., 260.
24. Ibid., 260.
25. Ibid., 257.
26. Ibid., 225.
27. Sam Gindin, "Breaking Away: The Formation of the Canadian Auto Workers," *Studies in Political Economy,* 29 (Summer 1989): 63.
28. Tuohy, *Policy and Politics in Canada,* 170.
29. Canadian Alliance for Trade and Job Opportunities, "Straight Talk on Free Trade," *Maclean's, 21* November 1988, 23; ECC, *Reaching Out,* 41; ECC, *Venturing Forth,* 22; J. Schlefer, "What Price Economic Growth," *The Atlantic,* 270 (December 1992): 115.
30. Drew Fagan, "Unemployment Rate Jumps to 7.6% in May," *Globe and Mail,* 11 November 1988, B1.
31. Daniel Girard, "Jobless Must Blame Recession Not Free Trade, Wilson Says," *Toronto Star,* 30 May 1992, D1.
32. CLC, *CLC Free Trade Briefing Document,* 7 (1991): 5.
33. Charlotte Yates, "Free Trade: Year 3," *Canadian Dimension,* 26, no. 1 (1992): 5; Jackson, *Job Losses in Canadian Manufacturing,* 334; Ian Austen, "Trade Disputes Aren't Being Solved Any Faster With Pact," *Sault Star,* 14 March 1992, A5; Ian Austen, "Canadians Believed Trade Deal Closed Factories, Poll Says," *Sault Star,* 8 April 1992, A6; Patricia Lash, John Heinzl and Chetan Lakshman, "165,000

Factory Jobs Vanished in Past Year, StatsCan Report Says," *Globe and Mail,* 9 June 1990, A1.

35. Yates, "Free Trade: Year 3," 5.
36. Harvey Enchin, "Canadian Branch Assets Slashed Before Gillette Announced Closing," *Globe and Mail,* 25 November 1988, A1; Janis Hags, "Québec Shore Plant Being Shut Because of Greater Competition," *Globe and Mail,* 28 November 1988, A22; Brenda Dalglish, "The Fight to Find a Job," *Maclean's,* 24 June 1991, 16; "General tire Closes Barrie Plant: 820 Workers Lose Jobs," *Sault Star,* 31 August 1991, B10; "Trade Deal With U.S. Linked to Plant Closing," *Sault Star,* 26 November 1988, A6.
37. Judy MacDonald, "Talkin' Trade," *This Magazine,* 23 (December 1989): 42.
38. Canada, *Inflation and the Canadian Economy,* 1-2.
39. Ibid.
40. S. Dale, "One Year After: Free Trade Fallout," *This Magazine,* 23 (January 1990): 11.
41. K. Yakabuski, "Wage Hikes Higher in January," *Toronto Star,* 16 March 1991, C1; Shawn McCarthy, "Jobless Rate Forecast to Stay High For Years," *Toronto Star,* 5 August 1992, F1.
42. Girard, "Jobless Must Blame Recession Not Free Trade, Wilson Says," D1.
43. Schlefer, "What Price Economic Growth?" 117.
44. Bluestone and Harrison, *The Deindustrialization of America,* 45.
45. Geoffrey Scotton, "Report Outlines Pitfalls in Three-way Free Trade," *Financial Post,* 18 July 1991, 28.
46. Randy Robinson, "Index on Free Trade," *Canadian Forum,* 69 (January 1991): 32.
47. M. Clark, "Brave New World," *Maclean's* 9 January 1989, 12.
48. Canada, Adjusting to Win: Report of the Advisory Council on Adjustment (Ottawa: Ministry of Industry, Science and Technology, 1989), 2.
49. Ibid.
50. "$27 Million Set Aside to Help Canadian Business in Free Trade," *Sault Star,* 2 March 1993, A5.
51. BCNI, "The Canada-United States Free Trade Agreement," 6.
52. Laurell Ritchie, "The Attack on UI," *This Magazine,* 23 (November 1989): 14.
53. CLC, *CLC Free Trade Briefing Document,* 2 (July 1989): 20.
54. John DeMont, "Paying the Piper: Ottawa Clamps Down on Unemployment Insurance," *Maclean's,* 18 December 1990, 42.
55. Ed Finn and Michael McBane, "Index on Unemployment Insurance," *Canadian Forum,* 68 (May 1990): 32.
56. Laurell, "The Attack on UI," 15.
57. Ibid.
58. Ibid.
59. Ibid.
60. Morand, "Canada: Our Model?" 22.
61. Shawn McCarthy, "Federal PCs Ram Through UI Bill Cutting Payment to Quitters," *Toronto Star,* 25 March 1993, A5.
62. Ted Byfield, "Federal Liberals Retreat on Left-wing Issues," *Financial Post,* 20

May 1995, 24; John Geddes, "Martin Steers Toward Blue Liberalism," *Financial Post*, 22 October 1994, 5; Mel Watkins, "Foreign Ownership '94 - Bye, Buy Canada," *This Magazine*, 27, no. 8 (1994): 30.

63. Edward Greenspon, "New UI Plan Would Cut Benefits," *Globe and Mail*, 10 June 1995, A1, A10.
64. M.J. Piore and C.F. Sabel, The Second Industrial Divide: Possibilities for Production (New York: Basic Books, 1984); Louis Uchitelle, "Use of Temporary Workers on Rise in Manufacturing," *New York Times*, 6 July 1993, A1, C2.
65. Michael Storper and Allen Scott, "The Geographical Foundations and Social Regulation of Flexible Production Complexes," in *The Power of Geography: How Territory Shapes Social Life*, Jennifer Wolch and Michael Dear, eds. (Boston: Unwin Hyman, 1989), 32.
66. Statistics Canada, *The Labour Force, April 1995* (Ottawa: Supply and Services, 1995), A8; Statistics Canada, *Historical Labour Force Statistics, 1991* (Ottawa: Supply and Services, 1992), 60 62.
67. Daniel Bell, *The Coming of the Post-Industrial Society* (New York: Basic Books, 1973); Fred Block, *Postindustrial Possibilities* (Berkeley, CA: University of California Press, 1990)
68. Statistics Canada, *Canadian Economic Observer*, (Ottawa: Supply and Services, 1993); Eric Beauchesne, "Fewer Canadians Producing Goods, StatsCan Reports," *Sault Star*, 9 March 1993, A5.
69. Brenda Dalglish, "On the Rebound," *Maclean's*, 28 June 1993, 25.
70. John Naisbitt and Patricia Aburdene, *Megatrends 2000: Ten New Directions for the 1990s* (New York: Avon Books, 1990), 25; William Orme, "Myth Versus Facts: The Whole Truth About the Half-Truths," *Foreign Affairs*, 75, no. 5 (1993): 4.
71. Robert Reich, *The Work of Nations* (New York: Alfred A. Knopf, 1991); Lester Thurow, *Head to Head: The Coming Battle Among Japan, Europe, and America* (New York: William Morrow and Company, 1992).
72. Statistics Canada, "Statistical Summary," *Canadian Economic Observer* (Ottawa: Supply and Services, 1995); Statistics Canada, *Canadian Economic Observer* (Ottawa: Supply and Services, 1993).
73. John Myles, "Post-Industrialism and the Service Economy," in *The New era of Global Competition*, Daniel Drache and Meric Gertler, eds. (Montréal: McGill-Queen's University Press, 1991), 354.
74. Drache, "The Systematic Search for Flexibility," 262.
75. Statistics Canada, "Statistical Summary," *Canadian Economic Observer* (Ottawa: Supply and Services, 1995).
76. Bluestone and Harrison, *The Deindustrialization of America*, 72; Edward Malecki, *Technology and Development* (New York: Longmans, 1991), 68.
77. Ross Laver, "Scrapping the Assembly Line," *Maclean's*, 12 August 1991, 28; Sayer and Walker, *The New Social Economy*, 183.
78. Andrew Sayer, "Industrial Location on a World Scale: The Case of the Semiconductor Industry," in *Production, Work, Territory: The Geographical Anatomy of Industrial Capitalism*, Allen Scott and Michael Storper, eds. (Boston: Unwin Hyman, 1988), 107.
79. Buroway, *The Politics of Production*, 143.

80. Mike Parker and Jane Slaughter, *A Union Strategy Guide for Labor-Management Participation Programs* (Detroit: Labor Notes, 1992), 1.
81. Ibid.
82. Ibid.
83. Ibid., 15.
84. Tuohy, *Policy and Politics in Canada*, 197.
85. John Daly, "Automotive Shakeout," *Maclean's*, January 15, 1990, 24.
86. Schlefer (1992, 118) quotes from the late Chilean economist Fernando Fajnzylber who believed that economic growth occurs most sustainably in countries promoting some measure of social equity. He argued that the key measure of equity promoting growth was income distribution because it implies social co-operation. Fajnzylber compared Japan, West Germany and the United States from 1960 to 1980. He found that during this period Japan had the most equitable distribution of income, followed by West Germany and then the United States. During the same period, Japan grew most rapidly, followed by West Germany, and then the United States. He went on to argue that given the tendency toward polarization in North America and the creation of trade blocs, it may be that Europe and Japan will outcompete North America because of the more equitable income policies in those areas. Of course the argument can be made that Japan and Germany grew more rapidly because of their newer, more productive capital stock put in place since the Second World War, but the impact of the maldistribution of income in the United States must not be overlooked as a source of slow growth.
87. Robert Swift, "Manufacturing Job Losses Cripple the Economy," *New York Times*, 4 July 1993, A14.
88. Kim Moody and Mary McGinn, *Unions and Free Trade: Solidarity Versus Competition* (Detroit: A Labor Notes Book, 1992), 1; Jim Sinclair, "Free Trade: The Canadian Way," *Z Magazine*, 6 (July/August 1993): 21.
89. Samuel Bowles, foreword to *Creating a New World Economy: Forces of Change and Plans for Action*, Gerald Epstein, Julie Graham and Jessica Nembhard, eds. (Philadelphia: Temple University Press, 1993), xvii.
90. Wonnacott and Hill, *Canadian and U.S. Adjustment Policies in a Bilateral Trade Agreement*; E.P. Neufeld, "Financial and Economic Dimensions of Free Trade," *Canadian-American Free Trade: Historical, Political and Economic Dimensions* (Halifax: The Institute for Research on Public Policy, 1987); Richard Lipsey and Robert York, *Evaluating the Free Trade Deal: A Guided Tour Through the Canada-U.S. Agreement* (Toronto: C. D. Howe Institute, 1988).
91. ECC, *Venturing Forth*, 21.
92. Harley Shaiken, "Will Manufacturing Head South," *Technology Review*, 24 (April 1993): 28.
93. Schlefer, "What Price Economic Growth," 115.
94. ECC, *Venturing Forth*, 27.
95. Stephen Franklin, "Whipsaw Debate on GM Policy," *The Chicago Tribune*, 26 February 1992, sec. 3, 3.
96. Michael Lynk, "The Labour Law Factor: What Effect Will the Free Trade

Agreement Have on the Legislative Gains Made by the Canadian Labour Movement? *Canadian Labour,* Spring (1988): 18.

97. Judy MacDonald, "Talkin' Trade," *This Magazine,* 23 (September 1989): 42.
98. V. Galt, "Small Town Hard Hit by 3 Plant Closings," *Globe and Mail,* 9 June 1990, A7.
99. John Fryer, "Canada-Mexico 'Free Trade': Worse than Canada-U.S. FTA," *Canadian Dimension,* 24 (September 1990): 33.
100. "GM 'Not Bluffing' About Closing Plant If Concessions Not Granted," *Sault Star,* 19 June 1991, A8.
101. "Uniroyal Conditions Leave Workers Bitter," *Sault Star, 21* June 1991, A6; Galt, "Small Town Hard Hit by 3 Plant Closings," A7.
102. R. Brehl, "NDP Accused of Frightening Business Off," *Toronto Star,* 18 June 1991, B3.
103. D'Arcy Jenish and Pat Chisholm, "Tighter Picket Lines," *Maclean's,* 10 August 1992, 44; Derek Ferguson, "Labour Plan Will Drive Retailers Into Bankruptcy," *Toronto Star,* 7 August 1992, A13.
104. "A Blunt Warning," *Maclean's,* 27 January 1992, 27.
105. Leo Panitch and Donald Swartz, "The Social Contract: Labour, the NDP and Beyond," *Canadian Dimension,* 27 (November 1993): 28; Laura Fowlie, "Union Rifts Cost Labour Credibility," *Financial Post,* 24 December 1994, 11.
106. Martin Mittelstaedt and Murray Campbell, "Harris Vows to Undo 'Damage' by NDP," *Globe and Mail,* 10 June 1995, A1.
107. Brenda Dalglish, "Goin' Down the Road," *Maclean's,* 28 June 1993, 28; John Davies, "British Columbia Vows to Fight NAFTA," *Journal of Commerce,* 29 March 1993, 1A.
108. McGaughey, *A U.S.-Mexico-Canada Free Trade Agreement,* 73.
109. Barbara Wickens, "A Fresh Breath of Optimism," *Maclean's,* 18 March 1991, 39; "Workers Stand Guard After Employer Pulls Out," *Sault Star,* 3 February 1993, A1; Patricia Chisholm, "Giving Up, Moving Out," *Maclean's,* 18 March 1991, 36; Patricia Chisholm, "The Stampede to Buffalo," *Maclean's,* 18 March 1991, 44; Clyde Farnsworth, "Free-trade Accord is Enticing Canadian Companies to the U.S.," *New York Times,* 9 August 1991, A1, C3; "Toronto Firm Decides on New York for Expansion," *Sault Star,* 29 February 1991, A7; "Defence Plant Heads South, 400 Lose Jobs," *Sault Star,* 2 April 1991, A6.
110. Kenneth Kidd, "Canadians Have an Eye on Buffalo for Business," *Toronto Star,* 19 November 1988, C1; Barbara Chisholm, "The Flight of Industry," *Maclean's,* 3 December 1990, 55; Chisholm, "The Stampede to Buffalo," 44.
111. Deborah Dowling, "Shuffling off to Buffalo: Exodus Worries Business, Political Leaders," *Sault Star,* 26 October 1991, A8.
112. CLC, *CLC Free Trade Briefing Document,* 2 (1989): 3.
113. The industrial heartland includes the following states: Connecticut, Illinois, Indiana, Kentucky, Massachusetts, Michigan, Missouri, New Jersey, Ohio, Pennsylvania, and Wisconsin. (Knox and Agnew, 1989, 146). Certainly, Michigan, Ohio, and even Pennsylvania could be considered to be border-states while New York could be considered to be central to the industrial heartland. However, states were categorized according to the nature of the firms that migrated

to each region. Border-states generally received investment from small Canadian-owned firms, while American multinational corporations in the industrial heartland closed down branch plants in Canada and moved production back to the parent company.

114. Mike Trickey, "Trade Offices Bring Message North: U.S. Open For Business," *Sault Star*, 29 June 1991, A1; "Unions May Scare Off U.S. Investment: Harvard," *Globe and Mail*, 1 December 1988, B9.
115. Wonnacott and Hill, *Canadian and U.S. Adjustment Policies in a Bilateral Trade Agreement*, 15; Farnsworth, "Free-trade Accord is Enticing Canadian Companies to the U.S.," A1.
116. Bertrand Marotte, "North Carolina's Anti-Union Reputation Pays Off," *Sault Star*, 1 August 1992, A7; John Keating, "North Carolina a Model of Success in Drawing Business, Investment," *Financial Post*, 17 September 1994, S17.
117. CLC, *CLC Free Trade Briefing Document*, 6 (August 1990): 1-2.
118. Hufbauer and Schott, *North American Free Trade*, 91; The term "maquiladora" comes from the Spanish word *maquilar*, which means to retain a portion of flour as payment for milling or processing somebody's wheat. Similarly, a *maquiladora* is any processor of goods to be returned to the original producer for resale. Inputs are imported duty-free into Mexico, but the importer posts a bond stating that no goods or only a certain portion of the finished goods will be sold in Mexico. Most or all of the goods must be exported. If not, duties are collected by the Mexican government.
119. Tom Barry, *Mexico: A Country Guide* (Albuquerque: Inter-Hemispheric Education Resource Center, 1992), 142-44.
120. Hufbauer and Schott, *North American Free Trade*, 91.
121. BCNI, "Canada-Mexico-United States Free Trade: A Canadian Perspective," (Ottawa: Unpublished Report of the BCNI, 1990), 1; U.S. Department of Commerce, *North American Free Trade Agreement: Generating Jobs for Americans* (Washington, DC: U.S. Government Printing Office, 1991).
122. Louis Uchitelle, "America's Newest Industrial Belt: Northern Mexico Becomes a Big Draw for High-tech Plants - and Jobs," *New York Times*, 21 March 1993, E1, E14.
123. Ibid.
124. Ibid.
125. Shaiken, "Will Manufacturing Head South?" 28.
126. Labor unions have a long history in Mexico but they have not been effective institutions representing Mexican workers. Over the past 10 years Mexican minimum wages have decreased 60 percent in real terms. Union corruption and the fact that the Mexican State maintains close control over unions also hinder the efficacy of organized labour to improve the lot of the Mexican workers (Barry 1992, 190).
127. American firms have been looking forward to NAFTA as well because it makes it even easier to coerce concessions out of American workers and localities or to actually move production to Mexico because of dropping trade barriers. A *Wall Street Journal* survey of 455 top U.S. executives asked their opinions about

NAFTA (Hightower 1993, 97). Fifty-five percent said that they would move at least some production to Mexico as a result of NAFTA. One-fourth of the executives admitted that the threat of relocation to Mexico would be used to force concessions out of workers.

128. "Learn How You Can Cut Manufacturing Costs Up to 50% in Mexico," *Wall Street Journal*, 6 April 1989, A2; Tim Golden, "Mexico Pulls Out of a Fund that has Roiled Trade Issue," *New York Times*, 18 February 1993, C1.
129. "Ottawa Warned Free Trade Had Some Firms Thinking of Leaving," *Sault Star*, 30 November 1992, B7.
130. Larry Rubstein, "A Mexican Miracle," *Newsweek*, 20 May 1991, 45; William Orme, "Myth Versus Fact: The Whole Truth About the Half-truths," *Foreign Affairs*, 72, no. 5 (1993): 5.
131. Chisholm, "Giving Up, Moving Out," 36.
132. Ibid.
133. "Free Trade Victims Likened to 'Flowers that Die'," *Toronto Star*, 24 November 1988, D1.
134. Bluestone and Harrison, *The Deindustrialization of America*, 71; Malecki, *Technology and Economic Development*, 41.
135. Eric Beauchesne, "Crow Wants Inflation in Line With U.S. Rate," *Sault Star*, 17 January 1992, A6.
136. ECC, *Reaching Out*, 41; ECC, *Venturing Forth*, 22.
137. Noam Chomsky, "Notes on NAFTA," *Open Magazine Pamphlet Series*, 24, no. 1 (1993): 5.

Chapter 5

The Canadian Welfare State and Free Trade

During the Fordist era, the State had a powerful legitimation role, utilizing social welfare programmes to minimize class and social conflicts in order to ensure stable economic growth. In the crisis of Fordism and the subsequent implementation of free trade, the State has at least partially abandoned its legitimation role to promote economic expansion. With its more overt focus on capital accumulation, the State has allowed greater social inequalities to develop in the name of economic growth. Canada is becoming a "post-national State," increasingly tied to a continental model of development that accepts social inequality as the price for economic growth.[1] The ability to implement social and political policy has become constrained due to the continental market forces unleashed by free trade. The fact that Jean Chrétien and the Liberals continued neoconservative policies after they ousted Mulroney in the 1993 elections testifies to this new reality. The Canadian electorate voted for the Liberals in part because the Liberals had promised to renegotiate the North American Free Trade Agreement (NAFTA) and to bolster Canada's social safety net. By 1995, it became clear to many Canadians that just the opposite had happened. Canada was deeply embedded in a continental free trade agreement and social spending had been cut further by Prime Minister Jean Chrétien and his Finance Minister Paul Martin. This chapter examines how free trade and related cuts to the Welfare State have been used by the Tories and the Liberals to accelerate Canada's transition from a Fordist to a post-Fordist model of development.

The Role of the State Under Fordism

Disagreement over free trade can be traced in part to differing views on the broader role of the State in a capitalist society. Supporters of free trade stated that Canadian social programmes and sovereignty would be unaffected by free trade because the FTA was an economic policy, not a political policy.[2] Neoconservatives adopted a "theory of the State in capitalism" which conceptualizes the role of the State as being separate from that of the economy.[3] They derive their view of the world from neoclassical economics which views economic crisis only indirectly. In the pure neoclassical model of the economy in which the State is imbedded, all markets are theorized as tending towards equilibrium. Growth and full employment are believed to be the norm. Any economic crises are viewed as resulting from external shocks such as an energy crisis or a blockage of the market mechanism by monopolies or militant unions. Furthermore, the State is conceived as a neutral institution where the issue of class is largely irrelevant. The neoclassical viewpoint focuses on the role of individual behavior in the marketplace or political arena. The State is deemed to be above the endemic conflicts of society and can therefore act as an impartial umpire in democratic conflicts.[4] This pluralist conception of the State as a servant of the citizenry is deficient because it fails to consider the interdependence of the State and economy, the class nature of capitalist society, the class bias of the State, and the role of the State in a time of crisis.

Many opponents to free trade adopt a "theory of the capitalist State" which attributes a central role to class struggle in the process of capitalist economic growth.[5] The capitalist State is a non-neutral institution imbedded within a class society where economic crisis is an inherent characteristic of that economy. Crisis does not occur from some exogenous shock such as a war or energy shortage. Crisis occurs because of the inherent qualities of capitalism including the tendency towards overproduction, class struggle and the rate of profit to fall.

According to this view, the development of the State is essential for capitalism to survive because it alone is able to ameliorate class struggle and counter the tendency toward economic decline. In the early development of capitalism, the State helped to develop the proletariat through such actions as the Enclosure Movement and the Corn Laws in England. The State also established the legal foundation for capitalism by protecting the concept of private property. Later, the State intervened to help centralize and monopolize capital and form the imperialist world market. Capital tends toward crisis and collapse, yet it seldom does because the State has been able to implement counter-cyclical economic, political and social policies.

A theory of the capitalist State also emphasizes the ideological-repressive functions of the State in the regulation of society. Capitalism depends upon a State which can regulate antagonistic social relations which would otherwise tear society apart. Viewed in this way, conceptions of the State, economy and society are combined in a relational and reciprocal totality referred to by Gramsci as a "historical bloc."[6] The idea of a model of development is based on Gramsci's concept because of the shared emphasis on the role of hegemony and a proactive State to generate ideological and societal consensus.

Hegemony can be defined as the political and ideological practices through which the dominant class or ruling interests maintain their dominant position within society. The goal of the hegemonic class is to convince the working class to consent to the social and economic conditions defining the current model of development. Hegemonic interests must do more than control workers in factories to perpetuate capitalism. Economic growth and the reproduction of class relations depends upon mass production as well as mass consumption. Because consumption occurs away from the factory, class struggle and consumption patterns must be regulated at sites away from the factory. The Welfare State built societal consensus by penetrating deep into the social relations that defined education, religion, the media and the family.[7] The worst social antagonisms within the Fordist model of development were effectively mediated through the implementation of the modern Welfare State. Unpopular government policies that favored business interests could be made more palatable to the working class, women and minorities if social spending was increased.

The Welfare State was rooted in the long traditions of progressivism in the late nineteenth century, union demands of the early twentieth century, and economic planning of the New Deal era.[8] Building on this legacy of social protection and altruism, the discourse surrounding the Welfare State generated an ideology that all people, regardless of class, gender, ethnicity or religion, were autonomous individuals who were free to make demands and compete on an equal basis for the realization of those demands. Inevitable conflicts were mediated by the State as an unbiased arbiter which gained its legitimacy from references to bureaucratic expertise, technical rationality and national interests.[9] The ideology of pluralism and equality of access to the resources of the State was central to the discourse surrounding the Welfare State. Social antagonisms were dispersed into a multiplicity of separate political spaces instead of being coalesced into overt class conflict. Public opinion within Fordist society paid scant attention to the various differences between the radical Left and the radical Right. The differences between these polar opposites were overshadowed by their common appeal to conflict and radical change, contrasting with the harmony, universality and social engineering of the Welfare State. The result of the hegemonic discourse of the Welfare State was that social antagonisms were sufficiently displaced so that the modern Welfare State could present itself as a unifying apparatus where all people within a particular country accepted the ideology of equality of opportunity.[10]

The Welfare State ensured the relative stability of Fordism through a number of institutional arrangements. First, societal relations were stabilized through a constant rotation of social minorities who were included and then subsequently excluded from the hegemonic bloc according to short term calculations. Minorities were given just enough access to the benefits of the Welfare State to manage conflict. Second, the wage relation was expanded so that mass consumption could keep up with mass production. Furthermore, the State moderated labour militancy by passing legislation such as the Wagner Act in the U.S. which recognized unions as legitimate representatives of the workers. Third, the worst aspects of intercapitalist rivalry were ameliorated within a Keynesian macroeconomic framework involving negotiation between capital, the State and unions. The Welfare State was an essential component of a system which promoted unprecedented economic growth from the late 1940s to the late 1960s in the industrialized democracies of North America and Western Europe.

The crisis of the modern Welfare State can be linked to the economic and political crises affecting most industrial democracies during the late 1960s. The lack of government revenues halted the stable articulation of the State, economy and civil society.[11] First, consider the relation between the State and the economy. During the most productive periods of the Fordism, the Keynesian State played a central regulatory role by spending money on infrastructural and welfare projects as a way of preventing serious recessions. When the economic crisis became manifest in the late 1960s, State interventions became increasingly politicized for two reasons. First, in order to combat the inflation accompanying the crisis almost every industrial democracy adopted high interest rates. The impact of these policies was to undermine the institutionalized guarantees of full employment, predictable wage increases and collective welfare provisions which had ameliorated class conflict and legitimated government activity on behalf of business interests. Second, in order for the Welfare State to be able to continue offering services, it had to raise taxes which further alienated capital and labour. The State was caught in a situation where no matter what it did, it could not avoid alienating a significant portion of society. The State had to provide assistance to ailing companies while at the same time providing support for increased numbers of unemployed workers. Lower tax revenues coupled with an increased need to spend money induced a fiscal and legitimation crisis of the State.[12]

Consider, secondly, the relation between civil society and the State which had also become a terrain of increased struggle during the crisis of the Welfare State. During the 1960s women and minorities were offered the hope of social equality based on the State's recognition of unions, the expansion of social spending and the linkage of real wage increases to improvements in productivity. The promise was almost realized with President Johnson's "Great Society" programmes in the 1960s.[13] However, the fiscal problems of the 1970s and Reaganomics of the 1980s undermined the role of the Welfare State as a cohesive force. New social movements rose up in this ideological power vacuum and challenged the Fordist model of development.

Finally, important changes occurred in the articulation of the economy and civil society. The production system under Fordism was characterized by mass production, unionization and wage increases that matched productivity increases. In the emerging post-Fordist production system, new technologies are being introduced which tend to segment the work force into skilled and unskilled labour. Unions are being weakened, the work force is being fragmented and greater flexibility is being sought after by capital who wants to be able to adapt to changing market conditions as rapidly as possible.

Recently, American unions have lost bitterly contested battles with management and the U.S. federal government. The ability of workers to strike has been greatly undermined because the U.S. Supreme Court and the National Labor Relations Board have worked to reverse 35 years of pro-labour legislation.[14] The most obvious attack by the State has been on the right of unionized workers to strike without losing their jobs. The Reagan Administration replaced striking air traffic controllers. Similarly, Greyhound Bus Lines, Hormel Meats, Pittston Coal, Eastern Airlines and Caterpillar Tractor have adopted the strategy of replacing striking union workers as a way to discipline the work force. These direct assaults on the labour movement have contributed to the declining importance of unions in U.S. society.

The bulk of the burden of increasing corporate flexibility is being carried by workers and their families. Large sectors of the population including minorities, militant unions, unskilled workers and underdeveloped regions have been excluded from the purported benefits of enhanced corporate efficiency. The unifying ideology of the Fordist Welfare State has been replaced by the post-Fordist ideology of globalization and industrial competitiveness based on labour force segmentation and polarization. Industrial democracies are increasingly being incorporated into models of development where societal inequality is an explicit aspect of the hegemonic State ideology.

Under Fordism, the accumulation role of the State in promoting economic growth was supported by the legitimation role of the Welfare State in promoting social equity. In the post-Fordist era, the legitimation role of the Welfare State has become an impediment to corporate profitability. Because capital mobility is an increasing requirement for corporate profitability, the Welfare State has become more of a hindrance than a help in the eyes of many neoconservatives. The discourse of the beneficent Welfare State has been replaced by the post-Fordist discourse of competitiveness and flexibility. State-capital alliances are no longer concerned with creating the facade of social and regional equality through the Welfare State. Corporations overtly exploit regional and social differences in order to make the greatest profit. Corporate interests do not want to pay the taxes needed to support the Welfare State because that would hinder their competitiveness. MNCs also resent government intrusion into the economy in the form of protectionism and regulatory policy.

In Canada, the trappings of the Welfare State were more widespread and have persisted longer than those in the United States. It is my contention that the FTA and NAFTA were implemented as a way to further erode the basis of the Welfare State in Canada, thus harmonizing Canadian conditions with those of the United States. Neoconservatives wanted to cut back on workers' benefits, health care and education expenditures because they dulled the competitive edge of the Canadian worker. As social spending is cut, workers have no option but to find work regardless of the wage or working conditions. Free trade therefore acts as a catalyst, driving down the social wage to create a more flexible and compliant Canadian work force.

Free Trade and the Decline of the Canadian Welfare State

The FTA makes no explicit reference to the Canadian Welfare State. The Economic Council of Canada (ECC) uses this fact to say that the FTA is in no way linked to Canada's social welfare programmes nor will the FTA be used to undermine Canada's UI programme, Medicare, education or any other programmes that form the foundation of Canada's social safety net.[15] In fact, the ECC predicted that the FTA would strengthen Canada's economy and thereby generate more tax revenue. Flora MacDonald, the federal minister of communication under Mulroney, agreed with this position and railed against free trade opponents who warned that free trade would lead to social spending cuts.[16] In the end, supporters of the FTA predicted that it would increase the capacity of the Canadian State to guard social programmes and Canadian culture. The discourse of the Welfare State and social equality was used repeatedly during the 1988 election campaign to dispel the doubts held by Canadians about the impacts of the FTA.

The FTA was designed to facilitate the restructuring of the Canadian economy and labour force. Due to the interdependence of the economy, society and the State, it is logical to argue that free trade would transform the State just as it has forced changes in the economy and work force. In 1988, many Canadians feared the potential consequences of the FTA for the structure of social welfare. They believed that it was Mulroney's intention to transform the very role of the State in their lives by promoting public policy harmonization between Canada and the United States.[17] As early as 1986, writers predicted that free trade would force the privatization of many programmes offered by the Welfare State, reduce the number of government employees, and harmonize the level of social programmes down to those of the United States.[18]

Predictions on the impact of the FTA were based on statements made by business leaders such as Mickey Cohen, former deputy finance minister to Michael Wilson and now president of Molson Companies Limited. Cohen believed that free trade would create intense pressures for the harmonization of standards between Canada and the United States. Pressures were predicted to come from both American and Canadian business interests in Canada who resented high Canadian taxes and the inflexible labour force that had unreasonably high access to social resources. Universal health care, social programmes and UI benefits would all become victims of free trade some time after 1989. Cohen's final pronouncement on the fate of the Welfare State was that Mulroney would not take direct action to trim social programmes because the body politic would not tolerate it.[19] Therefore, the Tories could be expected to rely on market forces and subterfuge to implement their agenda.

Attempts by Tories to rationalize the Welfare State have been described as the "politics of stealth."[20] From 1984 to 1988, they focused on an agenda of deficit reduction, tax reform and international competitiveness. Because they were reluctant to dismantle a Welfare State that ameliorated class, regional and linguistic antagonisms, the Progressive Conservatives chose "to incrementally chip away at the Welfare State."[21] Despite their attempts at restructuring, they were not effectively meeting neoconservative demands for change. The FTA represented a qualitative change in the politics of stealth because it could utilize continental market forces to accelerate the changes outlined within the neoconservative agenda.

Business interests wanted transformations in the State that would enhance their flexibility, mobility and competitiveness in a free trade area.[22]

One month before the implementation of the FTA, the CMA announced that it favored the establishment of a Royal Commission on Social Spending which could recommend how to make social spending cuts to enhance corporate competitiveness.[23] The Business Council on National Issues (BCNI) publicly announced that Canada needed to rally around a "competitiveness agenda" that included a two-year freeze on federal spending, constitutional reforms which reduced the role of government and a new social policy strategy that abandoned the principle of universality in order to maximize the benefits offered by the FTA.[24] The discourse of equality and universality was superseded by the discourse of competitiveness and inequality.

Canadians wondered how they would be helped by a free trade pact that promised to rationalize the institutions which formed the basis of the Canadian State in all its forms including the Welfare State, culture, and transportation system. Canadians might get more private goods in the form of commodities under the FTA, but it was probably impossible to do this without sacrificing some of the "public good" that makes up Canadian society.[25] Canadian productivity is lower than that of the United States, but the more collectively-oriented polity of Canada offers more noneconomic benefits than the United States. Canadian attitudes and expectations about unions, health care, education and regional development could be altered by free trade. It is necessary to ask whether it was wise to seek more private goods if they came at the expense of the noneconomic benefits that are provided by Canadian society, sovereignty and the Welfare State.

Transfer Payments for Education and Health Care

The State has always played a leading role in the development of the Canadian economy and society. The idea of a Fordist Welfare State was established by the 1945 federal *White Paper on Employment and Incomes.* This report advocated the creation of a social safety net designed to complement the rise of the modern industrial Nation-State. Leonard Marsh was commissioned to conduct this study because of two fears held by prominent Canadian political leaders. First, Canadian leaders worried that massive unemployment would occur when soldiers returned from the Second World War. A strategy was needed to ward off social unrest that was sure to follow. Second, political and business leaders feared the emergence of socialism as expressed through the Communist Party of Canada and the CCF. Government intervention via the Welfare State promised to ameliorate the worst aspects of capitalism without prompting voters to turn towards socialism.

The Welfare State was used to legitimate capitalist accumulation during a tumultuous time immediately after World War II. Since that time, the State has expanded into all aspects of Canadian society. Public enterprises such as the Canadian National Railroad (CNR) and Air Canada have influenced development in the transportation sector. Television and radio development has been influenced by CBC Television, CBC Radio and Radio Canada in Québec. Institutions such as Petro Canada and Ontario Hydro have played central roles in the development of Canadian energy resources. At various times the State has sought to manage natural resources and to ensure domestic security through commodity marketing boards and investment guidelines. The State has also developed a domestic industrial base through the use of tariffs and performance requirements for foreign investment. The Auto Pact used domestic content requirements to reinvigorate a deteriorating automotive industry in Canada in the 1960s. The State has spent millions of dollars through the Canada Council to promote Canadian culture. Finally, the State has used welfare programmes as a way to stimulate effective demand and as a policy tool for community building and social justice. National universal health care, UI benefits, family allowance benefits, national retirement benefits and regional development programmes all contribute to the Canadian standard of living. These programmes reduced social and regional inequalities thereby legitimating the accumulation process.

In the initial FTA debate, Canadians were promised that they could expect the same level of social services after free trade as before. The FTA was just an economic agreement that would lower tariffs between Canada and the United States. However, within a month of the 1988 Tory electoral victory, corporate interests lead by the CMA, BCNI and the Canadian Chamber of Commerce launched a campaign to cut the deficit and reduce spending on social services.[26] According to this group, the problem was not that American social welfare standards were too low. Rather, the problem was that the social wage in Canada was too high. To be competitive under free trade, Canada would have to role back social services to the levels available in the United States. Laurent Thibault, former president of the CMA, explained the corporate point of view in the following manner: "It is a simple fact that as we ask our industries to compete toe to toe with American industry ... we in Canada are obviously forced to create the same conditions in Canada that exist in the U.S., whether it is the UI scheme, workman's compensation, the cost of government, the level of taxation or whatever."[27]

Shortly after the FTA was implemented, it became clear that campaign promises would be broken. Deep social spending cuts were made to facilitate the implementation of the FTA. The Canadian Labour Congress (CLC) outlined three general mechanisms through which the FTA has affected the public sector in Canada.[28] First, competitive pressures unleashed by the FTA forced the Canadian government to create a level playing field so that firms in Canada could compete with firms from the United States. Part of the leveling or harmonization process included tax reform, cuts in social spending and labour reforms. Failure to enact these reforms was met with threats of plant relocation. Second, increased capital mobility and increasingly integrated financial markets made it difficult for the Canadian government to raise taxes on corporations and wealthy individuals. The FTA therefore weakened the fiscal capacity of the government. The third free trade factor influencing the State had to do with the interest rate policy. The Bank of Canada pursued a high interest rate policy to counter an alleged inflation problem. The high interest rate policy actually put intense pressure on the federal deficit and has created a climate of urgency to reduce government spending on social and regional development programmes.

The interest rate has a serious impact on the deficit because a one percent increase in the Bank of Canada interest rate adds approximately Can$1.5 billion a year to the cost of servicing Canada's national debt. The cost of servicing the debt masks the fact that the Tories have been cutting social spending since they came to power in 1984. Mulroney came into office in 1984 faced with a Can$17 billion operating deficit for social programmes. By 1992, the Tories had turned this deficit into a Can$9 billion surplus by cutting social programmes. The national debt kept growing because of the high interest charges related to the high interest rate policy followed by the Bank of Canada.

Here the politics of stealth worked most effectively. Neoconservatives complained that rising social spending was contributing to the national debt and hampering national competitiveness. Yet, as Figure 34 shows, social spending cannot be blamed because social spending as a percent of total federal government expenditures and as a percent of GDP was stable throughout Mulroney's tenure while the Canadian national debt grew dramatically.

Alternatively, Figure 35 shows that while social spending remained relatively stable during the late 1980s, the deficit as a percentage of the GDP dropped because revenues have risen. The debt problem was not a deficit problem based on excessive spending, but a high interest rate

Figure 34
Federal Government Spending on Social Programs

Year	As a % of Total Expenditures	As a % of GDP	Federal Debt (Can$ millions)
1984	55.6	26.2	160,768
1985	55.8	26.1	199,092
1986	56.9	26.3	233,496
1987	56.3	25.6	264,101
1988	56.5	24.8	292,184
1989	56.2	24.8	320,918
1990	56.7	26.3	357,811
1991	58.5	29.1	388,429

Source: Statistics Canada, *Canadian Social Trends* 36 (Spring 1995): 35.

problem.[29] The deficit was under control, declining as a percent of the GDP throughout the 1980s and into the free trade era. Figure 36 shows the composition of annual deficits in Canada, illustrating again that social spending was not exacerbating long-term debt. When the annual deficit is broken down into its component parts, high interest rates are shown to be the major culprit because they raised the costs of servicing the debt.

Despite this reality, neoconservatives targeted social programmes, not interest rates, as the major hindrance to corporate competitiveness. Once the FTA was in place, corporate lobbies became more aggressive and made public their attempts to restructure the Canadian Welfare State. Roger Hamel, an executive officer of the Canadian Chamber of Commerce, called for a Can$4 billion cut from UI benefits without any money going into retraining programmes. The Canadian Alliance for Trade and Job Opportunities (CATJO) and other business lobbies accused free trade opponents of being scaremongers for claiming the FTA would lead to cuts in social spending. Yet within months of the 1988 Tory electoral victory, neoconservatives were openly promoting social spending cuts. The Tories embraced the corporate agenda by cutting

Figure 35
Federal Revenues, Expenditures and Deficits as Percentages of the GDP

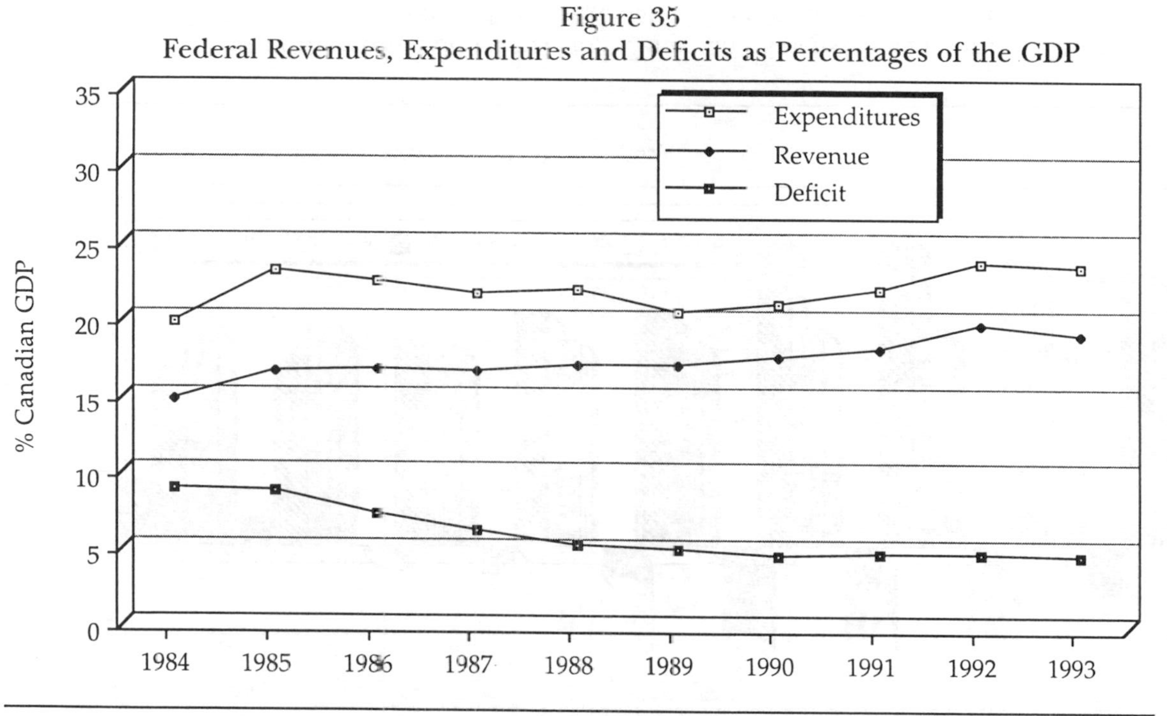

Source: Statistics Canada, Canadian Economic Observer (Ottawa: Supply and Services, 1995).

Figure 36
Canadian Federal Government Deficits

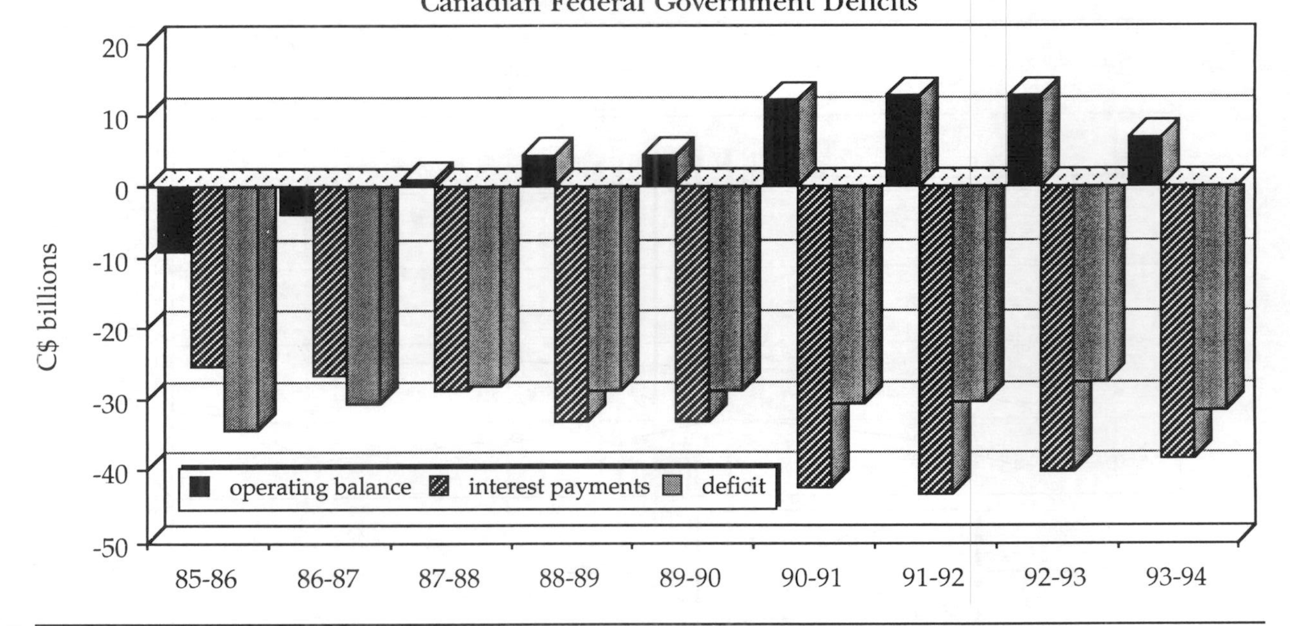

Source: "A Way Out of the Economic Wasteland," Canadian Dimension 26 (April 1992): 6; Statistics Canada, Canadian Economic Observer (Ottawa: Supply and Services, 1994).

nonmilitary spending from 20 percent of the GDP in 1988, to 16 percent of the GDP by 1992. Other cuts included 1989 UI reforms and Bill C-69, which in 1990 set in motion the gradual elimination of transfer payments from the federal government to help provinces run social welfare programmes.

In Canada, some of the most important Welfare State programmes such as education, health care and public housing are actually managed by the provinces. During the Fordist era, the federal government used the allocation of transfer payments as a means to ensure equality amongst all provinces. The Canadian federal system allowed provinces to design and manage a large portion of the Welfare State on a regional basis, but provinces were obligated to meet certain standards in order to receive money from Ottawa. In this way, the Canadian government guaranteed a certain level of regional autonomy while simultaneously ensuring a certain level of social and regional equality with regards to social spending.

During the transition to a post-Fordist model of development, the federal government shifted the burden of financing the Welfare State onto the provinces. As Figure 37 reveals, the Tories reduced transfer payments to the provinces that manage much of the Canadian Welfare State. Although there was a slight increase in transfer payments as a percent of total revenue in 1993, this does not hide the fact that federal contributions to provincial coffers have decreased since the start of the FTA negotiations in 1985.

This is akin to the "New Federalism" implemented by Ronald Reagan in the United States which also forced states to pay a larger proportion of the social welfare budget.[30] As transfer payments were reduced in Canada, the provinces had to either make up the difference or curtail services. This set up the potential for provinces to cut back on social spending in order to compete against each other for investment. Social and exacerbated regional inequality ensued just as it did in the United States under New Federalism.

Federal government transfer payments under the Tories came in three forms which were affected in different ways by Bill C-69. The first transfer payments, called equalization payments, transferred tax revenues collected in prosperous provinces such as Ontario, Alberta and British Columbia to poor provinces such as Newfoundland and New Brunswick. Their purpose was to ensure a basic level of social services from coast to coast regardless of location. Bill C-69 left equalization payments intact.

The second type of transfer payments come under the Canada Assistance Plan (CAP). CAP was established in 1966 and represented a major

Figure 37
Federal Transfer Payments to Provinces as a Percentage of Federal Revenue

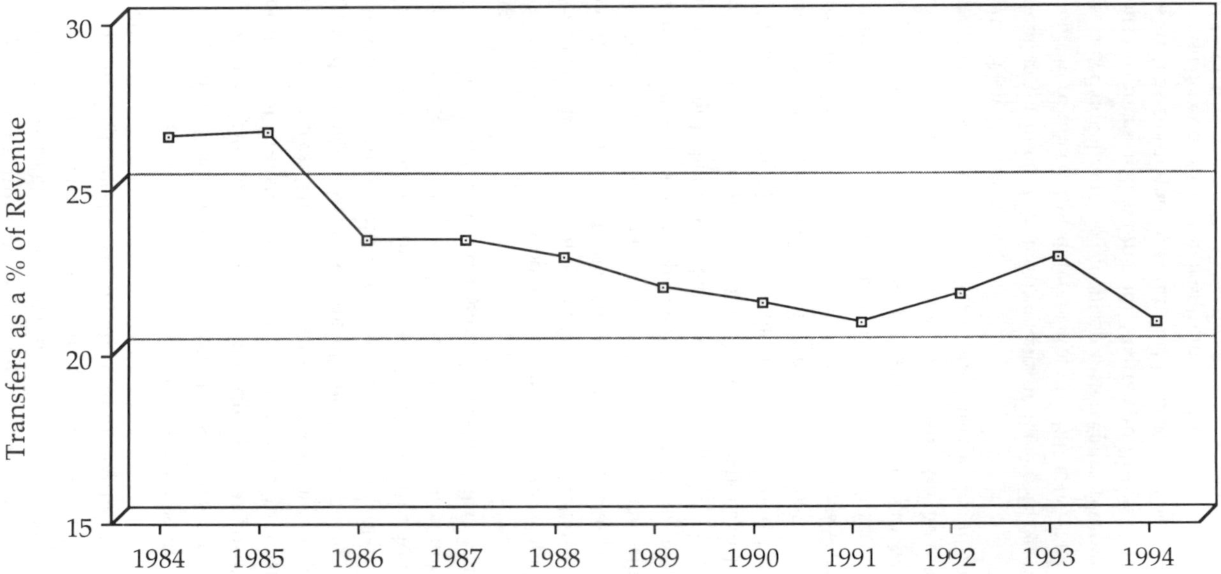

Transfers as a % of Revenue

30
25
20
15

1984 1985 1986 1987 1988 1989 1990 1991 1992 1993 1994

Source: Statistics Canada, National Income and Expenditure Accounts (Ottawa: Industry, Science and Technology, 1995).

element of Canada's Fordist development. It required the federal government to match provincial spending dollar-for-dollar on such social programmes as nursing care for the elderly, child care for low income families and public housing. Bill C-69 placed a funding freeze on the CAP for wealthy provinces such as Ontario, British Columbia and Alberta. Their CAP transfer payments did not increase by more than 5 percent per year even if provincial spending exceeded the 5 percent limit. It is estimated that the funding cap created a Can$160 million shortfall in its first year.[31] CAP payments to hinterland provinces were unaffected by Bill C-69.

The third category of transfer payments was called Established Programs Financing (EPF). These payments provided the main federal contributions to higher education and health care programmes managed by the provinces. Federal funding of the EPF was frozen at Can$20 billion per year which meant a reduction of Can$1 billion in real terms between 1990 and 1992.[32]

The multi-billion dollar shortfall in education shattered the Fordist ideal in Canada of universal access to higher education for all students with adequate secondary school grades. With federal funding cuts and provincial budget shortfalls, universities have raised tuition just to maintain the status quo. Since 1990, tuition costs at some schools have increased by as much as 50 percent.[33] Even with tuition increases, some schools have had to turn away students who met entrance requirements because the university lacked financial resources. For example, York University, in suburban Toronto, was forced to turn away 2,000 eligible students who wanted to enroll in September 1993 because of inadequate funding from the province of Ontario.[34] The province lacked the money because of the funding cuts to the EPF.

In another example of how the State in Canada has abandoned the Fordist ideal of universal access to education, the Ontario government stopped providing low income students with tuition grants in 1992. Traditionally under the Ontario Student Assistance Plan (OSAP), low and middle income students were given either a low-interest loan or a grant. The poorest students could at one time qualify for as much as Can$5,100 per year to defray tuition and dormitory costs. OSAP has now stopped the grant programme which means that thousands of qualified people will be unable to afford to go to university. Students may have to opt for a less-expensive community college education in order to attain skill development and training in order to ensure quicker job placement. This may be part of the overall agenda for creating a more flexible labour force.[35] Corporate interests are provided with a larger work force that has been trained in a community college with taxpayers money to work on the post-Fordist shop floor or service sector office.

Higher education was previously a central element of the Welfare State. Financial assistance removed barriers for students from lower-income families who could then enter institutions of higher learning. These students now have to consider greater indebtedness which to many lower-income families is as frightening as unemployment itself. The ripple effects of the EPF cuts are coursing through Canadian society, segmenting young Canadians into a privileged class who can choose to go to either a university or community college and the rest who can only go to a community college if they want to pursue a post-secondary education.

The Tories restructured the education system to complement the corporate competitiveness agenda by moving funding away from grade schools, high schools and universities and redirecting that money towards vocational training. Money was shifted from universities to community colleges and spending on university education decreased as a percent of total spending on education (Figure 38). This has occurred while spending on education as a percent of GDP has dropped since 1985 and while enrollment in colleges and universities has risen dramatically from 740,000 Canadian college and university students in 1984 to 878,660 students in 1991.[36] The federal government justified funding cuts for education because they claimed that social spending was out of control. Yet, data reveals that education costs were under control. The federal government expenditure per student actually dropped from about Can$4,600 in 1984 to Can$4,196 in 1991.[37] The restructured education system creates inequalities by not allowing all students to have access to the same educational training. And even then, Canada's most prestigious institutions do not provide the same level of education that they once did.

Sally Brown, the vice president of the Association of Universities and Colleges in Canada, said that even before the EPF cuts, the Tories had basically frozen funding of Canada's universities and colleges since 1988.[38] Because of moderate inflation and growing enrollments, the funding freeze translates into a funding cut in real terms per student. How do corporate interests justify this sort of restructuring and segmentation of the Canadian education system? David Vice, chairman of the CMA, said that "increasing competitiveness is the key to almost everything that matters in this country."[39] The competitiveness agenda encompasses the labour force and the education system. The student population is becoming segmented just like the labour force. This is no

Figure 38
Percentage Allocation of Federal Education Expenditures

Year	Primary and High School	University and College	Vocational Training	GDP % Spent on Education
1984	15.1	60.4	24.5	1.26
1985	13.7	56.0	30.3	1.31
1986	14.2	54.7	31.1	1.17
1987	14.2	55.5	30.3	1.20
1988	12.5	56.6	30.9	1.10
1989	13.1	56.0	30.9	1.05
1990	14.4	53.4	32.2	1.04
1991	13.7	48.2	38.1	1.13

Source: Statistics Canada, *Education Statistics Bulletin* (Ottawa: Supply and Services, 1992), 5.

coincidence because vocational training — comprising an increasingly large proportion of Canada's education system — is teaching workers to exist in a segmented and flexible work force.

Health care was also affected by the FTA and EPF funding cuts. In order to understand how free trade has affected health care in Canada, it is useful to examine how the Tories have approached health care during the free trade negotiation period extending from 1984 to 1988. During the 1984 election campaign, Mulroney promised that he would not negotiate an FTA with the United States and that he would direct more federal funding to the provinces to ensure universal access to health care.[40] Within one year in office he was negotiating a free trade agreement with the U.S. and he initiated a spiral of funding cuts that has had a devastating effect on Canada's health care system. In 1986, the Tories capped yearly expansion of federal contributions to health care at two percentage points below the growth in the Canadian economy. In 1989, Ottawa cut funding growth to three percentage points below economic growth. Then in 1990, the federal government froze all contributions to the EPF. With moderate inflation, rising health care costs and increasing demands placed on the Canadian health care system, this freeze was tantamount to a funding cut. In fact, the Tories planned to treat the Canadian health care system the same way it dealt with the UI programme. Gradually, the Tories planned to eliminate all federal funding to health care just as Mulroney halted federal government contributions to the UI scheme.[41] Once the federal government stops funding provincial health care through the EPF, the national universal health care system will fragment into a collection of ten regional health care plans of varying quality.

When a State-run health care system was implemented in Canada in 1971, the goal was to ensure universal access and the standardization of services regardless of geographic location or socioeconomic status of the patient. The federal government ensured the universality and equality of the system by controlling the allocation of a large proportion of necessary funds. Provinces failing to comply with national standards risked forfeiting federal funds. Here then was the discourse of equality. The health care system was a nation-building and centralizing programme because the federal government could use transfer payments as a lever to control the provinces.

As federal funding to the provinces was reduced, the federal government began to lose its mechanism for ensuring provincial compliance to national standards. More importantly, cuts to transfer payments reduced the ability of provinces to maintain existing levels of services. The discourse of inequality has been muted because Canadians would not tolerate a direct attack on their health care system. Hence, the Tories employed the politics of stealth by making incremental cuts to the health care portion of the Welfare State. Between 1990 and 1992, the Tories cut contributions to health care by 12 percent from Can$6.9 billion to Can$6.1 billion. Bill C-31 (passed in 1991) provided a formula for reducing federal transfer payments for health care to zero by the year 2004. Provinces that want to maintain pre-FTA standards for health care had to consider privatization and user fees. Only 17 percent of the hospitals in Canada were State-operated in 1990. The remaining 83 percent were managed by religious orders, philanthropic organizations and municipalities. Pressures to privatize were predicted to be greatest on these hospitals because they lacked the "deep pockets" of the State-run hospitals.[42]

Some provinces and hospitals could not afford to maintain service at previous levels even with creative financing and have therefore abandoned their commitment to universal access. Calgary's Foothills Hospital replaced some registered nurses with lower-wage nursing assistants. Québec has pursued the idea of user fees for each visit to a physician. An estimated 3,500 beds were closed in Ontario between 1990 and 1992 with a loss of 5,000 jobs.[43] The BCNI and other neoconservative commentators recommended that Canada introduce health management organizations (HMOs) as a way to privatize the system and cut costs at the same time. American-style HMOs are a real possibility because the FTA allows American health care corporations to enter the Canadian market in order to manage certain components of the health care system such as hospitals, nursing homes, diagnostic labs and blood donor clinics.

A study conducted by the Government of Alberta recommended that a two-tiered health care system be implemented in that province.[44] A basic level of health care would be funded by the State and additional services could be purchased by those who could afford them through supplemental private insurance. Preston Manning, leader of the Alberta-based Reform party, says that the provinces should be allowed to erode universal health care to suit their regional needs.[45] The ECC reassured Canadians that the FTA should "not be viewed as a threat [to] universal medicare in Canada."[46] After five years of free trade, Canadians witnessed the erosion of the Welfare State and universal access to health care. Just as there is growing segmentation in the work force and education system, inequality is being legislated into the Canadian health care system in the name of competitiveness, debt reduction and flexibility. Dennis Timbrell, president of the Ontario Hospital Association, commented on the end of universality in Canada by saying "Medicare as we know it has reached the end of an era."[47]

The corporate agenda should not be ignored when examining the relationship between free trade and Canada's crumbling public health care system. In 1993, the CMA openly advocated that the federal government cut spending on health care and welfare programmes to make Canadian industry more competitive. The manufacturing lobby went on to say that money cut from social spending should be used to create industrial subsidies (it was unclear how that would be compatible with the provisions of the FTA). The president of the CMA, Stephen van Houten, said that Can$2 billion redirected away from the social safety net to help manufacturing would result in Can$15 billion in additional industry revenues.[48] The subsidies to corporations would help Canada over the long term as the benefits trickled down to Canadian workers.

The multinational pharmaceutical industry has also played an important role in restructuring the Canadian health care system. In 1969, Pierre Trudeau passed legislation to promote a Canadian pharmaceutical industry which could provide low-cost pharmaceuticals to Canadian consumers. This legislation was called compulsory licensing and it allowed Canadian manufacturers to buy the right to produce generic versions of brand name drugs within four years of the drug first being introduced.[49] Canadians benefited by gaining access to lower-cost prescriptions, saving taxpayers about Can$500 million per year. Multinational pharmaceutical producers were angered by this policy because while they were still making profits, they were not making monopoly profits. They wanted to have their patents recognized for a longer time in order to reap greater revenues.

The FTA brought changes which favored the profit margins of multinational corporations. The American Pharmaceutical Manufacturers' Association used their clout to affect the FTA negotiation process. The Canadian government passed Bill C-22 in 1988 in response to pressures from the Reagan Administration and American pharmaceutical producers.[50] Bill C-22 extended the monopoly held by the multinational pharmaceutical firms from four to ten years. While the waiting time for generic pharmaceutical producers increased by 6 years, the corollary to Bill C-22 is that large pharmaceutical firms gained six more years of monopoly profits and in turn increased health care costs in Canada.

Despite Canadian acquiescence under Bill C-22, American trade officials harassed Canada for allowing generic pharmaceuticals to be produced even ten years after patent recognition. George Bush condemned Canada for allowing generic pharmaceuticals to be produced in any form.[51] Canada was placed on the "Super 301" list compiled by the office of the USTR in 1990 and 1991 because of unfair trading practices including compulsory licensing for generic drug production. Under the threat of continued harassment, and to ease NAFTA negotiations, the Tories passed Bill C-91 in 1992 extending the recognition of patents and monopoly profits in drug production from 10 to 20 years.

Canadian consumer affairs minister Pierre Blais claimed that Bill C-91 was actually good for Canada because it would create greater profits for multinational pharmaceutical manufacturers operating in Canada as well as for Canadian manufacturers of non-generic drugs. This would in turn stimulate greater investment in research and development within Canada. In the end, Canadians would benefit from a healthier Canadian pharmaceutical industry that is able to produce innovative and lower-priced remedies for a variety of maladies.

Critics of Tory policies eschew justifications for Bill C-91 which emphasizes the altruistic intentions of the Canadian government and multinational pharmaceutical manufacturers. Free trade opponents point to the fact that

Bill C-91 was modeled after the American proposal to NAFTA and GATT to protect intellectual property rights. Critics also note that the U.S. Pharmaceutical Manufacturers' Association was the first American industry association to endorse NAFTA. They saw that the NAFTA-inspired Bill C-91 was designed to protect U.S. intellectual property rights by eliminating compulsory licensing while providing few if any benefits to the Canadian health care system.[52] In fact, opponents and independent analysts of Bill C-91 predicted that the extension of patent recognition and monopoly profits to 20 years would greatly increase prescription prices. Stephen Schondelmeyer, a pharmacoeconomist at the University of Minnesota, testified before a Canadian House of Commons subcommittee that Bill C-91 could potentially increase drug costs in Canada by Can$7 billion over what they would be expected to increase without Bill C-91 during a twenty-year period. Ruth Collins-Nakai, a professor at the University of Alberta and a member of the Province of Alberta's Council on Science and Technology, supported Bill C-91 but conceded that rising pharmaceutical costs are the single greatest factor driving up health care costs in Canada.[53]

The federal government reduced transfer payments in a ploy to cut costs but then allowed Bill C-91 to pass, offsetting any savings which would have come from austerity programmes forced on the provinces. The FTA, and now NAFTA are central factors contributing to the dismantling of Canada's universal health care system. American multinational corporations were dissatisfied with profits derived from their existing intellectual property rights and they did not want to a have an alternative model for health care north of their border. The destruction of compulsory drug licensing in Canada is a "strategic wedge" designed to undermine the universal health care system in Canada while setting a precedent for the expanded American patent recognition.[54]

With inadequate funding and rising prescription costs, the provinces are having to consider private alternatives to maintain services. Canada is now confronted with a fragmenting health care system that opponents to health care reform in the U.S. can point to as inadequate. The Canadian system is disintegrating but few people understand that its inadequacies are due to funding cuts as opposed to inherent flaws in system. The system is inadequate because the very corporate interests which criticize it have persuaded their ideological supporters in the State to hobble it through legislation and funding cuts. The results of neoconservative health care policy and free trade can already be seen as provinces struggle to maintain a level of health care provision previously taken for granted. Social inequality has become a central theme in the post-Fordist model of development.

Canadian Culture and Communications

One of the most contentious elements in the free trade debate revolved around the production, control and dissemination of information, communication and culture. During the FTA negotiations, Canadians were told that cultural sovereignty would be preserved despite the fact that free trade would occur in goods, energy, services and finance capital. Free trade proponents stated that culture was not even on the bargaining table during the free trade negotiations.[55] This assertion only makes sense if information and culture can be isolated from all other sectors of the economy and society.[56] In reality this can never be done. Even in economic sectors such as resource extraction, agriculture and manufacturing, information-oriented work is essential. The service sector exists largely to process and disseminate information. This section explains how control over information flows and the production of culture in Canada has changed dramatically as a consequence of free trade.

The end point of information dissemination is knowledge. An information market enables the consumer to know something that was not known previously. Knowledge acquisition can occur in many ways such as through shared symbolic experiences, learning new facts or skills, or by purchasing a new commodity which changes or improves a person's habits, perceptions or opportunities.[57] The production, distribution and exchange of information is not necessarily synonymous with cultural activity, but the overlap is enormous. Information consists of symbols which are manipulated in such a way as to construct or represent particular meanings. Culture on the other hand consists of shared meanings, perceptions and values common to a group of people based upon a common pool of information. But as the commodification of culture through books, movies, computer software, television and radio accelerates, the line between culture and information vanishes. It is in this sense that one can say that all economic exchanges involve the exchange of culture and communication.[58] Given this argument, one must conclude that a free trade deal that promotes the free flow of goods, services, capital and energy must by definition promote the free flow of information and cultural commodities across international boundaries.

This is hardly a new idea. Harold Innis, Canadian scholar of communications and mentor to Marshall McLuhan, emphasized that economic activity of all kinds including resource extraction and transportation constituted communication. Consider the role of Canada's first transcontinental railroad which was completed in 1885. The history of the Canadian Pacific Railroad (CPR) is primarily the "history of the spread of western civilization over the northern half of the North American continent."[59] The CPR was an instrument used by the Canadian State to help settle a nascent and enormous Canadian Nation-State in the late nineteenth century. Concomitantly, the CPR united the new Nation-State and helped to disseminate cultural values distinct from those originating in the United States. Canada needed this transcontinental railroad to develop an east-west transportation and communications axis that redirected information flows from the existing north-south axis. The dissemination of information was crucial in the creation of a Canadian cultural monopoly of space.[60] In any one territorially-bounded region, only one culture can dominate if a Nation-State is to evolve. The CPR helped to secure that monopoly of space for Canada by spreading Canadian values originating in central Canada to Western Canada along an east-west axis. Although the CPR became a corporate entity owned by its stockholders, it was originally a creation of the Canadian State. The CPR represented the first in a series of major State efforts made over the last hundred years to preserve a cultural monopoly of space separate from the United States.

Throughout the twentieth century, Canadians have held an ambivalent attitude about American culture. In the past, Canadians have read and continue to read American books and magazines, watch American movies and television and listen to American music. At the same time, leaders of Canada's cultural elite worried that a home-grown Canadian culture would fail to mature without help from the State. Control of information dissemination and cultural development was viewed as an essential tool for policy legitimation and national sovereignty. Canadian political and intellectual leaders worried that their ability to shape Canadian development would be hindered by the encroaching American media. This sentiment grew stronger after the First World War when Canadians began to see themselves as "graduating from [under] British tutelage."[61]

At the same time, Canadian leaders warned against American cultural imperialism which threatened to replace British cultural dominance for one based in New York and Hollywood. In the 1920s, cultural leaders such as Graham Spry argued vociferously for a Canadian public radio broadcasting system that would unite Canada from sea to sea with an information infrastructure. In his view, it was either "the state or the United States."[62] The Canadian State had to take an active role in promoting domestic cultural development if Canada was to survive as an independent Nation-State. This vision became a reality in 1932 when the Canadian government enacted legislation to create what would later become the Canadian Broadcasting Corporation. The fact that a national radio network was launched in the depths of the Depression speaks to the perceived importance of a domestically controlled national media source that could reinforce the east-west communications axis on which Canadian culture was based. The creation of the CBC also represented a primary conduit for the discourse of universality and regional equality in Canada. The CBC was an early component of the mode of regulation underpinning Canada's permeable Fordism.

Canadian cultural nationalism continued unabated after 1945. The period immediately after the Second World War was perceived to be a "time of critical passage in national development [in which] an independent [Canadian] identity could be molded."[63] This national self-confidence was tempered by nagging doubts about the ability of Canada to maintain a distinctive Canadian cultural monopoly of space in the shadow of the United States. In 1948, the Canadian government was concerned enough about American domination of the Canadian book, movie, magazine, radio and television markets that it sponsored the Royal Commission on National Development in the Arts, Letters, and Sciences to evaluate Canadian media industries and cultural development. The *Massey Report*, as it was also known, concluded that Canada was in danger of being overwhelmed by American media giants if actions were not taken by the Canadian government. Increased funding by the State was required to keep Canadian cultural industries competitive with American cultural commodities entering Canada.[64] Specific recommendations included the establishment of a federally-funded Canada Council to promote and subsidize Canadian arts, humanities, and social sciences through competitive grant programmes. The *Massey Report* also concluded that Canadian universities needed increased governmental support for research, curriculum development and the training of Canadian scholars. Existing communications institutions such as the CBC and the National Film Board (NFB) were also targeted for increased State support in the face of American cultural domination.

The *Massey Report* confirmed to Canadians that the State was committed to the promotion and protection of a national culture that was universally accessible to all Canadians. In the 1960s and 1970s, the Canadian government implemented further policies to promote the Canadian magazine, film, book publishing, radio and music industries. The Canadian State was promoting national culture as a way to control the dissemination of information and cultural messages within its national boundaries. American magazine publishers such as *Time Magazine* and movie companies such as Gulf and Western resented the Canadian monopoly over information dissemination and made several attempts to pry open the Canadian market during this time. Canadians from varying socioeconomic backgrounds generally supported the protectionist actions of their government designed to protect Canadian cultural sovereignty and a distinctly Canadian way of life. Most Canadians believe that their culture differs from that of the United States. While Canadians and Americans share the same continent, they do not share the same cultural values. Canadian nationalists embrace the idea that Canada was born of evolution, not revolution as was the United States.[65] Canada is perceived to be a geographically distinct entity that has evolved along a different path than that of the United States. Part of the Welfare State has been given over to the support of Canada's distinctive culture. Many Canadians believed that cuts to the Welfare State that could accompany free trade posed a threat to Canadian culture.

It was not until the Tories came to power after 1984 that American politicians and media executives were able to effect changes in Canadian cultural policies. Every model of development rests upon a particular mode of regulation which is itself infused with a particular ideology and set of cultural values. Canada's permeable Fordism promoted national economic development with the help of a mode of regulation that was comprised of a national culture and information system. In 1984, American media executives began to challenge Canada's cultural monopoly of space more aggressively with the knowledge that the Tories were less protectionist than their predecessors. Also in 1984, American entertainment and publishing industry executives were polled by CBS television. The American executives responded that Canadian cultural policies and non-tariff barriers "imposed under the guise of political or cultural concerns represented a major impediment to [American] international commercial activities."[66] American media executives were upset with the long history of Canadian activities protecting cultural industries. They felt that Canada was a lucrative market that should not be protected. In addition, American executives were upset with the geopolitical and geocultural consequences of Canadian cultural policies. Using the geopolitical discourse of domino theory, American executives argued that Canada was setting a bad example to other countries that were also considering measures to protect their domestic cultural production against American media giants.[67]

The CBS poll identified ten protectionist activities by the Canadian government that needed to be changed. This list was submitted to the office of the USTR in the hope that they could effect change in Canadian policies. Problem areas named in the CBS poll included unfair competition caused by Canada's public funding of the CBC; public funding of film and television production through a federal agency called Telefilm Canada; public funding of production through the National Film Board (NFB) and provincial education networks; discriminatory tax policies including the Capital Cost Allowance (CCA) programme which provided a 100 percent deduction for private companies who invested in certified Canadian film and television productions; Bill C-58, passed in 1976 by Trudeau, which disallowed tax deductions for advertisements placed by Canadian companies in foreign print and electronic media but allowed tax breaks for advertising in Canadian publications; and Canadian content regulations which require Canadian television and radio stations to broadcast several hours of programming each day that had either been written, directed, performed or financed by Canadian citizens.[68] Other restrictions and actions identified by irate American media executives included restrictions placed on foreign ownership and control of Canadian broadcasting and publishing enterprises; cable substitution whereby cable operators in Canada broadcasting American shows simultaneously shown in both countries substituted American advertisements with Canadian advertisements; duties placed upon records, compact discs, videos; and Canadian attempts to limit American control of film and video distribution in Canada.

When the CBS poll findings are compared to what has been done to Canadian cultural policy since the beginning of the FTA negotiations, it is not difficult to link the FTA to the evisceration of Canadian cultural sovereignty. The continental model of development ushered in by Mulroney needed a new geographical basis for the creation, dissemination and control of information and ideology. The FTA is creating a "new information order" where power over the flows of information and ideology are being concentrated in the hands of the Americans.[69]

Two elements of culture are being manipulated under the FTA to erode Canada's cultural monopoly of space.[70] First, copyright protection and intellectual property rights linked to information and culture received enormous attention in the FTA, NAFTA and the Uruguay Round of the GATT negotiations. The United States has prioritized the strengthening of international copyright law in its trade relations. The philosophical basis of copyright legislation can be traced back to the notions of private property, commodity exchange and the laws of supply and demand in the market place. Works of art and information are distributed according to the willingness and ability of potential users to pay for the use of these commodities. The belief is that creators of works of art, books, computer software and so forth should be remunerated for their creativity and knowledge.

The problem lies with the indirect impact of strengthened copyright laws under the FTA.[71] Canadian producers of information and culture are forced to seek out ever wider markets. In the Canadian case, creators will have to factor in the marketability of their products in America when undertaking creations. Similarly, distributors of information in Canada may be persuaded to procure the rights to American material rather than Canadian material because production costs can be amortized over a much larger number of users. Canadian producers will be crowded out of the market unless they produce goods for a North American market rather than a narrow Canadian market. A simple example of this occurred with a best-selling Canadian cookbook developed and written by *Canadian Living Magazine*. In Canada, the book was marketed as the *Canadian Living Rush Hour Cookbook*. In the United States, the identical book was sold as the *Random House Rush Hour Cookbook*, making no mention of its Canadian origins. Thus, the situation arises that few distinctively Canadian cultural commodities sell in the United States. The copyright issue is also important because it locks into place the gap between the "information haves and have-nots."[72] This is true in the case of pharmaceutical production as well as for cultural commodities. More stringent copyright and intellectual property laws only exacerbate Canada's growing information and media dependence on the United States.

The second issue has to do with the relationship between free trade and information as a resource for cultural development. Information can be seen as a social resource that serves a different purpose than information produced for sale as a commodity. Information as a social resource enables other resources to function productively since it is the existence of this salient information that determines the value and existence of other resources. Information as a social resource provides the validation for other forms of culture and information. Canadian culture creates a social space for Canadian writers and artists to survive. Metaphorically speaking, information as a social resource can be seen as a computer operating system that permits other subsystems or programmes to function.[73]

This raises the question of who controls information that serves as a social, or publicly oriented resource? Copyrighted information entails a restriction in access to information, yet information and culture as a resource requires a wide and unhindered flow of information. At first glance this might seem compatible with the international free flow of information supported by the American trade negotiators. The problem resides in the fact that the international free flow of information and cultural commodities can overwhelm domestic production in small countries such as Canada. Control over film distribution in Canada shows how the FTA is implicated in the erosion of Canadian cultural sovereignty.

Government policies with regard to domestic film distribution can serve as a "litmus test" for how serious the State treats cultural issues in general.[74] Importance is placed on film distribution because movies represent a powerful medium for the creation and distribution of ideas, information, ideology and commodities. Whoever controls film distribution therefore acts as a societal gatekeeper determining which values and commodities are shown to the public.[75] Because Canadian film distributors understand this aphorism, they are upset knowing that they have to distribute 95 percent of Canadian films when they only have access to 5 percent of the Canadian market. In a healthy, self-sustaining industry, movie distribution revenues provide the capital to finance new production. This does not happen in Canada. In 1986, American movie distributors made over US$1 billion in the Canada yet only paid US$29 thousand to Canadian producers.[76] The vast proportion of the distribution revenues are funneled back to the United States to finance new American movies.

There is little incentive for American distributors to invest in Canadian productions. What makes matters worse is that major American movie production firms such as Columbia, MGM-UA, Paramount, 20th Century Fox, Universal Pictures and Warner Brothers all consider Canada to be an integral part of the American domestic market. Independent movie producers cannot sign separate contracts for Canadian and American distribution rights. The major U.S. distributors demand that independent producers sign for North American rights if they want access to the American market. Compounding the problem is the fact that Canadian distributors must face a virtual exhibition duopoly. Most of the movie theaters in Canada are operated by Famous Players or Cineplex-Odeon. Both of these corporations are vertically integrated into production and distribution activities of the major American movie producers such as Paramount, which owns Famous Players, and Universal, which runs the Cineplex-Odeon chain. In the face of this integration and concentration, Canadian distributors cannot present Canadian movies to their domestic market which ultimately means that Canadian distributors cannot get revenues to finance more Canadian films.

For 25 years, the Canadian government has attempted to end this "cycle of poverty."[77] The government tried a supply-side solution by establishing the CCA as a tax incentive programme. Private investors were allowed to claim 100 percent of their investments in Canadian films as a tax deduction. In 1973, 1975, 1978 and 1982, the Canadian and Ontario governments attempted to create space for Canadian films by establishing a quota system for film distribution in Canada. Each time, the Canadian film distribution legislation got bogged down in the Cabinet. Under the Mulroney government, a series of paradoxical events occurred that appeared to clear the way for greater distribution of Canadian movies in Canada. The first was the appointment of Marcel Masse as the Canadian Minister of Communication. The paradox here was that while Mulroney was implementing a free trade, free market agenda elsewhere, he appointed a Québecois and Canadian cultural nationalist to his Cabinet. As a member of the Québec national assembly, Masse helped to pass legislation which limited American film distribution in Québec. As a cabinet minister in the communications portfolio, Masse managed to ram through the Baie Comeau Policy which was designed to repatriate profits and ownership of Canadian book publishing. At a 1986 federal provincial cultural ministers' meeting, Masse identified Canadian control of film distribution as "the missing link" in cultural policies.[78]

By this time, Masse had raised the ire of American media giants. Gulf and Western (which owned Paramount Studios) was angry over the Baie Comeau Policy because it had blocked their attempt to take over Prentice-Hall's Canadian operations. When Gulf and Western heard that Masse planned to do for Canadian film distribution what he had helped do in Québec, they placed heavy pressure on the Canadian government to change its cultural policies. Gulf and Western organized other American film studios to force Québec to abandon its new film distribution guidelines by threatening to pull all American films from Québec. Pressure was placed on Mulroney by U.S. Secretary of State George Shultz who suggested that the FTA negotiations would be jeopardized if Masse's policies were approved. Clayton Yeutter, the USTR, claimed that Canada should be willing to risk its culture because he was willing to have America's culture on the bargaining table and take the risk of it being damaged by Canadian influences after a free trade arrangement.[79]

The Canadian cultural community was dumbfounded at Yeutter's ignorance or duplicity in making such as a statement. Prominent organizations in the Canadian cultural community such as ACTRA (Alliance of Canadian Cinema, Television and Radio Artists) campaigned against the FTA because they believed that Canada would not be an equal partner in the deal.[80] Mulroney was faced with a dilemma. He had to appease the Americans while making it appear to Canadians that he was not backing down on the issue of cultural sovereignty. His solution was to make Masse the new Canadian Minister of Energy. Flora MacDonald was appointed as the new Minister of Communications. However, she also proposed legislation which would increase the distribution of Canadian films.

MacDonald proposed that a quota be established that would increase Canadian film distributors' current share of the Canadian market from five to fifteen percent. The American response was strong, coming from the highest office in the land. When Reagan visited Mulroney in April 1987, he mentioned that MacDonald's policy was a threat to the FTA talks.[81] Jack Valenti of the MPAA flew to Ottawa to confront Flora MacDonald in person. By the summer of 1987, the House of Commons had recessed without passing the film distribution legislation. Under pressure from the United States, the legislation languished in a House of Commons subcommittee long enough to allow Mulroney and Reagan to sign and ratify the FTA by the summer of 1988. MacDonald finally presented her legislation to the whole House of Commons but it no longer contained the provision to allow Canadian film distributors access to fifteen percent of the Canadian market.

Mulroney initially allowed MacDonald to offer substantive changes in the film distribution legislation in order to assuage Canadian fears. This ploy "baited and hooked" Canadian cultural nationalists who opposed free trade.[82] Mulroney could then string the cultural nationalists along while delay tactics and modifications to the proposal were done to appease the Americans. The legislation was allowed to go forward only after it had received the free trade imprimatur. It no longer conflicted with American interests because it had been altered so much. Canadian film distributors ended up receiving Can$85 million to promote and show their films but they had to remain satisfied with access to only 5 percent of the movie theaters in Canada.[83]

Even after the film distribution legislation had failed in its original intent, the office of the USTR and Jack Valenti continued to berate Canadian movie makers for asking for help from the Canadian government.[84] In addition, the CCA programme designed to attract private funding for Canadian movie production was partially dismantled by Mulroney in 1987 to appease the office of the USTR. Previously, investors could claim 100 percent of their investments in Canadian movies as a tax deduction. After 1987, investors could only deduct 30 percent. The impact of this policy change has been a halt in the growth of independent film production in Canada. Between 1980 and 1989, total independent and television film production grew by 445 percent. In 1989, there was zero growth. Production of English language films actually decreased by 43 percent.[85] American media executives successfully used their access to the office of the USTR and the FTA negotiation process to scuttle Canadian cultural policy.

Film distribution was not the only issue that American executives and politicians wanted to change. In fact, they wanted to gain full access to the Canadian cultural and media market. Free trade supporters in Canada have repeatedly stated that Americans did not gain access to the Canadian market and that the FTA actually protects many Canadian cultural industries.[86] Of course the whole debate about cultural sovereignty depends upon how the idea of culture has been defined within the FTA.

Canada and the United States have a different perception about the nature of culture. Culture, according to the American view, has been defined as a purely marketable commodity. Canadians admit to, and care about the commodity aspects of culture, but they also see culture as a social resource or public good.[87] At first glance, the FTA does seem to exempt cultural industries from provisions of the FTA. The first paragraph of Article 2005 of the FTA text states that Canadian culture has indeed been protected. But the Canadian cultural community was slow to interpret the full meaning of Article 2005.[88] Gradually, a chorus of protest arose when the contradictory implications of it were understood.[89]

The FTA text contains four unambiguous statements which explicitly refer to cultural industries. First, tariffs were removed on compact discs, records, cassettes and videos entering Canada just as American executives had wanted. Second, the FTA left the Baie Comeau Policy, designed to protect Canadian book publishers from foreign buyers, largely intact. Third, the FTA forced Canadian cable operators to stop inserting Canadian commercials in place of American commercials when broadcasting American television shows at the same time they were being shown in the United States. It is estimated that this provision has resulted in a 25 percent decline in the number of commercials being produced in Canada. The fourth exception affects Bill C-58 and provisions in the Canadian Income Tax Code that penalized Canadian firms advertising in American print or electronic media. Advertisers can no longer be penalized under the Canadian Tax Code for placing an advertisement in a publication printed outside Canada. American magazines hold a 75 percent share of the Canadian magazine market. With the elimination of the advertising revenue generating Bill C-58, Canadian magazines will lose even more market share as profits decline.

While the cultural community was unhappy about these explicit revisions to Canadian cultural policy, the most troubling culture-related aspect of the FTA was the perceived ambiguity within Article 2005.[90] The first paragraph of Article 2005 clearly exempts cultural industries, but the second paragraph contains a "notwithstanding clause," implying that culture *is* part of the FTA.[91] Canadians can promote culture as much as they want but if American commercial interests are affected adversely, they can retaliate against other sectors of the Canadian economy notwithstanding the first paragraph of Article 2005 of the FTA text.[92] Instead of exempting culture from the FTA, the United States can retaliate if it judges that Canadian artists have used unfair subsidies, cultural grants or Canadian content rules to cause the loss of money-making opportunities to American firms operating in Canada. The subtle hook in the FTA lies in the fact that retaliation is not directly imposed against the Canadian cultural industry. Instead, the United States can retaliate through "measures of equivalent commercial effect" by raising duties in some other non-cultural area.[93] Yet, the fact remains that culture can still be targeted as a reason for retaliation. Therefore, culture is an integral part of the FTA.

The FTA not only provides a definition for culture, it also makes clear what is meant by a monopoly. The workhorse of the Canadian communications system has been the crown corporation, which carries out national or provincial goals as a public enterprise. The flagship crown corporation in Canada is the CBC. Other crown corporations in the cultural sphere include the National Film Board and Telefilm. All three have promoted Canadian culture "beyond the commodity sphere."[94] As part of Canada's information infrastructure, they have helped to maintain the east-west axis of national information flows. Under the FTA, the crown corporation could be defined as a monopoly and be subject to retaliation by the United States.

Monopoly provisions in the FTA effectively scuttled plans by the Province of Ontario to offer a single-payer, provincially-run automobile insurance plan similar to one that already exists in Manitoba. Under the monopoly provisions of the FTA text, the Province of Ontario would be susceptible to compensation claims by American insurance firms who are unable to compete in the Ontario insurance market. The amount of compensation is equal to lost profits now and in the future. For example, if an American insurance firm made a 3.5 percent profit per year over the past five years, it could be eligible to ask the provincial government to pay that annual rate of profit amortized over 20 years.[95] The accounting firm Coopers and Lybrand was commissioned by State Farm Insurance to study the Ontario auto insurance proposal. Coopers and Lybrand concluded that the Ontario taxpayers could be liable for as much as Can$3.6 billion. The fact that several American firms threatened to ask for this level of compensation convinced provincial officials that it would be too costly to implement their plan. The FTA has therefore limited Canadian political sovereignty by restricting the policy decisions that can be made.

The FTA also jeopardizes the ability of Canadians to control their own movie industry, publishing houses, television and radio networks and artistic community. In fact, the U.S. Department of Commerce anticipated that the FTA would "encourage the adoption of non-discriminatory policies in Canada" in the area of cultural industries.[96] Clayton Yeutter and the office of the USTR asserted that Article 2005 could serve as a disincentive to government subsidies of the arts in Canada. The fear of American retaliation would have a chilling effect on government support for existing cultural programmes and would act as a deterrent to the creation of future cultural programmes.[97] These predictions have been proven correct. The Tories were quick to take measures against Canadian cultural industries and organizations in order to appease Americans who might seek actions against Canada for supporting cultural industries.

Consider how the FTA has affected the CBC. In the twentieth century, the CBC has played a national development role equivalent to that played by the CPR in the nineteenth century. The CBC has a mandate to broadcast Canadian news and cultural programming to the large urban centres of central Canada as well as to the isolated hamlets of northern Canada. The CBC was designed to be a national institution that could unite a population distributed across enormous expanses of land. In order to secure this monopoly of space, the CBC has acted as a monopoly in the realm of radio and television broadcasting. Article 2010 of the FTA addresses the issue of monopolies. Paragraph one of this article states that the FTA does nothing to impede the establishment of a monopoly. Paragraph two qualifies this statement by saying that advance notification of the designation of the monopoly is required and the party seeking designation must engage in consultations prior to setting up the monopoly. This provision permits Canada to set up a new monopoly or crown corporation or maintain a pre-existing monopoly but there are serious consequences for doing so. If a monopoly is interpreted as an anti-competitive enterprise such as a crown corporation interfering in the activities of an American firm operating in Canada, the American firm has a right under the FTA to seek retaliatory measures. Funding cuts to the CBC have occurred in part to avoid having it called a monopoly by the American executives. The Tories planned to cut Can$140 million over five years from the Can$915 million annual CBC budget in 1989. Decreased funding forced the CBC to lay off 1,100 employees, curtail its short wave radio service, cancel funding for 160 programmes and to close 11 regional stations across Canada.[98]

Here again the discourse of equality and universal access has been cast aside. The broader agenda of the Mulroney government can be seen in the nature of the programmes that were cut and the stations that were closed. Almost all of the now-defunct programmes had one element in common. They usually focused on events and issues of importance to particular communities and regions outside of central Canada. Some of the 160 canceled shows include *Land and Sea*, a public affairs show that discussed issues important to Maritime fisherman, *Country Canada*, a programme that covered topics important to farmers in the Prairies, *Pacific Report*, which was the west-coast equivalent to *Land and Sea*, and *Down to Earth*, an environmental issues show produced out of the Vancouver studios of the CBC.

Besides the individual shows, the Mulroney government also shut down eleven CBC regional studios including the ones in Goose Bay and Corner Brook, Newfoundland, Sydney, Nova Scotia, Rimouski and Matane, Québec, Windsor, Ontario and Calgary, Alberta. These CBC stations are often the only television and radio stations that broadcast local news. Even Windsor, Ontario, in the media-shadow of metropolitan Detroit, has lost its local Canadian television programming as of 1991. It has been "abandoned in a sea of Americanism" according to one pundit.[99] The CBC now only provides Windsor with an Ontario-wide news broadcast that is produced in Toronto. Furthermore, the Tory government passed Bill C-40, also known as the Broadcast Act, which downgrades the traditional mandate of the CBC to "promote national unity." The CBC has only to "contribute to a shared national consciousness."[100] Former CBC president Pierre Juneau, decried the Tory treatment of the CBC, arguing that the network could no longer "reflect the regions" as it was originally intended.[101] In the view of Juneau, Mulroney has incrementally undermined the ability of the CBC to reach all Canadians.

Canadian neoconservatives and American media executives applauded the massive cuts to the CBC. Jack Valenti was never satisfied with the fact that Flora MacDonald's proposal for film distribution was defeated. He used the NAFTA negotiation process to prevent new Canadian film distribution laws from developing and to reduce subsidies to the CBC. According to conservative columnist Barbara Amiel, the CBC deserved to have its budget slashed because it is the last bastion of the New Left in Canada. She believes that the initials "CBC" actually stand for "consistently biased coverage" because of the anti-FTA editorial stance held by the CBC.[102] Members of the cultural community such as Peter Desbarats, the dean of the Graduate School of Journalism at the University of Western Ontario, believe that the Tories cut CBC funding in part to retaliate against the network for opposing free trade.[103] This perspective of the cultural community was confirmed when, after trimming the CBC budget, Mulroney appointed avid free trade supporter, John Crispo to be the president of the CBC. A professor at the School of Management at the University of Toronto, Crispo appeared on television and radio shows and authored many articles and books proclaiming the benefits of free trade for Canada. Amiel celebrated the appointment because Crispo represented a "small correction of balance" in Canadian reporting.[104] Free trade critics were appalled at Crispo's appointment because he openly called for funding cuts to the Welfare State as part of the broader neoconservative agenda and criticized the anti-FTA stance of the CBC.

The Tories also dismantled crown corporations other than the CBC. The neoconservative agenda called for cutting back the Welfare State. This goal, combined with the fact that a crown corporation could be considered a monopoly under the FTA, motivated the Mulroney government to dissolve 15 out of 57 crown corporations and their 134 subsidiaries. Between 1985 and 1990, the Tories managed to reduce the number of federal government employees from 224,000 to 215,000. In addition, 20 crown corporations were either fully or partially privatized. The Tories abandoned Canadian transcontinental passenger rail service offered by Via Rail and privatized Air Canada — Canada's national airline. Train service was cut by more than 50 percent. The Canadian government cut the number of trains from 405 to 191 in the heavily subsidized rail regions of Canada's hinterland.[105] Many communities in the Maritimes, Northern Ontario and the Prairie Provinces lost access to passenger rail service. After Air Canada was privatized, it downgraded the service on many isolated routes to concentrate on the profitable routes between Canada's major urban centres.

Efforts to provide universal access to Canada's transportation network have been abandoned by the Progressive Conservatives. Along with the cuts to the CBC, the Tories have dismantled the east-west transportation axis which has traditionally promoted national unity. Continental integration accelerated as Canada's transportation and communication infrastructure began to disappear. The east-west axis can no longer serve as an intervening opportunity to those Canadians who now travel or communicate in a north-south axis. At the same time, there is a greater inequality within Canada with regards to access to transportation and communications.

Recent actions by the CPR have also undermined Canada's east-west orientation that is essential for the Canadian monopoly of space. In 1885, the CPR united Canada in an east-west fashion. Later, the CPR built a luxury hotel in each major Canadian city or resort area. Together, the rail and hotel service became an integral part of the national consciousness. Despite its strong Canadian heritage, the CPR has also taken dramatic steps to adjust to free trade. As it cut back on its domestic east-west rail service, the CPR purchased stock in The Soo Line Railroad in the United States. This acquisition now allows the CPR to provide uninterrupted north-south service without having to rely on an American company. Canadian railways are also shipping an increasing amount of freight through the United States because unions are less militant, taxes are lower and regulations are less stringent.[106] The creation of a continental market is forcing Canadian railroads to abandon their traditional role uniting Canada.

The Canadian cultural community has suffered in the 1980s and 1990s. The problem, says Glenn Lowry of the Art Gallery of Ontario in Toronto, is that federal and provincial governments have cut funding to the arts as part of their competitiveness agenda. The problem is that several years of underfunding is causing the "cultural infrastructure" to erode.[107] Consider that ballet and theater groups spend years developing a repertoire, client base and reputation. With funding cuts, performance quality erodes because staff and performers are either cut or paid less well. After a period of deterioration and neglect, it is very difficult to restore the quality and reputation of a once-successful theater company or dance troupe.

The NFB has also had to cope with chronic underfunding. The NFB is a collection of award-winning film studios that have served a nation-building role by producing images of the various regions of Canada and showing Canadians that there can be unity in diversity. In 1985, the NFB had an annual budget of Can$72 million. Because government funding had not kept pace with inflation, the NFB suffered a Can$10 million funding shortfall in real terms by 1990. Cost-cutting measures at the NFB have forced the movie studio to lay off employees and to rely more upon part-time and contract workers. The NFB has had to sell its technical services and perform research and development for private industry instead of pursuing its own mission of producing Canadian films.

Critics of Tory cultural policies identify the funding cuts of the Canada Council as the single most damaging element in "the current arts crisis."[108] Founded in 1957 on the recommendation of the *Massey Report,* the

CanadaCouncil is the primary supporter of the arts in Canada and is the central reason why Canadian culture flourished in the 1960s through to the 1980s. Since the Tories came to power, the Canada Council has been devastated by funding cuts. After 1986 and the start of the FTA negotiations, the parliamentary appropriation to the Canada Council was frozen. This translated into a 20 percent funding decrease by 1991 given inflation. Actual funding cuts began to occur after 1989. In November 1990, Can$150 thousand was cut from the Canada Council purportedly to help finance the Gulf War. In February 1991, a further Can$280 thousand was cut from the base funding of Canada's largest supporter of the arts and humanities. In December 1993, the Canadian Finance Minister announced the largest budget cut in the history of the Canada Council. A total of Can$8.7 million was eliminated from the 1994 budget of Can$100 million and the reduced budget was frozen for the 1995 fiscal year.[109]

These cuts were directly linked to the combination of Article 2005 of the FTA text and NAFTA negotiations. The impact of the ambiguity in Article 2005 of the FTA has already been discussed. During NAFTA negotiations, Carla Hills in her role as the USTR, stated that culture is on the negotiating table. She implied that Canada could face retaliation under Article 2005 if it maintained its protectionist stance with regard to culture during NAFTA negotiations.[110] The Mulroney government responded that they were not going to put culture on the bargaining table. Representatives of the Canadian cultural community claimed that Mulroney was able to talk about culture not being on the bargaining table because he was "giving it away under the table."[111]

To add insult to injury, Allen Gotlieb was appointed to be the new head of the Canada Council in 1990. Gotlieb was Canada's ambassador to the United States and was a vocal supporter of free trade. Along with John Crispo who was appointed to head the CBC, Mulroney appointed two of his most loyal supporters to lead Canada's cultural institutions. Mulroney was sending a message to the United States that two stalwart supporters of free trade were now directing Canada's cultural institutions and that American media executives should not worry about unfair subsidies being given to Canadian artists and entertainers.

Contrary to the pundits who claimed that culture was exempted under the FTA, book publishing in Canada has also suffered either directly or indirectly as a result of free trade. Studies conducted by the Canadian Book Publishers' Council and the Canadian Department of Communications have concluded that Canadian-owned book publishers have been hurt by Tory policies related to free trade. In 1993, 37 percent of the 300

Canadian-owned book publishers lost money, up from 27 percent in 1992.[112] Reasons for the unstable condition of Canadian publishers include the GST, funding cuts to the Canada Council which has subsidized small publishing houses, sporadic enforcement of the Baie Comeau Policy, and the continued domination of the Canadian market by American and British publishing giants.

The GST has hurt sectors of Canada's economy that depend upon the discretionary spending of consumers. This value-added tax has made all books sold in Canada 7 percent more expensive. The problem rests in the fact that Canadian publishing houses are smaller then their foreign competitors.[113] Their small size prevents Canadian firms from achieving the economies of scale enjoyed by their foreign competitors. Canadian publishers have shorter production runs as well as more expensive per-book backlisting and storage costs than larger foreign firms. Diminutive Canadian firms are also affected to a greater extent by the increased internal costs of collecting the GST. The end result is that Canadian firms have narrower profit margins than larger foreign companies operating in Canada, making Canadian publishing houses more vulnerable to the vicissitudes of the marketplace.

The effects of budget cuts made to the Canada Council have rippled through the Canadian book publishing industry. Part of the mandate of the Canada Council has been to subsidize small Canadian publishers to print Canadian books that would otherwise not be published. With publishers receiving less support from the Canada Council, Canadian authors have fewer opportunities to find outlets for their work. For example, Oberon Press of Ottawa had its Canada Council subsidy cut by 30 percent in 1991 to Can$68 thousand and has had to cut back on its publishing plan.

The Baie Comeau Policy was implemented in 1986 in order to protect Canadian publishing houses from being taken over by foreign firms, thus preserving Canadian cultural sovereignty. It was enshrined in Article 1607 of the FTA text, and prevented foreign firms from directly securing controlling interest in a Canadian publishing enterprise. In addition, foreign firms that purchase publishing companies with Canadian subsidiaries must sell 51 percent of the Canadian subsidiary to a Canadian citizen or corporation within two years. If no Canadian buyer can be found in that time, the Canadian government has to purchase the company and manage it until a private Canadian investor can be found.

Canadian publishers and leaders of the cultural community defended these protectionist reforms because of the increasingly integrated nature of the communications industry. Media conglomerates integrate book publishing with periodical and newspaper publishing. The largest conglomerates also combine print media with television and movie production allowing them to promote and distribute their information and entertainment products throughout the world. Canadian book publishers could never compete against these multinational media behemoths with access to global resources. In addition, Canadian publishers lack the resources to fend off foreign acquisitions that would take corporate and editorial control out of Canada. The policy was applied effectively in 1986 against Gulf and Western which had purchased Prentice-Hall publishers and was reluctant to divest itself of the Canadian subsidiary of Prentice-Hall. The problem has been that the policy has been enforced in a very selective manner since the implementation of the FTA.

The machinations of Gulf and Western provide an example of how the American company was able circumvent aspects of the FTA-enshrined Baie Comeau Policy with the help of Congress and Article 2005 of the FTA text. Gulf and Western acquired Ginn Publishing which had a Canadian subsidiary. According to Article 1607 of the FTA, Gulf and Western had to sell that subsidiary to a Canadian buyer at a fair market price within two years. When confronted by officials of the Canadian government, Gulf and Western promised a "scorched earth policy" towards Canada if it was forced to divest its Canadian holdings.[114] The media giant submitted a brief to Congress in April 1989 calling for punitive action to be taken against Canada. The recipient of this brief was Congressman John Dingall (D-Michigan), chair of the U.S. House Subcommittee on Oversight and Investigations of the Committee on Energy and Commerce. Dingall was sympathetic to the cause of Gulf and Western and he wrote a ten-page brief condemning the Baie Comeau Policy which he placed into the *Congressional Record*.[115] The White House also involved itself in the fray by drawing up a Statement of Administrative Action condemning Canada for protecting cultural industries. In the end, Gulf and Western agreed to sell a 51 percent share in the Canadian subsidiary long after the two year limit but refused to sell it to a Canadian private enterprise or the Canadian government. The Canadian government also failed to enforce the divestiture of Macmillan Canada when Robert Maxwell purchased Macmillan Incorporated of the United States. The Canadian book publishing industry can find little protection in the provisions of the Baie Comeau Policy or the FTA.

The FTA compromised Canadian control over the dissemination of information and cultural values within Canada's borders. Canada's existence as an independent country has always been at odds with the concept of unrestricted north-south cross-border trade. With a cold climate, sparse population and a vast territory greater than that of the United States, the Canadian State has had to work hard to maintain east-west transportation, communications, and cultural axis in the face of a strong north-south pull. During the Fordist era, the Canadian government exerted considerable efforts to unify Canada. Weak industries and isolated regions were supported through subsidies, regulations, protectionism, and the east-west communications axis that underpinned the Canadian Fordist model of development.[116] In the post-Fordist era, the legitimation function of the Welfare State is no longer deemed essential. With development now organized at a continental scale, many national institutions have become obsolete in the eyes of neoconservatives. The FTA has been responsible either directly or indirectly for the elimination, erosion or privatization of national symbols such as Air Canada, Via Rail, the CBC, the NFB, and the Canada Council.

Canadian Tax Reform and Free Trade

One question remains given the neoconservative assault on the Welfare State. Why are Canadians paying higher taxes even though many programmes in the Welfare State have been restructured or eliminated? Taxes on individuals are higher to facilitate the implementation of the FTA and to enhance corporate profitability.

Canadian tax reforms have occurred in two stages since the beginning of free trade talks in 1985. First, the Canadian government embarked on a series of tax reforms designed to harmonize the Canadian Tax Code with that of the United States while the FTA negotiations were proceeding. When two countries enter into a free trade agreement, they must share similar policy preferences for public goods and income distribution. If a wide discrepancy exists between the two countries with regard to tax structure, third-party investment may favor the country with the lower corporate taxes. Corporations already in the free trade area may also relocate to regions or the country with lower corporate tax rates. Statements made by corporate interests corroborate this view. Eric Owen, the taxation manager of the CMA, said that Canadian businesses needed the tax reforms to restore competitiveness.[117] While business organizations such as the BCNI were lobbying the Canadian government on the issue of free trade, they were also pushing for tax reforms that would lower Canadian corporate taxes. Their goal was to co-ordinate trade and tax policy by harmonizing Canadian corporate tax rates with those of the United States.

Figure 39
Corporate and Individual Tax Burden in Canada

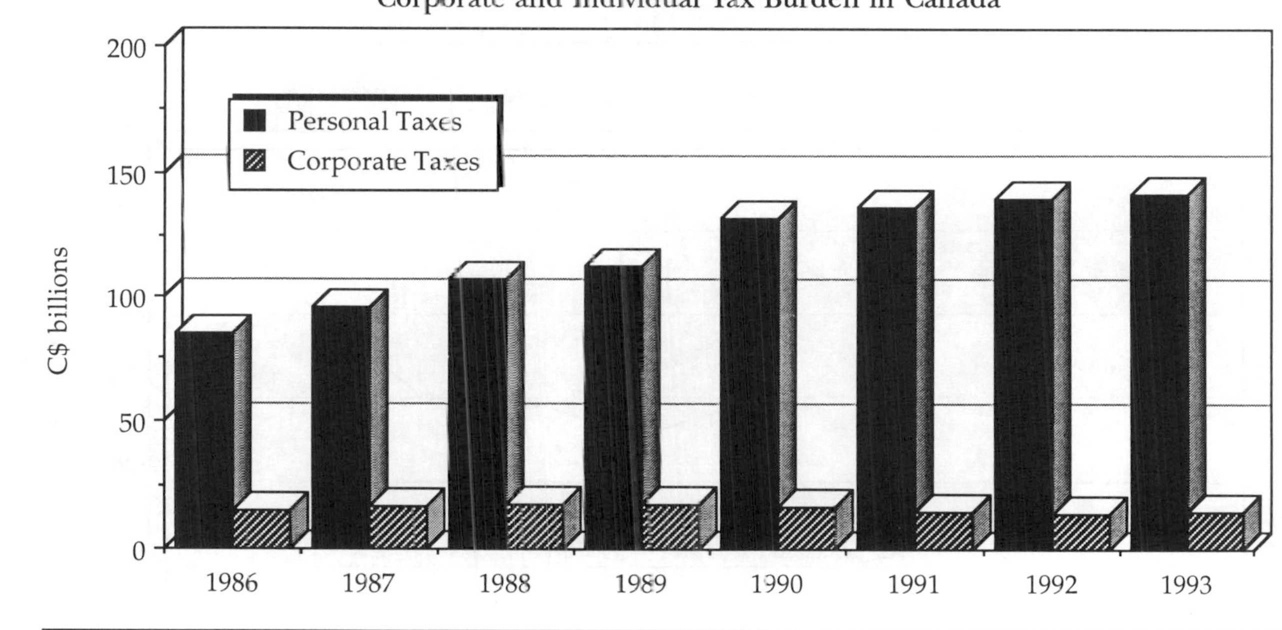

Source: Mel Hurtig, The Betrayal of Canada, 2nd ed., (Toronto: Stoddart Publishing, 1992); Statistics Canada, Canadian Economic Observer (Ottawa: Supply and Services, 1994).

Figure 40

Personal Direct Tax Burden as a Percentage of Federal Government Revenue

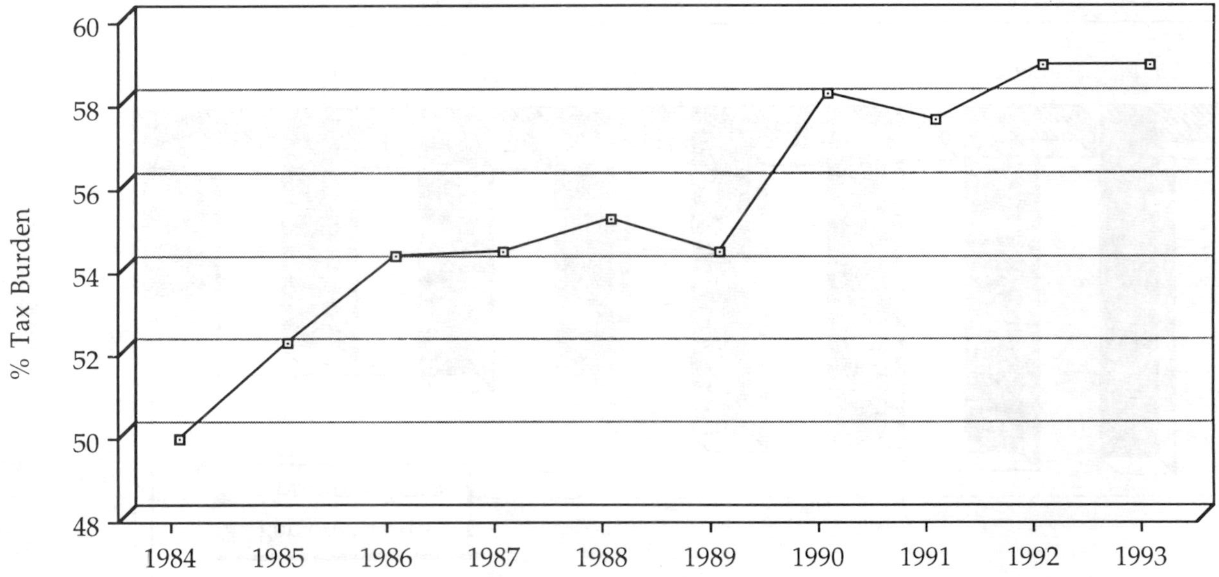

Source: Statistics Canada, Canadian Economic Observer (Ottawa: Supply and Services, 1990); Statistics Canada, Canadian Economic Observer (Ottawa: Supply and Services, 1995).

Donald Beach, a partner in the Canadian office of the multinational accounting firm of Coopers and Lybrand, argued that Canada has been forced into tax reform because of a combination of earlier tax reforms in the United States and the impact of the FTA.[118] Tax reforms initiated by Reagan had lowered the corporate tax rate in the United States. According to this view, if Canada did not implement comparable tax reforms, Canadian firms would not be able to compete under the FTA. Canadian firms would be forced to close or relocate to the United States. Foreign multinational firms with operations in both Canada and the United States stated that they would move their operations out of Canada if tax levels were not harmonized between the two trading partners. Finance Minister Wilson, with help from the FTA and pressure exerted by Canadian and multinational business interests, brought Canadian corporate and personal tax rates in closer harmony with those of the United States.[119]

Concomitant with this fiscal harmonization has been a shift in the tax burden from corporations onto the shoulders of individual taxpayers. Evidence for this shift is provided in Figure 39 which shows that the tax structure in Canada has become increasingly regressive in absolute dollar terms since the Tories took office in 1984. Figure 40 shows that the tax structure has become more regressive in proportional terms by placing a larger percentage of the tax burden on the shoulders of individuals.

Since 1985, the Tories have made over thirty major revisions to the Canadian tax code as a way to replace revenues lost because of lowered corporate tax rates. Tory strategy aimed to capture additional revenue from individuals and families by legislating ten changes in the personal income tax structure and by making twenty-three changes to Canadian sales and excise taxes. Between 1985 and 1990, the average annual tax burden for each Canadian household increased by Can$1,900 more than it would have without Tory tax reforms.[120] The reforms began in May 1985 with a 5 percent surcharge on personal income tax. In 1988, Canada's ten personal income brackets were reduced to three and the rate of taxation for the highest income bracket was reduced from 34 to 29 percent. In addition, the corporate tax rate was reduced from 36 to 28 percent. Between 1986 and 1989, corporate taxes as a percent of profits declined by 21 percent. In 1992, 93,405 profitable firms paid no income taxes on $27 billion in profits.[121]

A major reconfiguration of the Canadian tax structure came in 1990 and 1991. In 1990, the Tories froze or cut many of the transfer payments the federal government made to the provinces in support of social programmes. In 1991, the Tories implemented the 7 percent GST. Together, these policies combined to shift the tax burden from the federal government to the provinces and from corporations to individuals. The GST caused almost as much popular criticism as the FTA because the Canadian public perceived the Tory tax policy as inherently regressive.

The BCNI defended the tax reforms by stating that there was a "professional consensus" among Canadian economists, public finance scholars and economic forecasters that the GST would make Canadian industry more competitive in global markets.[122] Proponents of tax reform explained that the GST would make Canadian industry more competitive because it would replace a hidden 13.5 percent manufacturers' sales tax that was implemented back when manufacturing and natural resources provided the foundation for the Canadian economy. The manufacturers' sales tax was considered to be outmoded because it did not apply to the service sector which has played an ever-increasing role in the North American economy. By replacing the hidden manufacturers' sales tax with a tax on both goods and services, more tax revenue can be raised without hurting the manufacturing sector. The GST is a value-added tax because it is levied at every stage of the production process. This means that the GST applies to twice as many transactions as the manufacturers' tax it replaced. Policy-makers felt that the regressive aspects of the tax could be countered by giving low-income families special tax credits. Finance Minister Wilson went so far as to say that the GST was a progressive tax because it is levied on services which he claims are used disproportionately by the wealthiest people.[123]

In a counter argument, critics pointed out that the FTA eliminated tariffs which were an important source of government revenue. Tariff reduction could cost as much as Can$3 billion per year in lost revenues. The GST therefore provides an easy way to raise government revenue without impinging upon corporate profitability. A tax that raises revenue without cutting into corporate profitability is likely to be a regressive tax. A study conducted by Alan Tait of the IMF looked at the impact of the value-added tax in other countries and found that it was a regressive tax even when tax credits are provided to low-income groups.[124] Canadian critics of the GST describe it as one of the largest retreats from the progressive system of taxation used in Canada. Neil Brooks, a tax law professor at Osgoode Hall Law School in Toronto, concurs that the GST is a regressive tax. Brooks shows that a family with an income of Can$200 thousand would pay about 3.1 percent of its annual income on goods and services taxes. Families earning between Can$25 thousand and Can$35 thousand would pay almost 5.8 percent of their income. Brooks discounts the claim made by Tories that tax credits to low-income families will negate the regressivity of the GST. The tax credits are not appropriately indexed to account for inflation.[125] Even if they were properly indexed, the GST is still regressive because middle-income Canadians are paying more than upper-income Canadians.

Within a year of its implementation, it was clear that the GST was indeed regressive. The Canadian ministry of finance reported that government revenue from personal income tax jumped by 13.9 percent in the first three months of 1991. During the same period, government revenues from corporate taxes dropped by 12 percent. Finance Minister Mazankowski was at a loss to explain the sharp jump in personal income tax receipts at a time when the Canadian unemployment rate hovered near the 10 percent level.[126] The Consumers' Association of Canada conducted a survey that provides the Finance Minister with a possible answer. Supporters of the new tax said that the GST would not make consumer goods more expensive. In order to allay the fears of skeptical Canadians, the federal government released a list of fifty products in April of 1990 that they claimed would drop in price if the GST replaced the manufacturers' tax. The Consumers' Association of Canada studied the price of the fifty products before and after the implementation of the GST. Their research found that only eighteen of the fifty products dropped in price. Twenty-nine products increased in price by as much as 11 percent. Confirming the suspicions of many taxpayers, Revenue Canada reported that the tax structure in Canada was becoming more regressive. Between 1984 and 1991, personal income taxes rose 66 percent while corporate taxes dropped 34 percent.[127]

Canadian taxpayers and consumers have not been sanguine about Tory policies. Mulroney touted the FTA for its ability to lower Canadian consumer prices. When it become evident that the GST was increasing consumer prices, Canadians showed their displeasure by flocking across the border to shop in the United States in order to avoid paying the new federal tax. Canadians disliked the GST so much that they referred to it as the "go south tax."[128] The unintended consequences of the GST were that it drove millions of Canadians to shop in the United States instead of shopping in Canada. The high value of the Canadian dollar relative to the American dollar further persuaded Canadians to shop in the United States. Canadian one-day shopping trips to the United States increased almost 25 percent during 1991. This represented Can$5 billion in lost revenues to Canadian retailers. Cross-border shopping by Canadians contributed to the record number of retail bankruptcies in Canada. Mayors from Canadian border communities proposed that a regional tax break be used to lure Canadian shoppers back into Canada. The Canadian government only offered to hire more customs officials to levy the GST on goods brought into Canada from the United States.

At the same time as Canadian localities along the border suffered, American border communities prospered as a result of the FTA and GST. Merchants in American cities located close to the Canadian border such as Bellingham, WA, Grand Forks, ND, Sault Ste. Marie, MI, and Plattsburgh, NY aggressively advertised in Canada to attract Canadian shoppers. The factory outlet mall in Niagara Falls, NY, contains 85 stores sprawling over 400,000 square feet of commercial space with parking spaces for 1,900 vehicles. In 1991, the parking lot was full almost every Saturday. Over 50 percent of the cars had Ontario license plates. Gallup Canada surveyed Canadians in the summer of 1991 and found that 18 percent of Canadian households had at least one person who had traveled to the United States between April and June of 1991 for the specific purpose of shopping for goods that were also available in Canada but at a higher price.[129] The Canadian government was only able to staunch the flow of Canadian consumers to the United States after the Canadian dollar began to drop against the American dollar. More stringent border inspections and the lower value of the Canadian dollar caused the numbers to begin dropping in late 1992. Unfortunately for many Canadian retailers, this reprieve came too late.

The Fragmentation of the Canadian State

Tory policies caused the decentralization and fragmentation of the Canadian federal system. Two interlocking factors created this political fragmentation: FTA-inspired cuts to the Welfare State and attempts at constitutional reform. This section contends that the two most debated issues in recent Canadian history are intertwined. Free trade and attempts at constitutional reform in the Meech Lake and Charlottetown Accords were part of the same neoconservative agenda to weaken the influence of the Canadian federal government that had traditionally promoted social democratic ideals.

The geography of transportation and communications played a crucial role in the creation and maintenance of Canada's status as an independent Nation-State. Transportation, communications, and economic policy were used by the State to promote the idea of an independent Canada to a disparate population. The State first relied upon the CPR and the National Tariff system to unite Canada and to nurture a domestic manufacturing sector. Later came unemployment insurance, the CBC, the Canadian National Railroad, Air Canada, the NFB, and an expanding

Welfare State that tied the Canadian federal system together. By the 1960s, Canada was exhibiting all the outward manifestations of Fordist national development. In 1965, Canada abandoned the Union Jack and created its own national flag with the maple leaf. In 1967, Canada celebrated 100 years of national independence by holding the World's Fair in Montréal. In the 1970s, Canada established its national health care system and was spending millions of dollars promoting Canadian culture. At the same time that Canada was concentrating on issues of class and regional unity, it was also attempting to quell nationalist sentiment in Québec. French was given the status of Canada's other official language. The federal government spent millions of dollars in order to offer government services in both of Canada's official languages.

Since 1985, the Tories have used *laissez-faire* economics and the idea of free trade to reduce the role of the government in national affairs. Mulroney consciously adopted economic and political policies which have profoundly restructured the Canadian federal system that developed after World War II. Deregulation and privatization of large segments of the Welfare State resulted in the dramatic withdrawal of federal agencies and institutions from their role in promoting national development. A significant component of this restructuring came in the form of reduced transfer payments to the provinces who used this money to pay for health, welfare and education. Neoconservatives supported these cuts as a way to give the provinces greater freedom, authority and responsibility. After the cuts, provinces had the ability to restructure or downgrade services, or they could raise taxes to maintain or improve upon current service levels. The decentralization of power is viewed positively by neoconservatives as a form of enhanced regional autonomy. Bill Vander Zalm, former Premier of British Columbia, supports decentralization as a natural worldwide evolution towards local empowerment.

Critics of Tory policies see nothing benevolent or benign in the decentralization and fragmentation of the Canadian State. In their view, the Tories are dismantling institutions that have maintained Canadian national unity. As national institutions erode, Canada's federal system will become a patchwork confederation with regionally varying standards for health care, education, transportation and economic opportunity. By reducing federal funding for many provincially-run programmes, Ottawa is reversing a decades-old trend.

The provinces were granted authority to manage social programmes at Canadian independence in 1867. The Depression exposed the unwillingness or inability of the provinces to support social programmes. As a result, the federal government intervened. Starting with unemployment relief benefits, the Canadian State became increasingly involved in supporting Canada's expanding welfare programmes. As federal government spending increased, it stipulated that the provinces had to abide by common national standards to qualify for federal funds. The Tory cuts to transfer payments, UI benefits, transportation subsidies and other services undermine those national standards. At a supra-national level, deregulatory legislation governing such areas as telecommunications and foreign investment has been cemented into the FTA as an international treaty. Neoconservatives have renounced the role of the federal government to set national standards, to regulate the national economy and to maintain national unity. The post-Fordist State has become a post-national State as well.

The claim that the Canadian State has abandoned efforts to maintain national unity might seem paradoxical given Tory attempts to adopt constitutional reforms purportedly designed to assuage Québec separatists and other regional malcontents. On closer analysis, it can be shown that failed constitutional reforms such as the Meech Lake Accord and the Charlottetown Accord were not noble gestures to promote regional empowerment and national unity.[130] Constitutional reforms, the FTA and NAFTA were all designed to entrench neoconservative principles into fundamental documents that cannot be easily changed by a legislative assembly. The following brief history of proposed constitutional reforms shows how they are linked to free trade and neoconservative policies.

The issue of constitutional reform is rooted in the presence of Québec within Canada. As a conquered linguistic minority within Canada, the French-speaking people of Québec have long felt that their cultural and economic needs were ignored by the English-speaking population of Canada. Even in Québec, the positions of power had been traditionally held by Anglophones. French Canadian culture survived in Anglo-North America by retreating into the Roman Catholic Church and the farming communities of the Québec countryside. French Canadian culture was marked by its obedience to the church, rural introversion, large extended families, and its avoidance of Anglo-dominated commercial enterprise. Church leaders proclaimed that French Canadian culture could only be preserved through isolation. After World War II, it became obvious to French Canadian secular intellectuals that Canada was being transformed by urbanization and industrialization. French Canadians had to move into the city and away from the Church if they were to keep up with the rest of Canada. The introverted cultural nationalism of rural

Québec was replaced by an extroverted economic nationalism focused on Montréal and Québec City. By 1960, this transformation had been called Québec's Quiet Revolution. French Canadians were encouraged to obtain university degrees so that they could seize positions of power in business and government that had been traditionally held by Anglophones. The culmination of the Quiet Revolution came in 1976 when René Levesque, the leader of the Parti Québecois, was elected to be premier of Québec on a separatist platform.

Levesque promised to hold a referendum on the issue of Québec sovereignty in 1980. Prime Minister Trudeau was alarmed by growing separatist sentiment in Canada's second most populous province. As an avowed federalist, Trudeau believed that he could convince French Canadians to stay in Canada if they were given a special place in a revised Canadian constitution. The Canadian Prime Minister promised the people of Québec that a new constitution would give that province the status of a "distinct society" within Canada.[131] The proposed constitutional changes would transform Canada from a federal system comprised of ten individual provinces, to one consisting of two equal cultures. The people of Québec voted to stay in Canada, and Trudeau managed to gain approval for the 1982 Constitution Act. When political leaders from Québec examined the new constitution they refused to ratify it because it appeared to them that Québec was not given more autonomy or special status within Canada. The two-nation model of Canada promised by Trudeau had not replaced the ten-province model of Canada that would give Québec equal status. In fact, it appeared to some analysts that Canada would become more centralized than before if the new constitution was implemented.

When Mulroney came to power in 1984, the Québec government drew up a list of constitutional conditions under which it would endorse the 1982 Constitution Act. Some of those conditions included the constitutional recognition of Québec as a distinct society and expanded power over issues such as immigration and cultural policy. These conditions plus proposals developed by the Tories were included in a constitutional reform package that came to be known as the Meech Lake Accord (MLA).

It is important to note that the FTA negotiations were going on at the same time that the MLA discussions were taking place. This fact explains why the MLA included many provisions that decentralized Canada while embedding neoconservative values into a constitutional document. In fact, the MLA and the FTA were designed to reinforce each other by devolving many powers to the provinces.[132] The risk of decentralization, whether proposed by the FTA or the MLA, is that it erodes the ability of the federal government to set national standards or to protect Canadian social programmes in the face of continental market forces. Under the MLA, the provinces would assume greater responsibility for health, education and welfare. This goal was achieved under the FTA by cutting transfer payments. The MLA proposed to further entrench intellectual property rights in the constitution thus prioritizing the rights of the individual over the common good. This policy was discussed at length in the FTA and NAFTA negotiations as well.

The MLA retained the Charter of Rights and Freedoms that had been part of the 1982 Constitution Act promulgated by Pierre Trudeau. This charter was modeled after the Bill of Rights embedded in the American Constitution. The Canadian Charter has the potential to change Canada by focusing more attention on individual rights. Canadians had previously asked Parliament or the Crown for privileges. The new Charter as part of the MLA puts limits on the State and encourages Canadians to fight for individual rights. This represents a change from Canada's "traditional group-centredness."[133] By emphasizing individual rights to a greater extent, Canada would become a more classically liberal and libertarian society like the United States. The Tories also proposed that the Bank of Canada be forced to ensure "price stability" through a constitutional mandate.[134] Mulroney planned to embed monetarism and the pursuit of a zero inflation rate within the Canadian constitution. The Tory constitutional reforms were designed more to protect neoconservative policies than to provide protection for Québecois culture.

If the MLA and the FTA were designed with the same goals in mind, it is worth considering why the Tories were able to implement the FTA in 1989 and why they were not able to implement constitutional reforms in 1990. In the 1960s, English-speaking intellectuals on the Left supported Québec nationalism. The Anglo-Left cheered as the Québec proletariat voted out its corrupt politicians, rejected the paternalism and conservatism of the Church, and overthrew the privileged English upper class that had controlled the Québec economy for centuries. Leftists from English-speaking Canada supported the independence movement in Québec because they believed that they shared the same social-democratic ideals.[135]

It came as quite a shock to Anglophones on the Canadian Left when a majority of the popular vote in Québec voted for Mulroney and free trade in 1988. The English-speaking Left opposed the FTA and they believed that there should have been a *quid pro quo* for all the support they had offered to French Canadians in the past. The intelligentsia on the

Left supported Trudeau whose socialist and nationalist policies such as the NEP and the FIRA also included the expenditure of billions of dollars in the province of Québec. In order to appease Québec nationalists during the 1980 referendum, Trudeau spent Can$90 billion more in Québec than was extracted from the province in taxes. The Anglo-Left supported official bilingualism and spending for nationalist policies whether they buttressed the French Canadian or English Canadian national identity. The Parti Québecois had at one time applied for membership in the Socialist International, leading leftist intellectuals to believe that there was a basis for mutual respect and understanding.

Despite its earlier affiliations, the Parti Québecois had broken with its social democratic past. Jacques Parizeau replaced René Levesque as the head of the Parti Québecois. He and his party espoused a free market and pro-business philosophy. The Parti Québecois also shared with Alberta a distaste for federal policies which intruded on the policy-making powers of the provinces. Québec wanted more power to control regional cultural, immigration and energy policy. Alberta wanted more control over natural resources. Albertans also wanted guarantees that the federal government would never implement another NEP. Hugely unpopular in the West, the NEP was perceived to have transferred oil revenues from Alberta into the federal treasury in Ottawa.

Mulroney understood the regional politics at work in Canada. He appealed to the nationalist and entrepreneurial spirit in Québec. He promised constitutional reform in the guise of the MLA if the people of Québec would support him on the issue of free trade. Robert Bourassa, Liberal premier of Québec and alleged federalist, supported the FTA on the grounds that the MLA would keep Québec in Canada by granting that province more autonomy. Parizeau, as leader of the Parti Québecois, openly supported the FTA because free trade and the MLA could accelerate the independence of Québec by decentralizing the federal power structure.[136] He believed that the FTA would weaken English Canada while opening up new north-south links that could benefit manufacturers in Québec. The FTA and the MLA were promoted by Québec separatists and federalists alike because they both believed that the Tory policies reduced federal institutions supporting the east-west communications axis in Canada and diluted the impact of policies designed in Ottawa and Toronto. In Alberta, Mulroney had little difficulty in garnering support for the FTA or the MLA. Albertans perceived that the FTA would prevent another NEP from occurring. The MLA also promised to restrict federal powers.

As Paul Bunner of the *Alberta Report* noted, the MLA was not offered out of the "pristine belief in the ideals of self-determination, but as a Machiavellian maneuver to bribe Québec into supporting the FTA."[137] Mulroney's gambit was effective in the short run because the Tories were able to win the 1988 election and approval of the FTA with less than 50 percent of the popular vote. All of the English-speaking provinces except Alberta voted against the FTA. In Québec, the Tories won 53 percent of the popular vote which translated into 63 out of a possible 75 seats. If the vote was held only in English Canada, the Tories would have lost and the FTA would not have been implemented.

It can be argued that the FTA was imposed on English Canada by Québec voters. A broad consensus of voters in Québec supported free trade. Provincial Liberals, the Parti Québecois and the French Canadian media promoted the benefits of free trade to the electorate in Québec. Voters in Québec decided that their political future was logically grounded in Tory policies which offered economic sovereignty under the FTA and increased political control under the decentralized influence of the MLA.[138]

The Anglophone intelligentsia understood the threat to English Canadian political sovereignty posed by the FTA and the MLA. Anglo-Canadians repaid French Canadian support of the FTA by rejecting the MLA and its later incarnation, the Charlottetown Accord.[139] Discussions concerning Canadian constitutional reform remain at an impasse. The level of distrust between Canada's two official linguistic groups is as high as it has been since the 1980 Québec referendum. Tory machinations have only served to further polarize French and English Canadians.

The failure to implement constitutional reforms may have also generated a possible problem for the Tories. They had promised to implement the MLA if the people of Québec voted for the FTA in 1988. The Tories were unable to follow through on their promise and this may have cost them French Canadian votes in the 1993 Canadian federal election. Did the Tory strategy result in a Pyrrhic victory? Possibly, because they managed to pass the FTA and NAFTA but they were then soundly defeated in the 1993 federal election. It is unclear whether or not the Progressive Conservatives will recover as a national party. What is clear is that their strategies have radically transformed the Canadian State. Free trade and the MLA represented "twin body blows aimed at the capacity" of the federal State to maintain a national political community.[140] The Tories were unable to mount an overt challenge to Canada's Fordist economic, social and political institutions. Free trade and attempts at constitutional reform represent a covert, incremental strategy to establish a neoconservative model of development in Canada. The national Welfare State and the discourse of universality were replaced by the limited entrepreneurial State that promoted economic growth on the basis of enhanced capital mobility with little regard for social justice or national unity.

From Trudeau Liberalism to Neoliberalism

The story of free trade did not end with the defeat of the Progressive Conservatives in the 1993 federal election. The Tories lost the election but their legacy lives on in the practices of the Liberal Party and its leader, Prime Minister Jean Chrétien. To many Canadians, the neoliberal turn of the party that erected the Welfare State has come as quite a surprise. During the 1960s and 1970s, the Liberal Party put in place the very cornerstones of Canada's Fordist model of development including the FIRA, expanded health care, the NEP, and official bilingualism. The Liberal Party under Pierre Trudeau promoted economic nationalism and an expanded Welfare State that defined the apex of Canadian Fordist development.

By 1993, Canadians had become disenchanted with Tory policies that had reduced real wages and the standard of living of working Canadians. Canadians voted for the Liberal Party that had emphasized their social democratic legacy during the election campaign. The fact that Jean Chrétien had helped Pierre Trudeau expand Canada's social safety net during the 1970s was utilized by Liberal campaign strategists. As recently as the 1988 federal election, the Liberals campaigned on an anti-FTA platform. Chrétien promised that if elected in 1993 he would renegotiate NAFTA and restore spending to many programmes that had been gutted by the Tory government. The implicit message was that the Liberals were going to restore Canada to its social democratic past.

Canadians would eventually find out, however, that the Liberal Party had been transformed after almost a decade out of power. The social democratic ideals of Pierre Trudeau had all but disappeared. A new cadre of "blue Liberals" with ties to corporate Canada had attained positions of power within the Liberal Party during the early 1990s.[141] Trudeau Liberalism had given way to neoliberalism. This fact would not become clear until after the Liberal election victory.

During the election campaign, Liberals such as Paul Martin, Roy Maclaren and John Manley downplayed their anti-deficit and pro-business views. Paul Martin, for example, campaigned on the message that the deficit was just a symptom of a faltering economy that had been besieged by faulty policies from a previous government. It was implied that if the Liberals were elected, Keynesian policies could be implemented that would spur economic growth, create jobs, and boost tax revenue thereby alleviating the deficit problem. After the Liberal victory, Martin was appointed by Jean Chrétien to be Canada's finance minister. Martin then reversed the cause and effect relationship between economic growth and Canada's deficit problem.[142] Martin took the position that in order to generate jobs and economic growth, the deficit had to be eliminated first. Deficit reduction meant cuts to social spending, tax reforms and the continuation of many policies that had been put in place by the Progressive Conservative Party.

Within a month of gaining office, the neoliberal transformation of the Liberal Party was clearly manifest. In order to set the stage for future pro-business initiatives, Jean Chrétien appointed three business-oriented Members of Parliament to key Cabinet economic portfolios. Besides Paul Martin as Finance Minister, Chrétien appointed Roy Maclaren as minister of trade and John Manley as minister of industry. In November 1993, Paul Martin used his first major public speech to call for a national consensus to reduce the deficit. The challenge confronting the Liberals was how to cut the Welfare State without losing political credibility in the eyes of the Canadian electorate. The solution was to continue relying on the discourse of competitiveness that had been used to justify free trade. Martin argued that Canada would not be able to compete in a continental and increasingly global economy if its deficit was too large. Paul Martin echoed statements made by the BCNI, the C. D. Howe Institute, the OECD and many political commentators that Canada's "extravagant social policy framework constructed in the 1950s and 1960s no longer meets Canada's needs or its means."[143]

Neoconservatives in Canada have taken cues from Republican politicians in the United States who have proposed a balanced budget amendment. Ralph Klein, Premier of Alberta, has been called the "Newt of the North" because of his tax cuts and vigorous attacks on welfare spending.[144] In this continental harmonization of deficit rhetoric, pundits note that 31 U.S. states have balanced budget amendments in their constitutions. Canada and its provinces should also adopt tax and expenditure limits. Only through such ironclad measures will Canadians be able to "cut waste," reduce the Canadian deficit and promote the "national interests" of economic growth.[145] "Special interests" such as women, children and the unemployed were blamed for the deficit because they have become dependent on an exorbitantly expensive Welfare State.

Of course the deficit discourse hides the fact that neoconservatives really want to continue harmonizing Canadian social standards with those of the United States. The Liberals understand, as did the Tories before them, that an overt attack on remaining elements of the Welfare State would be politically untenable. Emphasizing the enormity of Canada's accumulated debt masks the true corporate agenda. Are Canada's social programmes really so extravagant that they are no longer affordable? Canada actually spends far less on social programmes than many OECD countries. Canada ranks thirteenth in social spending, sixteenth in unemployment insurance spending and fifteenth in maternity-leave provisions. Yet Canada ranks third in child poverty, second in unemployment and third in the gap between men and women's salary.[146] Clearly, Canada does not have an extravagant Welfare State.

More importantly, Canada can actually afford its Welfare State. In 1984, the Progressive Conservatives inherited an accumulated federal debt of Can$207 billion. By the middle of 1993, that figure had reached Can$453 billion, an increase of Can$246 billion under the Tories who had promised to control the debt. Interest charges during this period were Can$279 billion. By subtracting the interest payments of Can$279 million from the Can$246 million debt increase, the final figure turns out to be a Can$33 billion surplus.[147] If federal corporate taxes had remained unchanged between 1978 and 1993, Can$105 billion would have been collected. If interest rates had remained stable during the late 1980s, accumulated debt would have been between Can$65 billion and Can$95 billion lower.[148] Canada's social spending, at around 18 percent of GDP, is far less than the European average of 25 percent of GDP. Statistics Canada shows that up to 90 percent of the national debt is due to excessively high interest rates and uncollected or falling corporate taxes.[149]

Free trade is intimately linked to the deficit issue because the increased mobility afforded to capital hinders the ability of the government to increase corporate taxes. Organizations such as the BCNI and Chamber of Commerce bemoan the size of the deficit yet many of their individual corporate members are unwilling to pay their fair share of the taxes. Each year thousands of corporations making billions of dollars in profits pay no taxes due to tax loopholes. In 1991, 62,000 profitable firms in Canada paid no taxes. The Conference Board of Canada says that raising corporate taxes would force some corporations to leave Canada.[150] Many firms already believe that Canadian taxes, labour costs and transportation costs are excessive. Increased taxes could trigger the exodus of companies to the United States where taxes and production costs are lower.

The Liberals also argue that they have no choice but to cut social spending because international financial markets are losing confidence in the ability of Canada to honour its debts. Even though Canada's deficit has been shrinking due to social spending cuts, the debt keeps growing because of interest payments on the national debt. International agencies such as the IMF, the OECD and New York debt rating agencies such as Moody's, have targeted Canada for its profligate spending on the Welfare State.[151] Canada was warned to cut its social spending or have its debt ratings lowered. A lower debt rating means higher interest rates in international commercial lending markets which would compound Canada's debt service costs.

It appears that Paul Martin and the Liberals have few options. They inherited a huge debt and ongoing deficit problem from the Tories. Free trade has tied their hands so that corporate tax increases are difficult. International financial institutions have warned Canada that its social programmes are too generous. The only solution appears to be cuts to social spending if the deficit is going to be controlled. The discourse of the deficit has largely achieved its goal of justifying social spending cuts.

The Liberals never discussed the fact that there are many deficit management strategies available that don't involve massive cuts to social spending.[152] The Bank of Canada could reduce the real interest rate. The Canadian government finances its operating deficit by selling bonds. A 2 percent drop in interest rates would save the government over Can$2 billion in debt service costs per year. A job creation plan similar to the one described by Paul Martin during the 1993 election campaign could bolster tax revenues. A one percent drop in the unemployment rate could generate Can$6 billion in tax revenue. Some critics of the Liberal government suggest that some corporate tax loopholes could be closed without risking capital flight. Thousands of profitable firms in Canada pay zero taxes. If these firms would pay their fair share, up to Can$25 billion could be collected in corporate tax revenue. Up to Can$30 billion could be generated by imposing a 1 percent GST on stock and bond transactions. Canada could easily manage its deficit while supporting a generous Welfare State. Unfortunately, the Liberals, like the Tories before them, lack the desire or political will to adopt these alternative strategies. Instead, the Liberals have placed the burden of paying for the deficit on the backs of people least able to carry it — the poor, the infirm, children, students and the unemployed.

In 1994, Paul Martin's first federal budget made deep cuts in Canada's social programmes. Unemployment insurance was cut Can$3.1 billion over three years. Benefits for UI recipients were reduced from 57 to

55 percent of the claimant's wages. Workers also had to be employed for 12 weeks in order to be eligible for UI benefits. Public sector salaries were frozen until 1997. Federal transfer payments to the provinces were frozen as well.[153] Despite the depth of the cuts, international bond rating agencies, the BCNI and the OECD claimed that Canada had to do more to reduce its deficit. Social spending was blamed again for initiating the deficit crisis in Canada.

In the summer of 1994, Moody's lowered the rating on Canada's foreign currency bonds claiming that Canada was becoming a credit risk. In late 1994, many economists and foreign investors in Canada warned that Canada's debt had grown to unmanageable proportions. The C. D. Howe Institute and the governor of the Bank of Canada ratcheted the deficit hysteria upwards when they urged the Liberals to cut social spending even further because Canada could face a "lenders' strike."[154] There was an increasing chance that an abrupt withdrawal of foreign lending could occur if Canada did not halt the growth of its debt. All this despite the fact that investment dealers such as Goldman Sachs of New York were recommending that investors allocate a significant share of their bond portfolios to Canadian securities.[155] Despite the deficit rhetoric portraying Canada as a bad credit risk, foreign investment was occurring in Canada at a record pace. The fact that Canada was actually still a good credit risk in the eyes of many foreign investors did not hinder the ability of the Liberals to use the rhetoric of a deficit crisis to cut social spending.

The Liberals satisfied the concerns of many neoconservatives in 1995 when discussions of UI reforms proposed a new "national framework" for UI.[156] Planned UI reforms include a two-tier system that will provide lower benefits to repeat claimants. The Liberals also envision a UI system that would permit provincial variations in benefits. The proposed regionalization scheme would dismantle the national system of old that pooled the risk of unemployment across all regions and sectors. The Liberals are proposing UI reforms that would balkanize Canada's system, harmonizing it with that of the United States. The American system currently allows state-by-state variations that permit states to compete with each other by offering lower-cost UI programmes to attract investment.

The 1995 federal budget worked in tandem with free trade to accelerate the Americanization of Canada through social spending cuts. The Liberals targeted two elements within Canada's transportation system that had traditionally maintained Canada's east-west transportation infrastructure. The Crow Rate, a transportation subsidy to Prairie farmers, was deemed expendable by the Liberals because it was a trade irritant and a drain on the federal budget.[157] The Canadian National Railroad (CNR) was targeted for privatization. It was losing money as a State-run enterprise. As a private enterprise, the railroad would not cost the Canadian government any money. The end of the Crow Rate and the possible privatization of the CNR are two more factors leading to the deterioration of the east-west axis in Canada and the strengthening of the north-south ties between Canada and the United State.

The Liberal budget reduced funding to the arts and humanities in Canada. The Liberals plan to cut federal spending by Can$9.8 billion, a 19 percent reduction over three years. Heritage and cultural programmes will be reduced by Can$676 million, representing a 23 percent reduction. Funding reductions to specific institutions included a Can$300 million cut to the CBC, a 2.5 percent cut to the Canada Council, a 50 percent cut to book publishing subsidies, and a 5 percent cut to the NFB and Telefilm.[158] Despite these cuts, the USTR continues to identify Canada's protection of its cultural industries as the greatest trade irritant between the United States and Canada.

The most profound budget reductions have restructured the transfer payments between Ottawa and the provinces. Recall that three major transfer payments, the CAP, the EPF and equalization payments were made by the federal government to help the provinces run social programmes. The Liberals have taken the CAP and the EPF and combined them to form a single payment called the Canada Social Transfer (CST). The CST will receive Can$1.8 billion less funding from Ottawa and there will be fewer federal restrictions on how the money is to be spent.[159] Transfers have become block grants with greater freedoms given to the provinces. Social activists fear that the CST will lead to the further erosion of national standards for health care and education.

Neoconservatives would like to privatize the Canadian health care system. The OECD analyzed the rising costs of health care and compared OECD countries on their health care expenditure as a percent of GDP. They argued that increased privatization and market incentives would be the best way to manage health care costs.[160] While Canada spends about 10 percent of its GDP on health care, it has contained cost increases over the past three decades better than most OECD countries (Figure 41). Despite this fact, health care transfer payments have been targeted for dramatic cuts by the Liberals. In the face of large budget cuts, health care services can only be maintained if provincial taxes are raised or if privatization of the system is permitted. The FTA and NAFTA permit large portions of the Canadian system to be managed by American enterprises. The Kaiser Foundation and other Health Maintenance Organizations and insurance companies in the

Figure 41
Health Care Expenditures as a Percentage of GDP

Country	1960	1992	% Increase
United States	5.3	14.0	260
Italy	3.6	8.5	240
Japan	3.0	6.9	230
France	4.2	9.4	220
Germany	4.8	8.7	180
United Kingdom	3.9	7.1	180
Canada	5.5	10.2	180
G-7 Average	4.3	9.3	220
OECD Europe	3.8	8.0	210
Total OECD	3.9	8.4	220

Source: Maitland MacFarland and Howard Oxley, "Reforming Health Care," *OECD Observer* 192 (February 1995): 23-26.

United States have targeted Canada as the next "growth market."[161] The budget cuts embedded in the CST will allow greater fragmentation, privatization and a greater American presence in the Canadian health care system.

Education has also come under attack by the 1995 Liberal budget. The merging of the EPF with the CAP ultimately means funding cuts to provinces which run the Canadian university system. Government transfers per student steadily declined under the Tories. The Liberals propose that federal government funding to post-secondary education be reduced to zero.

Paul Martin's budget cuts have been so draconian that even neoconservative columnists such as David Frum are convinced that the Liberals have become neoliberals. According to Frum, Paul Martin's budget announcement "ripped the guts out" of social democracy as a governing political idea in Canada.[162] The Fordist Welfare State erected by the Liberals in the 1960s now stands condemned by that same party and is in the process of being dismantled. Frum concluded that the 1995 Liberal budget could have gone even further, but it still remains the most radical turn away from statism and "toward freedom" since the Second World War.[163] Neoconservatives need not have worried about their future under Jean Chrétien. The post-Fordist principles of free trade and a limited Welfare State are alive and well within the new Liberal party.

Notes

1. Clarkson, "Disjunctions: Free Trade and the Paradox of Canadian Development," 117.
2. Economic Council of Canada, *Venturing Forth*, 28.
3. Peter J. Taylor, *Political Geography: World Economy, Nation-State, Locality*, 2nd ed. (London: Longmans, 1989), 157-58.
4. Martin Carnoy, *The State and Political Theory* (Princeton, NJ: Princeton University Press, 1984), 37.
5. Bob Jessop, "Recent Theories of the Capitalist State," *Cambridge Journal of Economics*, 1 (1977): 353.
6. Gramsci, *An Antonio Gramsci Reader*, 192; Robert Cox, *Production, Power, and World Order* (New York: Columbia University Press, 1987), 6.
7. Vera Chouinard and Ruth Fincher, "State Formation in Capitalist Societies: A Conjunctural Approach," *Antipode*, 19 (19987): 339.
8. Jacob Torfing, "A Hegemony Approach to Capitalist Regulation," in *State, Economy and Society*, Rene Bertramsen, Jens Peter Frolund and Jacob Torfing, eds. (London: Unwin Hyman, 1991), 86.
9. Ibid.
10. Ibid.
11. Ibid., 89.
12. James O'Connor, *Accumulation Crisis* (New York: Basil Blackwell, 1984), 221.
13. Bluestone and Harrison, *The Deindustrialization of America*, 206.
14. Davis, *Prisoners of the American Dream*, 140.
15. Economic Council of Canada, *Venturing Forth*, 28.
16. Tom McCoag, "MacDonald Slams Opposition Tactics," *Halifax Chronicle-Herald*, 7 November 1988, 34.
17. Leonard Shifrin, "Free Trade in Social Programs," *Perception*, 12, no. 1 (1988): 27.
18. Mel Watkins, "Ten Good Reasons to Oppose Free Trade," *This Magazine*, 20 (April 1986): 13.
19. Don McGillivray, "Free Trade Puts Pressure on Canadian Values," *Sault Star*, 30 November 1988, A4.
20. Hilary Grammer, "Social Policy by Stealth," *Canadian Dimension*, 25 (June 1991): 19.
21. Keith Banting, "Neo-conservatism in an Open Economy: the Social Role of the Canadian State," *International Political Science Review*, 13, no. 2 (1992): 150.
22. BCNI, "Canadian Trade, Competitiveness and Sovereignty," 13.

23. "CMA Wants Royal Commission on Social Programs," *Sault Star,* 21 December 1988, A1.
24. BCNI, "National Economic Priorities: Challenges and Opportunities. A Perspective on the Canadian Economy by the BCNI," (Ottawa: Unpublished Report of the BCNI, 1991), 5.
25. Tim Hazledine, "Canada-U.S. Free Trade? Not So Elementary, Watson," *Canadian Public Policy,* 14, no. 2 (1988): 209.
26. S. Dale, "One Year After: Free Trade Fallout," *This Magazine,* 23 (January 1990): 10.
27. Jim Sinclair, "Free Trade, the Canadian Way," 23.
28. CLC, *CLC Free Trade Briefing Document,* 7 (January 1991): 12.
29. Hugh Winsor, "In Grey Pre-budget Ottawa, Prime Minister's Agenda Doesn't Add Up," *Globe and Mail,* 28 November 1988, A2.
30. Bluestone and Harrison, *The Deindustrialization of America,* 209.
31. Chris Hill, "Ontario Joins B.C. Challenge of Federal Limits for Social Programs," *Sault Star,* 28 February 1990, A1.
32. Allan Maslove, "Reconstructing Fiscal Federalism," in *How Ottawa Spends: The Politics of Competitiveness,* Francis Abele, ed. (Ottawa: Carleton University Press, 1992), 60.
33. D'Arcy Jenish, "A Cry of Protest: Rising Tuition Fees Stir Campus Discontent," *Maclean's,* 9 March 1993, 44.
34. "York to Turn Away 2,000 First-year Students," *Sault Star,* 11 March 1993, A7.
35. Charles Hill, "Who Can Afford To Go To University?" *Western Gazette,* 69, no. 4 (1993): 34.
36. Statistics Canada, *Education Statistics Bulletin* (Ottawa: Supply and Services, 1992), 5.
37. Ibid.
38. "Report Documents Declining Federal Education Funding," *Sault Star,* 30 November 1992, A1.
39. CLC, "Submission by the CLC to the House of Commons Standing committee on External Affairs and International Trade: Canada's Role in U.S.-Mexico Free Trade Negotiations," (Ottawa: Unpublished Document from the CLC, 1990), 12.
40. Frances Russell, "The Americanization of Medicare: Will that be Visa or Mastercard?" *Canadian Forum,* 69 (August 1990): 17-19.
41. Lois Sweet, "Medicare May Need Miracle to Survive," *Toronto Star,* 9 March 1991, A1.
42. Russell, "The Americanization of Medicare," 18.
43. Nora Underwood, "Cross-border Checkup," *Maclean's,* 25 November 1991, 58.
44. Russell, "The Americanization of Medicare," 18.
45. P. Todd, "Manning Would End Federal Role in Medicare," *Toronto Star,* 15 June 1991, A1.
46. Economic Council of Canada, "Health Care Policies Safe," *Au Courant,* 9, no. 2 (1988): 9.
47. D'Arcy Jenish, "Facing Radical Surgery," *Maclean's,* 13 January 1992, 38.
48. "CMA Demands Ottawa Trim Social Programs," *Sault Star,* 30 January 1992, A6.

49. Glen Allen, "Strong Medicine," *Maclean's,* 21 December 1992, 10.
50. Cameron, "The Dealers," 18.
51. Canadian Centre for Policy Alternatives, *Which Way for the Americas? Analysis of NAFTA Proposals and the Impact on Canada* (Ottawa: CCPA, 1992), 41.
52. Ibid.; John Dillon, "NAFTA is a Very Big Deal," *Action Canada Dossier,* 36 (March 1992): 2.
53. Allen, "Strong Medicine," 11.
54. Bacon, "Quick Reaction," A1; "Liberal Senators Call Drug Patent Bill a Tragedy," *Sault Star,* 23 January 1993, A6.
55. Richard Lipsey, "Sovereignty: Culturally, Economically, and Socially," in *Free Trade: The Real Story,* John Crispo, ed. (Toronto: Gage Educational Publishing, 1988), 154.
56. R. Babe, "Copyright and Culture," *Canadian Forum,* 67 (February 1988): 26.
57. Ibid.
58. Ibid.
59. Ibid.
60. Harold Innis, *The Bias of Communication* (Toronto: University of Toronto Press, 1951), 129.
61. Paul Litt, "The Massey Commission, Americanization, and Canadian Cultural Nationalism," *Queen's Quarterly,* 98, no. 2 (1991): 375.
62. Babe, "Copyright and Culture," 27.
63. Litt, "The Massey Commission," 376.
64. Finlay and Sprague, *The Structure of Canadian History,* 394; Gwyn, *The 49th Paradox,* 44.
65. Seymour Martin Lipset, *Continental Divide* (New York: Routledge, 1990), 2; Manjunath Pendakur, *Canadian Dreams and American Control: The Political Control of the Canadian Film Industry* (Detroit: Wayne State University Press, 1990), 252.
66. Colleen Fuller, "Fade to Black: Culture Under Free Trade," *Canadian Forum,* 70 (August 1991): 6.
67. Bob Davis, "Free-trade Pact's Details Are Sparking Squabbles as Congress Takes Up Review," *Wall Street Journal,* 8 September 1992, A2.
68. Charles Falzon, "Film, TV Central to Sense of Nationhood," *Toronto Star,* 17 June 1991, A21.
69. Vincent Mosco, "Toward a Transnational World Information Order: The Canada-U.S. Free Trade Agreement," *Canadian Journal of Communications,* 15, no. 2 (1990): 46.
70. Babe, "Copyright and Culture," 27.
71. Ibid.
72. Anthony Smith, *The Geopolitics of Information: How Western Culture Dominates the World* (New York: Oxford University Press, 1980), 52.
73. Babe, "Copyright and Culture," 28.
74. Tom Perlmutter, "The Flora Solution: The Politics of Film Distribution," *Canadian Dimension,* 23, (March 1989): 6.
75. Leaders of the Canadian cultural community fear cultural integration into the United States because of American censorship of Canadian movies. It is not enough that Canadian film distributors cannot easily show their movies in

Canada or the United States. The United States has actually censored and then banned the showing of Canadian movies such as the NFB production *If You Love This Planet* (Roberts 1991, 27). This film was banned because of its stance against nuclear war and the American military-industrial complex. The Canadian cultural community also worried about American censorship of Canadian artists and writers holding contrary political views. Canadian author Farley Mowat has already been denied entry into the United States because of his radical political perspectives. Mowat planned to give presentations at universities in California and Washington State but was prevented from traveling into the United States. His name had been placed on a list of subversive writers and intellectuals who are not allowed into the United States under provisions of the 1952 McCarran Act (Mowat 1985, 1).

76. Perlmutter, "The Flora Solution," 6.
77. Ibid.
78. Ibid.
79. Ibid.,9.
80. "Stop Talks, Says ACTRA," *Cinema Canada,* 139 (March 1987): 38; Garry Neil, "Election Countdown: Cultural Policy Options," *Cinema Canada,* 157 (November 1988): 14.
81. "Stop Talks, Says ACTRA," 43.
82. Perlmutter, "The Flora Solution," 11.
83. Falzon, "Film, TV Central to Sense of Nationhood," A21.
84. "Valenti Praises Canadian Talent, Raps Government Intervention," *Cinema Canada,* 168 (1989): 27; Jack Valenti, "Why Canada Must Never Restrict Imported Films," *Canadian Speeches,* 3, no. 7 (1989): 35.
85. Fuller, "Fade to Black," 6.
86. Lipsey, "Sovereignty: Culturally, Economically, and Socially," 154.
87. de Kerckhove, "Control of the Collective Mind. Free Trade and Canada's Cultural Industries," *Canadian Forum,* 67 (October 1989): 20; Babe, "Copyright and Culture," 6.
88. The term "cultural community" includes individual artists and performers as well as Canadian-controlled businesses that profit from merchandising Canadian cultural commodities such as music, books and paintings. The Canadian artistic community and Canadian cultural industries such as book publishers and recording studios survive because of their symbiotic relationship. Without the Canadian-controlled cultural industries, most Canadian artists would not have a commercial outlet for their work. American companies are unlikely to produce goods with Canadian themes to a North American audience. Without Canadian artists, Canadian cultural industries would not have a distinctive product to sell to Canadian consumers. These companies would not survive if they only had American products to sell because American companies can produce books and recordings more efficiently. It is important to distinguish between individual artists and cultural industries, but these two groups within Canada's cultural community shared a common critical view of the FTA.
89. W.H. New, "If Anyone Knows," *Canadian Literature,* 118 (Autumn 1988): 3; "Artviews Report: The Free Trade Agreement," *Artviews,* 15, no. 1 (1989): 15.

90. Michael Bergman, "Trick or Treaty," *Cinema Canada,* 151 (February 1988): 15.
91. John DeMont, "Standing On Guard: A Majority Now Opposes Free Trade," *Maclean's,* 18 December 1989, 50.
92. Susan Crean, "Reading Between the Lies: Culture and the FTA," *This Magazine,* 22 (May 1988): 29.
93. Richard and Dearden, *The Canada-U.S. Free Trade Agreement,* 311.
94. Mosco, "Toward a Transnational World Information Order," 49.
95. Linda McQuaig, "Pact Could Scuttle Insurance Scheme," *Globe and Mail,* 13 December 1988, A3; Mike Trickey, "Public Insurance Plan Will Cost $3.6 Billion, 10,000 Jobs -Study," *Sault Star,* 14 August 1991, A1.
96. U.S. Department of Commerce, *Canada-U.S. Free Trade Agreement: Summary of Provisions* (Washington, DC: International Trade Commission, 1987), 7.
97. Congress, House, Committee on Foreign Affairs, *Oversight of the U.S.-Canada Free Trade Agreement: Hearing Before the House of Representatives Committee on Foreign Affairs and Its Subcommittee On International Economic Policy and Trade, and On Western Hemisphere Affairs,* 100th Congress, 2nd sess., March 16, 1988, 152; Congress, House, Committee on the Judiciary, *Summary of the U.S.-Canada Free Trade Agreement: Hearing Before the Subcommittee on Courts, Civil Liberties, and the Administration of Justice of the House Committee on the Judiciary,* 100th Congress, 2nd sess., 28 April 1988.
98. Christopher Waddell, "A Nagging Question: Is Canadian Culture In Or Out?" *Globe and Mail,* 12 November 1988, D3; Edward Comer, "The Department of Communication Under the Free Trade Regime," *Canadian Journal of Communication,* 16 (1991): 250; John Ferguson, "Short Wave Radio Service Slashed," *Toronto Star,* 23 March 1991, A7; Antonia Zerbisias, "Fiscal Drama Unfolding at CBC-TV," *Toronto Star,* 16 March 1991, A1.
99. Howard Pawley, "CBC Back Talk," *Maclean's,* 17 December 1990, 18.
100. Anthony Wilson-Smith, "Cutting the CBC," *Maclean's,* 17 December 1990, 12.
101. Antonia Zerbisias, "Cuts Put CBC on 'Slippery Slope' Down, Juneau Says," *Toronto Star,* 23 March 1991, G3.
102. Barbara Amiel, "In Defence of Crispo, Fecan and the CBC," *Maclean's,* 29 April 1991, 13.
103. Wilson-Smith, "Cutting the CBC," 11.
104. Amiel, "In Defence of Crispo, Fecan and the CBC," 13.
105. John Burns, "Trains to be Cut in Canada," *New York Times,* 5 October 1989, B25.
106. Mark Hallman, "CN on Private Track," *Financial Post,* 1 October 1994, 1; Helen Forsey, "Railroading Into Oblivion," *Canadian Forum,* 74 (November 1994): 33.
107. Victor Dwyer, "Culture in Crisis," *Maclean's,* 22 April 1992, 46.
108. Ibid.
109. Canada Council, "Government Budget Cuts Affect Canada Council," *Canada Council Bulletin,* 39 (1993): 2.
110. Jeff Silverstein, "Canada Wants to Guard Culture in North American Pact," *Christian Science Monitor,* 13 November 1991, 8.
111. Nigel Hunt, "The Theory of Devolution," *This Magazine,* 25, no. 4 (1991): 24.
112. Brian Bergman, "Publish and Perish," *Maclean's,* 17 October 1994, 52.

113. Rowland Lorimer, "Book Publishing in English Canada in the Context of Free Trade," *Canadian Journal of Communications,* 16 (1991): 63; Pamela Young, "Taxing Culture," *Maclean's,* 14 January 1991, 48.
114. Lorimer, "Book Publishing in English Canada," 67.
115. Ibid.
116. Randy Robinson, "Colonizing Canada: A Year and a Half of Free Trade," *Multinational Monitor,* 11 (May 1990): 10.
117. BCNI, "Taxation Reform 1987: A Response to the Federal Government White Paper," (Ottawa: Unpublished Report of the BCNI, 1987), 9.
118. Donald Beach, "Sales Tax Reform is Needed But It's Hard to Get," *Toronto Star,* 21 November 1988, C2.
119. John Geddes, "Canada Corporate Tax Slightly Higher," *Financial Post,* 17 December 1994, 7.
120. Ed Finn, "Index on Federal Taxes," *Canadian Forum,* 68 (March 1990): 32; "U.S., Canada Near Accord to Cut Withholding Tax," *Wall Street Journal,* 28 April 1992, A2; Peter Newman, "Wilson's Vain Struggle with a Killer Debt," *Maclean's,* 4 March 1991, 46.
121. Sandra Sorenson, "Corporate Tax Avoidance," *Canadian Forum,* 72 (May 1994): 48.
122. BCNI, "The Goods and Services Tax: A Vehicle for Needed Tax Structure Reform. Submission to the House of Commons Standing Committee on Banking, Trade and Commerce" (Ottawa: Unpublished Document of the BCNI, 1990), 16.
123. Michael Wilson, Interview, *Maclean's,* 25 September 1989, 41.
124. Fred Langan, "Canadians Flocking to US Shops," *Christian Science Monitor,* 29 May 1991, 7; Brian Bergman, "The Tax in Effect," Maclean's, 2 October 1989, 22.
125. Brenda Dalglish, "They All Hurt," *Maclean's,* 8 October 1990, 23.
126. John Ferguson, "Ottawa Hauls in Windfall From GST," *Toronto Star,* 8 June 1991, A1.
127. Kaye Fulton, "Mad as Hell Over Taxes," *Maclean's,* 17 June 1991, 18.
128. Langan, "Canadians Flocking to US Shops," 7.
129. Gallup Canada, "18% of Households Have U.S. Shopper," *Toronto Star,* 17 June 1991, A19.
130. Grammer, "Social Policy by Stealth," 19.
131. Roger Gibbins, "Canadian Federalism: The Entanglement of Meech Lake and the Free Trade Agreement," *Publius,* 19 (Summer 1989): 187.
132. Donald Smiley, "Meech Lake and Free Trade," *Canadian Public Administration,* 32, no. 3 (1989): 470; Jack McArthur, "Meech is not a One-shot Solution," *Toronto Star,* 8 June 1990, F2; David Crane, "Big Shift of Powers to Provinces may Prove Too Costly for Canada," *Toronto Star,* 6 April 1991, D2.
133. Lipset, *Continental Divide,* 39.
134. Canadian Centre for Policy Alternatives, *Briefing Notes on the Tory Constitutional Proposals* (Ottawa: CCPA, 1991), 22.
135. Paul Bunner, "Divorce, Canadian Style. How Free Trade Estranged Québec From the Anglo Left," *Alberta Report,* 17, no. 1 (1990): 15.
136. Benoit Aubin, "Bourassa Makes Another Strong Pitch for Free-trade Deal,"

Globe and Mail, 17 November 1988; Benoit Aubin, "Re-election of Tory Majority a Blow for PQ," *Globe and Mail,* 25 November 1988; Robert McKenzie, "Trade Deal Boosts Separatism PQ Says," *Toronto Star,* 23 November 1988, A1; Jacques Parizeau, Interviewed by Tom Velk in *Canadian-American Free Trade: Historical, Political and Economic Dimensions,* Alvin Riggs and Tom Velk, eds. (Halifax, NS: IRPP, 1987), 213.

137. Bunner, "Divorce, Canadian Style," 15.
138. Reg Whitaker, "No Laments for A Nation. Free Trade and the Election of 1988," *Canadian Forum,* 67 (March 1989): 12.
139. David McNally, "Beyond Nationalism, Beyond Protectionism: Labour and the Canada-U.S. Free Trade Agreement," *Review of Radical Political Economics,* 22, no. 1 (1990): 185.
140. Whitaker, "No Laments for a Nation," 12.
141. Geddes, "Martin Steers Towards Blue Liberalism," 22.
142. Ibid.
143. Deirdre McMurdry, "The Tie that Binds," *Maclean's,* 31 October 1994, 50; Hannes Suppanz, "Canada: Recasting Social Assistance," *The OECD Observer,* 192 (February 1995): 49; Douglas Knight and Diane Francis, "Debt and Taxes," *Financial Post,* 28 January 1995, DT1-DT9.
144. Deirdre McMurdry, "A State of De-Klein," *Maclean's,* 6 February 1995, 47.
145. Melvin Smith, "Ironclad Resolve is Needed to Cut Waste," *Financial Post,* 28 January 1994, DT6; Michael Walker, "We've Caught the Balance-the-Budget Religion," *Financial Post,* 28 January 1995, DT9; Patrice Martin, "The Kiss of Debt," *Canadian Forum,* 74 (March 1994): 20.
146. Ed Finn, "No Alternatives," *Canadian Forum,* 74 (1994): 47.
147. "Demystifying the Debt," *Canadian Forum,* 73 (1993): 10.
148. Ibid.
149. Ed Finn, "Deficit Doctors," *Canadian Forum,* 74 (1994): 47.
150. Peter Morton, "Martin's Options Limited. Closing Business Tax Loopholes May Drive Corporations Elsewhere," *Financial Post,* 11 February 1995, 7.
151. Greg Ip, "Canadians Starting to Live Within Their Means," *Financial Post,* 24 December 1994, 35.
152. Finn, "No Alternatives," 47.
153. Ibid.
154. Greg Ip, "Lenders' Strike Alert: All Eyes on Martin as Debt Fears Unsettle the C$," *Financial Post,* 15 October 1994, 5.
155. "U.S. Bullish on Canada," *Maclean's,* 6 February 1995, 48.
156. Laurell Ritchie, "Flying Without a Net," *This Magazine,* 28, no. 1 (1994): 34.
157. Scott Haggett, "As The Crow Rate Flies," *Financial Post,* 13 May 1995, 4.
158. "$676 million hacked from Federal Support to Cultural Sector," *Bulletin of the Canadian Conference of the Arts,* February, (1995): 1.
159. Peter Hall, "Austerity Budget Brings Structural Change," *Canada Outlook,* 10, no. 3 (1995): 22.
160. MacFarlan and Oxley, "Reforming Healthcare," 23.
161. Ecumenical Coalition for Economic Justice, "Free Trade and Healthcare," *Canadian Review of Social Policy,* 33, no. 1 (1994): 96.

162. David Frum, "Martin's Speech Renounced All the Liberals Have Stood For," *Financial Post,* 4 March 1995, 22.
163. Ibid.

Chapter 6

Conclusion

Free Trade as Catalyst: Market Forces and Social Change

At the outset of this book it was noted that the Canada-United States FTA was neither free, nor about trade, nor a popularly-supported agreement. It was (and is) not free because Canada has had to pay a high price to gain greater access to American and Mexican markets. Canadian consumers have seen prices rise because of the FTA-inspired GST. Thousands of Canadian jobs have been lost. The 1995 Canadian unemployment rate still hovers above 10 percent. The FTA is also not primarily about trade. Free trade has been shown to be more about the creation of a new continental model of development for the regulation of capitalism. Free trade was implemented to serve as a corporate bill of rights that entrenches deregulation and market orientation in an international treaty. More importantly, free trade was implemented to erode national economic, social and political institutions on which Fordist development was based. The crisis of Fordism prompted corporate managers to search for an alternative model of development that could reduce restrictions placed upon them by the Nation-State. Finally, the FTA was not an agreement bargained in good faith because a majority of Canadians voted against the Tories in the 1988 federal election. The Liberals campaigned against the FTA in 1988 and NAFTA in 1993. The Tories went ahead and adopted the FTA against the wishes of Canadians. The Liberals reneged on their promise to renegotiate NAFTA. Free trade was used by both the Tories and the Liberals as a way to clear the ground for the implementation of a broader neoconservative and neoliberal agenda.

Neoconservatives in Canada and the United States desired a deregulated continental model of development that could increase capital mobility as a measure for restoring profitability. With open access to an entire continent, corporate managers could drive down wages and Welfare State spending by playing communities off against each other. The overall goal was to harmonize and integrate Canadian standards and institutions with those of the United States. After six years of free trade, it is reasonable to conclude that this agenda has been largely put into effect. The Canadian economy, political system and labour practices have been significantly altered as a result of closer articulation with the economy of the United States. Canada has been forced to acquiesce to a continental model of development by continental market forces and the geopolitical pressures of the United States. In the language of Regulation theory, neoconservatives abandoned Canada's Fordist model of development based on the Nation-State. In its place a post-Fordist model of development was promoted, organizing capitalist regulation at a continental territorial scale.

The FTA had been promoted as a universally beneficial economic policy that had no negative political or social implications for Canada. Because this study argues to the contrary — that free trade was intentionally designed to restructure society to suit corporate needs — it was necessary to reveal the intentions of free trade promoters. Chapter two was therefore written to show the underlying intent of the free-trade proponents. Promoters of the FTA consistently relied upon the discourse of neoclassical economics and the purportedly objective laws of comparative advantage to justify free trade. The use of Foucault's discourse theory allowed the facade of objectivity to be penetrated. It could therefore be shown that the theory of free trade is not based on any natural law but is instead a socially constructed idea that has been used in different places during different times to suit different political and economic purposes.

After the genealogy of abstract theories of free trade was presented, chapter two examined the concrete case of free trade between Canada and the United States. Supporters of free trade relied upon a neutral social scientific discourse to deflect attention away from their value-laden continentalist agenda. In reality, the neoclassical model of free trade has little to say about the geopolitics and the realpolitik of international trade in the late twentieth century. Despite this criticism, supporters of the FTA continued to include the law of comparative advantage in their discourse because it projected an aura of neutral science and objectivity. In contrast, anti-FTA discourse emphasized the threat posed to communities by capital with enhanced geographic mobility. Opponents to free trade also stressed that the FTA would force many Canadian policies to be harmonized with those of the United States. By examining the regional impacts of free trade, it was shown that free trade was not a universally beneficial policy. Certainly, many people have benefited from free trade. Even more people have been hurt.

The burden of free-trade driven restructuring was shared unequally on a national, regional, class, and gender basis. In the process, Canadian sovereignty has been compromised to a much greater degree than that of the United States. Free trade has been the central factor driving Canada from a Fordist model of development based on the Nation-State to a post-Fordist model of development based on a broader vision of the North American continent. This reality was revealed by examining the impact of free trade on the Canadian economy, labour movement and the Welfare State. By focusing on the performance of economic institutions before and after the implementation of free trade, it was possible to elucidate how continental market and geopolitical forces have forced Canada to adopt a post-Fordist model of economic development. Much to Canada's detriment, its economic institutions and policies have become increasingly harmonized with those of the United States. Consider the entertainment industry and pharmaceutical industries. In both cases Canada had attempted to foster greater autonomy for Canadian movie distribution and health care costs. Both of these attempts were scuttled either in the FTA negotiating process or in the FTA itself. Continental standards for movie distribution and tightened intellectual property rights have replaced Canadian policies.

The development of the Canadian manufacturing sector has relied upon certain protectionist policies enforced by the Fordist Canadian State. The NEP was designed to increase Canadian control over Canadian energy resources. The Auto Pact was designed as a managed trade agreement in automobiles and parts to ensure that Canadian workers and communities were able to produce cars in proportion to the number of cars sold in Canada. The FIRA was designed to screen foreign investments to ensure that they met certain Canadian performance requirements. All three of these policies were eliminated or restructured under the FTA. Canada lost considerable control over domestic economic and industrial policy as a result of free trade. In hindsight, this is not a surprising outcome. A researcher from the American Enterprise Institute testified before the U.S. House of Representatives that the FTA was good for the United States because it eliminated Canadian performance requirements for foreign investors. The president of Dow Chemical Canada, stated that Canada had to "mesh its economic and tax policies with those of the United States or lose big under free trade."[1]

Canadian corporate culture has also harmonized with that of the United States. The prospect of continental competition sparked a merger spree in Canada. Accompanying the merger-driven expansion of Canadian companies, has been an increasing tendency to remunerate Canadian executives along an American model with "performance-based pay plans."[2] In addition to salary increases, chief executive officers are given stock options and a percentage of net corporate profits. Canadian executive paychecks have grown because there is a shortage of competent business leaders in North America capable of leading the increasing number of large firms.

Free trade has also permitted American geopolitical pressures to be disguised as trade policy. The as yet unresolved issue of subsidies has confounded Canadian economic development strategy. With no definition of what constitutes an unfair subsidy, Canada has been increasingly targeted by the United States for unfairly subsidizing Canadian exporters. The United States has used the strategy of harassment related to the subsidy issue to force changes in policy with regard to Canadian wood exports, agriculture and automobile manufacturing. Three of Canada's most important industries have been hurt by free trade in this manner. This problem has no immediate solution due to the lack of a provision to resolve the subsidy definition issue in NAFTA.

Mulroney promised during the FTA debates that Canada was not entering into a customs union, common market or any other arrangement that would affect the ability of Canadian officials to make foreign policy aimed at third parties. The Canadian Importers Association (CIA) now sees the shift to a customs union as inevitable. Yasuo Noguchi, Japanese Consul General to Canada, presaged the pronouncements of the CIA in the June 21, 1989 edition of the *Financial Post* when he stated that the FTA is a precursor to the creation of a North American customs union.[3] Currently, Canada has a higher average of tariffs on imports from non-Mexican third-party countries than the United States. If the current gap in third-party tariffs is maintained, high Canadian tariffs will deflect trade and investment to the United States. The Canadian International Trade Tribunal has heeded these warnings and has recommended that Canada lower third-country tariffs to American levels in some economic sectors such as textiles. This provides further evidence that Canadian sovereignty related to the ability to set and control economic policy has been compromised as a direct result of the FTA. The ramifications of this development have been felt throughout Canada because the surrender of economic sovereignty foreshadows the loss of political sovereignty.[4]

By examining labour relations before and after the FTA, it becomes apparent that free trade has been undermining Canada's Fordist labour relations. A new capital-labour accord has emerged that is dramatically different from the one that prevailed over the postwar, golden age of Fordist labour relations. The post-Fordist era ushered in by free trade relies on domination instead of negotiation. Canadian workers have been increasingly subjected to the "whipsaw process" which has enabled businesses to force concessions out of workers in the areas of wages, benefits and work rules. Managers want a more flexible and lower-cost labour force that will increase competitiveness. Failure to acquiesce to corporate demands can and has resulted in the relocation of production out of Canada to regions in the United States and Mexico that actually advertise the fact that their workers are paid lower wages and benefits.

Canadian workers have suffered as a result of free trade in other ways as well. The FTA-generated jobs promised by Mulroney have never materialized. Canada experienced a net loss of manufacturing jobs as a result of free trade. Canada's 1994 unemployment rate was considerably higher than the 1988 rate (10.0 percent versus 7.8 percent). Many Canadian corporations complain that free trade has heightened the degree of competition in the marketplace. In a strategy to cut costs, companies have been relying more and more on un-unionized part-time and seasonal labour. These workers are paid lower wages and fewer benefits, thus lowering production costs. The Tories and the Liberals also restructured the UI programme so that it is more difficult for unemployed workers to receive benefits. The overall conclusion reached is that the continental model of development has lead to a polarization and segmentation of the Canadian labour force. The FTA and now NAFTA have successfully begun to roll back Canadian labour conditions that unions struggled for decades to achieve. After decades of divergence in workers' rights between Canada and the United States, free trade has managed to force a convergence and harmonization of Canadian labour standards with those of the United States with regard to wages, benefits and work rules.

Finally, the fate of the Welfare State under the influence of continental market forces was examined. The legitimation role of the Welfare State was essential to the mode of regulation for Canada's permeable Fordist development. The central theme in Canada's Welfare State was the creation of an east-west transportation and communications axis with the help of transportation subsidies, the CBC and the NFB. Regional inequalities were ameliorated by transfer payments that ensured every region in Canada had access to a certain standard of health care facilities and educational opportunities. The Canada Council spent hundreds of millions of dollars promoting Canadian artists, writers and performers from all regions within Canada. The Canadian government also attempted to reduce linguistic conflict by spending millions of dollars to establish official bilingualism in Canada. The discourse of universality and equality was indispensable to Canadian Fordist development in the postwar era.

As a result of free trade, social inequality and segmentation have replaced the discourse of universality. The Welfare State, rooted in national institutions, has become an impediment to profitability in the eyes of business. Adopting the "politics of stealth," neoconservatives have used the FTA to incrementally chip away at the foundations of the Welfare State in Canada.[5] Deregulation, budget cuts and privatization linked to free trade have undermined Canada's east-west infrastructure. Via Rail, the CBC and Air Canada no longer provide service to all regions of Canada. As a result, Canadians now confront increased regional variation with respect to communication and transportation.

Brian Mulroney, and now Jean Chrétien, reduced the value of transfer payments made to the provinces in support of education, health care and public housing. In a retreat from universality, Canada's national health care system is becoming a patchwork of ten provincial health care systems offering different standards of service. At the same time that Canada was negotiating the FTA, Canada restructured its tax code to be more compatible with that of the United States. Canada has followed the American lead of implementing an increasingly regressive taxation system. Finally, the link was made between constitutional reform and free trade. The Meech Lake Accord (MLA) was designed to be a neoconservative political counterpart to the FTA. Instead of unifying Canada, the MLA was designed to decentralize Canadian federalism, thereby reinforcing north-south links between the Canadian provinces and the United States. Although constitutional reforms have yet to be implemented, the debate over reforms has also had a divisive and fragmenting impact on Canadian unity.

The Welfare-State ideals of national unity and universal access to the resources of the State have been replaced by a neoconservative State that promotes corporate profitability at the expense of social equality. Social segmentation is now an acceptable byproduct of a capitalist system regulated at a continental scale. The position of capital has been enhanced within the capital-State-labour relationship. The Business Council on National Issues (BCNI), with its multinational membership, has achieved its goal of diminishing the impact of State boundaries in North America. As a key representative of the hegemonic bloc in Canada, the BCNI was willing to sacrifice small Canadian businesses and workers in the name of corporate profitability. As a result, a mode of regulation based on national institutions cannot be maintained under the pressures of a continental market. In simpler words, free trade has been used by corporate interests to reorganize the North American economy by reducing the checks and balances once provided by unions and the Welfare State.[6]

With its focus on the political and social consequences of international trade, this study borrows elements from geo-economics and critical geopolitics.[7] However this study moves beyond these approaches by examining a specific free trade agreement to study the impact of supranational market and geopolitical forces on social, political and economic institutions rooted at the level of the Nation-State. These institutions have been restructured or eliminated by continental forces. In order to study these changes, we cannot rely upon state-centered research that has characterized much of the social sciences. A more thorough understanding of changes in the global economy can only be achieved by looking at the interaction between the Nation-State and new supranational forms of economic regulation.

The FTA as Prelude to NAFTA

The implementation of NAFTA changes none of the conclusions reached in this study which focuses primarily on the Canada-U.S. FTA. Indeed, the passage and implementation of NAFTA only serves to confirm the conclusions reached about the fate of Canada under a continental model of development. This assertion can be confidently made because NAFTA was modeled directly after the Canada-U.S. FTA.[8] This section outlines how NAFTA is merely an extension of the existing FTA. By looking at the NAFTA debate and text it can be shown that the FTA and NAFTA should not be seen as two discrete events. Instead, they should be seen as part of a multi-step process to deregulate the continent and eventually the entire hemisphere.

In the early 1980s, President Reagan had discussed the issue of free trade with Mexican officials. In 1987, Canada and Mexico discussed the possibility of opening free trade negotiations. Article 102 of the Canada-U.S. FTA text declares that the objective of the Canada-United States FTA is "to lay the foundation for further bilateral and multilateral cooperation to expand and enhance the benefits of this Agreement."[9] In 1989, Canada became a member of the Organization of American State (OAS). In October 1989, the Canadian Embassy in the United States co-sponsored a conference in El Paso, Texas called "Region North America" which included Mexican, American and Canadian delegates. In March of 1990, Mulroney led a delegation of Canadian business leaders to Mexico where he signed a framework trade agreement. On June 11, President Bush and President Salinas announced their plans to negotiate a free trade agreement. On September 25, Canada officially joined the discussions to create a trilateral free trade agreement. The point here is that even before the FTA was implemented, there was discussion about including Mexico in a free trade agreement. The FTA was only a few months old when government and business officials from all three countries were actively working to expand the free trade area. Less than two years after the implementation of the FTA, official NAFTA negotiations had begun. On January 1, 1994 NAFTA was implemented.

It is not surprising that NAFTA debate in the United States unfolded in a similar manner as the FTA debate occurred in Canada. Neoclassical rhetoric promised a more efficient allocation of resources and the creation of new jobs. The U.S. ITC predicted that North American free trade could generate a one percent increase in American jobs.[10] Government officials and economists promised that NAFTA could generate prosperity from the "Yukon to the Yucatan" with jobs created for Canadians, Americans and Mexicans.[11] Canadian Trade Minister Wilson promised that NAFTA would create more jobs for Canadians and Bush promised more jobs for Americans.[12] In contrast to the genteel and objective discourse in support of NAFTA, opponents to NAFTA were described as coming from "the loony left."[13] Opponents to NAFTA were diagnosed as having succumbed to "a Canadian disease: 'emporiophobia' — literally, fear of trade."[14] Free trade opponents were accused of being "populists" whose "bad arguments tend to drive out the good."[15] Supporters of NAFTA descended to the level of name-calling in order to be heard above the din of the free trade debate.

The debate over NAFTA also included massive expenditures by corporate interests to swamp any opposition to free trade in a sea of pro-NAFTA rhetoric. Just as American and Canadian business organizations spent over Can$60 million promoting Canada-U.S. free trade, an even larger amount of money was spent by Canadian, American and Mexican business organizations and governmental agencies promoting NAFTA to the North American public and legislative officials. The Mexican government spent close to US$35 million promoting free trade in Mexico, Canada and the United States. Corporate and government expenditures promoting free trade in the United States could exceed US$25 million.[16]

An impressive list of former U.S. governors, congressmen, and government officials from the U.S. Treasury, the office of the USTR, the U.S. Information Agency and the State Department were hired by business organizations such as the Business Roundtable, the National Association of Manufacturers, USA*NAFTA and the U.S. Chamber of Commerce to serve as pro-NAFTA lobbyists. Included in this list of lobbyists were former Secretary of Labor, William Brock and the former Governor of New Mexico, Toney Anaya. USA*NAFTA was founded by the chief executive officers of Kodak and American Express. This is noteworthy because American Express was one of the most vocal American supporters of the FTA. After NAFTA was signed by representatives from Canada, the United States and Mexico, a seven-page advertisement appeared in the *New York Times* promoting the benefits of NAFTA.[17] This supplement was paid for by multinational corporations and the American and Mexican governments.

In a remarkable display of group-think, the NAFTA debate also included a ringing endorsement from academic economists. During the FTA debate over free trade between Canada and the United States, 250 Canadian economists signed a statement in support of free trade that was then submitted to the Canadian Parliament. In a similar fashion, 300 economists ranging from conservatives like Milton Friedman to liberals including Paul Samuelson signed a letter to President Clinton supporting the North American Free Trade Agreement.[18]

Opponents to North American free trade relied upon the same arguments that were used in opposition to the FTA. Union leaders protested that NAFTA would further accelerate job losses and deindustrialization that had occurred under the FTA. The chief economist for the Montréal Trust predicted that NAFTA will cost Canada even more jobs than were lost under the FTA.[19] Other Canadian critics predicted that NAFTA would be used by American negotiators to weaken any remaining protectionist provisions of the FTA.[20] These fears were well-founded because the Auto Pact and rules of origin, intellectual property rights, pharmaceutical production, Canadian culture and the subsidy issue were all negatively affected by NAFTA.[21] In the end, former Canadian trade negotiator Simon Reisman concluded that Canada had little to gain from free trade. Former assistant to Reisman, Gordon Ritchie stated that Canada had little to gain and much to lose by entering into NAFTA.[22] The defining characteristic of NAFTA is that it merely extends and clarifies provisions within the FTA, modifying the existing bilateral agreement to accommodate Mexico. The subsidy issue has been unsatisfactorily clarified by agreeing to never define an unfair subsidy. At least under the FTA, Canada and the United States had agreed to define the meaning of a subsidy by 1996. Mexico and Canada are now subject to constant and perpetual harassment by the United States on the issue of unfair subsidies and regional development strategies.

In 1995, the possibility of hemispheric free trade has become a reality. Chile has applied to enter into NAFTA. Ironically, the first meetings to consider Chile's application to join NAFTA were held in Toronto. Jean Chrétien promised to alleviate the damage done to Canada by NAFTA yet all the Liberals can seem to do is preside over a conference to expand the influence of free trade. Chile is an ideal candidate to join the post-Fordist model of development embodied in NAFTA. It has abandoned any pretense of promoting a Welfare State. Its environmental laws are lax. Chilean unions were broken during the fascist rule of General Augusto Pinochet and taxes are low for corporations and the wealthy. From a neoconservative perspective, Chile is "the star of the South American economies."[23] For Canadians, accession of Chile to NAFTA means further erosion of the remaining vestiges of Canadian sovereignty and social democratic ideals.

Overall, Canada has lost much of its economic and political sovereignty by entering into the FTA and NAFTA. Canadian voters passed judgment on this new reality in the fall of 1993 when the Tories were voted out of office. The Progressive Conservatives won only two of 295 parliamentary seats. The virtual collapse of one of Canada's traditionally powerful political parties indicates just how dissatisfied Canadians had become with free trade and its attendant neoconservative policies. The problem, however, was that the damage had been done. The neoconservative agenda has been largely implemented and entrenched in an international treaty far from the hands of meddling leftist politicians. Continental free trade has helped to create a neoconservative utopia where issues such as social justice and regional equality have become relics of a bygone Fordist era.

Notes

1. Congress, House of Representatives, Committee on Energy and Commerce, *Hearing Before the Subcommittee on Commerce, Consumer Protection, and Competitiveness*, 100th Congress, 2nd Sess., March 22, 1988, 238; John Lewis Orr, "Talkin' Trade," *This Magazine*, 24 (September 1990): 42.
2. John Daly, "Paying the Boss," *Maclean's*, 21 June 1993, 34.
3. CLC, *CLC Free Trade Briefing Document*, 2 (July 1989): 21.
4. A. Lower, "The Americanization of Canada," *Canada and the World*, 55, no. 7 (1990): 13.
5. Banting, "Neo-conservatism in an Open Economy," 150.
6. Kim Moody and Mary McGinn, *Unions and Free Trade: Solidarity Versus Competition* (Detroit: A Labor Notes Book, 1992), 1.
7. Stephen Cohen, "Geo-economics and America's Mistakes," in *The New World Economy in the Information Age: Reflections On Our Changing World*, Martin Carnoy, et. al., eds. (University Park, PA: Pennsylvania State University Press,

1993), 97; Simon Dalby, "Critical Geopolitics: Discourse, Difference, and Dissent," *Environment and Planning D: Society and Space,* 9 (1991): 261.

8. G. Norcliffe, "Regional Labour Market Adjustment in a Period of Structural Transformation: An Assessment of the Canadian Case," *Canadian Geographer,* 38 (1994): 7.
9. Canada, *Preliminary Transcript: Canada-U.S. Free Trade Agreement, Elements of the Agreement* (Ottawa: Supply and Services, 1987), 1.
10. Stephen Franklin, "Jobs Still No. 1 Free Trade Issue," *Chicago Tribune,* 14 February 1993, sec. 1, 1.
11. Roger Dornbush, "Free Trade With Mexico," *The Senior Economist,* 7, no. 2 (1991): 3; Kim Johnson, "Unprecedented Opportunity from the Yukon to the Yucatan," *Canadian Speeches,* 5, no. 3 (1991): 46; Jaime Serra Puche, *Partners in Trade: A North American Free Trade Zone* (Mexico City: Government of Mexico, 1991), 1; Mickey Kantor, "At Long Last, A Trade Pact to be Proud Of," *Wall Street Journal,* 17 August 1993, A14.
12. Linda Diebel, "Closed-door Trade Talks Denounced," *Toronto Star,* 5 August 1992, A10.
13. "The NAFTA Tapes. Special Report: Transcript of a Conference Call Between Senior Trade Ministerial Aides," *Maclean's,* 21 September 1992, 21.
14. Gary Hufbauer and Jeffrey Schott, "Prescription for Growth," *Foreign Policy,* 93, no. 1 (1993): 104.
15. Paul Krugman, "The Uncomfortable Truth About NAFTA. It's Foreign Policy Stupid," *Foreign Affairs,* 72, no. 5 (1993): 14.
16. "NAFTA Lobbying Cost $25 Million," *Canadian Free Trader,* 6, no. 6 (1993): 71; Jim Hightower, "NAFTA -We Don't Hafta!" *Utne Reader,* July 1993, 99; Charles Lewis and Margaret Ebrahim, "Can Mexico and Big Business USA Buy NAFTA?" *The Nation,* 14 June 1993, 826.
17. Macleod Group, "NAFTA: North American Free Trade Agreement," *New York Times,* 21 July 1993, C10-C16.
18. Naser, "A Primer: Why Economists Favor Free Trade Agreements," A1.
19. John Ferguson, "Trade Wrangle Puts Thousands of Jobs in Peril," *Toronto Star,* 3 August 1992, A9.
20. "U.S. Wants End to Culture Protection," *Toronto Star,* 24 November 1991, A2.
21. Canada, *North American Free Trade Agreement* (Ottawa: Supply and Services, 1993), 4-6; Peter Truell and Bob Davis, "Administration Releases Text of Trade Accord," *Wall Street Journal,* 9 September 1992, A2.
22. Brenda Dalglish, "Trading in Signals," *Maclean's,* 2 December 1991, 76; Gordon Ritchie, "A Canada-Mexico-U.S. Free Trade Agreement: Watch Out!" *Business Quarterly,* 55, no. 3 (1991): 18.
23. Howard Waitzkin, "Next in Line for NAFTA? Images from Chile," *Monthly Review,* 46, no. 10 (1995): 17; "And Chile Makes Four," *Globe and Mail,* 10 June 1995, D4.

Appendix

Job Relocations from Canada since 1989

Corporation Name	Location in Canada	Location in U.S. or Mexico (MX)	Jobs Shifted
Advanced Gibson Canada	Windsor, ON	PA	36
Alcon Canada Inc.	Mississauga, ON	NJ	48
Allbright and America	Long Harbour Nfld	NC	290
Allied-Signal Inc.	Mississauga, ON	KY	400
Allied-Signal Inc.	London, ON	NC	270
Amerlock	Meaford, ON	IL	140
Arnold Manufacturing	Windsor, ON	KY	100
Arvin Automotive	Ajax, ON	MX	32
BASF Canada Inc.	Cornwall	MX	100
BASF Canada Inc.	Cornwall	NJ	200
BC Packers Limited	Steveson, BC	WA	200
Beckman Industries	Etobicoke, ON	MX	80
Bendix Safety	Collingwood, ON	AL	200
Bendix Safety	Collingwood, ON	MX	200
BF Goodrich	Kitchener, ON	OH	70
Bilt-Rite Furniture	Toronto, ON	MS	750
Black and Decker	Montreal, PQ	MX	150
Black and Decker	Brockville, ON	MX	45
Black and Decker	Trenton, ON	MX	100
Black and Decker	Trenton, ON	CT	264
Bovie, MFG	Lindsey, ON	MX	60
Bristol-Myers Squib	Candiac, PQ	IL	62
Bristol-Myers Squib	Candiac, PQ	NY	62
Bundy of Canada	Cambridge, ON	OH	250
Burlington Carpets	Bramelea, ON	GA	150
Burlington Carpets	Bramelea, ON	VA	150
Burlington Carpets	Bramelea, ON	IL	150
C.P. Trucks	Toronto, ON	WI	600
Campell Soup	Port LaPrairie, MB	MX	168
Canadian Transport	Toronto, ON	MI	153

Canadian Coleman	Toronto, ON	KS	107
Canadian Coleman	Toronto, ON	TX	107
Canasphere Industries	Moose Jaw, SK	AZ	5
Canron, Inc.	Etobicoke, ON	SC	20
Carter Automotive	Bramalea, ON	TN	230
Caterpillar Canada	Brampton, ON	IL	200
Caterpillar Canada	Brampton, ON	NC	200
Celenese	Kingston, ON	NJ	108
Chrysler, Canada	Ajax, ON	MX	400
Clairol Canada	Knowlton, PQ	CT	228
Clearwater Fine Foods	Port Mouton, NS	ME	150
Clevite Elastomer	St. Thomas, ON	OH	50
Cobi Foods	Whitby, ON	MI	250
Colgate Palmolive	Toronto, ON	NY	250
Combustion Engineering	Ottawa, ON	MX	104
Cooper Industries	Cobourg, ON	AL	200
Croyden	Cambridge, ON	IL	360
Croydon Furniture	Cambridge, ON	IL	360
Custom Trim	Waterloo, ON	MX	25
D.G. Trim	Petrolia, ON	KY	32
Dicon Systems	Toronto, ON	MX	15
Dixon Ticonderoga	Newmarket, ON	MT	100
Dixon Ticonderoga	Newmarket, ON	PA	100
Dominion Textiles	Yarmouth, NS	GA	430
Dubarry Furniture	Toronto, ON	NY	42
Eastman Kodak	Toronto, ON	MX	450
Echlin, Canada	Rexdale, ON	MX	125
Echlin, Canada	Niagara Falls, ON	MX	58
Electrolux	Montreal, PQ	MX	68
Fiberglass Canada	Mission, BC	OR	90
Fiberglass Canada	Mission, BC	WA	90
Fiberglass Canada	Sarnia & Guelph, ON	MX	442
Fleck Manufacturing	Centralia, ON	MX	200
Ford Motor Company	St. Thomas, ON	MX	140
Ford Motor Company	Windsor, ON	MX	1716
Freedland Ind.	Kingsville, ON	MI	235
Frigidaire Co.	Montreal, PQ	SC	25
Friskies Pet Prod.	Mississuaga, ON	OH	115
Galtaco	Orillia, ON	MI	400
General Electric	Peterborough	MX	100

General Tire	Barrie, ON	OH	400
General Tire	Barrie, ON	MX	472
General Electric	Montreal, PQ	MX	200
Gerber Canada	Niagara Fall, On	MI	150
Gillette Canada	Toronto, ON	MA	60
Gillette Canada	Montreal, PQ	MA	530
Glidden Canada	Bramelea, ON	NJ	40
GM Vans	Scarborough, ON	MX	2700
GM Trim Plant	Windsor, ON	OH	255
GM	Boisbriand, PQ	MX	1700
GM	Oshawa, ON	MX	400
GM	Oshawa, ON	MX	800
GM	St. Catherines, ON	MX	369
GM	St.Therese, PQ	MX	240
H.J. Heinz	Leamington, ON	MI	200
Harding Carpets	Collingwood, ON	TN	180
Hartz Canada	St. Thomas, ON	OH	26
Harvard Industries	Ashburn, ON	TN	150
Honeywell	Toronto, ON	MX	100
Hunt-Wesson	Tilbury, ON	OH	80
Hunt-Wesson	Tilbury, ON	CA	60
Ideal Equipment	Montreal, PQ	MX	25
Int'l Playing Card	Bramelea, ON	OH	35
International Bag	Toronto, ON	NY	25
ITW Shakeproof	Mississauga, ON	TN	45
J.H. Warsh	Toronto, ON	NY	45
JCI Explosives	McMasterville, PQ	TX	200
Johnson Controls	St. Thomas, ON	WI	170
Johnson Controls	Port Perry, ON	TN	153
Johnson and Johnson	Montreal, PQ	MX	86
K.D. Manufacturing	Kingston, ON	NY	62
K.T. Industries	Winnipeg, MB	IN	20
Kaufman Furniture	Collingwood, ON	NC	100
Kraft General Foods	Cobourg, ON	IL	20
L-Tec Canada	Mississauga, ON	MI	30
Leviton Manufacturing	Montreal, PQ	MX	253
Marr's Leisure Prod.	Brandon, MB	SC	40
Midas Canada	Scarborough, ON	WI	140
Miscelleneous Shifts	BC	WA	1,285
Mitel	Kanata, ON	MX	30

Motor Wheel Corp.	Chatham, ON	MI	550
Motorola, Canada	Brampton, ON	MX	175
Murata Erie	Trenton, ON	CA	400
National Sea Products	Canso, NS	ME	625
National Sea Products	St. John's, NF	ME	492
New Wave Fisheries	Pt.de l'Eglise, NS	MA	100
Newcor	Windsor, ON	MI	40
Northern Telecom	St. Laurent, PQ	MX	250
Northern Telecom	Brockville, ON	MX	145
Northern Telecom	Aylmer, PQ	MX	680
Northern Telecom	Belleville, ON	MX	240
Northern Telecom	Bramelea, ON	MX	120
Norton Abrasives	Cap-de-la Mad., PQ	MX	116
Nygard International	Saskatoon, SK	CA	50
Nygard International	Toronto, ON	CA	200
Nygard International	Winnipeg, MB	CA	50
Olan Mills	Kingston, ON	NY	95
Ortho Diagnostic	North York, ON	NJ	16
Outboard Marine Corp	Peterborough, ON	MX	290
Peraflex Hose	Mississuaga, ON	NY	15
Picker International	Bramelea, ON	OH	160
Pittsburgh Paint	Etobicoke, ON	PA	140
Playtex Apparel	Renfrew, ON	MX	160
Premium Automotive	P. Hawkesbury, NS	NH	70
Prestolite	Cambridge, ON	MX	33
Progress Company	St. Laurent, PQ	PA	75
Raytheon	Kitchener, ON	MX	184
Redirack Limited	Toronto, ON	IL	136
Robertson Controls	Etobicoke, ON	VA	150
Rockwell Int'l	Barrie, ON	MX	45
Schlegel of Canada	Burlington, ON	TN	64
Schlegel of Canada	Burlington, ON	OK	40
Scholl-Plough	Scarborough, ON	MX	105
Schwitzer	Stratford, ON	NC	80
Sea Fair Enterprises	Wood Harbour, NS	ME	60
Sealy Furniture	Concord, ON	VA	235
Sheller-Globe	Kingsville, ON	MX	410
Siemen Automotive	Chatham, ON	MX	127
Sivaco	Ingersoll, ON	NY	125
Sklar-Pepplar	Hanover, ON	MO	42

Speedo	Carleton Pl., ON	KY	70
Square D Canada	Port Colbourne, ON	MX	107
Square D Canada	Edmunston, NB	MX	156
Square D Canada	Arnprior, ON	MX	70
St. Lawrence Starch	Mississuaga, ON	IL	230
Star Kist Tuna	Bayside, NB	NH	125
Star Suspension	Mississauga, ON	MI	32
Star Kist Tuna	Bayside, NB	ME	125
Sterling Drug	Aurora, ON	PR	180
Stevens Controls	Renfrew, ON	OH	49
Sunar-Hauseman	Waterloo, ON	MI	280
Sunbeam Corporation	Toronto, ON	MX	75
Sunbeam Corporation	Brantford, ON	MX	228
Takahashi Industries	Vancouver, BC	WA	25
Thermo disc	St. Thomas, ON	MX	300
Thompson Transport	Talbotville, ON	MI	250
Toro Corporation	Steinbach, MN	MN	68
Tridon Limited	Burlington, ON	TN	550
Tupperware Canada	Morden, MB	TN	80
Tupperware Canada	Morden, MB	SC	80
Twincraft Limited	Montreal, PQ	VT	60
Unisys	St. Laurent, PQ	CA	115
Unisys	St. Laurent, PQ	MX	115
United Maple Products	Delta ON	VT	18
United Technologies	St. Thomas, ON	MI	200
United Technologies	St. Thomas, ON	MX	119
Valenite Modco	Windsor	MI	32
Varity	Toronto, ON	NY	45
Varta Batteries	Winnipeg, MB	MX	175
Wang Canada	Toronto, ON	MA	65
Warnaco	Carleton Place, ON	MX	70
Warnaco	Montreal, PQ	MX	140
Warner Lambert Canada	Brockville, ON	SC	35
Wayne Canada	Windsor, ON	IN	145
WCI Canada	Cambridge, ON	MN	100
WCI Canada	Cambridge, ON	MX	100
Westinghouse Canada	Renfrew, ON	MX	147
Westinghouse Canada	Hamilton, ON	MX	147
Westinghouse Canada	Mount Forest, ON	SC	45
Whirlpool (Inglis)	Toronto, ON	OH	650

Whirlpool (Inglis)	Toronto, ON	MX	650
Whirlpool (Inglis)	Montmorency, PQ	MX	220
Wilton Grove Bendix	London, ON	KY	15
Wilton Grove Bendix	London, ON	NC	15
Wilton Grove Bendix	London, ON	MX	16
Woodbridge INOAC	St. Jerome, PQ	MX	270

The total loss from these corporate relocations is 42,062 Canadian jobs.

Sources:"Frigidaire Move Means 250 Jobs," *Sault Star,* 18 March 1992; Maude Barlow, *Parcel of Rogues* (Toronto: Key Porter Books, 1990); Barry Came, "The Colour of Despair," *Maclean's,* 12 November 1990; Cameron, "The Dealers,"; CLC, *CLC Free Trade Briefing Document,* 2 (July 1989); CLC, *CLC Free Trade Briefing Document,* 3 (September 1989); CLC, *CLC Free Trade Briefing Document,* 4 (January 1990); CLC, *CLC Free Trade Briefing Document,* 7 (January 1991); "Heinz shifting pickle production to Michigan," *Sault Star,* 21 January 1991; "Woman tells of beating after plant went south," *Sault Star,* 28 January 1991; "U.S. Investment in Canada down sharply," *Sault Star,* 5 April 1991; "Auto parts plant to be closed," *Sault Star,* 12 April 1991; "Uniroyal conditions leave workers bitter," *Sault Star,* 21 June 1991; "Windsor steel firm plans move to Detroit," *Sault Star,* 8 August 1991; "General tire closes Barrie plant; 820 workers lose jobs," *Sault Star,* 31 August 1991; "Colgate to move production to U.S.," *Sault Star,* 13 September 1991; "20 Kraft jobs to go to the U.S.," *Sault Star,* 1 January 1992; "U.S. auto parts company closures to idle 670 Ontarians," *Sault Star, 1* January 1991; "Auto parts plant heads home to U.S. parent," *Sault Star,* 4 February 1991; "Toronto firm decides on New York for expansion," *Sault Star,* 29 February 1991; "Defence plant heads south, 400 lose jobs," *Sault Star,* 2 February 1992; "350 more jobs lost in Ontario," *Globe and Mail,* 30 May 1992. "Workers stand guard after employer pulls out," *Sault Star,* 2 March 1993; Patricia Chisholm, "The Winners and the Losers," *Maclean's,* 18 December 1989; Patricia Chisholm, "Giving Up, Moving Out," *Maclean's,* 18 March 1991; Brenda Dalglish, "Goin' Down the Road," *Maclean's,* 28 June 1993; Clyde Farnsworth, "Free-trade is Enticing Canadian Companies to the U.S.," *New York Times,* 9 August 1991; Clyde Farnsworth, "U.S. Pact a Spur to Canada," *New York Times,* 22 July 1992; V. Galt, "Small Town Hard Hit by 3 Plant Closings," *Globe and Mail,* 9 June 1990; Bert Hill and Kelly Egan, "Ontario's Industrial Heartland Devastated by Plant Closings," *Sault Star* 16 February 1991; Kenneth Kidd and Tony Van Alphen, "Gillette Axes 600 Jobs, Critics Cite Trade Deal," *Toronto Star,* 24 November 1988; Deirdre McMurdy, "Three for the Show," *Maclean's,* 8 March 1992; Bob Mitchell and Bruce Campion-Smith, "Caterpillar Denies that Trade Pact Linked to Brampton Job Loss," *Toronto Star,* 13 April 1991; Randy Robinson, "Colonizing Canada: A Year and Half of Free Trade," *Multinational Monitor,* 11 (May 1990); John Saunders, "Shufflin' off to Sample Buffalo's Pleasure," *Globe and Mail,* 4 July 1991; Barbara Wickens and John Daly, "Riches to Rags," Maclean's, 25 September 1991.

Bibliography

"$27 Million Set Aside to Help Canadian Business in Free Trade." *Sault Star,* 2 March 1993, A5.

"$676 million hacked from Federal Support to Cultural Sector." *Bulletin of the Canadian Conference of the Arts,* February, (1995): 1.

"20 Kraft jobs to go to the U.S." *Sault Star,* 1 January 1992.

"350 more jobs lost in Ontario." *Globe and Mail,* 30 May 1992.

"A Blunt Warning." *Maclean's,* 27 January 1992, 27.

Aglietta, Michel. *The Theory of Capitalist Regulation: The American Experience.* Translated by David Fernback. New York: Verso, 1979.

________. "World Capitalism in the Eighties." *New Left Review* 136 (November 1982): 5-41.

Allen, Glen. "Strong Medicine." *Maclean's,* 21 December 1992, 10.

Amiel, Barbara. "In Defence of Crispo, Fecan and the CBC." *Maclean's,* 29 April 1991, 13.

"And Chile Makes Four." *Globe and Mail,* 10 June 1995, D4.

Armstrong, Pat, Andrew Glyn and John Harrison. *Capitalism Since 1945.* New York: Basil Blackwell 1991.

"Artviews Report: The Free Trade Agreement." *Artviews* 15 (1989): 15.

Atwood, Margaret. "Free Traders Don't Eat Quiche." *Globe and Mail,* 17 November 1988, A7.

________. *Survival: A Thematic Guide to Canadian Literature.* Toronto: Anansi, 1972.

Aubin, Benoit. "Bourassa Makes Another Strong Pitch for Free-trade Deal." *Globe and Mail.* 17 November 1988.

________. "Re-election of Tory Majority a Blow for PQ." *Globe and Mail,* 25 November 1988.

Austen, Ian. "Canadians Believed Trade Deal Closed Factories, Poll Says." *Sault Star,* 8 April 1992, A6.

________. "Trade Disputes Aren't Being Solved Any Faster With Pact." *Sault Star,* 14 March 1992, A5.

"Auto parts plant heads home to U.S. parent." *Sault Star,* 4 February 1991.

"Auto parts plant to be closed." *Sault Star,* 12 April 1991.

Babe, R. "Copyright and Culture." *Canadian Forum* 67 (February 1988): 26-29.

Bacon, Kenneth. "Quick Reaction: Trade Pact is Likely to Step Up Business Even Before Approval." *Wall Street Journal,* 13 August 1992, A1, A10.

"Bankruptcies Down." *Maclean's,* 15 August 1994, 29.

"Bankruptcies Hit Record." *Sault Star,* 4 February 1992, B16.

Banting, Keith. "Neo-conservatism in an Open Economy: the Social Role of the Canadian State." *International Political Science Review* 13 (1992): 149-170.

Barlow, Maude. *Parcel of Rogues: How Free Trade is Failing Canada.* Toronto: Key Porter Books, 1990.

Barry, Tom. *Mexico: A Country Guide.* Albuquerque, NM: Inter-Hemispheric Education Resource Center, 1992.

BCNI. "A Business Perspective on the Reform of the Unemployment Insurance Program. Notes for a Presentation of the House of Commons Standing Committee on Labour, Employment and Immigration." Ottawa: Unpublished Report of the BCNI, 1987.

________. "Canada-Mexico-United States Free Trade: A Canadian Perspective." Ottawa: Unpublished Report of the BCNI, 1990).

________. "Canadian Trade, Competitiveness and Sovereignty: The Prospect of New Trade Agreements with the United States." Ottawa: Unpublished Report of the BCNI, 1985.

________. "Economic Priorities and the National Agenda." Ottawa: Unpublished Report of the BCNI, 1986.

________. "Economic Priorities for Canada." Toronto: Unpublished Report of the BCNI, 1988.

________. "National Economic Priorities: Challenges and Opportunities." Ottawa: Unpublished Report of the BCNI, 1991.

________. "Social Policy Reform and the National Agenda." Ottawa: Unpublished Report of the BCNI, 1986.

________. "Taxation Reform 1987: A Response to the Federal Government White Paper." Ottawa: Unpublished Report of the BCNI, 1987.

________. "The Canada-United States Free Trade Agreement: Submission to the House of Commons Standing Committee on External Affairs and International Trade." Ottawa: Unpublished Report of the BCNI, 1987.

________. "The Canada-United States Free Trade Agreement: Submission to the Ontario Select Committee on Economic Affairs." Toronto: Unpublished Report of the BCNI, 1988.

________. "The Goods and Services Tax: A Vehicle for Needed Tax Structure Reform. Submission to the House of Commons Standing Committee on Banking, Trade and Commerce." Ottawa: Unpublished Document of the BCNI, 1990.

Beach, Donald. "Sales Tax Reform is Needed But It's Hard to Get." *Toronto Star,* 21 November 1988, C2.

Beauchesne, Eric. "Crow Wants Inflation in Line With U.S. Rate." *Sault Star,* 17 January 1992, A6.

________. "Fewer Canadians Producing Goods, StatsCan Reports." *Sault Star,* 9 March 1993, A5.

________. "Joint Committee Will Settle Port Standoff - Crosbie." *Sault Star,* 16 April 1991, A1.

Bell, Daniel. *The Coming of the Post-Industrial Society.* New York: Basic Books, 1973.

Bergman, Brian. "Publish and Perish." *Maclean's,* 17 October 1994, 52.

________. "The Tax in Effect." *Maclean's,* 2 October 1989, 22.

Bergman, Michael. "Trick or Treaty." *Cinema Canada* 151 (February 1988): 14-15.

Berry, John. "Economists Say Blocs May Block Free Trade, Regional Accords Seen As Troubling." *Washington Post,* 4 September 1991.

Best, Steven and David Kellner. *Postmodern Theory: Critical Interrogations.* New York: The Guilford Press, 1991.

Bijur, Peter. "Deregulation, Competition and Trade Drive Canadian Economy. Address Given to the Empire Club of Canada." *Canadian Speeches* 1 (1988): 11-14.

Black, Errol and Guy Landry. "Guess Who Wants High Interest Rates?" *Canadian Dimension* 23 (1989): 17.

Block, Fred. *Postindustrial Possibilities.* Berkeley, CA:University of California Press, 1990.

________. *The Origins of International Economic Disorder: A Study of United States Interna-*

tional Monetary Policy from World War II to the Present. Berkeley: University of California Press, 1977.

Block, Stephen. "Free Trade on Television: The Triumph of Business Rhetoric." *Canadian Journal of Communications* 17 (1992): 75-94.

Bluestone, Barry and Bennett Harrison. *The Deindustrialization of America: Plant Closings, Community Abandonment, and the Dismantling of Basic Industry.* New York: Basic Books, 1982.

Bothwell, Robert. *Canada and the United States: The Politics of Partnership.* New York: Twayne Publishers, 1992.

Bowker, Marjorie. *On Guard for Thee: An Independent Review of the Free Trade Agreement.* Ottawa: Voyageur Publishing, 1988.

Bowles, Samuel. *Foreword to Creating a New World Economy: Forces of Change and Plans for Action.* Edited by Gerald Epstein, Julie Graham and Jessica Nembhard. Philadelphia: Temple University Press, 1993.

Boyer, Robert. *The Regulation School: A Critical Introduction.* Translated by Craig Charney. New York: Columbia University Press, 1990.

Bradsher, Ken. "U.S. Told to Review Lumber Duty." *New York Times,* 27 July 1993, C5.

Braudel, Fernand. *The Perspective of the World: Civilization and Capitalism, 15th - 18th Century,* Vol. 3. New York: Harper and Row, 1984.

Braverman, Harry. *Labor and Monopoly Capital: The Degradation of Work in the Twentieth Century.* New York: Monthly Review Press, 1974.

Brehl, R. "NDP Accused of Frightening Business Off." *Toronto Star,* 18 June 1991, B3.

Brenner, Robert and Mark Glick. "The Regulation Approach: Theory and History." *New Left Review* 188 (July/August 1991): 45-120.

Brett, E.A. *International Money and Capitalist Crisis: Anatomy of Global Disintegration.* Boulder, CO: Westview Press, 1983.

Brown, Craig. "The Nationalism of the National Policy." *Nationalism in Canada.* Edited by Peter Russell. Toronto: McGraw-Hill, 1966:155-163.

Bulloch, John. "Restructuring of Canada Driven by Global Economy. Speech Given to the Sales and Marketing Executives of Vancouver." *Canadian Speeches* 5 (1991): 1-20.

Bunner, Paul. "Divorce, Canadian Style. How Free Trade Estranged Qubec From the Anglo Left." *Alberta Report* 17 (1990): 15.

Burns, John. "Canadians Urged to Accept Pact." *New York Times,* 10 November 1988, 53.

________. "Trains to be Cut in Canada." *New York Times,* 5 October 1989, B25.

Buroway, Michael. *The Politics of Production: Factory Regimes Under Capitalism and Socialism.* New York: Verso, 1985.

Byfield, Ted. "Federal Liberals Retreat on Left-wing Issues." *Financial Post,* 20 May 1995, 24.

Came, Barry. "In Search of the Bigger Gulp." *Maclean's,* 30January 1989, 36.

________. "The Colour of Despair." *Maclean's* 12 November 1990.

Cameron, Duncan and Daniel Drache. "Outside the Macdonald Commission: Reply to Richard Simeon." *Studies in Political Economy* 26 (Summer 1988): 173-180.

Cameron, Duncan. "Crow Rates." *Canadian Forum* 69 (September 1990): 10-15.

________. "Free Trade Looks Good — For the Americans." *Canadian Dimension* 69 (February 1990): 2.

________. "The Dealers: We Didn't Get What We Wanted and Gave Away a Lot. So Why is Our Business Class So Happy with Free Trade?" *This Magazine* 21 (1988): 18-23.

Campbell, Bruce. "A Critique of 'The Global Trade Challenge.'" *A Tory Trade Tabloid.* Ottawa: CCPA, 1992.

________. "Beggar Thy Neighbour." *The American Review of Canadian Studies* 21 (1991): 22-29.

Canada Council. "Government Budget Cuts Affect Canada Council." *Canada Council Bulletin* 39 (1993): 2.

"Canada Grasps the Future." *New York Times,* 23 November 1988, 22.

Canada. *Preliminary Transcript: Canada-U.S. Free Trade Agreement, Elements of the Agreement.* (Ottawa: Supply and Services, 1987), 1.

________. *Adjusting to Win: Report of the Advisory Council on Adjustment.* Ottawa: Industry, Science and Technology, 1989.

________. *Elements of a Canada-United States Free Trade Agreement: Synopsis.* Ottawa: Supply and Services, 1987.

________. *Foreign Direct Investment in Canada.* Ottawa: Information Canada, 1972.

________. *Inflation and the Canadian Economy: A Report by the Department of Finance.* Ottawa: Supply and Services, 1991.

________. *North American Free Trade Agreement.* Ottawa: Supply and Services, 1993.

________. *Royal Commission on Canada's Economic Prospects.* Ottawa: Queen's Printer, 1958.

Canadian Alliance for Trade and Job Opportunities. "Straight Talk on Free Trade." *Maclean's,* (Advertising Supplement) 21 November 1988, 24.

Canadian Centre for Policy Alternatives. *Briefing Notes on the Tory Constitutional Proposals.* Ottawa: CCPA, 1991.

________. *Which Way for the Americas? Analysis of NAFTA Proposals and the Impact on Canada.* Ottawa: CCPA, 1992.

"Canadian Elections Hinge on Trade Pact." Des Moines Register, 19 August 1988, 8S.

Canadian Manufacturers' Association, The Canadian Chamber of Commerce, and The BCNI. "Joint Statement on the National Economy." Ottawa: Unpublished Press Release, 1990.

Canadian-American Committee. *A Possible Plan for a Canada-U.S. Free Trade Area.* Montréal: Canadian-American Committee of the National Planning Association and the Private Planning Association of Canada, 1965.

________. *Cooperative Development of the Columbia River Basin.* Washington, DC: Canadian-American Committee of the National Planning Association and the Private Planning Association of Canada, 1959.

________. *The Perspective of Canadian-American Relations.* Washington, DC: Canadian-American Committee of the National Planning Association and the Private Planning Association of Canada, 1962.

________. *Toward a More Realistic Appraisal of the Automotive Agreement.* Washington, DC: Canadian-American Committee of the National Planning Association and the Private Planning Association of Canada, 1970.

Carchedi, Guglielmo. *Frontiers of Political Economy.* New York: Verso, 1991.

Carnoy, Martin. *The State and Political Theory.* Princeton, NJ: Princeton University Press, 1984.

Carr, Shirley. "Why Canadian Labour Opposes Free Trade." *Canadian Speeches* 1 (1988): 4-6.

Caves, Richard, Jeffrey Frankel, and Ronald Jones. *World Trade and Payments: An Introduction.* Glenview, IL: Scott, Foresman and Company, 1990.

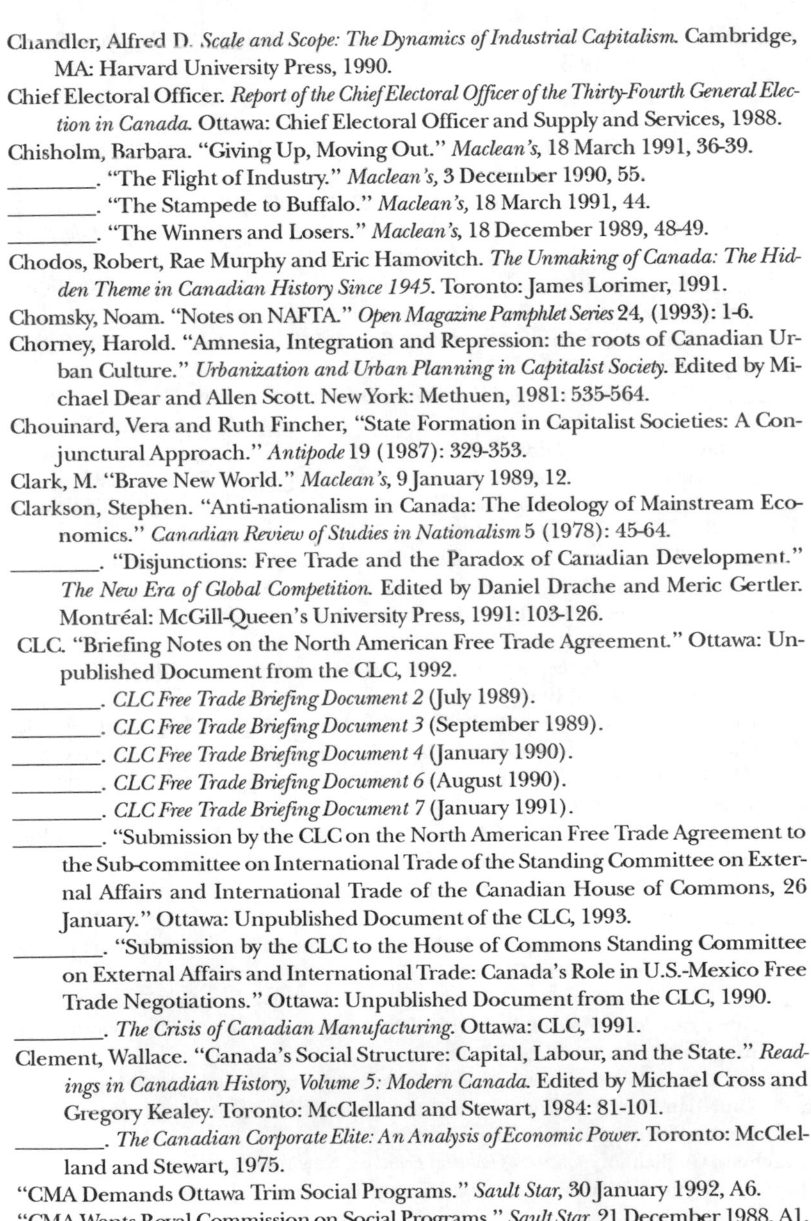

Chandler, Alfred D. *Scale and Scope: The Dynamics of Industrial Capitalism.* Cambridge, MA: Harvard University Press, 1990.

Chief Electoral Officer. *Report of the Chief Electoral Officer of the Thirty-Fourth General Election in Canada.* Ottawa: Chief Electoral Officer and Supply and Services, 1988.

Chisholm, Barbara. "Giving Up, Moving Out." *Maclean's*, 18 March 1991, 36-39.

________. "The Flight of Industry." *Maclean's,* 3 December 1990, 55.

________. "The Stampede to Buffalo." *Maclean's,* 18 March 1991, 44.

________. "The Winners and Losers." *Maclean's*, 18 December 1989, 48-49.

Chodos, Robert, Rae Murphy and Eric Hamovitch. *The Unmaking of Canada: The Hidden Theme in Canadian History Since 1945.* Toronto: James Lorimer, 1991.

Chomsky, Noam. "Notes on NAFTA." *Open Magazine Pamphlet Series* 24, (1993): 1-6.

Chorney, Harold. "Amnesia, Integration and Repression: the roots of Canadian Urban Culture." *Urbanization and Urban Planning in Capitalist Society.* Edited by Michael Dear and Allen Scott. New York: Methuen, 1981: 535-564.

Chouinard, Vera and Ruth Fincher, "State Formation in Capitalist Societies: A Conjunctural Approach." *Antipode* 19 (1987): 329-353.

Clark, M. "Brave New World." *Maclean's*, 9 January 1989, 12.

Clarkson, Stephen. "Anti-nationalism in Canada: The Ideology of Mainstream Economics." *Canadian Review of Studies in Nationalism* 5 (1978): 45-64.

________. "Disjunctions: Free Trade and the Paradox of Canadian Development." *The New Era of Global Competition.* Edited by Daniel Drache and Meric Gertler. Montréal: McGill-Queen's University Press, 1991: 103-126.

CLC. "Briefing Notes on the North American Free Trade Agreement." Ottawa: Unpublished Document from the CLC, 1992.

________. *CLC Free Trade Briefing Document 2* (July 1989).

________. *CLC Free Trade Briefing Document 3* (September 1989).

________. *CLC Free Trade Briefing Document 4* (January 1990).

________. *CLC Free Trade Briefing Document 6* (August 1990).

________. *CLC Free Trade Briefing Document* 7 (January 1991).

________. "Submission by the CLC on the North American Free Trade Agreement to the Sub-committee on International Trade of the Standing Committee on External Affairs and International Trade of the Canadian House of Commons, 26 January." Ottawa: Unpublished Document of the CLC, 1993.

________. "Submission by the CLC to the House of Commons Standing Committee on External Affairs and International Trade: Canada's Role in U.S.-Mexico Free Trade Negotiations." Ottawa: Unpublished Document from the CLC, 1990.

________. *The Crisis of Canadian Manufacturing.* Ottawa: CLC, 1991.

Clement, Wallace. "Canada's Social Structure: Capital, Labour, and the State." *Readings in Canadian History, Volume 5: Modern Canada.* Edited by Michael Cross and Gregory Kealey. Toronto: McClelland and Stewart, 1984: 81-101.

________. *The Canadian Corporate Elite: An Analysis of Economic Power.* Toronto: McClelland and Stewart, 1975.

"CMA Demands Ottawa Trim Social Programs." *Sault Star*, 30 January 1992, A6.

"CMA Wants Royal Commission on Social Programs." *Sault Star,* 21 December 1988, A1.

Cohen, Stephen. "Geo-economics and America's Mistakes." *The New Global Economy in the Information Age: Reflections on Our Changing World.* Edited by Martin Carnoy, Manuel Castells, Stephen Cohen and Fernando Henrique Cardoso. University Park, PA: The Pennsylvania State University Press, 1993: 97-147.

"Colgate to Move Production to U.S." *Sault Star,* 13 September 1991.

Comer, Edward. "The Department of Communication Under the Free Trade Regime." *Canadian Journal of Communication* 16 (1991): 239-261.

Congress, House of Representatives, Committee on Energy and Commerce. Hearing Before the Subcommittee on Commerce, Consumer Protection, and Competitiveness, 100th Congress, 2nd Sess., 22 March 1988, 238.

Congress, House, Committee on Energy and Commerce. U.S.-Canada Free Trade Agreement: Hearing before the Subcommittee on Consumer Protection, and Competitiveness, 100th Cong., 2nd Sess., 22 March 1988, 243.

Congress, House, Committee on Foreign Affairs. Oversight of the U.S.-Canada Free Trade Agreement: Hearing Before the House of Representatives Committee on Foreign Affairs and Its Subcommittee On International Economic Policy and Trade, and On Western Hemisphere Affairs, 100th Congress, 2nd Sess., 16 March 1988, 152.

Congress, House, Committee on the Judiciary. Summary of the U.S.-Canada Free Trade Agreement: Hearing Before the Subcommittee on Courts, Civil Liberties, and the Administration of Justice of the House Committee on the Judiciary, 100th Congress, 2nd Sess., 28 April 1988.

Cook, Peter. "Free Trade Fears: Zap, Zap, Zap You're Frozen." *Globe and Mail,* 11 November 1988, B2.

Coupland, Douglas. *Generation X: Tales for an Accelerated Culture.* New York: St. Martin's Press, 1991.

Cox, Robert. *Production, Power, and World Order.* New York: Columbia University Press, 1987.

Crane, David A. "Big Shift of Powers to Provinces may Prove Too Costly for Canada." *Toronto Star,* 6 April 1991, D2.

Crean, Susan. "Reading Between the Lies: Culture and the FTA." *This Magazine* 22 (May 1988): 29-32.

Crispo, John. "Conclusion." *Free Trade: The Real Story.* Edited by John Crispo. Toronto: Gage, 1988: 188-205.

________. *Making Canada Work: Competing in the Global Economy.* Toronto: Random House, 1992.

Crosbie, John. "International Trade Minister's Remarks from Debate in the House of Commons, August 29." *Canadian Speeches* 2, Special Supplement (August 1988): 22.

Crow, John. "Monetary Policy Must Aim for Zero Inflation." *Canadian Speeches* 3 (1990): 23-27.

d'Aquino, Thomas and John Bulloch. "The Canada-United States Trade Initiative: A Joint Statement by the President of the President of the BCNI and the President of the Canadian President of the Canadian Federation of Independent Business." Ottawa: News Conference Press Release, 1986.

Dalby, Simon. "Critical Geopolitics: Discourse, Difference, and Dissent." *Environment and Planning D: Society and Space* 9 (1991): 261-283.

Dale, S. "One Year After: Free Trade Fallout." *This Magazine* 23 (January 1990): 10-14.

Dalglish, Brenda. "Free Trade: A Cutthroat?" *Maclean's,* 7 January 1991, 28.

________. "Goin' Down the Road." *Maclean's,* 28 June 1993, 28.

________. "On the Rebound." *Maclean's,* 28 June 1993, 25.

________. "The Fight to Find a Job." *Maclean's,* 24 June 1991, 16.

________. "They All Hurt." *Maclean's,* 8 October 1990, 23.

________. "Trading in Signals." *Maclean's,* 2 December 1991, 76.

Daly, Herman and John Cobb. *For the Common Good: Redirecting the Economy Toward Community, the Environment, and a Sustainable Future.* Boston: Beacon Press, 1989.

Daly, John. "A Triple Threat." *Maclean's,* 8 October 1990, 48.

________. "Automotive Shakeout." *Maclean's,* 15 January 1990, 24.

________. "Paying the Boss." *Maclean's,* 21 June 1993, 34.

Damsell, Keith and Peter Morton. "Open Trade Door, Maclaren Warns." *Financial Post,* 24 September 1994, 1.

Davies, John. "British Columbia Vows to Fight NAFTA." *Journal of Commerce,* 29 March 1993, 1A.

Davies, Robertson. "Signing Away Canada's Soul: Culture, Identity, and the Free Trade Agreement." *Harper's,* January 1989, 45.

Davis, Bob. "Free-trade Pact's Details Are Sparking Squabbles as Congress Takes Up Review." *Wall Street Journal,* 8 September 1992, A2.

Davis, Mike. *Prisoners of the American Dream.* New York: Verso, 1986.

Daw, James. "Interest Rate Strategy 'Crude' Executive Says." *Toronto Star,* 8 June 1990, F1.

________. "Michigan to Resume Fight If Deal Dies." *Toronto Star,* 18 November 1988, C1.

de Vroey, Michael. "A Regulation Approach Interpretation of Contemporary Crisis." *Capital and Class,* 23 (Summer 1984): 45-66.

de Kerckhove, D. "Control of the Collective Mind. Free Trade and Canada's Cultural Industries." *Canadian Forum,* 67 (October 1989): 20-23.

"Defence Plant Heads South, 400 Lose Jobs." *Sault Star,* 2 April 1991, A6.

Demers, Michael. "Responding to the challenges of the global economy: the competitiveness agenda." *How Ottawa Spends: The Politics of Competitiveness, 1992-1993.* Edited by Frances Abele. Ottawa: Carleton University Press, 1992: 151-179.

DeMont, John. "Paying the Piper: Ottawa Clamps Down on Unemployment Insurance." *Maclean's,* 18 December 1990, 42.

________. "Spreading the Net Widely." *Maclean's,* 3 July 1989, 76.

________. "Standing On Guard: A Majority Now Opposes Free Trade." *Maclean's,* 18 December 1989, 50.

________. "Takeover Fever." *Maclean's,* 28 August 1989, 36.

"Demystifying the Debt." *Canadian Forum,* 73 (1993): 10.

Diebel, Linda. "Closed-door Trade Talks Denounced." *Toronto Star,* 5 August 1992, A10.

Dillon, John. "NAFTA is a Very Big Deal." *Action Canada Dossier* 36 (March 1992): 2.

Dobbin, Murray. "Thomas d'Aquino: The Defacto PM." *Canadian Forum,* 71 (November 1992).

Doern, Bruce and Brian Tomlin. *Faith and Fear: The Free Trade Story.* Toronto: Stoddart Publishing Company, 1991.

Dornbush, Roger. "Free Trade With Mexico." *The Senior Economist* 7, (1991): 3-4.

Dowling, Deborah. "Shuffling off to Buffalo: Exodus Worries Business, Political Leaders." *Sault Star,* 26 October 1991, A8.

Drache, Daniel. "The Systematic Search for Flexibility: National Competitiveness and New Work Relations." *The New Era of Global Competition: State Policy and Market Power.* Edited by Daniel Drache and Meric Gertler. Montréal: McGill-Queen's University Press, 1991: 251-269.

Driver, Felix. "Geography's Empire: Histories of Geographical Knowledge." *Environment and Planning D: Society and Space,* 10 (1992): 35.

Drohan, Madelaine. "U.S. Cuts Rates, Canada Doesn't: Wilson Sees Problems in Following the U.S. Lead." *Globe and Mail,* 14 July 1990, B1.

Dunford, Michael. "Theories of Regulation." *Environment and Planning D: Society and Space,* 8 (1990): 297-321.

Dwyer, Victor. "Culture in Crisis." *Maclean's,* 22 April 1992, 46.

ECC. *A New Frontier: Globalization and Canada's Financial Markets.* Ottawa: Supply and Services, 1989.

________. *First Annual Review, Economic Goals for Canada to 1970: A Statement by the Economic Council of Canada.* Ottawa: Supply and Services, 1970.

________. "Health Care Policies Safe." *Au Courant* 9 (1988): 9.

________. *Reaching Outward: A Statement by the Economic Council of Canada.* Ottawa: Supply and Services, 1987.

________. *Venturing Forth: An Assessment of the Canada U.S. Trade Agreement.* Ottawa: Supply and Services, 1988.

Ecumenical Coalition for Economic Justice. "Free Trade and Healthcare." *Canadian Review of Social Policy,* 33 (1994): 96-98.

Eden, Lorraine. "Free Trade, Tax Reform, and Transfer Pricing." *Canadian Tax Journal,* 39 (1991): 90-112.

Enchin, Harvey. "Canadian Branch Assets Slashed Before Gillette Announced Closing." *Globe and Mail,* 25 November 1988, A1.

Ernst, Alan. "From Liberal Continentalism to Neoconservatism: North American Free Trade and the Politics of the C.D. Howe Institute." *Studies in Political Economy,* 39 (Autumn 1992): 109-140.

Esping-Anderson, Gosta. *The Three Worlds of Welfare Capitalism.* Princeton: Princeton University Press, 1990.

External Affairs Canada. *Canada's New Free Trade Agreement: How It Benefits Women.* Ottawa: Supply and Services, 1988.

________. *Canada's New Free Trade Agreement: Key Benefits.* Ottawa: Supply and Services, 1988.

________. *Trade Negotiations: Securing Canada's Future.* Ottawa: Supply and Services, 1987.

Fagan, Drew. "Alberta May Lose $14 Billion in Projects: IDA." *Globe and Mail,* 11 November 1988, B6.

________. "Unemployment Rate Jumps to 7.6% in May." *Globe and Mail,* 11 November 1988, B1.

Falzon, Charles. "Film, TV Central to Sense of Nationhood." *Toronto Star,* 17 June 1991, A21.

Farnsworth, Clyde. "Canadians Seek Freer Trade in Steel." *New York Times,* 20 July 1992, C5.

________. "Economic Spur Set by U.S. and Canada in New Pact." *New York Times,* 5 October 1987, A1.

________. "Free-trade Accord is Enticing Canadian Companies to the U.S." *New York Times,* 9 August 1991, A1, C3.

________. "U.S. and Canada Decide to speed cuts in Tariffs." *New York Times,* 21 March 1991, C6.

________. "U.S. Pact a Spur to Canada." *New York Times,* 22 July 1992.

Federal Reserve Bank of St. Louis. *International Economic Conditions.* February (1995).

________. *International Economic Conditions.* May (1992).

Fennell, Tom, et. al. "A Free Trade Anniversary." *Maclean's*, 18 December 1989, 44-47.
Ferguson, Derek. "Labour Plan Will Drive Retailers Into Bankruptcy." *Toronto Star*, 7 August 1992, A13.
Ferguson, J. "Ottawa Hauls in Windfall From GST." *Toronto Star*, 8 June 1991, A1.
________. "Reisman Accuses Americans of Thuggery in Trade Dealings." *Toronto Star*, 18 January 1992, B16.
________. "Short Wave Radio Service Slashed." *Toronto Star*, 23 March 1991, A7.
________. "Trade Wrangle Puts Thousands of Jobs in Peril." *Toronto Star*, 3 August 1992, A9.
Fillmore, Nick. "The Big Oink: How Business Won the Free Trade Battle." *This Magazine*, 23 (March 1989): 13-20.
Finlay, John and Douglas Sprague. *The Structure of Canadian History*, 2nd ed. Scarborough, ON: Prentice-Hall, 1984.
Finn, Ed and Michael McBane. "Index on Unemployment Insurance." *Canadian Forum* 68 (May 1990): 32.
Finn, Ed. "Deficit Doctors." *Canadian Forum* 74 (1994): 47.
________. "Index on Federal Taxes." *Canadian Forum* 68 (March 1990): 32.
________. "No Alternatives." *Canadian Forum* 74 (1994): 47.
"Foreign Trade Legislation: Forward." *The Congressional Digest* 65 (1986): 193.
Forest, Anne. "Labour Legacy in Question." *Canadian Dimension* 29 (February 1995): 29
"Foresters Chop Down U.S. Softwood Proposal." *Sault Star*, 8 April 1992, A6.
Forsey, Helen. "Railroading Into Oblivion." *Canadian Forum* 74 (November 1994): 33-35.
Foucault, Michel. *The Archeology of Knowledge and the Discourse on Language*. New York: Pantheon Books, 1972.
Fowlie, Laura. "Union Rifts Cost Labour Credibility." *Financial Post*, 24 December 1994, 11.
Francis, Diane. *Controlling Interest: Who Owns Canada?* Toronto: McClelland-Bantam, 1987.
Francis, Diane. "Myths about the Free Trade Agreement." *Maclean's*, 29 January 1990, 15.
________. "Opposing Free Trade is like Opposing Gravity." *Maclean's*, 27 April 1992, 13.
Franklin, Stephen. "Jobs Still No. 1 Free Trade Issue." *Chicago Tribune*, 14 February 1993, 1.
________. "Whipsaw Debate on GM Policy." *The Chicago Tribune*, 26 February 1992, 3.
"Free Trade Victims Likened to 'Flowers that Die'." *Toronto Star*, 24 November 1988, D1.
"Frigidaire Move Means 250 Jobs." *Sault Star*, 18 March 1992.
Frum, David. "Martin's Speech Renounced All the Liberals Have Stood For." *Financial Post*, 4 March 1995, 22.
Frye, Northrop. *The Bush Garden*. Toronto: Anansi, 1971.
Fryer, John. "Canada-Mexico 'Free Trade': Worse than Canada-U.S. FTA." *Canadian Dimension* 24 (September 1990): 33-35.
Fuller, Colleen. "Fade to Black: Culture Under Free Trade." *Canadian Forum 70 (August 1991): 6.*
Fulton, Kaye. "Mad as Hell Over Taxes." *Maclean's*, 17 June 1991, 18.
Furlong, Kieran and Douglas Moggach. "Efficiency, Competition, and Full Employment in Canadian Free Trade Literature." *Studies in Political Economy*, 33 (Autumn 1990): 135-159.
Gallup Canada. "18% of Households Have U.S. Shopper." *Toronto Star*, 17 June 1991, A19.
Galt, V. "Small Town Hard Hit by 3 Plant Closings." *Globe and Mail*, 9 June 1990, A7.

Geddes, John, "Canada Corporate Tax Slightly Higher." *Financial Post*, 17 December 1994, 7.

________. " Martin Steers Toward Blue Liberalism." *Financial Post*, 22 October 1994, 5.

"General tire Closes Barrie Plant: 820 Workers Lose Jobs." *Sault Star*, 31 August 1991, B10.

Gibbins, Roger. "Canadian Federalism: The Entanglement of Meech Lake and the Free Trade Agreement." *Publius* 19 (Summer 1989): 185-198.

Gilpin, Robert. *The Political Economy of International Relations.* Princeton: Princeton University Press, 1987.

Gindin, Sam. "Breaking Away: The Formation of the Canadian Auto Workers." *Studies in Political Economy*, 29 (Summer 1989): 63-89.

Girard, Daniel. "Jobless Must Blame Recession Not Free Trade, Wilson Says." *Toronto Star*, 30 May 1992, D1.

"GM Not 'Bluffing' About Closing Plant if Concessions Not Granted." *Sault Star*, 19 June 1991, A8.

Golden, Tim. "Mexico Pulls Out of a Fund that has Roiled Trade Issue." *New York Times*, 18 February 1993, C1.

Gooderham, Mary. "Election Officials' Hands Tied on Flood of Late Ads." *Globe and Mail*, 17 November 1988, A10.

Gordon, David, Richard Edwards and Michael Reich. *Segmented Work, Divided Workers: The Historical Transformation of Labor in the United States.* Cambridge: Cambridge University Press, 1982.

Grammer, Hilary. "Social Policy by Stealth." *Canadian Dimension* 25 (June 1991): 19-20.

Gramsci, Antonio. *An Antonio Gramsci Reader, Selected Writings: 1916-1935.* Edited by David Forgacs. New York: Shocken Books, 1988.

Granatstein, J.L. "Free Trade: The History of an Issue." *The Future on the Table: Canada and the Free Trade Issue.* Edited by Michael Henderson, North York, ON: Masterpress, 1987): 1-34.

Gray, Earle. "Maude Barlow, Hobgoblin of Little Minds, and Terrors of Free Trade." *Canadian Speeches*, 6 (1992): 65-67.

Greenspon, Edward. "New UI Plan Would Cut Benefits." *Globe and Mail*, 10 June 1995, A1, A10.

Gwyn, Richard. *The 49th Paradox: Canada in North America.* Toronto: Totem Books, 1986.

Haggett, Scott. "As The Crow Rate Flies" *Financial Post*, 13 May 1995, 4.

Hags, Janis. "Qubec Shore Plant Being Shut Because of Greater Competition." *Globe and Mail*, 28 November 1988, A22.

Hall, Peter. "Austerity Budget Brings Structural Change." *Canada Outlook* 10 (1995): 22-24.

Hall, Peter. *Cities of Tomorrow: An Intellectual History of Urban Planning and Design in the Twentieth Century.* New York: Basil Blackwell, 1988.

Hallman, Mark. "CN on Private Track." *Financial Post*, 1 October 1994, 1.

________. "No Special Deal in Cars." *Financial Post*, 30 October 1991, 3.

Harvey, David. "From Space to Place and Back Again: Reflections on the Condition of Post-Modernity." *Mapping the Futures: Local Cultures, Global Change.* Edited by Jon Bird, et. al., New York: Routledge, 1993: 3-30.

________. *The Condition of Postmodernity.* Cambridge, MA: Basil Blackwell, 1989.

Hazledine, Tim. "Canada-U.S. Free Trade? Not So Elementary, Watson." *Canadian Public Policy* 14 (1988): 204-213.

________. "What Do Economists Know About Free Trade?" *Canadian-American Free*

Trade: Historical, Political and Economic Dimensions. Edited by Alvin Riggs and Tom Velk, Halifax, NS: The IRPP, 1987: 141-158.
Heilbroner, Robert. *The Worldly Philosophers,* 6th ed. New York: Simon and Schuster, 1989.
"Heinz shifting pickle production to Michigan." *Sault Star,* 21 January 1991.
Held, Peter. "Why we must understand the competitiveness issue. Speech given to the Canadian Institute of Chartered Accountants." *Canadian Speeches,* 5 (June 1991): 53-55.
Hepburn, Bob. "Reagan Promises 'co-operation' of Free Trade." *Toronto Star,* 18 November 1988, A3.
Hightower, Jim. "NAFTA - We Don't Hafta!" *Utne Reader,* July 1993, 99.
Hill, Bert and Kelly Egan. "Ontario's Industrial Heartland Devastated by Plant Closings." *Sault Star,* 16 February 1991.
Hill, Charles. "Who Can Afford To Go To University?" *Western Gazette,* 69 (1993): 34.
Hill, Chris. "Ontario Joins B.C. Challenge of Federal Limits for Social Programs." *Sault Star,* 28 February 1990, A1.
Holmes, John. "Industrial Restructuring in a Period of Crisis: An Analysis of the Canadian Automobile Industry." *Antipode* 20, (1988): 19-51.
Honderich, John. "A Leap of Faith Not Worth Taking." *Toronto Star,* 19 November 1988, D2.
Hufbauer, Gary and Jeffrey Schott. *North American Free Trade: Issues and Recommendations.* Washington, DC: Institute for International Economics, 1992.
________. "Prescription for Growth." *Foreign Policy,* 93 (1993): 104-114.
Hunt, Nigel. "The Theory of Devolution." *This Magazine* 25 (1991): 22-26.
Hurtig, Mel. *The Betrayal of Canada,* 2nd ed. Toronto: Stoddart Publishing, 1992.
Hymer, Stephen. "Direct Foreign Investment and the National Economic Interest." *Nationalism in Canada.* Edited by Peter Russell. Toronto: McGraw-Hill Co. of Canada, 1966: 191-202.
Innis, Harold. *The Bias of Communication.* Toronto: University of Toronto Press, 1951.
Ip, Greg. "Canadians Starting to Live Within Their Means." *Financial Post,* 24 December 1994, 35.
________. "Lenders' Strike Alert: All Eyes on Martin as Debt Fears Unsettle the C$." *Financial Post,* 15 October 1994, 5.
Jackson, Andrew. *Job Losses in Canadian Manufacturing: 1989-1991.* Ottawa: CLC, 1991.
Jackson, Kenneth. *Crabgrass Frontier: The Suburbanization of the United States.* New York: Oxford University Press, 1985.
Jenish, D'Arcy and Pat Chisholm. "Tighter Picket Lines." *Maclean's,* 10 August 1992, 44.
Jenish, D'Arcy, John Daly and Bruce Wallace, "Takeover Fever Hits Canada." *Maclean's,* 19 September 1989, 30.
Jenish, D'Arcy. "A Cry of Protest: Rising Tuition Fees Stir Campus Discontent." *Maclean's,* 9 March 1993, 44.
________. "A New Hard Line on Trade." *Maclean's,* 22 May 1989, 31.
________. "Facing Radical Surgery." *Maclean's,* 13 January 1992, 38.
________. "Merger Wave Rolls On." *Maclean's,* 6 February 1989, 28-30.
Jenson, Jane. "'Different' but not 'Exceptional': Canada's Permeable Fordism." *Canadian Review of Sociology and Anthropology* 26 (1989): 69-94.
Jessop, Bob. "Recent Theories of the Capitalist State." *Cambridge Journal of Economics* 1 (1977): 353-373.

________. "Regulation Theories in Retrospect and Prospect." *Economy and Society* 19 (Spring 1990): 153-216.

Johnson, Kim. "Unprecedented Opportunity from the Yukon to the Yucatan." *Canadian Speeches*, 5 (1991): 46-49.

Kantor, Mickey. "At Long Last, A Trade Pact to be Proud Of." *Wall Street Journal*, 17 August 1993, A14.

Keating, John. "North Carolina a Model of Success in Drawing Business, Investment." *Financial Post*, 17 September 1994, S17.

Kidd, Kenneth and Tony Van Alphen. "Gillette Axes 600 Jobs, Critics Cite Trade Deal." *Toronto Star*, 24 November 1988.

Kidd, Kenneth. "Canadians Have an Eye on Buffalo for Business." *Toronto Star*, 19 November 1988, C1.

Knight, Douglas and Diane Francis. "Debt and Taxes." *Financial Post*, 28 January 1995, DT1-DT9.

Krugman, Paul. *Geography and Trade*. Cambridge, MA: MIT Press, 1991.

________. "Is Free Trade Passe?" *Economic Perspectives*, 1 (1987): 131-144.

________. "The Uncomfortable Truth About NAFTA. It's Foreign Policy Stupid." *Foreign Affairs*, 72 (1993): 13-19.

Kuttner, Robert. "Forward." *The Political Economy of North American Free Trade*. Edited by Ricardo Grinspun and Maxwell A. Cameron. New York: St. Martin's Press, 1993.

Lachica, Eduardo. "U.S. Issues Rule Against Canada Lumber Imports." *Wall Street Journal*, 18 May 1992, A2.

Lamorie, Andrew. *How They Sold Our Canada to the U.S.A.* Gravenhurst, Ontario: Northern Books, 1964.

Langan, Fred. "Canadians Flocking to US Shops." *Christian Science Monitor*, 29 May 1991, 7.

Langille, David. "The Business Council on National Issues and the Canadian State." *Studies in Political Economy*, 24 (Autumn 1987): 49-57.

Lash, Patricia, John Heinzl and Chetan Lakshman. "165,000 Factory Jobs Vanished in Past Year, StatsCan Report Says." *Globe and Mail*, 9 June 1990, A1.

Laver, Ross. "A Collision Course." *Maclean's*, 1 July 1992, 84-85.

________. "Scrapping the Assembly Line." *Maclean's*, 12 August 1991, 28-29.

"Learn How You Can Cut Manufacturing Costs Up to 50% in Mexico." *Wall Street Journal*, 6 April 1989, A2.

Leborgne, Daniel and Alain Lipietz. "New Technologies, New Modes of Regulation: Some Spatial Implications." *Environment and Planning D: Society and Space* 6 (1988): 263.

Lee, Charlene. "Canadian Dollar Falls to 28-month Low on Signs Ottawa May Seek Cut in Rates." *Wall Street Journal*, 12 May 1992, C15.

Lemco, Jonathon, Richard Belons and Laura Subrin, "The Free Trade Agreement: Initial Winners and Losers." *Canada-U.S. Outlook 2 (1990): 3-19.*

Levitt, Kari. *Silent Surrender*. Toronto: Macmillan of Canada, 1970.

Lewington, Jennifer. "It Began as a Case of Self-Defence." *Globe and Mail*, 12 November 1988, D1.

Lewis, Charles and Margaret Ebrahim. "Can Mexico and Big Business USA Buy NAFTA?" *The Nation*, 14 June 1993, 826.

"Liberal Senators Call Drug Patent Bill a Tragedy." *Sault Star*, 23 January 1993, A6.

Lipietz, Alain and Jane Jenson, "Rebel Sons: The Regulation School. Jane Jenson Interviews Alain Lipietz." *French Politics and Society* 5 (Fall 1987): 18.

Lipietz, Alain. " The Debt Problem, European Integration and the New Phase of World Crisis." *New Left Review* 178 (November 1989): 39.

________. *Mirages and Miracles: The Crisis of Global Fordism.* Translated by David Macey. London: Verso, 1987.

Lipset, Seymour Martin. *Continental Divide.* New York: Routledge, 1990.

Lipsey, Richard and Robert York. *Evaluating the Free Trade Deal: A Guided Tour Through the Canada-U.S. Agreement.* Toronto: C.D. Howe Institute, 1988.

________. "U.S.-Canada Free Trade Agreement: Handshake Across the Border." *New York Times,* 27 February 1989, 29-32.

Lipsey, Richard. "Sovereignty: Culturally, Economically, and Socially." *Free Trade: The Real Story.* Edited by John Crispo, Toronto: Gage, 1988: 148-60.

________. "The Economics of a Canadian-American Free Trade Association." *The Future on the Table: Canada and the Free Trade Issue.* Edited by Michael Henderson, North York, ON: Masterpress, 1987: 35-45.

Litt, Paul. "The Massey Commission, Americanization, and Canadian Cultural Nationalism." *Queen's Quarterly,* 98 (1991): 375-387.

Little, Bruce. "Howe Study Finds Free-trade Winners." *Globe and Mail,* 20 October 1992, B1.

Lorimer, Rowland. "Book Publishing in English Canada in the Context of Free Trade." *Canadian Journal of Communications 16 (1991): 58-72.*

Lovering, John. "Fordism's Unknown Successor: A Comment on Scott's Theory of Flexible Accumulation and the Re-emergence of Regional Economies." *International Journal of Urban and Regional Research* 14 (1990): 159-174.

Lower, A. "The Americanization of Canada." *Canada and the World 55 (1990): 13-16.*

Lumsden, Ian, ed., *Close the 49th Parallel Etc.: The Americanization of Canada.* Toronto: University of Toronto Press, 1970.

Lynk, Michael. "The Labour Law Factor: What Effect Will the Free Trade Agreement Have on the Legislative Gains Made by the Canadian Labour Movement?" *Canadian Labour,* Spring (1988): 18-20, 36.

Lyon, Peyton. "CUFTA and Canadian Independence." *Canadian-American Free Trade: Historical, Political and Economic Dimensions.* Edited by Alvin Riggs and Tom Velk, Halifax, NS: The IRPP, 1987: 195-198.

MacDonald, Judy. "Talkin' Trade." *This Magazine,* 23 (December 1989): 42.

________. "Talkin' Trade." *This Magazine,* 23 (December 1989): 42.

________. "Talkin' Trade." *This Magazine,* 23 (May 1989): 42.

________. "Talkin' Trade." *This Magazine,* 23 (September 1989): 42.

Macdonald, Donald. "A Leap of Faith: The Canadian Decision for Free Trade." *The American Review of Canadian Studies* 21 (1991): 155-161.

Maclean's/Decima. "Sex, Politics, and Dreams: the Poll Texts." *Maclean's,* 9 September 1991, 35.

Macleod Group. "NAFTA: North American Free Trade Agreement." *New York Times,* 21 July 1993, C10-C16.

Mahant, Edelgard and Graeme S. Mount. *An Introduction to Canadian-American Relations.* Toronto: Methuen, 1984.

Mahon, Rianne. "Post-Fordism: Some Issues for Labour." *The New Era of Global Com-*

petition: State Policy and Market Power. Edited by Daniel Drache and Meric Gertler, Montréal: McGill-Queen's University Press, 1991: 316-332.

Malecki, Edward. Technology and Development. New York: Longmans, 1991.

Mandel, Ernest. *Late Capitalism.* Translated by Joris de Bres. New York: Verso, 1975.

Marotte, Bertrand. "North Carolina's Anti-Union Reputation Pays Off." *Sault Star,* 1 August 1992, A7.

Martin, Patrice. "The Kiss of Debt." *Canadian Forum* 74 (March 1994): 20-22.

Maslove, Allan. "Reconstructing Fiscal Federalism." *How Ottawa Spends: The Politics of Competitiveness.* Edited by Francis Abele. Ottawa: Carleton University Press, 1992: 57-78.

Massey, Doreen. *Spatial Divisions of Labour: Social Structures and the Geography of Production.* London: Macmillan, 1984.

McArthur, Jack. "Compared to Global Statistics, We've Been in a Long Slump." *Toronto Star,* 18 June 1991, B2.

________. "Meech is not a One-shot Solution." *Toronto Star,* 8 June 1990, F2.

McCambly, James. "North American Free Trade Demands a Charter of Labour. Speech Given by the President of the Canadian Federation of Labour to the Americas Society in New York." *Canadian Speeches,* 4 (1991): 47-48.

McCarthy, Shawn. "Economists See 'Glimmer' in the Gloom." *Toronto Star,* 1 June 1991, C1.

________. "Federal PCs Ram Through UI Bill Cutting Payment to Quitters." *Toronto Star,* 25 March 1993, A5.

________. "Jobless Rate Forecast to Stay High For Years." *Toronto Star,* 5 August 1992, F1.

McCoag, Tom. "MacDonald Slams Opposition Tactics." *Halifax Chronicle-Herald,* 7 November 1988, 34.

McGaughey, William. *A U.S.-Mexico-Canada Free Trade Agreement: Do We Just Say No?* Minneapolis, MN: Thistlerose Publications, 1992.

McGillivray, Don. "Free Trade Puts Pressure on Canadian Values." *Sault Star,* 30 November 1988, A4.

McKenzie, Robert. "Trade Deal Boosts Separatism PQ Says." *Toronto Star,* 23 November 1988, A1.

McMurdy, Deirdre. "A Show of Strength." *Maclean's,* 28 October 1991, 40.

________. "A State of De-Klein." *Maclean's,* 6 February 1995, 47.

________. "Packaged for Growth." *Maclean's,* 12 August 1991, 31.

________. "The Tie that Binds." *Maclean's,* 31 October 1994, 50.

________. "Three for the Show." *Maclean's,* 8 March 1992, 22-23.

McNally, David. "Beyond Nationalism, Beyond Protectionism: Labour and the Canada-U.S. Free Trade Agreement." *Review of Radical Political Economics* 22 (1990): 179-194.

McParland, Kelly, "Cross-border Trade Issues Unresolved." *Financial Post,* 24 December 1993, C5.

McQuaig, Linda. "Pact Could Scuttle Insurance Scheme." *Globe and Mail,* 13 December 1988, A3.

Merrett, Christopher D. *Crossing the Border.* Orono, ME: University of Maine Press, 1991.

Mitchell, Bob and Bruce Campion-Smith. "Caterpillar Denies that Trade Pact Linked to Brampton Job Loss." *Toronto Star,* 13 April 1991.

Mittelstaedt, Martin and Murray Campbell. "Harris Vows to Undo 'Damage' by NDP." *Globe and Mail,* 10 June 1995, A1.

Moody, Kim and Mary McGinn. *Unions and Free Trade: Solidarity Versus Competition.* Detroit: A Labor Notes Book, 1992.

Moody, Kim. *An Injury to All: The Decline of American Unionism.* New York: Verso, 1988.

Morand, Martin. "Canada: Our Model?" *Monthly Review* 42 (1990): 40-47.

Morici, Peter. "The Environment for Free Trade." *Making Free Trade Work: The Canada-U.S. Agreement.* Edited by Peter Morici, New York: Council on Foreign Relations, 1990: 1-26.

Morton, Peter. "Martin's Options Limited. Closing Business Tax Loopholes May Drive Corporations Elsewhere." *Financial Post,* 11 February 1995, 7.

Morton, W. *The Canadian Identity.* Toronto: University of Toronto Press, 1972..

Mosco, Vincent. "Toward a Transnational World Information Order: The Canada-U.S. Free Trade Agreement." *Canadian Journal of Communications* 15 (1990): 46-63.

Mowat, Farley. *My Discovery of America.* Toronto: Seal Books, 1985.

Mulroney, Brian. "Social and Cultural Goals Underlie Canada's Pursuit of Freer Trade. Speech to the Chambre de Commerce de la Rive-Sud, Longueuil, Qubec." *Canadian Speeches,* 2, Special Supplement (1987): 9.

Myles, John. "Post-Industrialism and the Service Economy." *The New Era of Global Competition.* Edited by Daniel Drache and Meric Gertler, Montréal: McGill-Queen's University Press, 1991: 351-366.

"NAFTA Lobbying Cost $25 Million." *Canadian Free Trader,* 6 (1993): 71.

"Nafta before health." *Wall Street Journal,* 18 August, A10.

Naisbitt, John and Patricia Aburdene. *Megatrends 2000: Ten New Directions for the 1990s.* New York: Avon Books, 1990.

Naser, Sylvia. "A Primer: Why Economists Favor Free Trade Agreements." *New York Times,* 17 September 1993, A1, C4.

Neil, Garry. "Election Countdown: Cultural Policy Options." *Cinema Canada* 157 (November 1988): 14.

Neufeld, E.P. "Financial and Economic Dimensions of Free Trade." *Canadian-American Free Trade: Historical, Political and Economic Dimensions.* Edited by Alvin Riggs and Tom Velk, Halifax, NS: The IRPP, 1987: 177-185.

New, W.H. "If Anyone Knows." *Canadian Literature,* 118 (Autumn 1988): 2-6.

Newman, Peter C. "Sliding Down the Path to Third World Status." *Maclean's,* 25 February 1991, 36.

________. "Wilson's Vain Struggle with a Killer Debt." *Maclean's,* 4 March 1991, 46.

________. "The Dark Side of Merger Mania." *Maclean's* 6 February 1989, 31.

Noel, Alain. "Accumulation, Regulation, and Social Change: An Essay on French Political Economy." *International Organization* 41 (Spring 1987): 303-333.

Norcliffe, G. "Regional Labour Market Adjustments in a Period of Structural Transformations: An Assessment of the Canadian Case." *The Canadian Geographer* 38 (1994): 2-17.

O'Connor, James. *Accumulation Crisis,* New York: Basil Blackwell, 1984.

________. *The Meaning of Crisis: A Theoretical Introduction.* New York: Basil Blackwell, 1987.

O'Hagen, Dan. "Free Trade, Our Canada or Theirs: Workers Confront the Corporate Blueprint." *Canadian Labour,* September (1986): 15-18.

OECD Observer. "OECD Economic Outlook." *OECD Observer,* 161 (February 1991): 33.

Olver, Lynne. "MP Hails End of 'Devastating' Lumber Tax." *Sault Star,* 4 September 1991, A6.

Orchard, David. "What They Don't Want Us to Know About Free Trade." *NeWest Review* 14 (1989): 8-14.

Orme, William. "Myth Versus Fact: The Whole Truth About the Half-truths." *Foreign Affairs* 72 (1993): 2-12.

Orr, John Lewis. "Talkin' Trade." *This Magazine* 24 (September 1990): 42.

"Ottawa Warned Free Trade Had Some Firms Thinking of Leaving." *Sault Star*, 30 November 1992, B7.

Palmer, Bryan. *Working Class Experience: Rethinking the History of Canadian Labour, 1800-1991*, 2nd ed. Toronto: McClelland and Stewart, 1992.

"Panel Rejects Ruling of Unfair Subsidies for Canadian Hogs." *Wall Street Journal*, 20 May 1992, B3.

Panitch, Leo and Donald Swartz. "The Social Contract: Labour, the NDP and Beyond." *Canadian Dimension* 27 (November 1993): 28.

Panitch, Leo. "Capitalist Restructuring and Labour Strategies." *Studies in Political Economy* 24 (Autumn 1987): 131-157.

Parizeau, Jacques. "Tom Velk interviews Jacques Parizeau."*Canadian-American Free Trade: Historical, Political and Economic Dimensions*. Edited by Alvin Riggs and Tom Velk, Halifax, NS: IRPP, 1987: 213-218.

Parker, Mike and Jane Slaughter. *A Union Strategy Guide for Labor-Management Participation Programs*. Detroit: Labor Notes, 1992.

Pattison, Jim, "Paradise Postponed." *Maclean's*, 3 December 1989, 56.

Pawley, Howard. "CBC Back Talk." *Maclean's*, 17 December 1990, 18.

Pendakur, Manjunath. *Canadian Dreams and American Control: The Political Control of the Canadian Film Industry*. Detroit: Wayne State University Press, 1990.

Perlmutter, Tom. "The Flora Solution: The Politics of Film Distribution." *Canadian Dimension* 23, (March 1989): 6-11.

Phillips, Paul. *Canadian Political Economy: An Economic Introduction*. Toronto: Garamond Press, 1990.

______. "The National Policy Revisited." *Journal of Canadian Studies* 14 (1979): 3-13.

Piore, M.J. and C.F. Sabel. *The Second Industrial Divide: Possibilities for Production*. New York: Basic Books, 1984.

Plourde, Andre. "The NEP Meets the FTA." *Canadian Public Policy* 17 (1991): 14-24.

Pollen, Robert and Alexander Cockburn. "A Haunted House: Capitalism and Its Specters — the World, the Free Market, and the Left." *The Nation*. 252 (July 1991): 224-236.

Puche, Jaime Serra. *Partners in Trade: A North American Free Trade Zone*. Mexico City: Government of Mexico, 1991.

Reagan, Ronald. "An Historic Step Toward World Economic Renewal. Speech Given to the Canadian House of Commons." *Canadian Speeches*, 1 (1987): 10-12.

Reich, Robert. *The Work of Nations*. New York: Alfred A. Knopf, 1991.

Reisman, Simon. "Free Trade Will Strengthen Canada's Ability to Survive as a Strong Free Nation." *Canadian Speeches*, 1 (1987): 2-5.

"Report Documents Declining Federal Education Funding." *Sault Star*, 30 November 1992, A1.

Richard, John and Richard Dearden. *The Canada-U.S. Free Trade Agreement: Final Text and Analysis*. Toronto: Commerce Clearing House Canadian Limited, 1988.

Riggs, Alvin R. and Tom Velk. *Canadian-American Free Trade: Historical, Political and Economic Dimensions*. Halifax, NS: The IRPP, 1987.

Ritchie, Gordon. "A Canada-Mexico-U.S. Free Trade Agreement: Watch Out!" *Business Quarterly*, 55 (1991): 18-26.

________. "The Free Trade Agreement Revisited." *The American Review of Canadian Studies*, 21 (1991): 207-214.

________. "The Negotiating Process." *Free Trade: The Real Story*. Edited by John Crispo. Toronto: Gage, 1988: 16-22.

Ritchie, Laurell. "Flying Without a Net." *This Magazine* 28 (1994): 34-36.

________. "The Attack on UI.." *This Magazine* 23 (November 1989): 14-17.

Roberts, Bill. "Positively Canadian: Culture on the Free Trade Table." *Our Times* 7 (December 1991): 27-29.

Roberts, Wayne and John Bullen. "A Heritage of Hope and Struggle: Workers, Unions, and Politics in Canada." *Readings in Canadian History, Volume 5: Modern Canada*. Edited by Michael Cross and Gregory Kealey, Toronto: McClelland and Stewart, 1985: 105-140.

Robinson, Randy. "Colonizing Canada: A Year and a Half of Free Trade." *Multinational Monitor* 11 (May 1990): 10-14.

________. "Index on Free Trade." *Canadian Forum* 69 (January 1991): 32.

Rocher, Francois. "Canadian Business, Free Trade and the Rhetoric of Economic Continentalization." *Studies in Political Economy* 35 (Summer 1991): 135-154.

Romain, Ken. "Steel Industry Under Pressure From U.S. Actions." *Globe and Mail*, 11 November 1988, B1.

Rosenbaum, David. "Good Economics Meets Protective Politics." *New York Times*, 19 September 1993, 5E.

Rotstein, Abraham and Gary Lax, eds., *Independence: The Canadian Challenge*. Toronto: Committee for an Independent Canada, 1972.

Rotstein, Abraham. "Foreign Control of the Economy: A Screening and Ownership Policy." *Getting It Back: A Program for Canadian Independence*. Edited by Abraham Rotstein and Gary Lax. Toronto: Clarke, Irwin and Company, 1974: 22-33.

Rubstein, Larry. "A Mexican Miracle." *Newsweek*, 20 May 1991, 45.

Rugman, Alan. "Free Trade Opponents have 'Mickey Mouse' Criticism." *Halifax Chronicle-Herald*, 7 November 1988, 7.

Russell, Frances. "The Americanization of Medicare: Will that be Visa or Mastercard?" *Canadian Forum* 69 (August 1990): 17-19.

Sabel, Charles and Jonathon Zeitlin. "Historical Alternatives to Mass Production: Politics, Markets and Technology in Nineteenth-Century Industrialization." *Past and Present*, 108 (August 1985): 133-176.

Safire, William. "Canada's Comeback Kid." *New York Times*, 23 March 1992, A13.

Saunders, John. "Shufflin' off to Sample Buffalo's Pleasure." *Globe and Mail*, 4 July 1991.

Sayer, Andrew and Richard Walker. *The New Social Economy: Reworking the Division of Labor*. Cambridge, MA: Blackwell, 1992.

Sayer, Andrew. "Industrial Location on a World Scale: The Case of the Semiconductor Industry." *Production, Work, Territory: The Geographical Anatomy of Industrial Capitalism*. Edited by Allen Scott and Michael Storper. Boston: Unwin Hyman, 1988: 107-123.

Schlefer, J. "What Price Economic Growth." *The Atlantic* 270 (December 1992): 114-118.

Schor, Juliet. "The Great Trade Debates." *Creating a New World Economy: Forces of Change and Plans for Action*. Edited by Gerald Epstein, Julie Graham and Jessica Nembhard, Philadelphia: Temple University Press, 1993: 274-286.

Scott, Allen. "Flexible Production Systems and Regional Development." *International Journal of Urban and Regional Research* 12 (1988): 171-185.

Scott, Gavin. "Free-for-all." *Time,* 18 May 1992, 37.

Scotton, Geoffrey. "Report Outlines Pitfalls in Three-way Free Trade." *Financial Post,* 18 July 1991, 28.

Shaiken, Harley. "Will Manufacturing Head South." *Technology Review* 24 (April 1993): 28-29.

Sheppard, Robert. "Wilson Calls Turner Liar, Coward, Defends National Sales Tax Plan." *Globe and Mail,* 11 November 1988, A16.

Shifrin, Leonard. "Free Trade in Social Programs." *Perception* 12, (1988): 27-29.

Silverstein, Jeff. "Canada Wants to Guard Culture in North American Pact." *Christian Science Monitor* 13 November 1991, 8.

Simeon, Richard. "Inside the MacDonald Commission." *Studies in Political Economy* 22 (Spring 1987): 167-179.

Simon, Bernard. "Bank Governor is Hero After Fall in Inflation." *Financial Times,* 9 December 1992, 24.

Sinclair, Jim. "Free Trade: The Canadian Way." *Z Magazine* 6 (July 1993): 21-23.

"Small Business Not So Sure About Trilateral Trade Deal Survey Says." *Sault Star,* 10 October 1991, A10.

Smiley, Donald. "Meech Lake and Free Trade." *Canadian Public Administration* 32 (1989): 470.

Smith, Adam. *The Wealth of Nations.* New York: Modern Library, 1937.

Smith, Anthony. *The Geopolitics of Information: How Western Culture Dominates the World.* New York: Oxford University Press, 1980.

Smith, Melvin. "Ironclad Resolve is Needed to Cut Waste." *Financial Post,* 28 January 1994, DT6.

Smith, Susan. "Toyota's Canadian Strategy." *Financial Post,* 8 April 1995, 16.

Sorenson, Sandra. "Corporate Tax Avoidance." *Canadian Forum* 72 (May 1994): 48-49.

Statistics Canada. *Canada's Balance of International Payments, Fourth Quarter.* Ottawa: Supply and Services, 1993.

Statistics Canada. *Canada: A Portrait.* Ottawa: Supply and Services, 1989.

________. *Canadian Economic Observer,* August. Ottawa: Supply and Services, 1993.

________. *Canadian Economic Observer,* May. Ottawa: Supply and Services, 1990.

________. *Canadian Economic Observer,* May. Ottawa: Supply and Services, 1995.

________. *Canadian Economic Observer: Historical Supplement.* Ottawa: Supply and Services, 1991.

________. *Canadian Social Trends, 24* (Summer 1992).

________. *Canadian Social Trends, 36* (Spring 1995).

________. *Education Statistics Bulletin.* Ottawa: Supply and Services, 1992.

________. *Employment Earnings and Hours* (May). Ottawa: Supply and Services, 1993.

________. *Historical Labour Force Statistics, 1991.* Ottawa: Supply and Services, 1992.

________. *The Labour Force, April 1995.* Ottawa: Supply and Services, 1995.

________. *Canada's Balance of International Payments.* Ottawa: Supply and Services, 1995.

________. *Manufacturing Industries of Canada: National and Provincial Areas, 1989.* Ottawa: Industry, Science and Technology, 1992.

________. *Manufacturing Industries of Canada: National and Provincial Areas, 1991-1992.* Ottawa: Industry, Science and Technology, 1995.

"Stelco finds trade deal not working." *Sault Star,* 26 January 1991, A7.

Stinson, Marian. "Dollar Zooms to a 7-year High as Buying Clamor Hits Markets." *Globe and Mail*, 1 December 1988, B1.

"Stop Talks, Says ACTRA." *Cinema Canada*, 139 (March 1987): 38.

Storper, Michael and Allen Scott. "The Geographical Foundations and Social Regulation of Flexible Production Complexes." *In The Power of Geography: How Territory Shapes Social Life*. Edited by Jennifer Wolch and Michael Dear, Boston: Unwin Hyman, 1989: 19-40.

Story, Christopher. "The Canadian Dollar." *International Currency Review*, 20 (1989): 125-135.

Suppanz, Hannes. "Canada: Recasting Social Assistance." *The OECD Observer* 192 (February 1995): 49-51.

Sweet, Lois. "Medicare May Need Miracle to Survive." *Toronto Star*, 9 March 1991, A1.

Swift, Robert. "Manufacturing Job Losses Cripple the Economy." *New York Times*, 4 July 1993, A14.

Taylor, Peter J. *Political Geography: World Economy, Nation-State, Locality*, 2nd ed. London: Longmans, 1989.

"The NAFTA Tapes. Special Report: Transcript of a Conference Call Between Senior Trade Ministerial Aides." *Maclean's*, 21 September 1992, 21.

Thurow, Lester. *Head to Head: The Coming Battle Among Japan, Europe, and America*. New York: William Morrow and Company, 1992.

Todd, P. "Manning Would End Federal Role in Medicare." *Toronto Star*, 15 June 1991, A1.

Torfing, Jacob. "A Hegemony Approach to Capitalist Regulation." *State, Economy and Society*. Edited by Rene Bertramsen, Jens Peter Frolund and Jacob Torfing. London: Unwin Hyman, 1991: 35-93.

"Toronto Firm Decides on New York for Expansion." *Sault Star*, 29 February 1991, A7.

"Trade Deal With U.S. Linked to Plant Closing." *Sault Star*, 26 November 1988, A6.

Tremblay, Rodrigue. "250 Economists Say Its Our Best Option. Excerpts From an Address to the House of Commons Legislative Committee on Bill C-130, A Bill to Enact the Canada-U.S. Free Trade Agreement." *Canadian Speeches* 2, Special Supplement (August/September 1988): 5-6.

Trickey, Mike. "Public Insurance Plan Will Cost $3.6 Billion, 10,000 Jobs - Study." *Sault Star*, 14 August 1991, A1.

________. "Trade Offices Bring Message North: U.S. Open For Business." *Sault Star*, 29 June 1991, A1.

Truell, Peter Bob Davis. "Administration Releases Text of Trade Accord." *Wall Street Journal*, 9 September 1992, A2.

Tuohy, Carolyn. *Policy and Politics in Canada: Institutionalized Ambivalence*. Philadelphia: Temple University Press, 1992.

"U.S. Auto Parts Company Closures to Idle 670 Ontarians." *Sault Star*, 1 January 1991.

"U.S. Bullish on Canada" *Maclean's*, 6 February 1995, 48.

U.S. Department of Commerce. *Canada-U.S. Free Trade Agreement: Summary of Provisions*. Washington, DC: International Trade Commission, 1987.

________. *North American Free Trade Agreement: Generating Jobs for Americans*. Washington, DC: U.S. Government Printing Office, 1991.

"U.S. Investment in Canada down sharply." *Sault Star*, 5 April 1991.

"U.S. Wants End to Culture Protection." *Toronto Star*, 24 November 1991, A2.

"U.S., Canada Near Accord to Cut Withholding Tax." *Wall Street Journal*, 28 April 1992, A2.

Uchitelle, Louis. "America's Newest Industrial Belt: Northern Mexico Becomes a Big Draw for High-tech Plants - and Jobs." *New York Times*, 21 March 1993, 1, 14.

________. "Use of Temporary Workers on Rise in Manufacturing." *New York Times*, 6 July 1993, A1, C2.

Underwood, Nora. "Cross-border Checkup." *Maclean's*, 25 November 1991, 58.

"Unions May Scare Off U.S. Investment: Harvard." *Globe and Mail*, 1 December 1988, B9.

"Uniroyal Conditions Leave Workers Bitter." *Sault Star*, 21 June 1991, A6

"Valenti Praises Canadian Talent, Raps Government Intervention." *Cinema Canada* 168 (1989): 27.

Valenti, Jack. "Why Canada Must Never Restrict Imported Films." *Canadian Speeches* 3 (1989): 34-38.

Van Alphen, Tony. "Dollar, Trade Pact at Odds, Lougheed Says." *Toronto Star*, 1 January 1991, B1.

Veilleux, Gerard. "Do We Need and Can We Afford the CBC?" *Canadian Speeches* 5 (1991): 54-59.

Waddell, Christopher. "A Nagging Questions: Is Canadian Culture In Or Out?" *Globe and Mail*, 12 November 1988, D3.

Waitzkin, Howard. "Next in Line for NAFTA? Images from Chile." *Monthly Review* 46 (1995): 17-26

Walker, Michael. "We've Caught the Balance-the-Budget Religion." *Financial Post*, 28 January 1995, DT9.

Wallace, Bruce. "A Warning From Ottawa: Regulating the Merger Wave." *Maclean's*, 30 January 1989, 38.

Wallerstein, Immanuel. *The Capitalist World Economy*. Cambridge: Cambridge University Press, 1979.

Warnock, John. *Free Trade and the New Right Agenda*. Vancouver: New Star Books, 1988.

Watkins, Mel. "Foreign Ownership '94 - Bye, Buy Canada." *This Magazine* 27 (1994): 30-32.

________. "Forum." *Queen's Quarterly* 98 (1991): 492-496.

________. "Ten Good Reasons to Oppose Free Trade." *This Magazine* 20 (April 1986): 13-16.

"We Can Impose Import Laws with the Deal - U.S." *Sault Star*, 17 November 1988, A6.

"What's the Point of NAFTA?" *Des Moines Register*, 17 August 1993, 6A.

Whitaker, Reg. "No Laments for A Nation. Free Trade and the Election of 1988." *Canadian Forum* 67 (March 1989): 9-13.

White, Robert. "Control of Canada is Free Trade Issue." *Canadian Speeches* 2 (1988): 18-22.

Wickens, Barbara and John Daly. "Riches to Rags." *Maclean's*, 23 September 1991, 55.

Wickens, Barbara. "A Fresh Breath of Optimism." *Maclean's*, 18 March 1991, 39.

________. "Hammered By Trade Laws, Canadian Steel Producers Face U.S. Penalties." *Maclean's*, 5 July 1993, 21

"Wilson Credits FTA for Gained Share of U.S. Markets." *Sault Star*, 16 April 1992, A6.

Wilson, Michael. "Interview." *Maclean's*, 25 September 1989, 41.

Wilson-Smith, Anthony. "Cutting the CBC." *Maclean's*, 17 December 1990, 12.

"Windsor steel firm plans move to Detroit" *Sault Star*, 8 August 1991.

Winsor, Hugh. "In Grey Pre-budget Ottawa, Prime Minister's Agenda Doesn't Add Up." *Globe and Mail*, 28 November 1988, A2.

Wohlfarth, Tony. "Honda: What's at Stake?" *Action Canada Network Dossier* 36 (March 1992): 4.

Wolfe, David A. "The Rise and Demise of the Keynesian Era in Canada: Economic Policy, 1930-1980s." *Readings in Canadian Social History, Volume 5: Modern Canada, 1930-1980s.* Edited by Michael Cross and Gregory Kealey, Toronto: McClelland and Stewart, 1985: 46-78.

"Woman tells of beating after plant went south." *Sault Star,* 28 January 1991.

Wonnacott, Paul and Roderick Hill. *Canadian and U.S. Adjustment Policies in a Bilateral Trade Agreement.* Washington, DC: Canadian-American Committee Representing the C.D. Howe Institute and the National Planning Association, 1987.

Wonnacott, Paul. "The Auto Pact: Plus or Minus." *Free Trade: The Real Story.* Edited by John Crispo, Toronto: Gage, 1988: 54-65.

Wonnacott, Ronald J. and Paul Wonnacott. *Free Trade Between the United States and Canada: The Potential Economic Effects.* Cambridge, MA: Harvard University Press, 1967.

Wood, Chris. "A Distrust of Government." *Maclean's,* 1 January 1990, 23.

"Workers Stand Guard After Employer Pulls Out." *Sault Star,* 3 February 1993, A1.

World Bank. *World Development Report.* Oxford: Oxford University Press, 1988.

________. *World Development Report.* Oxford: Oxford University Press, 1991.

Yakabuski, K. "Wage Hikes Higher in January." *Toronto Star,* 16 March 1991, C1.

Yates, Charlotte. "Free Trade: Year 3." *Canadian Dimension* 26 (1992): 5-13.

"York to Turn Away 2,000 First-year Students." *Sault Star,* 11 March 1993, A7.

Young, Pamela. "Taxing Culture." *Maclean's,* 14 January 1991, 48.

Young, R.A. "Political Scientists, Economists, and the Canada-U.S. Free Trade Agreement." *Canadian Public Policy* 15 (1989): 49-56.

Zerbisias, Antonia. "Cuts Put CBC on 'Slippery Slope' Down, Juneau Says." *Toronto Star,* 23 March 1991, G3.

________. "Fiscal Drama Unfolding at CBC-TV." *Toronto Star,* 16 March 1991, A1.

Index

Also published by

COMMON CENTS **Media Portrayal of the Gulf War and Other Events**
James Winter

Objectivity is the theme of these five case studies which deal with how the media covered the Gulf War, the Oka standoff, the Ontario NDP's budget, the Meech Lake Accord and Free Trade.

Like Chomsky, he enjoys contrasting the "common-sense" interpretation with views from alternative sources. As facts and images clash, we end up with a better grasp of the issues at hand
Montréal Gazette

304 pages, index
Paperback ISBN: 1-895431-24-7 $23.99
Hardcover ISBN: 1-895431-25-5 $52.99

ELECTRIC RIVERS **The Story of the James Bay Project**
Sean McCutcheon

... a book about how and why the James Bay project is being built, how it works, the consequences its building will have for people and for the environment, and the struggle to stop it... it cuts through the rhetoric so frequently found in the debate.
Canadian Book Review Annual

Electric Rivers *is a welcome contribution to the debate... a good fortune for readers who would like to better understand a story that is destined to dominate the environmental and political agenda.*
Globe and Mail

194 pages, maps
Paperback ISBN: 1-895431-18-2 $18.99
Hardcover ISBN: 1-895431-19-0 $47.99

POLITICAL ECOLOGY **Beyond Environmentalism**
Dimitrios Roussopoulos

Examining the perspective offered by various components of political ecology, this book presents an overview of its origins as well as its social and cultural causes.

A useful and timely history of the environmental movement and its philosophical bases.
Books in Canada

180 pages
Paperback ISBN: 1-895431-80-8 $15.99
Hardcover ISBN: 1-895431-81-6 $44.99

BANKERS, BAGMEN, AND BANDITS

Business and Politics in the Age of Greed

R.T. Naylor

From the shadowy underworld of business, the shady side of politics, and the twilight zone the two share, comes a collection of articles based on Naylor's widely read column.

An eminently readable book, with outré insights into the corrupt underside of world affairs in each chapter...Read it, wake up, and weep.
Canadian Book Review Annual

Without exception, the essays make very interesting reading... Naylor's book is an exhilarating if sometimes frightening or distressing roller coaster ride through the real world.
The Alternative Voice

250 pages
Paperback ISBN: 0-921689-76-4 $18.99
Hardcover ISBN: 0-921689-77-2 $47.99

THE DECLINE OF THE AMERICAN ECONOMY

Bertrand Bellon and Jorge Niosi

translated by Robert Chodos and Ellen Garmaise

Two prominent economists examine the decline of U.S. industry, covering the post-World War period to the Reagan era.

A convenient summary of a vast amount of research... packed with facts and figures.
The Village Voice

242 pages, index, bibliography
Paperback ISBN: 0-921689-00-4 $16.99
Hardcover ISBN: 0-921689-01-2 $45.99

TOWARD A HUMANIST POLITICAL ECONOMY

Phillip Hansen and Harold Chorney

A collection of essays written between the late 70s and the present day that focus attention on the neglected cultural side of society in order to chart the progress of political change. As background some of the insights of writers as diverse as Hannah Arendt and John Maynard Keynes are examined.

... the themes are relevant for those trying to fathom the post-Reaganite political world of the 1990s.
Canadian Book Review Annual

... their publication in one volume is a welcome addition to both the Canadian political economy literature and the literature on western Canada.
Prairie Forum

224 pages, index
Paperback ISBN:1-895431-22-0 $19.99
Hardcover ISBN:1-895431-23-9 $48.99

GLOBAL VISIONS Beyond the New World Order

Jeremy Brecher, John Brown Childs and Jill Cutler, eds.

All over the world, grassroots movements are forging links across national boundaries to resist the New World Order. Their aims are to restore the power of communities. This book initiates a crucial worldwide discussion on what such an alternative might be — and on how to create it.

Most remarkable for the refreshing plurality of its voices.
Alternatives

Highly recommended to those persons to whom the idea of a world order is more than just a slogan.
Études internationales

317 pages, index
Paperback ISBN: 1-895431-74-3 $19.99
Hardcover ISBN: 1-895431-75-1 $48.99

SHOCK WAVES Eastern Europe after the Revolutions

John Feffer

In *Shock Waves*, John Feffer paints a vivid picture of the political and economic conflicts that are dramatically reshaping daily life in today's Eastern Europe.

...his [Feffer's] analysis is sound... In each chapter, there is a sensitive discussion of economics.
Canadian Book Review Annual

The reality that Feffer tentatively speculates about in his analysis... provides valuable insights into the brief period when utopian ideas battled free market orthodoxy for currency.
Imprint

350 pages, index
Paperback ISBN: 1-895431-46-8 $19.99
Hardcover ISBN: 1-895431-47-6 $48.99

SPIRITUAL WARFARE The Politics of the Christian Right

Sara Diamond

If you think Margaret Atwood's Handmaid's Tale *was a fantasy, try thinking a bit harder. Sara Diamond...has documented, footnoted and analyzed the meticulously planned moves of the Christian Right toward authoritarian power in the secular world.*
The Humanist in Canada

Sara Diamond's new book scares the living hell out of you. But that's the point.
University of Western Ontario Gazette

304 pages, index
Paperback ISBN: 0-921689-64-0 $19.99
Hardcover ISBN: 0-921689-65-9 $48.99

BLACK ROSE BOOKS

has also published the following books of related interest

The Trojan Horse: Alberta and the Future of Canada, *edited by Gordon Laxer and Trevor Harrison*

The Permanent Debt System: Dependence or Democracy, *by Jacques B. Gélinas*

The Former State Communist World: A Left Analysis, *edited by David Mandel*

From Camp David to the Gulf: Negotiations, Language and Propaganda, and War, *by Adel Safty*

Frist Person Plural: A Community Development Approach to Social Change, *by David Smith*

The Legacy of the New Left, *edited by Dimitrios Roussopoulos*

The Political Economy of International Labour Migration, *by Hassan N. Gardezi*

Private Interest, Public Spending, *by William E. Scheurerman and Sidney Plotkin*

Dissidence: Essays Against the Mainstream, *by Dimitrios Rousspoulos*

Partners in Enterprise: The Worker Ownership Phenomenon, *edited by Jack Quarter and George Melnyk*

Toward a Humanist Political Economy, *by Phillip Hansen and Harold Chorney*

The Myth of the Market: Promises and Illusions, *by Jeremy Seabrook*

Race, Gender and Work: A Multi-Cultural Economic History of Women in the United States, *by Teresa Amott and Julie Matthaei*

Dominion of Debt: Centre, Periphery and the International Economic Order, *by Jeremy Brecher and Tim Costello*

Bringing the Economy Home from the Market, *by Ross V.G. Dobson*

The Economy of Canada: A Study of Ownership and Control, *by Jorge Niosi*

Is the Canadian Economy Closing Down?, *edited by Fred Caloren*

send for a free catalogue of all our titles
BLACK ROSE BOOKS
P.O. Box 1258
Succ. Place du Parc
Montréal, Québec
H3W 2R3 Canada

Printed by the workers of
Les Éditions Marquis
Montmagny, Québec
for Black Rose Books Ltd.